REFORM
AND RESISTANCE

GENDER,

DELINQUENCY,

AND

AMERICA'S

FIRST

JUVENILE

COURT

Anne Meis Knupfer

Routledge
New York London

Published in 2001 by

Routledge
29 West 35th Street
New York, NY 10001

Published in Great Britain by

Routledge
11 New Fetter Lane
London EC4P 4EE

Routledge is an imprint of the Taylor & Francis Group.

Copyright © 2001 by Routledge

Printed in the United States of America on acid-free paper.

Library of Congress Cataloging-in-Publication Data
Knupfer, Anne Meis, 1951–
    Reform and resistance : gender, delinquency, and America's first
    juvenile court / Anne Meis Knupfer
        p.   cm.
    Includes bibliographical references and index.
    ISBN 0-415-92597-5 (hb) —   ISBN 0-415-92598-3 (pb)
    1. Illinois. Juvenile Court (Cook County)—History. 2. Juvenile courts—
Illinois—Cook County—History. 3. Female juvenile delinquents—Legal
status, laws, etc.—Illinois—Cook County—History. 4. Juvenile delinquency—
Illinois—Cook County—History. I. Title.

    KFI1796 .K58 2001
    364.36'09773'1—dc21   00-045730

            10 9   8   7   6   5   4   3   2   1

To my mother, Dorothy Mae Hart Meis,
and, once again, to my son, Franz Paul Knupfer

Contents

Acknowledgments

As with most scholarly endeavors, this book would not have been completed without the assistance of professionals, colleagues, and family and friends. I would like to thank the Spencer Foundation for its financial support for two years, as well as the Purdue University Library for a Library Scholar's Grant.

Earlier versions of chapters 3, 7, and 8 appeared as "Professionalizing Probation Work in Chicago, 1900–1935," in *Social Service Review* 73 (1999): 145-63; "'Rectifying the Hampering Causes of Delinquency': The Chicago Home for Girls, 1900 to 1935," in the *Illinois Historical Journal* 1 (1999): 52–68; and "'To Become Good, Self-Supporting Women': The State Industrial School for Delinquent Girls at Geneva, Illinois, 1900–1935," in *Journal of the History of Sexuality* 9 (2000): 420–46.

Many librarians and archivists in Chicago were tremendously helpful in locating primary materials for the book. I would like to thank those at the Regenstein Library of the University of Chicago, the Chicago Historical Society, the Municipal Reference Collection of the Harold Washington Public Library, Northwestern University's Government Publications, and the Joseph Cardinal Bernadin Archival Research Center in Chicago. Special thanks to Mary Bamberger of Special Collections of the University of Illinois at Chicago, who is so knowledgeable about Chicago women's history; and to Archie Motley of the Chicago Historical Society, who although retired still finds time to assist historians. For assistance with photographs for the book, I would like to thank Zita Stukas and Patricia Bakunas at the University of Illinois at Chicago, and Debra Levine at the University of Chicago. My heartfelt gratitude goes to Sister Lourdes Langenfeld at the House of the Good Shepherd for assisting me with access to their archives.

I would like to thank the following scholars and colleagues who, in reading drafts, commenting at conference sessions, sharing their writing, and asking good questions, prompted me to rethink and rewrite: Mara Dodge, David Tanenhaus, Suellen Hoy, Kriste Lindenmeyer, Kathleen Jones, Joanne Goodwin, J. Herbie DiFonzo, Charlene Haddock Seigfried, and Ala Samarapungavan. I am also grateful to the anonymous reviewers and editors of the *Social Service Review*, the *Illinois Historical Journal*, and the *Journal of the History of Sexuality* for helpful criticism of articles from which specific chapters were carved.

Vikram Mukhija and Nicole Ellis of Routledge also deserve thanks for their editorial expertise and enthusiasm in the manuscript.

On a personal note, I wish to thank Bob Cary for opening his home to me so that I could continue my research and writing in Chicago. And for his curiosity, as we wound our way through Chicago, reconstructing what life must have been like for delinquent girls at the turn of the century. Finally, and once again, I want to thank my son for simply being who he is: he gives me such joy and inspiration.

Introduction

That Chicago was a crucial site of social reform during the Progressive Era is unquestionable. To date, most historical scholarship has focused on its social settlements, the women's clubs, ethnic voluntary associations, and the University of Chicago's School of Sociology and School of Social Service Administration (SSSA).[1] There has not, however, been a thorough examination of the Cook County Juvenile Court (CCJC), the first juvenile court established in the United States (in 1899). It was no coincidence that this juvenile court was created within a decade of the Chicago School of Sociology and alongside the flourishing activism of the Hull House and women's clubs. Indeed, the very impulse for the CCJC arose largely from the Chicago Woman's Club (CWC). The CWC, as well as other maternalist organizations, sustained its involvement in the juvenile court in multiple ways: funding sociological studies of delinquency; publishing surveys on the dangers of Chicago's dance halls, saloons, pool rooms, movie theaters, and roadhouses; underwriting the salaries of probation officers; and assisting the judges in their deliberations about delinquent girls in the early juvenile court years. Further, prominent club members and female social reformers spearheaded the Juvenile Psychopathic Institute, the first psychiatric clinic affiliated with a juvenile court.

Initially, club women worked in conjunction with fledging professionals. To be sure, many professionals nurtured their affiliations with club women, who assisted them through financial support, volunteer activities, and public advocacy of their research and programs. Over time, however, sociologists, social workers, psychologists, and psychiatrists distanced themselves from the club women through their professional discourses and practices. In effect, professional fields distinguished themselves through their own genres or "narratives": case studies, medical diagnoses, sociological theories and maps, community surveys, ethnographic studies, probation reports, annual reports, psychological profiles, court proceedings, and even the delinquents' "own stories." Essentially, delinquency became a contested terrain upon which sociologists, social workers, and others built their professional authority. Similarly, maternalists and "professional" maternalists gained a professional foothold for women by advocating for their employment as probation officers, policewomen, social workers, and even judges.[2] Predicating their social and moral authority upon gender, women argued that only they could deliberate on the distinct problems of delinquent girls, especially those pertaining to immorality. The roots of maternalism, then, remained pervasive in Chicago's juvenile court, despite the court's portrayal of itself as "sociological" and "scientific."

As a matter of course, the court's expansion entailed, and even necessitated, a proliferation and intensification of professional discourses. Following a Foucauldian analysis, I argue that sexuality—be it through prescriptions, diagnoses, or classifications—saturated the issue of female delinquency. This was, perhaps, to be expected, as immorality accounted, in some years, for nearly 80 percent of the court's female charges.[3] Concurrently, the other common charge—incorrigibility—frequently masked immorality to protect the delinquent girls' reputations. The legal definition of incorrigibility was correspondingly enlarged to accommodate a host of indiscrete activities on the girls' part: riding in a closed automobile; loitering in a department or drug store; shimmying on the dance floor of a roadhouse; or occupying a furnished room with a young man. As such, the court expanded its role as *parens patriae* to police young girls' improprieties, even though its benevolent and kindly language indicated otherwise. Not unlike other progressive reforms, the juvenile court was poised between the dialectics of compassion, middle-class prescriptions for female behavior, and scientific classifications of "others."

This is not to insinuate that delinquent girls were victims of social control or scientific measurements. Rather, the girls, too, contributed to the assemblage of discourses about delinquency through their own narratives and "scripts." In a critical theorist vein, I examine how they transposed scenes and characters from melodramas, popular romances, and white slave novels to their confessions before judges and probation officers. Similarly, letters and progress reports from paroled girls to matrons and superintendents of reform institutions were often "scripted"—that is, formulaic in their contriteness, their diligent listings of household chores, and requests to visit male friends. Conversely, others' bold and defiant behaviors in the reform institutions—rioting, beating up matrons, engaging in interracial lesbian affairs, and exhibiting hysterical and psychopathological symptoms—illustrated how rebellious girls resisted the monotony, domestication, and expected codes of behavior there. Their behaviors, detailed in institutional medical and psychiatric reports, provide ample evidence that not all girls passively accepted their commitments or paroles. Although the reform institutions inflated the number of delinquent girls who "made good," their numbers likewise spoke increasingly of girls who "put one over" on them.

To these myriad narratives this book deliberately adds its own: the frameworks of poststructuralism and critical theory. I seek to confound, as well as to clarify, issues surrounding female delinquency to more fully portray the complexity of the subject (delinquency), as well as subjects (the girls themselves). Discourse analysis challenges the very narrative structures embedded in the court records, the professional literatures, and the club women's reports, and illuminates how thickly texted the juvenile court was. Such an analysis also allows for comparisons among professional discourses, and how they drew, as well as disengaged, from one another. Further, comparisons between professional discourses and their practices often demonstrated how inflated such language became. Probation officers, for example, often relied upon the traditional methods of club women, settlement workers, and charity workers, despite their bolstered images of "social doctors." Lastly, discourse analysis and critical theory highlight the lived experiences and agency of delinquent girls.

Who exactly were Chicago's delinquent girls? Not surprisingly, court records revealed that most were working-class and poor daughters of immigrants and African-American migrants. Girls of Polish, German, American, and Irish parentage were most often brought to court. Although the numbers of German and Irish delinquent girls decreased over time, the numbers of African Americans, native-born white Americans, and Polish Americans rose dramatically. Regardless of their ethnicity, most delinquent girls appeared in court only once; those who were repeat offenders did not usually commit the same offense (although this may have been an artifact of the court's reluctance to name the charge of immorality). Girls, more so than boys, were more often arrested in groups, perhaps attesting to the peer influences and the social nature of their activities. In accordance with sociological theories about family disorganization, most delinquent girls lived in two-parent households "broken" by alcoholism, poverty, neglect, divorce and/or remarriage, lack of supervision, and immoral conduct.

But the court statistics on "disorganized" homes belied the complicated conditions of delinquent girls' family lives, their neighborhoods, and marginalization in employment. This was especially true for immigrant girls. Sociologist William I. Thomas's concerns about immigrant girls' adjustment to urban American life became vivified in Judge Mary Bartelme's court room. There, Bartelme mediated intergenerational conflicts between immigrant parents and their daughters. Frequently, Bartelme functioned as a cultural broker, encouraging parents to allow their daughters to keep a portion of their wages rather than turning their money over to the households. Similarly, she illustriously scolded the daughters, pointing out how disrespectful and unbecoming their slang, cheap dress, and makeup were. Many of these incidents corroborate Mary Odem's conclusions that parents often used the juvenile court system to coerce compliance from their daughters.[4] But girls, too, negotiated the court process, often requesting a new guardian or commitment to an institution to avoid the strident threats of a new stepmother or the painful experiences of incest.

Despite Bartelme's wise and kindly advice, the delinquent girls' road to rehabilitation was not an easy one. Structural problems in the juvenile court system—delayed court hearings, an untrained probation and parole staff, overcrowded reform institutions, and traditional reeducation programs—undermined the capacity for reform. Moreover, judges sadly noted, many of the girls returned to the very homes and neighborhoods that had led them astray. What the judges, probation officers, and volunteer club women had not anticipated was that many girls wished to continue their sexual adventures. Further, many could not live otherwise. Given the menial wages of factory, waitress, and department store work, working-class and poor girls could barely afford to live independently. For those who mustered the money to rent a furnished room and buy the necessary accoutrements of silk hosiery and willow plumes for evening attire, little remained for admission tickets to the dance hall or movie theater. Young men, however, were willing to pay the girls' way, sometimes in exchange for a good time. How the girls negotiated these situations varied. Some became charity girls and swindlers; some proudly remained virgins, engaging only in petting. Others were less fortunate, becoming victims of rape.

However, even these testimonies were sometimes scripted in order to protect a boyfriend, to seek revenge, or to outboast another girl. The challenge in teasing out fiction from fact, "true" stories from overwrought story plots, is an immense one. Admittedly, there were times I wondered who "pulled one over" on whom. People's lives and historians' versions of those lives are both cultural productions. There is, then, no one veritable story, be it told by delinquent girls, probation officers, judges, or even historians. The collision, even collusion, of these stories is at the heart of this book.

Overview of the Book Chapters

Chapter 1 begins with an examination of the alliances fostered between Chicago School sociologists and maternalists and professional maternalists. Although historians have pointed out how male sociologists increasingly distanced themselves from the volunteer work of female reformers, they have neglected points of mutual engagement. Indeed, Chicago sociologists had much to gain from cultivating the interests of women's clubs and organizations. First and foremost, female organizations, most prominently the CWC and the Juvenile Protective Association (JPA), provided funding for their research and eventual publications. Individual philanthropists Ethyl Sturges Dummer, Helen Culver, and Louise de Koven Bowen nurtured the fledgling sociologists while also remaining faithful to the progressive reform of the Hull House. Second, female volunteers assisted sociologists by collecting data for the delinquency studies. Paradoxically, even though sociologists insisted upon objectivity, they drew from the JPA's anecdotal surveys of the moral dangers of dance halls, saloons, and roadhouses. Although the club women and the Chicago School's original faculty shared moral sentiments, this did not completely account for the use of such unscientific data by later faculty.

Despite these points of convergence, there were distinct ways in which the Chicago School faculty and the Hull House reformers conceptualized their "social laboratories." Reflecting her own enactment of social motherhood, Jane Addams interiorized her conception of community through the establishment of clubs, classes, a kindergarten and nursery. In a similar vein, the Hull House's maps did not simply record incidents of poverty, crowded tenements, and child labor. Rather, as Kathryn Kish Sklar has so poignantly elaborated, the Hull House residents acted upon their findings through the promotion of child labor laws and municipal improvements.[5] Sociologists, on the other hand, exteriorized issues of family and home life through maps that detailed the frequency of dependency, delinquency, relief and charity cases, prostitution, and vice areas. Their stance presumed the scientific objectivity of George Simmel's "sociological stranger." Sociologist Robert Park was, in fact, decidedly skeptical of the role social science played in social reform; he was equally distrustful of female reformers, even claiming they were responsible for Chicago's social upheavals. Needless to say, the earlier tradition of sociology, borne out in Charles Henderson's ministry to prisons and maternity homes, was muted by Park.

Instead, Park deliberately chose his community affiliations for their research, not activist, potential. One example was the Chicago Urban League. But Park's motivations pointed to another larger conundrum: the uneasy relationship between mainstream sociologists and their African-American counterparts. Just as Chicago sociologists' relationships with female organizations were often self-serving, so too were their relationships with African-American organizations and affiliate sociologists. That W. E. B. Du Bois's rigorous community studies were virtually ignored by Chicago sociologists until the 1920s is ironic, given the school's keen interest in African-American migrants' adjustment to urban life. Paradoxically, the school drew upon Thomas's immigrant prototype to account for patterns of accommodation and assimilation among African Americans, while also insisting that African Americans had no cultural legacy or homeland.

The issues of adjustment and accommodation, as well as amorality and disorganization measured at the community, family, and individual levels, spoke directly to the issue of delinquency. According to sociologists, all ethnic groups cycled through stages of disorganization, transition, and organization, evident in the intergenerational conflicts of immigrant and migrant parents and their daughters. Through the process of individuation, female adolescents broke away from their parents' cultural traditions, preferring instead the Americanized versions of young women heroines and victims on the movie screen, in romance magazines, and on dance floors. Often torn by home conditions of poverty, alcoholism, and remarriage, these girls sought independence in order to spend their own wages as they saw fit, to enjoy the companionship of young men, and to engage in their own enactments of sexual freedom. Although the Chicago School correlated delinquency to residential areas of crime, poverty, and proximity to vice areas and unwholesome recreation, it did not attend to the amelioration of social conditions within families and communities that led to delinquency.

Chapter 2 focuses on one set of professionals who contributed to the medicalization of delinquency theory: psychiatrists, psychologists, and sexologists. As Elizabeth Lunbeck has so powerfully argued, the moral categories of degeneracy and dissoluteness became reinscribed through the scientific classifications of feebleminded, psychopathic, pathological liars, and perverted females.[6] To illustrate, feebleminded girls were thought to be unable to distinguish moral from immoral activities. Given their sexual vulnerability as well as contamination to others, these girls demanded constant supervision and, in many cases, institutionalization. Psychopathic girls, though, required surveillance for another reason: they were shrewd, cunning, and susceptible to sexual rampages. Further, they were highly prone to suggestibility, hysteria, and the "male prerogative."[7] Although the intelligence quotient of mentally defective girls hovered around the borderline, psychopathic girls often tested at normal and even superior levels.

Another complication for psychiatrists was that the sexual partners of psychopathic girls were not always men. Some were inclined toward other women. Distinguishing between homosexual identity and behavior, some sexologists and psychiatrists argued that young girls would naturally outgrow their preadolescent crushes and develop an interest in the opposite sex. But as incidents in the later chapters point out, many did not outgrow their initial preferences. At the State Industrial School for Delinquent Girls at Geneva, some inmates transgressed expected gender and racial codes of behavior, engaging in interracial lesbian affairs, insubordination, and hysterical "spells." A closer analysis of their medical reports, however, revealed that the all-too-frequent classifications of "psychopathic" and "hysterical" were often the psychiatrists' diagnoses of exasperation. To complicate matters, the girls' misbehaviors frequently masked attempts to escape or to undermine the authority of doctors and matrons. Not to be outdone, the doctors were well aware of how deliberate and calculated some girls' defiance was. To not imperil their own professional status, doctors and psychiatrists often camouflaged the girls' motives, referring to their egocentric tendencies, their attempts at self-mutilation, and abhorrent sexual inclinations.

Chapter 3 brings the reader closer to the court process in its discussion of the female probation officers' training and practices. Although probation work was to undergird the juvenile court system, the lack of initial funding from the Illinois legislature for the officers' salaries jeopardized Chicago's juvenile court's success. Nonetheless, the CWC, handmaiden to the Juvenile Court Act of 1899, funded the court's first probation officers until the county assumed fiscal responsibility in 1906. However, the club women's volunteer work with the juvenile court became problematic for probation officers who wanted to standardize their work. Despite the probation officers' adoption of medical language, as they crossed the threshold from "moral" to "social" physicians, the maternalist influence persisted. Additionally, large caseloads, poor salaries, and meager training vexed the probation staff's success with delinquent girls. By the 1930s, Edith Abbott had become so disenchanted with Chicago's probation officers that she recommended a community approach similar to the Chicago School's Chicago Area Project (CAP). As such, she advised that community members cooperate with social agencies, schools, and police to straighten the forked paths of delinquent youth.

The second part of the chapter examines the different training and employment opportunities for African-American female social workers. Although some had received their social work degrees under Sophonisba Breckinridge and Edith Abbott at the SSSA, many attended the historically black institutions of Fisk and Atlanta Universities. All three institutions' programs were rigorous, but the latter two focused more upon the specific problems African Americans faced—most notably the lack of access to viable employment, social and health services, and affordable and decent housing. Given these imperatives, most social workers were employed by the Chicago Urban League (CUL) and other African-American facilities. Unlike the later juvenile court, which distinguished the activities of professionals from volunteers, the CUL drew heavily from the club women. As I have discussed elsewhere, this esprit de corps exemplified how social and self uplift were indelibly enmeshed in the African-American community of Chicago.[8]

The scripts and narratives that circumscribed delinquent girls' lives are explored in chapter 4. As detailed in chapter 3, probation officers' reports were themselves an admixture of stories told by neighbors, parents, employers, and the girls themselves. That the girls were familiar with the narratives of seduction and abandonment was clear in their confessions to the judge. This should come as no surprise given the saturation of sexual discourse in movies, romance novels, white slave narratives, and vaudeville shows. Moreover, popular sites of consumption, including department stores, amusement parks, and palatial movie theaters in downtown Chicago lured young women after work. In their own right, many working-class girls became not only spectators but spectacles with their fetishes of beaver hats, willow plumes, and silk hosiery. Reinscribing their economic and social dependence upon men, young girls often competed for free admission to a movie, room on the dance floors, and the best men to pickpocket.

Such evening amusements may have softened the drudgery of a ten-hour factory shift or the sparse furnishings of a rented room. Female reformers thought differently, pointing out how fraught with moral dangers working-class girls' employments and recreations were. They considered hotels, restaurants, and department stores sites of temptation not only because of the low wages but because of the unscrupulous men who preyed upon working girls' desires for fashion and entertainment. The girls argued to the contrary: their purchases of fine clothing gave them sexual capital, as well as respect from their peers.

Chapter 5 closely examines the dispositions, characteristics, commitments, and outcomes of the delinquent girls brought before the CCJC. The chapter begins with an explication of the founding and development of Chicago's juvenile court. Prominent club women and professional maternalists—Julia Lathrop, Jane Addams, and Lucy Flower—were politically savvy in recognizing that the passage of the juvenile court bill necessitated their deference to male legislators, lawyers, and businessmen. Accordingly, they worked in tandem with prominent men, assuming a less visible role. Once the bill was passed, the club women and reformers continued their activism: subsidizing probation officers; helping to write a competitive examination for probation officers; and later, voting for the first female judge in the juvenile court, Mary Bartelme. Her position as judge did not, however, please everyone. Her determination to usher in progressive measures made her unpopular with evangelistic matrons and superintendents at reform institutions. For example, when the superintendent of the Chicago Home for Girls was recalcitrant in taking up Bartelme's recommendations, Bartelme responded swiftly: she simply cut back the number of delinquent girls committed to the institution, thus weakening the monetary pulse of the Home.

The last section of chapter 5 illuminates how contradictory many of the juvenile courts' practices were. The analysis also reveals the extent to which the court discriminated against immigrant and African-American girls. To illustrate, more African-American girls than foreign-born or native-born white girls were placed on probation, despite the dearth of African-American probation officers. One reason for this was that institutions discriminated against African Americans, accepting only a small percentage. In contrast, native-born white girls' cases were more often dismissed, perhaps because they and their parents had a better understanding of how to manipulate the court system. The dispositions to reform facilities also revealed differences. Pregnant, native-born white girls were more often committed to reform institutions, thus ensuring them greater access to maternity and prenatal care. Likewise, institutionalization was most often reserved for native- and foreign-born white girls who had engaged in multiple sexual relations or who required protection because of feeblemindedness or volatile home violence. Detention and institutionalization, then, served different purposes, depending upon the girls' ethnicity, social class, the types and frequency of sexual activities, and the girls' potential for moral restitution.

Despite the prodigious amount of time Judge Bartelme spent with delinquent girls, the number of those who "made good" was actually quite low. This was especially true for those committed to reform institutions. The House of the Good Shepherd had the highest failure rate at 65 percent. Nonetheless, the court continued to send more first-, second-, and third-time offenders there than any other institution. However, the higher success rates at the two other institutions, the Chicago Home for Girls and the Geneva School, should be questioned (as should the House of the Good Shepherd). In the case of the Chicago Home for Girls, it recorded a high number of girls who "made good" to ensure continued contributions from philanthropists and businesses, as well as to convince the juvenile court to commit more girls. The success rates at both institutions should also be questioned because there were too few officers to supervise the girls during their paroles. Subsequently, it was fairly easy for young girls to elude parole officers by running away from home or forging their parents' signatures on parole reports.

Additionally, the criteria of what actually constituted reform was never explicitly formulated, though one could surmise that it meant not being recommitted or falling back into immoral behavior. Indeed, many girls were simply clever enough not to get arrested by police officers or to be closely supervised by probation officers. Given the girls' frequent attempts at escape from reform institutions, one can only imagine the schemes devised by girls to evade supervision, much less recommitment, once released. The monotony and ineffectiveness of the reform institutions' program of reform—which emphasized domesticity, religiosity, and industrial arts—also vexed the issue of reform. Although the institutions claimed to make girls "self-supporting," this rhetoric rang hollow. Instead, the institutions helped to reinforce the girls' delinquency, as most girls were trained and paroled as domestic servants even though domestic workers constituted the highest number of employees brought before the juvenile court. However, reform institutions were not so concerned with viable employment as much as containing the girls' sexuality through marriage, motherhood, and home life.

Chapter 6 focuses on the Chicago Detention Home and Juvenile Psychopathic Institute, both affiliated with the CCJC. For safety and health reasons, it was sometimes necessary for delinquent girls to be detained in the Home prior to their court dates. Additionally, the services of the institute were deemed necessary to determine cases of feeblemindedness, epilepsy, psychopathology, and other psychiatric problems. Judge Merritt Pinckney, in fact, so relied upon the deliberations of the institute's director, Dr. William Healy, that he asked Healy to assist him in the court decisions. Healy was not comfortable with this arrangement, as he found the causes of delinquency to be multiple and complex. Psychological problems, he believed, were compounded by physical ailments, heredity, and family and community strife. One way to resolve the delinquents' problems, Healy believed, was to have a sit-down chat in order to elicit the delinquent's "own story." In a method remarkably similar to Judge Bartelme's conversations with girls and their parents, Healy coaxed youth to talk about their childhood memories, motivations, and feelings. Their stories, in turn, assumed various purposes and genres: supporting evidence for the judge, case studies for a social workers' textbook, and data for child guidance clinics.

The Chicago Detention Home provided the clientele for Dr. Healy's institute, but it also provided much needed medical and dental services: the treatment of venereal diseases; the removal of infected adenoids and tonsils; and the correction of dietary deficiencies with three sound meals a day. Although the Home was overcrowded, it functioned largely as a welfare institution, providing children and youth with safe accommodations, medical and dental care, and educational resources. The credit for these provisions again rested with the female reformers and club women, who founded and financially sustained the Home until 1906, when the county assumed responsibility. Again, in arguing that women were best suited to care for dependent children and delinquent girls, the club women created employment for women as matrons, teachers, and principals at the Home.

Chapters 7 though 9 respectively examine the Chicago Home for Girls, the Geneva School, and the House of the Good Shepherd. The commonalities of these institutions' curricula—manual labor, domestic skills, and religious devotions—spoke to the motifs of social and moral redemption. The largely untrained staff of matrons, teachers, and superintendents reinforced gendered codes of dependency and morality as well. Yet each institution was unique in its own fiscal challenges, as well as its relationship to the juvenile court. As noted, differences in ideologies often occurred as Bartelme and the court probation officers attempted to wrestle control from the hands of evangelical spinsters, suburban socialites, and, infrequently, devoted nuns. As such, the transition from rescue to rehabilitation was not an easy one. And yet, the administrators of the institutions had little choice if they wanted to reap the benefits of court monies. Compliance with the court's demands that institutions make use of services that medicalized delinquency—child guidance clinics, psychiatric research institutes, maternity hospitals, and psychological testing services—became increasingly apparent in the institutions' annual reports of the 1920s and 1930s. Reform and rehabilitation, then, were at crossroads, reflecting tensions among psychiatrists and doctors, progressive reformers, court officials, institutional administrators, and, not least of all, the delinquent girls themselves.

This history of female delinquents and their reeducation reveals the complexities and contradictions of one of the Progressive Era's most ambitious reforms: the juvenile court system. While not always succeeding in reforming the girls, the juvenile court did contribute to the growth of professional fields of psychiatry, psychology, social work, probation and police work. The court also provided its own forms of social welfare through medical services, room and board, and prenatal and maternal care. The attendant growth of reform institutions provided another kind of "social laboratory" where reform measures could be enacted upon delinquent girls. The one calculation that had been underestimated were the girls themselves, with their own scripts and acts of rebellion. They made the terrain of delinquency even more contested.

Part One

The Professionalization of Delinquency

1

Female Delinquency

Social Reform and Sociology

He would give the "right" sociological touch. He would be vaguely alarming, then vaguely reassuring, about the Morals of the Young.

—Floyd Dell, *Love without Money*

Female and Male Dominions

Founded in 1889 by Jane Addams and Ellen Gates Starr, the Hull House provided opportunities for young, middle-class women to live independently while also engaging in the social experiment of living among poor immigrants. As such, even before the Chicago School of Sociology conceived of the city as a "social laboratory," the Hull House had successfully conjoined social investigation to advocacy through its prodigious surveys, maps, and corresponding outreach. Although no Chicago sociologist would make use of these materials, some sociologists would recognize Jane Addams's sphere of influence in the world of social reform; fittingly, the Chicago School would offer her a part-time faculty position in 1913. Addams refused it, as she had already received national recognition for her work. She may have also been concerned that the university would attempt to subsume the settlement.[1] Assuming their own gender privilege, Jane Addams and the Hull House's "female dominion" realized that they had more to gain from affiliations with their sister organizations—including the Chicago Woman's Club (CWC) and the Juvenile Protective Association (JPA)—than from an all-male department. The first wave of Chicago sociologists, too, would recognize the advantages of associating with these maternalist organizations and with their wealthy members. This discussion of sociology and female delinquency appropriately begins, then, with how female reformists nurtured sociological research while at the same time sustaining their own activist enterprises.

Addams and her female coresidents conceptualized the Hull House as an enlargement of the domestic sphere, what scholars have referred to as "social motherhood." The settlement's kindergarten, children's clubs, and mothers' classes exemplified this approach. The women's utilization and expansion of interior space within the Hull House anticipated social workers' focal concerns with domestic and family life. This is not to suggest, however, that the Hull House women isolated family issues from those of poverty, crowded tenements, unfair labor laws, and a livable family wage. Rather, by design and necessity, the Hull House women conjoined social research to activism in specific gendered ways. As Florence Kelley, one member of the "female dominion" stated, "In the field of sociology there is brain work waiting for women which men cannot do."[2] Her investigations of Chicago's sweatshop system and its attendant child labor led to a state position as first chief factory inspector, in which her enforcement of the eight-hour work day law for women and children confirmed the ideology of social motherhood both within the home and workplace.

So too did Hull House residents Sophonisba Breckinridge and Edith Abbott distinguish their social science projects from the Chicago School's. Indeed, much of the women's research relating to delinquency, immigrants' adjustments, and family strife preceded the Chicago School's. Their attentiveness to historical and legal aspects of social and economic welfare, as well as their keen analysis of statistical data, attested to their rigorous scholarship as well. But they were far less theoretical than Chicago School sociologists in their interpretations and conclusions. To illustrate, it was not sufficient for Abbott and Breckinridge to correlate frequencies of delinquency, prostitution, and crime with specific urban areas or zones. Nor did they attempt to simply understand the social worlds of taxi-dance halls, hobohemia, and gang territories. Instead, the women wedded their research findings to the formation of public policy and legislative reform, thereby seeking to improve the economic, social, and legal status of women, children, and other disenfranchised groups. This they accomplished, despite years of professional marginalization at the University of Chicago, through the support of the Hull House and maternalist organizations.[3]

Indeed, many of Abbott's and Breckinridge's recommendations focused on the administration of the very social institutions and programs that maternalist organizations had supported: the juvenile court, mothers' pensions programs, detention homes and jails, and state reformatories. For example, Edith Abbott's investigation of jail conditions in Illinois prompted her to criticize the ineffectiveness of local and county authorities, and to advocate state intervention. Her state-building plan was not simply directed at efficiency. Ever mindful of the economic welfare of women and children, she argued that the establishment of state "work-house farms" could provide some means of financial support for male prisoners' families. Detention in county jails, on the other hand, was counterproductive. Similarly, she criticized Chicago's police courts for imprisoning poor men because they could not pay their fines. Decrying that it was not only "demoralizing" but "unjust" to jail men for fines that averaged fifty dollars or less, she thought it more prudent to let them return to work so they could support their families, as well as pay their fines incrementally.[4]

Likewise, Abbott's examination of the mothers' pensions administration in Illinois in 1917 pointed to the need for more state supervision of county welfare offices. Because mothers' pension programs were in their infancy, she found little consistency in the criteria used in the selection of recipients. Confounding the process was a lack of qualified social workers who conducted home investigations. In turn, social workers' unstandardized practices and record keeping distorted data so vital for social policy reform. But most important, mothers who were not given pensions could not adequately care for their children. Like Kelley, Abbott saw the critical relationship between wages and family welfare. Noting the high numbers of applicants for mothers' pensions in Illinois, she argued that if men received higher wages for their work, their families could be provided for after their deaths.[5] In her assessment, then, the need for mothers' pensions originated from other economic injustices.

Such economic inequities directly affected delinquency and truancy rates. For one, children's school nonattendance rates correlated with poor mental and physical health, aggravated by poverty and parental negligence. Second, many girls who became truants did so because they had to care for their younger siblings while their mothers worked. It was not surprising to Breckinridge and Abbott that many of these truants later became delinquents. However, the two women did not recommend that more truant officers be hired, as the officers simply brought nonattending schoolchildren to court. Bridging educational to social and economic needs, the two women instead advised that visiting teachers, trained in social work and education, be employed. The CWC would take up Breckinridge and Abbott's suggestion and sponsor a visiting teacher the same year.[6] This example demonstrated how female social scientists and maternalists clubs worked together to link research to advocacy.

Most dramatically, Abbott and Breckinridge pointed to how "civic neglect"— the lack of wholesome recreation, separate facilities for the mentally and physically disabled, crowded tenements, and abuse of child labor laws—had a direct bearing upon delinquency. Their map of delinquency, the first of its kind in Chicago, divided the city by wards. This was in contrast to the delinquency maps of the Chicago School, whose zones and districts depoliticized the conditions of overcrowded neighborhoods and family poverty.[7] Breckinridge and Abbott's finger pointing was intentional, holding the aldermen and the city's political machinery accountable. Purposefully, they published their findings in 1912, one year before women were allowed to vote in Chicago's aldermanic elections. Again, research and advocacy were indelibly connected.

In contrast to the Hull House and female social scientists, the Chicago School's "male dominion" distinguished itself by concentrating on the exterior features of community and family strife, that is, those features that could be objectified and quantified. Incidents of delinquency, dependency, desertion, and illegitimacy dotted their social research maps, corroborating the proclivity of disorganized households in Chicago. Crowded tenements, rooming houses, illicit public amusements, and vice areas registered as patterns of density on their spot and rate maps, amplifying causal relationships to "broken" families and demoralized individuals, rather than structural inequalities in employment and housing.[8] As such, their measurements were less concerned with social amelioration than with understanding immigrants' and migrants' accommodations to city life.

The city of Chicago was an ideal social laboratory for sociological engagement by the Chicago School. The topographical features of its urban geography—saloons, cabarets, black and tans, prostitute houses, single-room registries, and roadhouses—were associated with high rates of delinquency, crime, and vice. These correlations assumed another form of spatiality as well: zones circumscribing and radiating from the city's core, expanding to the outlying suburbs and towns. Most of the city's disorganized areas were proximal to its decaying industrial center. In contrast, the organized neighborhoods—measured by home ownership, stable marriages, and low percentages of delinquency and crime—were most distal from the city's core.[9]

This conceptual approach differed significantly from the Hull House maps, which did not attribute poverty, ill health, and lack of wholesome recreation for children to individual or community disorganization. Instead, in keeping with their municipal housekeeping ideology, the female settlement workers campaigned for legislative reform to protect tenement dwellers and wage earners from unscrupulous landlords and factory owners, respectively. Consonant with their vision of the Hull House as a grand social experiment, the female residents opened their settlement doors to the neighboring immigrant mothers, fathers, and children. Certainly, the reformers' class and ethnic privileges eclipsed their ability to fully understand their neighbors' cultural habits.[10] Yet they interacted daily with their neighbors, as well as visited the families when constructing the Hull House maps; this was vastly different from sociologists who preferred to remain professional strangers.

As a further point of comparison, the Hull House women and Chicago School sociologists noted how immigrant girls' ties to their "mother" cultures loosened as they gravitated toward dance halls, new styles of dressing, and slang. But the reformers' and sociologists' approaches to such knowledge varied. Sociologist William I. Thomas, for one, relied upon juvenile court records and autobiographical materials to theorize about the girls' love of adventure and desire for recognition.[11] The Hull House women, on the other hand, enacted programs to prevent delinquency and to minimize mother–daughter tensions. They sponsored girls clubs, dances, and nickelodeons, although not all girls were enticed by these events. They also created a cultural museum where daughters could watch their mothers engage in traditional crafts, thereby creating an intergenerational bridge of understanding. In conjunction with the Hull House, the JPA and the later Immigrant Protective League, Edith Abbott's sister Grace worked to ensure the protection of immigrant girls against white slave traffickers, purportedly unscrupulous men who duped innocent girls into prostitution. Her observation about how difficult it was for largely rural and uneducated immigrant girls to adjust to an American urban landscape preceded William I. Thomas and Florian Znaniecki's well-known 1917 publication, *The Polish Peasant in Europe and America.*[12]

The Hull House could literally afford such social programs because it had its own community of female philanthropists. These women, reformers in their own right, contributed to the Hull House's goals of municipal improvement and building female leadership at the city, state, and federal levels. Helen Culver, owner of the Hull House, not only donated the house and adjacent property for settlement purposes but gave generous sums of money. Louise de Koven Bowen—treasurer of the Hull House, president of the JPA, and chair of the Juvenile Court Committee—contributed nearly half a million dollars to the Hull House during her lifetime.[13] And Ethyl Sturges Dummer, former student of Hull House cofounder Ellen Gate Starr, fostered the aspirations of settlement residents Sophonisba Breckinridge and Edith Abbott as founding trustee of the Chicago School of Civics and Philanthropy in 1908. Indignant about child labor, Dummer joined the National Child Labor Committee and the JPA. Sharing Julia Lathrop's concern for the mentally ill, Dummer underwrote the costs for the Juvenile Psychopathic Institute in 1909, affiliated with Chicago's juvenile court and detention home.[14]

Strategically, the Hull House women were members of prominent maternalist organizations, especially the CWC and the JPA. Through their cosponsorship of state legislation relating to child welfare, women's organizations were largely responsible for the first juvenile court system in Chicago, detention homes, parental schools, reformatories, and girls' homes. In creating interstitial layers of advocacy with legislators, judges, and social reformers, maternalists and professional maternalists ensured the passage of critical legislation. Their efforts, however, sometimes entailed taking a secondary, even deferential, role. As detailed in subsequent chapters, in order to secure the passage of the Juvenile

Court Act of 1899, male lawyers and judges—not club women—forwarded the bill.[15] But in documenting and publishing the conditions of dance halls, five- and ten-cent theaters, department stores, and hotels and restaurants that employed girls, women's groups such as the JPA took the lead in activism by closing theaters and dance halls that violated city codes. And although their surveys were considered unscientific, their publications created a nexus between reformers and sociologists, as some Chicago School sociologists used the JPA surveys to corroborate their own theories and conclusions.[16]

When female reformers and organizations began to fund studies by Chicago School sociologists, they did so partly to advance their own state-building agendas. Helen Culver and Ethyl Dummer funded studies by Chicago sociologist William I. Thomas, which resulted in his publications of *The Polish Peasant in Europe and America*, *The Unadjusted Girl*, and *The Child in America*. Thomas's scholarship reflected Dummer's steadfast concerns with child labor, child study programs, and prostitution. Dorothy Swaine Thomas, his wife, provided the necessary entrée to these philanthropic connections through her membership in the CWC and JPA; she was also indispensable to her husband as a trained social scientist and coauthor of *The Child in America*. Ernest Burgess, too, received monies raised by Dummer and Jane Addams. His directorship of the Illinois Vigilance Association, which crusaded against Chicago's white slave traffic and red light districts, fueled Dummer's cause for the rehabilitation of prostitutes. Burgess, too, nurtured close connections with the JPA, which financially underwrote his student Paul Cressey's study. And Clifford Shaw, a former parole officer for the JPA, completed his graduate sociology studies largely through the CWC's support.[17] The CWC would later provide funding for a project on delinquent boys to the University of Chicago's Local Community Research Committee, an umbrella agency that funded, supervised, and disseminated research on economic, political, and social aspects of Chicago's diverse populations. In turn, the committee echoed the reform agenda of the CWC and other maternalist organizations. Between 1923 and 1929, it published numerous books, book chapters, and journal articles on social welfare issues.[18]

On a larger scale, University of Chicago President William Rainey Harper, who envisioned collaborations between academic departments and social agencies, fostered connections between sociologists and social reformers.[19] The Chicago School of Civics and Philanthropy (CSCP) was one such pragmatic outcome. Predecessor to the School of Social Service Administration (SSSA), the CSCP provided yet another illustration of how men's and women's social visions coalesced as well as diverged. Like the Hull House, the CSCP was a forerunner to the Chicago School's social laboratory model. CSCP students conducted field studies and worked in Chicago's social agencies long before sociology students did. But the ambitions of affiliate faculty Julia Lathrop, Edith Abbott, and Sophonisba Breckinridge extended beyond Chicago's welfare institutions to state and federal agencies. As a member of the Illinois Board of Charities, Lathrop astutely understood the importance of linking women's professional experiences to state-building activities. Along with Breckinridge, she organized CSCP students' visits to state schools for delinquent girls and boys, the feebleminded, and the epileptic. SSSA students later trained at the Illinois Division of Criminology, again preceding sociology students' fieldwork there.[20] In contrast to the female faculty, CSCP cofounder Graham Taylor emphasized more of a social gospel approach, not unlike Chicago School sociologist and Baptist minister Charles Henderson. Taylor's reformist stance eschewed the SSSA's emphasis on theory, as well as the interdisciplinary study of history, politics, economics, and sociology.

As of World War I, the Chicago School reflected President Harper's vision. Some of the faculty engaged in social welfare research and encouraged their graduate students to write theses on social welfare institutions, labor issues, and "civic neglect." This may have been the partial influence of the Hull House, where as early as 1894, Sociology Chair Albion Small had sent his students.[21] The ministerial predilections of the department also swayed the Chicago School toward social welfare issues. As noted, Charles Henderson was a minister; Albion Small and Ernest Burgess were sons of ministers. However, their interest in social welfare did not rule out the call for objectivity, which would eventually drive a wedge between sociologists and social reformists and social workers.[22] With the arrival of Robert Park to the Chicago School in 1916, sociologists increasingly dissociated themselves from social reformers and social work professionals, described by one student as reminiscent of "the chill that is characteristic of the feelings between divorced couples."[23] One scholar has suggested that the Chicago School initially courted the female reformers for their philanthropic support, only to later distance themselves when the school became known.[24] The concept of objectivity, played out in research methodologies and design, also vexed this alliance, especially when Park joined the faculty.

Park was especially skeptical of Abbott and Breckinridge, and occasionally hurled verbal abuses at them. Publicly, he referred to Breckinridge as an "elderly spinster," perhaps because she refused to lend him case files.[25] In one particular letter, he referred to the two "distinguished ladies" of the SSSA whom he particularly disliked, undoubtedly Abbott and Breckinridge. He was equally distrustful of female social reformers, remarking at one point how most of Chicago's problems resulted from women's meddling, not from the city's political or police corruption.[26] Assuming George Simmel's stance of the "sociological stranger," Park drew fixed boundaries between social science and social reform. Accordingly, the local affiliations he chose, such as the Chicago Urban League (CUL), were ones that advanced his sociological research.[27]

In effect, "social distance" became the hallmark of the Chicago School's sociologists after World War I. Yet even prior to Park, William Thomas had insisted that sociologists be objective in their observations and stance. Yet as Jennifer Platt has so well documented, Thomas did not always follow his own advice. For one, his reliance upon letters and autobiographies reflected his literary training, not just his sociological pursuits.[28] His vignettes of delinquent girls, extracted from juvenile court records, revealed a predilection for dramatic episodes that corroborated his idea of young girls' wishes for excitement and adventure. Second, Thomas did not consider the "truthfulness" of the multiple narratives within the probation officers' reports. Gossipy neighbors, vindictive relatives, and even recalcitrant delinquent girls confounded any objective recording of events. Given the youthfulness of sociology itself, methodological concerns relating to subjectivities had not yet emerged. As such, Thomas's aim to vivify the inner desires of young girls more closely resembled that of social psychology, not the objective stance of sociology.

One could also question Park's reliance upon objectivity. In contrast to some female reformers and their morally freighted language, Park and other sociologists advanced the concept of social distance as scientific and amoral. Park adamantly declared, "A moral man cannot be a sociologist."[29] As noted, his idea of social distance drew heavily from his German professor, George Simmel, who conceived of urban life as alien and dislocated from traditions. But Park also drew heavily from his journalistic career and insisted that sociology's methods were akin to journalism's. As he stated, "a sociologist is merely a more accurate, responsible and scientific reporter."[30] Clearly, Park was distancing himself from the muckrakers and sensational journalists who wrote of white slave traffickers and Chinese opium dens, and from those female reformers who published moral tracts.

Ironically, the stance of the sociological stranger mirrored not just the sociologists' social distance but their alienation from the marginal social groups they studied: delinquents, taxi-dance-hall girls, prostitutes, and gangs. But just as Chicago's neighborhoods were ideal for sociologists to study marginality, so too were they ideal for young girls trying out new gendered experiences. As a matter of course, the city's permeable boundaries encouraged the girls' own cultural adaptations and their "superficial" and "adventitious" behaviors.[31] One could argue, then, that the city functioned as a social laboratory not just for sociologists and reformers but for adventurous girls.

Sociologists attempted to understand such populations and to resolve some of the internal contradictions of early sociological research through scientific detachment. Some of these studies focused on wayward girls and women. Paul Cressey, in his study of Chicago taxi-dance halls, remained ever attentive to balancing his objective observations with a *verstehen* approach. He was keenly aware of how theories could dictate, not just frame, one's sociological findings. As he recalled, "I had to be careful to see that what I was observing was not an indication of disorganization but rather—perhaps—a perfectly normal mani-

festation of the folkways and mores of the cultural groups to which they belong." However, his interpretations sometimes revealed the very moralism sociologists sought to avoid. Cressey's analysis for why the girls attended taxi-dance
halls echoed Thomas's: it was their desire for freedom, new experiences, and
recognition. But Cressey concluded that in order for the dancers to adapt to
the social conditions, they had to develop "abnormal types of behavior."[32]
What he did not consider was the girls' need for some kind of wage, not just
excitement. Nonetheless, Cressey was far more objective than sociologist Clara
Roe, who expressed shock over the dance-hall couples' intimacy. Her own
middle-class mores became the filter for her observation notes: "The men
stood around between dances with their arms around the girls in a much more
open fashion than they do at the dances to which I am accustomed." Her disso-
ciation from the girls certainly extended beyond sociological detachment: "The
men looked as if they would have higher I.Q.s than the girls, if they had been
mentally tested."[33]

Similarly, the Chicago sociologists' quest for objectivity was compromised
by their sources of data. As noted, sociologists did not consider the issue of subjectivity in their use of diaries, letters, and other autobiographical materials.
Other primary sources were also problematic, such as the JPA's surveys on
dance halls and saloons in which the women, respectably accompanied by their
husbands, tallied the numbers of underage youth and their draughts of beer.[34]
Thomas, Shaw, and E. Franklin Frazier drew heavily from these surveys and the
juvenile court's case records, despite the probation officers' sundry sources of
evidence. Other sociologists excerpted data from the police department, social
agencies, and vice commissions reports, all questionable sources in terms of objectivity.[35] Ironically, the very female reformers' activism from which Park had
so adamantly dissociated himself became part and parcel of much of the
Chicago School's scholarship.

Here, the presence of female sociology students in the Chicago School demands some acknowledgment, as some conjoined sociological frameworks to
social welfare concerns. During the 1890s and 1900s, the University of Chicago
had the largest number of female graduate students in the social sciences. Expanding this time period, from 1893 to 1935, almost 9 percent of students receiving Ph.D.s from the Chicago School were women; nearly 25 percent who
received their master's degrees were women.[36] An analysis of their dissertations
and master's theses indicated that many of the female students and graduates
were concerned with social amelioration and reform, not just theories of
accommodation and adjustment. Of the fourteen women who received their
doctorates from the Chicago School from 1893 to 1935, half wrote their dissertations on some aspect of disorganization, such as delinquency, crime, suicide,
and mental disease. Of the other half, three wrote about the public schools or
labor unions; and two on aspects of social psychology. (The other two disserta-

tions were anthropological.) But of the fifty-eight female students who wrote
their master's theses, almost one-third focused on female reformist issues: female
labor, mothers' pensions, social agencies, poverty, children, and delinquent
girls.[37]

This requires us to rethink how female sociologists might have established
their own gendered professional authority by focusing on issues related to families and children. This was, as noted, a strategy used by professional maternalists
Breckinridge, the Abbott sisters, Kelly, Lathrop, and Addams. In many cases, female sociologists followed the functionalist approaches of their professors, especially on topics relating to aspects of disorganization. But others attempted to
"get at" their subjects' perspectives through interviews and "participant observation." For the purposes of this chapter, brief descriptions of two publications
by female sociologists affiliated with the Chicago School must suffice. Ruth
Shonle Cavan, in her 1929 study of business girls (who, she claimed, constituted
a cultural group), interviewed the girls about their customs, traditions, and
ideas. This group of predominantly white, middle-class girls worried about
their lack of male friends and, hence, marriageable partners. Echoing Thomas's
desire for security, some of these girls worried that if they were too successful
in business they would be less attractive to men.[38]

Frances Donovan, affiliated with the Chicago School, also illustrated how
female sociologists used their gender to gain entry into unfamiliar settings and
establish rapport with their subjects. Rather than relying upon surveys or interviews, Donvan took positions as a department store clerk and as a waitress to
more fully understand the girls' social lives and economic constraints. She
found that many of the girls had little money to live on and so relied upon men
by sexual treating. Like William Thomas and Jane Addams, she found that after
a hard day's work, most girls wanted a night of excitement and adventure.[39] To
be sure, Donovan's concerns more closely resembled those of Breckinridge and
Abbott than the Chicago School faculty: women's employment, inequitable incomes, and sexual vulnerability.

Gender differences not only emerged within the field of sociology but between sociology and social work. Because social work was a largely feminized
profession, gender accounted in part for expected professional behaviors. Yet
working with troubled youth and indigent parents required not social distance
or objectivity, but sympathy on the part of social workers. Indeed, as Northwestern University Sociology Professor Thomas Eliot pointed out, social workers could not be emotionally distant from their clients. In fact, he continued, if
a caseworker did not become engaged in her case, she was "merely a case-ob-
server."[40] Nonetheless, social workers and probation officers seized upon the
idea of objectivity to bolster their professional status. As will be more fully discussed in chapter 3, they wedded maternal sympathy to their roles as "social
physicians." Eliot, however, confounded the very notion of objectivity for both

social workers and sociologists, questioning whether one could be both scientific and sympathetic. Phrased differently, he asked whether it was possible to preserve objectivity in subjective experiences. Nonetheless, Eliot concluded that the "pure sociologist," that is, the "sociological stranger," could accomplish both. But not so with the social worker.[41]

As would be expected, methodologies differed in social work and sociology. Sociologists described social workers as engaged in social investigation, yet conceived of their work as social research. Worded differently, social workers *diagnosed*, whereas sociologists *analyzed*. Although diagnosing social work cases might entail categories of analysis, it also required emotional engagement. As such, social workers' and probation officers' personalities became paramount in drawing out clients to reveal their home conditions, family backgrounds, and other pertinent information. And what better way to do so than through sympathy? Social distance would only hinder, not facilitate, social workers' case work. In fact, the only social workers who attained objectivity, some sociologists argued, were psychiatric social workers who bridged traditional social work methods to sociology through the "suppress[ion]" of their personalities.[42]

Despite avowed professional differences, sociologists continued to use social workers' case records for their own research through the 1920s and 1930s. But to better serve sociologists, Burgess urged that social workers write more complete records that detailed family budgets, social agencies' visits, residential changes, and families' adjustments. He also advised that social workers not use the word *individual* but *person*, the latter a sociological term denoting status and group membership.[43] Thomas Eliot criticized case records for an entirely different reason: their "stylistic flatness." He noted that even fiction writers who were handed some of the more interesting cases "could not even get a plot out of them."[44] Burgess concurred, but remained adamant about their sociological currency. Distrustful of social workers' accuracy, he recommended that they write verbatim reports so that sociologists could more fully analyze the clients' social interactions and situations. Here, Eliot rejoined that quotation marks and exact language would not contribute to more objectivity or accuracy, only a more heightened sense of drama. Other sociologists countered that if social workers studied dramatic writing, they might enliven their reports as well as sharpen their analyses. Clearly, these recommendations echoed little concern for the social workers' heavy caseloads and paper work.[45] Ironically, such recommendations would have compromised the very objectivity sociologists sought.

Sociologists not only criticized social workers' writing but their interviewing techniques, which again were of little benefit to them. First, social workers aimed toward a particularistic determination of pathologies and subsequent treatments. Although they might interview extended family members, neighbors, employers, and social agency providers, their main purpose was to establish the most effective plans of treatment for individuals. Sociologists, on the other hand, aggregated individual accounts to generalize about group processes and so map their preponderance. Second, social workers' interviews were accompanied by impressionistic, not systematic, observations.[46] As a result, their records revealed class and ethnic biases. In contrast, sociologists—including those who were "regulars" at the unsavory sites of roadhouses, taxi-dance halls, and saloons—portrayed themselves as analytical, objective, and unbiased. But as noted in earlier examples, moral and gender biases sometimes confounded their studies.

In order that sociologists might make better use of social workers' interviews, Burgess proposed several procedures. First, he recommended that they use first-person language to establish better rapport with their clients. Second, he suggested that they plan their interviews on "the democratic and friendly basis of sharing experience."[47] But how could these meetings be democratic, when social workers gathered information that affected mothers' pensions or young girls' wages? Here, ironically, Burgess promoted the emotional capital of sympathy and consolation in the name of democracy. Third, Burgess argued, an interview handled in such a friendly and straightforward fashion would provide a personal document, as well as objective material. In turn, sociologists and social workers could arrive at their own interpretations.[48]

It could be argued that social workers were more concerned with the truthfulness of their clients' stories, not the quest for objectivity. As discussed later, many delinquent girls did fabricate stories to protect themselves, their boyfriends, and family members. Social workers, probation officers, and court officials, though not always able to ferret the truth from delinquent girls or their families, soon realized their inability to do so. Psychiatric categories of pathological lying would later confirm the female propensity toward fabrication and "falsities."[49] Sociologists, on the other hand, did not usually question the authenticity of stories told to them. Park, for one, thought there were "good reasons" given by the confessants for why they behaved as they did. Sociologist Shaw, fashioning a research technique based on psychiatrist William Healy's "own story," accordingly asked delinquent boys to conjecture why they did what they did, thus combining narrative with methodology. Preceding Michel Foucault's concept of the transfer of the confessional to the professional, sociologist Reed Bain concluded, "There is sound sociology back of the Catholic confessional."[50] Whether and how sociologists teased out contradictions of first-person accounts from their "objective" observations was not discussed in the early sociological literature. Perhaps such admissions would have undermined their very concept of objectivity.

To be sure, social workers had their own dose of criticism for sociologists. Joint conferences with sociologists and social workers corroborated Thomas Eliot's survey findings that social workers had little use for sociological theory and knowledge. Instead, social workers found the study of economics and psychology more useful. The schism between social work and sociology was also reflected in the contents of their professional journals. Not surprisingly, most social-work journals published few sociological articles; similarly, the premier sociological journal, the *American Journal of Sociology*, published few articles of interest to social workers.[51] A new journal, *Social Forces*, was launched in the 1920s to bridge the two disciplines. *Social Service Review*, founded by Edith Abbott and Sophonisba Breckinridge in the late 1920s, likewise fostered connections between social work and sociology. Although the latter journal featured numerous articles by Addams, Kelley, Breckinridge, and the Abbott sisters, it also included sociological works by Burgess, Shaw, Eliot, T. V. Smith, and Howard Becker. Consistent with their state-building interests, Abbott and Breckinridge published a number of articles related to social welfare issues, including child and women's labor, mothers' pensions, race discrimination, and corresponding legislation.[52]

Mapping Disorganization and Delinquency: The Chicago School

The Chicago School's social research maps reflected a structuralist approach toward various types of disorganization, including delinquency, desertion, dependency, divorce, prostitution, and crime. Following the ecological model of the biological sciences, sociologists argued that the urban topography of industry, railroads, crowded tenements, and vice districts influenced a person's alienation, detachment, and amorality. On the other hand, those areas most distal from the city's core, the suburbs, conveyed a different pattern of land use. There, spacious parks, boulevards, and homes with trimmed lawns reflected community stability and organization.[53] These distributive uses of urban space and attendant human interactions became the catalyst for Burgess's configurations of the city into concentric and radial zones. In turn, other Chicago sociologists charted the frequency of male and female delinquency, gangs, divorce and desertion, suicides, and mental disorders within these zones.[54] Not surprisingly, their data supported the theoretical basis of Burgess's prototypical maps: people's individual and collective behaviors were influenced by, and "embodied," the physical structures of their environment.

Mapping behavior did not mean, however, that social groups remained static. Rather, Chicago sociologists argued that disorganization, resulting from environmental changes, was inevitable. Further, most social groups cycled through stages of disorganization, transition, and organization as they accommodated change. This cycle occurred on four different levels: racial and ethnic groups; communities; families; and individuals. These levels were not necessarily nested within one another, although many demoralized individuals (including delinquents) came from "broken" families who resided in disorganized communities. In contrast, many nondelinquent youth lived in two-parent families in communities characterized by low crime, home ownership, and stable institutions.[55]

There were, of course, exceptions. Regardless, the juvenile court and reform institutions appropriated the language of the Chicago School and correlated delinquency with homes "broken" by divorce, desertion, death, immorality, drunkenness, and poverty. Similarly, the communities in which many delinquents lived were cast as disorganized, unstable, and vice ridden. Court officials and administrators of reform institutions sometimes distorted Chicago sociologists' studies of immigrants' and migrants' adjustments to urban life, speaking degradingly of immigrant and migrant mothers and their delinquent daughters as morally and mentally unfit. In effect, they disembodied sociological theory from empirical findings. The following examination of the four levels of disorganization—race, community, family, and individual—amplifies the Chicago School's theories, especially as they pertained to disorganization and delinquency.

According to the Chicago School's ecological model, a change in spatial relationships, be it through migration or immigration, prompted a political or economic competition of resources. This, in turn, required some kind of accommodation by ethnic groups. In Robert Park's formulation of the race-cycle theory, these adjustments were structural and inevitable, not pathological or haphazard. African Americans, Cajuns, Appalachian whites, Chinese Americans, Polish Americans, and other migrants and immigrants—all were conceptualized as prototypical peasant groups who experienced anomie or alienation in their adjustments from rural settings to urban frontiers.[56] To be expected, these conflicts occurred not only within a single generation but between generations. William Thomas's studies of strife between immigrant daughters and their parents spoke most poignantly to adolescent girls' desires for adventure, which created an amorality far different from traditions honored by parents.[57]

Of all ethnic groups, however, African Americans most confounded the Chicago model. Unlike immigrant groups, sociologists argued, African Americans did not have a homeland or culture. Further, William Thomas contended that they had lost their most favorable African traits during slavery and emancipation. Although he had little evidence to support this argument, his intent was to refute the then-popular hereditarian model of racial inferiority. In Boasian fashion, he attributed their moral ideas to experiences and environment, not to heredity or racial "endowment."[58] Albeit in a racist tenor, Robert Park also refuted the notion of African retentions, concluding that the slave "left behind him almost everything but his dark complexion and his tropical temperament." Even their superstitions, he noted, were not African, but "products of people who live[d] in an intellectual twilight." Translated differently, African Americans were in a profound state of disorganization.[59]

To some degree, Park's position was curious. As speechwriter and journalist for Booker T. Washington, Park had ample opportunity to observe African-American community life in the South. What is most disconcerting is that neither Park nor any other Chicago School sociologist examined the retentions of southern cultural traditions and institutions in northern cities such as Chicago. Perhaps if they had consulted W. E. B. Du Bois's Atlanta studies on racial etiquette, social uplift programs, the black churches, and other community institutions in the South and the North, they would have realized how enduring and "stable" many cultural practices were. Yet Chicago sociologists neglected this rich material. Albion Small and Du Bois had, in fact, studied under the same German professor, yet Small never acknowledged Du Bois's work. Park and Burgess, too, never cited DuBois's nor any other African-American sociologists' work, except that of their own students.[60]

Rather, it was the African-American graduate students at the Chicago School who bridged the theories of Park and Burgess to Du Bois. Although they utilized Park's race-cycle theory and Burgess's social research maps, they also acknowledged the dire effects of discrimination in housing, employment, and access to social welfare institutions on migrants' "disorganized" lives. Like Park, E. Franklin Frazier conceptualized disorganization as a "throwing off" of old ideas and attitudes, and the subsequent adoption of new ones. To this prototypical model, however, he added the negative aspects of racism. Although not as vocal as Du Bois about the virulent effects of discrimination, Frazier concluded that African Americans as a group could never fully assimilate because of segregation.[61] William Oscar Brown, another of Park's African-American protégés, revised Park's race-cycle theory as well. The son of a Texas sharecropper, Brown found little difference between race antipathy and prejudice in the South and North respectively. The race problem, as he conceived it, was not simply one of disorganization but rather of the failure to be given opportunities to "achieve" accommodation.[62] After all, he pointedly asked, how could African Americans accommodate to American society when there were segregated facilities, clubs, and organizations?

However, Brown and Frazier were not the only sociologists aware of Chicago's segregated communities. Some of the Chicago School's faculty also attempted to understand this phenomenon through their social research maps. As mentioned, the city's physical layout of industry, commercial and vice areas, railroad lines, and tenement districts influenced patterns of collective and individual behaviors, variously categorized as disorganized, transitional, and organized. The criteria of an organized community included group homogeneity, standard age and sex distribution, stable family life, and participation in community life expressed through long-term residency, home ownership, and institutional memberships.[63] In contrast, high residential mobility, disproportionate age and sex ratios, a preponderance of rooming and prostitution houses, and high rates of divorce, desertion, delinquency, and dependency were the usual forms of disorganized communities. These characteristics of disorganization occurred for a number of reasons: cultural and economic conflicts; individuals' alienation from group norms; the deterioration of stable community institutions; and disruption in community "metabolism," which most often resulted from an influx of "outside" groups.[64]

Burgess's sociological maps divided Chicago into five radial or concentric zones, originating downtown and extending to the outlying towns. Each zone was not discrete, as his model suggested, but rather permeated the adjacent one. Accordingly, zone 1, comprised of the downtown business district, merged with zone 2, a transitional area where residences deteriorated as industry encroached. The rooming-house area west of the Gold Coast was typical of the second zone with its high resident mobility, nearby slums, "faltering" community organizations, and "moral climate" associated with vice and immorality. In this zone's neighborhoods, most of the residents were detached individuals: shop girls, office help, waitresses, salespeople, and bohemian art students.[65] The proximal zone, zone 3, was primarily a residential area where many immigrant factory workers lived in flats. A number of their daughters worked in the downtown Loop, frequented nearby movie theaters and dance halls, and hoped to eventually move to a better residential area in one of the last two zones, those of the middle-class and the commuters.[66]

As noted, sociologists correlated specific zones with high rates of delinquency. Drawing from the records of probation officers and the juvenile court from 1917 to 1923, Clifford Shaw and his colleagues created their own spot maps from the residences of over 43,000 juvenile delinquents. Their maps were not the first, however, as Breckinridge and Abbott had published spot maps of delinquency in the Hull House neighborhood. But unlike the earlier maps, the sociological maps encompassed the entire city. Further, in converting their spot maps to rate maps, sociologists measured the real frequency (and likelihood) of delinquency by comparing the number of delinquents with the number of same-aged peers per square mile. To be expected, these rate maps indicated that delinquency was not evenly distributed throughout the city but was prevalent in zones characterized as disorganized or transitional.[67]

The areas of high delinquency corresponded to zones 1 and 2, where many immigrant and migrant families lived. Yet Shaw and his colleagues found that those areas of delinquency remained persistently high, even after the dispersion of immigrants to other zones. These conclusions attributed delinquency, then, to human ecology, not cultural influences. This is not to say that Shaw and his collaborators did not take ethnic or familial aspects into consideration, as they observed that community disorganization was compounded by ethnic groups' "weakening" of social controls and traditions typically found in their indigenous institutions.[68] But in adhering to their prototypical models Shaw and his colleagues neglected significant differences among immigrant groups, such as social class, levels of educational attainment, and levels of discrimination.

Sociology student Betty Marwood Hill modified their conclusions in her thesis. In her examination of residential dispersion, she observed that only certain ethnic groups, such as German Americans and Swedish Americans, achieved economic or social mobility, whereas Italian Americans and African Americans did not. As such, she argued, the rate maps distorted the frequency of delinquency. That is, rate maps did not account for why specific groups remained overrepresented in delinquency; they only confirmed that high concentrations of delinquency persisted in certain parts of the city.[69]

Hill did not fully examine African-American communities, perhaps because their dispersion was limited more than other groups by restrictive covenants, red-lining tactics, and other forms of discrimination. By 1920, 90 percent of African Americans in Chicago lived in the southside Black Belt.[70] Alongside racial segregation in the Black Belt, social class differentiation ensued, often resulting in intramobility rather than intermobility. Frazier took note of this phenomena, expanding Burgess's model to seven graduated zones within the Black Belt. He found that most African-American migrants, upon their arrival to the city, settled in the disorganized communities located in zones 1 through 4. High rents exacerbated tenement deterioration there, as single-family structures were frequently converted to multifamily dwellings and kitchenette apartments. To be expected, most male and female delinquents resided in the disorganized and transitional neighborhoods of the Black Belt. Alternately, African-American professionals, who comprised only 3 percent of Chicago's African-American population by 1930, lived in the outermost zones, zones 5 through 7. Communities in those zones registered few or no delinquents, at least as of 1930.[71]

Generally speaking, low delinquency rates were attributed not only to organized communities but to stable family life. Concurrent with theories of adjustment and accommodation, the family unit was not conceptualized as static but as subject to change.[72] In Burgess's words, families had lost their collective identities and had become instead a "mere unity of interacting personalities."[73] This is hardly surprising given the momentous demographic, political, and social changes in early-twentieth-century cities. Massive immigration and migration, an increased presence of women in the labor market and in higher education, the demand for female suffrage, and the avowals of women's sexual independence portrayed in public and in commercial images had a tremendous impact on family structures and roles. Some sociologists, most notably Ernest Mowrer, argued that an increase in the divorce, remarriage, and desertion rates supported the concept that families, like ethnic groups, cycled through stages of disorganization, transition, and organization.[74] (By 1924, one out of seven marriages ended in divorce.[75]) Other sociologists, though, were disconcerted by the dissolution of the traditional family and family roles. Burgess, while noting that the nuclear family was a recent phenomenon, nonetheless elevated mothers' domestic roles, curiously reminiscent of the republic of motherhood ideology. Burgess felt that "[t]o preserve the nation, its foundation must rest upon true domestic life and a higher and more equal public conscience. Whatever destroys home life, what poisons the womb of human generation, or depraves the rising and coming life of the race is treason and destruction against the nation."[76]

This idea was consistent with much of the prescriptive literature that described the mother's emotional capital as critical in the development of her children's personalities. Daughters were to confide in their mothers, especially on sexual matters, although it became apparent, at least to juvenile court officials, that many delinquent girls did not. Sons, too, were to develop close relationships with their mothers, expressed in their frequent conversations and demonstrations of affection. Even African-American sociologist Earl Moses measured family stability by the degree to which adolescent males demonstrated close bonds with their mothers—for example, by kissing their mothers goodbye before school.[77]

By comparison, disorganized families were those "broken" by a host of factors: desertion, divorce, remarriage, dependency, delinquency, death, immorality and intemperance. Typically the designator *broken* referred to homes in which one or both biological parents were absent. Many of these families were immigrants or migrants who found adjustment from rural to urban communities particularly difficult. For example, some Italian-American men, used to communal and extended familial support, found their roles as primary breadwinners in the United States untenable. Consequently, they deserted their families. Stuart Alfred Queen, a graduate of the Chicago School, developed a typology for these deserters in concert with varying aspects of disorganization: the "spurious deserter," the "gradual deserter," the "intermittent husbands," the "temperamental deserter," the "ill-advised marriage type," and the "last resort type."[78] The juvenile and domestic courts, however, were not so interested in such typologies as much as in ascertaining the negative effects of absent parents on their children.

Family stability excluded the presence of lodgers, even in two-parent households, as they contributed to family disorganization and female delinquency.[79] Here, the concern was that a male lodger would take advantage of a young girl's sexual vulnerability or that the power of suggestibility might overwhelm her. Yet many immigrant and African-American families had little choice except to take in lodgers because of high rents. Of the 2,400 Chicago African-American families Irene Graham studied, nearly 34 percent received money from lodgers; 67 percent lowered their rent costs by sharing their residences with relatives. Relatives in particular were not just economic but social resources as they often assisted with child care and household duties.[80] Indeed, such extended families were not simply functional but culturally veritable for African Americans and many immigrants. Nonetheless, lodgers and even extended family members were thought to be indicators of family disorganization.

To be sure, many professionals thought family disorganization a contributing factor to juvenile delinquency. Consistently, the juvenile court records corroborated this idea, noting that most delinquent boys and girls resided in "broken" households. But family disorganization was only one cause of delinquency. In Hill's thesis she concluded that family disorganization was not as serious a factor for those children who lived in high delinquency areas. For these children, it was community disorganization that placed them at a greater risk for delinquency. However, for those children who lived in low delinquency areas, family disorganization was more often the leading cause for delinquency. Certainly Hill acknowledged that poverty affected delinquency rates, although she claimed that it did so indirectly because it influenced where a family lived. Translated differently, poor delinquent children were more likely to reside in deteriorating tenements located in disorganized communities.[81]

Clifford Shaw and his colleagues, too, were interested in the effects of family disorganization upon delinquents. Questioning the commonly accepted idea that delinquency was caused by "broken homes," they conducted a statistical study and found that this was not entirely true. In the case studies they examined, they found evidence of delinquency in both stable and broken homes. In one case from an "organized" community, an aunt brought her fourteen-year-old niece to the juvenile court for dressing "like a flapper" and engaging in sexual delinquency. Clinic examinations indicated that her IQ was average and that she had no emotional problems except "mental conflicts" with her aunt. As discussed in chapters 5 and 6, such cases were not unusual. Indeed, they exemplified the *sturm und drang* of adolescence. In contrast, an African-American mother brought her fifteen-year-old "illegitimate" daughter to a South Side clinic because of her truancy and sex delinquency. Her psychological examination revealed that she had an IQ of 83, classifying her as dull normal. Further tests categorized her as "egocentric and generally aggressive." Although she lived in what was considered a disorganized community, Shaw and his coauthors correlated her behavior with family disorganization, evident in desertion, an extended family, and the stepfather's racist attitudes toward the girl.[82] Although we are given relatively little information about the two girls' backgrounds, one cannot help but wonder to what extent race, social class, and residence influenced the sociologists' conclusions.

Perhaps it would be more accurate to conclude that delinquency could be correlated with family strife, not simply family disorganization. Psychologists theorized that emotional instability, a high degree of suggestibility, a desire for excitement, and hormonal fluctuations were part and parcel of a young girl's transition to adulthood. Sociologists, though, had their own prototypical versions of individual strife and demoralization. To be expected, individual disorganization often occurred within the larger contexts of racial, community, and family disorganization. As society changed, Thomas conjectured, so too did its individuals. But this did not mean that each individual responded to change in the exact same way. Rather, as Thomas pointed out, "There are rival definitions of the situation, and none of them is binding."[83] Like Max Weber, he emphasized the importance of understanding how individuals made sense of their experiences and the world around them. As such, individual and social attitudes were conjoined by what Thomas referred to as "experience complexes."[84]

To understand individual personalities and their interactions with social environments, Thomas often relied upon autobiographical materials. In *Polish Peasants in Europe and America*, Thomas and his coauthor, Florian Znaniecki, used private letters (762, to be exact), life histories, newspapers, and reports from social agencies and the courts to chronicle Polish families' transitions to the United States. They especially noted the overall disintegration of collective life through the process of individuation. More precisely, the social cohesion of traditional communities and families weakened as Polish-American youth assimilated to American life.[85] To illustrate, Polish parents and their daughters disagreed about many things: whether the daughters should hand over their weekly wages; whether they could attend dance halls and other public amusements; how they dressed or if they could wear makeup; and if they should have dowries. But the "wishes" of these girls—for new experiences, security, response, and recognition—were consonant with those of most adolescent girls. Not surprisingly, some immigrant girls drifted from traditional mores as they experimented with their newfound social and sexual independence. Thomas argued that what was commonly referred to as the "demoralization" of these girls entailed a shift, not a downward turn, in standards. They were not *immoral*, he argued, but *amoral*.[86]

To some extent, Thomas's position on amorality reflected his earlier scholarship on female sexual habits and instincts, which relied upon instinct theory and a historicoanthropological approach similar to that of Havelock Ellis. To illustrate, Ellis, in tracing the "primitive" histories of sexual practices, relished the age-old female trait of modesty. One of his examples of modest dress was the "petticoat of shredded bark" that primitive women wore. Thomas followed suit, arguing how the allure of modest clothing harked back to the primitive woman's "girdle of deer skin."[87] Ellis's ideas about female coquettish behavior were also elaborated by Thomas in his discussion of the female adventuress and the "sporting-woman." Focusing on the female "wooing instinct," Thomas drew parallels between the human and animal worlds, noting how male displays of color and nuanced techniques attracted females. In contrast, the female human display was coyness. Returning to the animal world, Thomas pointed to the female cuckoo, whose mating call was "an alluring laugh," followed by a mad chase. Women, too, he thought, employed this kind of strategy when they consented to sex, even though they demonstratively asserted they would never do so. Unlike men, who were ostentatious, women were more evasive and cunning. This was not immoral, he thought, but simply a "protective instinct" and a means of ensuring survival. Because a woman's capital was her "personal charm and wits," not her economic power, she had little choice except to use these behaviors to her advantage.[88]

Drawing further upon instinct theory, Thomas described two types of women: the "adventuress" and the "sporting-woman." Thomas thought that adventure for women was simply a demonstration of their instincts and their own understanding of "peril." As such, adventuresses were too intelligent and energetic to devote themselves to the drudgery of housework, and so sought the perils of a more fast-paced world. These women, usually single and unattached, craved stimulation and gratification for psychological, not economic, reasons. Thomas argued that the adventuress was not biologically abnormal; rather, it was her interests that were "defective." Like the adventuress, the "sporting-woman" wanted her own share of physical stimulation.[89] These two types of women would be refashioned later by psychiatrists as psychopathic women and sex deviants. As Elizabeth Lunbeck has argued, psychopathic women simply assumed the male prerogative of sexual gratification.[90]

Vestiges of instinct theory, especially as they related to female behavior, continued in Thomas's later work on immigrant girls. Once detached from their parents and communities, immigrant girls "loosened" their inhibitions. As Thomas conjectured, "There are thousands of girls leading irregular lives in our large cities whose parents think they are in factories, stores, and business positions."[91] The onset of female delinquency, then, began with a desire for freedom, adventure (or peril), and new experiences, but also with a desire to better one's circumstances. As such, the desire for security sometimes entailed provocative clothing, attendance at dance halls and roadside inns, and bold behaviors, not unlike the behavior of the adventuress.[92] Thomas's description of one delinquent girl's sexual impropriety and her frequent escapes from authorities—"she was as fleet as a deer"—exemplified her desires for adventure and freedom.[93]

Influenced by Thomas, sociology graduate student Evelyn Buchan examined the disorganization of delinquent girls as part of a complex process of accommodation. Like Thomas, she argued that there was no definitive authority upon which these girls could base their decisions. Rather, situations and the girls' adaptations constantly changed. These situations, however, were particularly problematic for immigrant girls, many of whom were juvenile court wards. More precisely, in their immigrant communities, there were fewer sex taboos and so they were more often exposed to sexual activities in overcrowded tenements.[94] Although Buchan used the sociological concepts of "the situation" and accommodation, she also voiced concerns reflective of Breckinridge and Abbott: overcrowded tenements, the presence of lodgers, and the correlation between poverty and delinquency.

Individual demoralization, then, especially for delinquent girls, took two interactive turns. The first centered on how the moral and physical environments affected a person. Detrimental aspects—faltering community institutions, crowded tenements, encroaching industry, and high rates of mobility—had a negative effect upon delinquent girls. The second focused on how individuals interpreted and adjusted to varying situations within their environments. Those girls who took a downward spiral—adventuresses, sporting women, prostitutes, and charity girls—reacted against a set of environmental constraints by willfully choosing to break traditional gender roles. Yet as Thomas observed, such decisions often arose from their desires for adventure, security, and recognition or love. As one charity girl reasoned, "'There was no one to care! Why should I slave and work when I might have the things I wanted? And not the least of these was the intimate touch and glance of a man—even it were only half make-believe—someone to talk intimately with; someone to come home to; someone to ask where you've been; these, too, are things one cannot live without.' "[95]

Sociologists were not the only professionals to wrestle with theories of individual disorganization. Psychiatrists and psychologists, too, diagnosed, measured, and treated young women's mental, emotional, and sexual aberrations. To some extent, they appropriated the sociological language of "broken" homes and disorganized communities to account for etiologies and causative factors. But unlike sociologists and the social reformers, they were interested in the interior mapping of an individual's subconscious desires, emotions, and memories. Accordingly, delinquent girls' sexual misbehaviors arose from buried childhood traumas, egocentric tendencies, and compulsive inclinations.

2

Psychomedical Models of Delinquency

I never knew what it was all about until I read that set of Havelock Ellis.

—Floyd Dell, *Love without Money*

The Medicalization of Heterosexuality

The juvenile court system promoted various professional fields whose knowledges contributed to a fuller understanding of delinquency. Psychologists, for one, developed a battery of intelligence, personality, vocational, and moral discrimination tests to ascertain how mentally capable and deliberate youth were when committing acts of delinquency and deviance. Psychiatrists, too, assisted in the diagnoses of those youth with the most intractable of behavioral problems: the feebleminded, psychopathic, hysterical, epileptic, "inverted" (homosexual), and egocentric. Juvenile court judges often relied on these tests and diagnoses to determine which dispositions were most conducive for delinquent youths' reform. Not surprisingly, gendered categories of pathologies for delinquent girls emerged. Despite the proliferation of psychological and psychiatric classifications purporting to be scientific, moral prescriptions persisted. As Carrol Smith-Rosenberg has argued, in relegating the "new woman" to the status of sexual object (or object of study), sexologists and doctors allowed the state to regulate female behavior and identity.[1]

Indeed, the professional discourses were saturated with the subject of sexuality. In their elaborations of "sexual heterogeneities"—inversions, perversions, autoeroticisms, and heterosexual promiscuities—professionals developed their own disciplinary genres from clients' narratives.[2] For example, psychiatrists coaxed childhood memories, dreams, and traumas from their patients. They interrogated delinquent girls about their fantasies, desires, and indulgences. These confessions became the basis for medical histories, case studies, institutional reports, and casework records. Psychoanalysts, to some degree, shaped delinquents' interpretations and narratives of childhood events through their directed questions.[3] Assuming the role of a fatherly confidante, Dr. William Healy, director of Chicago's Juvenile Psychopathic Institute from 1909 to 1914, created his own research tool for eliciting delinquents' "own stories." Correlating their autobiographical accounts with anthropometric measurements, psychological test results, family histories, and juvenile court records, Healy hoped to ascertain the exact causes of delinquency. He would reduce this information into psychograms, postcard-sized profiles, textbook illustrations of delinquency types.[4]

Parents, as before, were no longer the primary agents responsible for their children's sexual behaviors. Psychiatrists and psychologists, working in conjunction with juvenile courts, guided delinquent girls' rehabilitation through their diagnoses and treatment plans. Delinquent girls' reform expanded to include "bad" parents whose pathologies included promiscuity, alcoholism, feeblemindedness, and insanity. What purpose did this "whole thicket of disparate sexualities" serve? I argue that professionals had more to gain from these classifications than did the delinquent girls themselves. In essence, the juvenile courts and the behavioral sciences entered into an alliance, a system of regulations based on scientific conceptions of what constituted appropriate sexual behavior. Those who deviated from these established norms were subject to a "technology of control": psychopathic hospitals, mental hygiene and child guidance clinics, industrial schools, reformatories, or to use the kindlier designation, "homes."[5]

Although the behavioral sciences and medical fields disfavored a strictly hereditarian model in determining the etiology of delinquency, they still emphasized physiological factors. For example, children of female "drunkards" did not necessarily inherit the proclivity to drink, but they did bear the associated effects of "ill-nourished tissues" and "a badly developed brain and nervous system."[6] Moreover, parents' excessive drinking led to their children's moral degeneracy. Dr. Le Grain, in following four generations of alcoholics from 215 families, concluded that over 85 percent of family members were either "degenerates" or "morally irresponsible."[7] Although he did not fully specify their behavioral aberrations, he was most likely referring to their feeblemindedness and lack of sexual restraint.

Some psychologists and psychiatrists used anthropometrical measurements to correlate physical and mental abnormalities. They found that chemical and glandular imbalances, or skeletal and muscular defects, predisposed youth to delinquent behaviors. To illustrate, nearly 25 percent of the students in the truant class of the Chicago Parental School possessed physical and mental abnormalities. At Chicago's John Worthy School for delinquent boys, students were found to be "inferior" in all physical measurements. These defects were attributed to opium smoking, a weak-willed character, speech impediments, and deafness.[8] What remained largely unexamined were the long-term physical and psychological effects of poverty and malnutrition found in many children and youth presented to Chicago's juvenile court.[9]

Some psychiatrists and psychologists, however, argued that the causes of delinquency were complex. William Healy and his associate (and later wife) Dr. Augusta Bronner, conjectured that there was no single cause of delinquency. Rather, many physiological, psychological, environmental, and social factors contributed to such misbehaviors. Healy nonetheless remained concerned with heredity and physiological aspects, noting that many delinquents' parents were alcoholics, psychotics, and criminals. Although he thought that dissoluteness of home life through poverty, alcoholism, desertion, insanity, and immorality accounted for many delinquent cases, he also insisted that hereditary and physiological factors could not be completely ruled out. Accordingly, he remained attentive to delinquent girls' childhood illnesses, the onset of menstruation and breast development, their weight, height, physical appearance, and the presence of physical defects.[10]

Through their multivariate framework, Healy and Bronner refuted Henry Goddard's contention that a disproportionate number of delinquent girls were congenitally feebleminded. In one of many studies, Goddard and his associates had concluded that fifty-two of fifty-six delinquent girls they studied were feebleminded.[11] Other psychologists confirmed these findings. Margaret Otis, in her investigation of 172 delinquent girls in the New Jersey State Home, classified 75 percent of them as feebleminded. In his examination of state industrial boys and girls in 1915, C. S. Bluemel concluded that girls were generally more mentally defective than boys, especially among youth brought in on charges of immorality.[12] Healy and Bronner disagreed with these conclusions, noting that 63 percent of the delinquent children in Chicago they studied had average or above average IQs. Of the five hundred cases from Chicago's Juvenile Psychopathic Institute, they found that only 10 percent tested at the level of feebleminded.[13]

Like other mental aberrations, feeblemindedness was subject to various typologies. Characterizing feeblemindedness as any type of mental deficiency, Goddard categorized idiots as those with a mental age of two years or lower, imbeciles with a mental age of three to seven years, and morons from eight to

twelve years. In terms of IQs, high-grade feebleminded persons had a score of
70 or above; low graders tested below 70. Professionals generally agreed that
low-grade feebleminded individuals were incapable of distinguishing right
from wrong. While high-grade feebleminded youth could do so, they could not
fully comprehend the consequences of their actions.[14] Dr. Herman Adler of the
Chicago branch of the Institute for Juvenile Research (IJR), however, was less
sanguine in his appraisal of their capacities. He described low-grade feebleminded persons as "the healthy, stupid type" but high-grade persons as those
"by nature more intelligent, but do not teach its capacity" [sic].[15]

Historians who have examined the eugenics debate have documented how
sterilization laws targeted mostly poor white and immigrant females, many of
whom were classified as feebleminded.[16] Finding that approximately 40 to 50
percent of the immigrants he tested were feebleminded, Goddard favored their
sterilization, arguing that many feebleminded girls were descendants of feebleminded parents. Concerned with race suicide and the mongrelization of races,
some psychologists and public reformers, too, pointed out that sterilization
protected society, as well as the feebleminded females themselves, who were
vulnerable to unscrupulous males.[17]

Although the Chicago juvenile court did not keep records on the ethnicity
of girls classified as feebleminded, reformatory and rescue-home records provided some information. Not surprisingly, immigrant and poor native-born
white girls, many of the latter from the South, were more often classified as
such. To illustrate, Helena, a thirteen-year-old Bohemian girl, was one example of a feeblemindedness that doctors considered beyond repair. She had been
placed in a subnormal classroom but had made little progress there because
she talked incessantly about sex. She was also an inveterate masturbator. When
her teacher and school nurse discovered that she had "had sex" with several
classmates, they informed her parents who in turn did nothing. Helena was
then brought before the juvenile court where, based upon test results, the
judge recommended the Lincoln State School for the Feebleminded. But her
parents vehemently disagreed with this decision and so retained a doctor and
lawyer to represent her. As a consequence, the court continued her case. For
the next four years Helena remained at home because her former school refused to readmit her. She returned to the juvenile court at the age of seventeen
when she accused several boys of rape. The boys were indicted and Helena was
institutionalized this time, perhaps to the Lincoln State School for the Feebleminded. But that did not mean that juvenile court staff thought her capable of
reform. As one volunteer probation officer with the Juvenile Protective Association surmised about Helena's future, "One does not like to think what will
happen when she is released—a girl weak in self-control, sexually precocious
and perverted, with no one to protect her but a family whose moral standards
are very low."[18]

There were few published cases of African-American feebleminded girls. This may seem surprising, given the prevailing ideas that African Americans were childlike in their mental capacities and savage in their sexual appetite. Institutional racism may partly have accounted for the few cases of feeblemindedness because such a diagnosis would have warranted accommodations in facilities that were already overcrowded. To date, I have located only one African-American feeble-minded case, one that was highly publicized in Chicago's African-American news-paper. A juvenile court judge sent a fourteen-year-old African-American girl to the State Industrial School for Delinquent Girls in Geneva, Illinois, following the death of her parents. This disposition was contradictory because she had no charges of delinquency such as incorrigibility or immorality. But the Geneva re-formatory was one of the few institutions that accepted African-American girls. She was later paroled to a North Side Chicago family, who after two years time decided to commit her to the Dixon State School for the Uneducable Feeble-minded. According to the records at Dixon and Geneva, however, she had never been given a mental examination. Yet she was classified as feebleminded. Even so, the Dixon school staff entrusted her with caring for young crippled children, as well as cutting patients' hair with scissors and razors. No explanations were given by school officials for her commitment or for the fact that she was not re-leased until thirteen years later at the age of twenty-nine.[19]

Regardless of the ethnicity of feebleminded girls, the pressing issues for the juvenile court were twofold: how to determine if such girls were capable of giving accurate testimony; and to what degree they were capable of reform. Among the battery of tests given to delinquent girls was the Aussage test, which determined their ability to provide accurate statements about their cases. This was especially critical for determining cases of rape or incest. Augusta Bronner also considered the test's administration an issue of gender justice, pointing out that men sometimes went "scot-free" in rape cases simply because the judges refused to accept feebleminded girls' testimonies.[20] Al-though Bronner and Healy argued that many feebleminded girls were inca-pable of telling the truth, they did not consider another alternative, that some girls classified as such may have *chosen* not to tell the truth.[21] Perhaps threat-ened by parents or encouraged by the promise of marriage, some girls may have deliberately exaggerated or falsified their stories to the judge, psycholo-gists, and probation officers.

The issue of treatment for feebleminded girls was also problematic. Depend-ing upon the extent of their mental defectiveness, feebleminded girls might re-quire institutionalization or simply close supervision in their communities. By the late 1920s, a number of professionals estimated that up to 90 percent of fee-bleminded persons could live in their neighborhoods, where they could partic-ipate in clubs and organizations. In fact, many high-grade mentally subnormal persons could be self-supporting if they received special training in the public schools.[22] Instead, too many girls classified as feebleminded were sent to correctional schools, such as the State Industrial School for Delinquent Girls at Geneva. This was, as noted, because the institutions for the feebleminded were usually overcrowded. When a state colony for epileptics eventually opened in Illinois with few inmates, feebleminded patients were sent there to alleviate overcrowding at the Lincoln State School for the Feebleminded.[23]

In contrast to feebleminded girls, other girls possessed aggressive personalities, demonstrated in their acts of running away, destroying property, and teaching "bad habits" (usually of a sexual nature) to others. These girls were alternately classified as egocentric, hysterical, inverted, or psychopathic. The IJR in Chicago tested one such sixteen-year-old girl who was destructive during her stay at the Chicago Detention Home. During her first examination, she refused to talk with the staff, except to say that her mother had "peached on her." She later consented to a mental test that indicated she was of normal intelligence and had "superior constructive ability." Although she thereafter refused to take another exam, the judge noted that according to court and probation reports her mother was a prostitute and that the girl had been her accomplice since childhood. According to the girl's story, her mother became jealous when the male clients preferred her daughter and so dragged the girl to court. The judge sent the daughter to Geneva, where she was found to be pregnant as well as infected with syphilis. (Unfortunately, there was no discussion of whether the court charged the mother as an accomplice in her daughter's immorality.) Because of lack of complete case records, the girl's version cannot be verified. Nonetheless, the psychiatrist, Dr. Herman Adler, acknowledged her horrendous childhood, yet diagnosed her as "extremely egocentric," the cause of most of her difficulties.[24] Rather than attributing her delinquency to parental neglect or questionable home conditions, he specifically cast the problem as one of individual pathology.

Psychopathic girls, too, were considered egocentric, although not necessarily deficient in intelligence. If anything, many of the psychopathic females whom Elizabeth Lunbeck has analyzed had normal or even superior levels of intelligence. Nonetheless, they were considered subnormal, even though IQ tests could not determine the etiology of their deficiencies. Instead, those with a psychopathic personality were said to possess a "defective" memory and will, evident in their resistance to suggestions, especially those dispensed by professionals. Translated differently, psychopathic females were headstrong, independent, and openly defiant. Dr. Winifred Richmond, psychologist for the Government Hospital for the Insane in Washington, D.C., summed up her assessment of them as follows: "The psychopathic girl is a law unto herself."[25]

Psychopathic girls exhibited any number of peculiar symptoms. Dr. Goddard enumerated mania, hallucinations, and insanity, with the more usual characteristics of nervousness, "cunning," and stubbornness. Noting that many were truants, liars, or sexual "perverts," he added that they could be either feeble-minded or of average intelligence. One way that Goddard measured their psychopathology was through a word association test. But how he distinguished whether their lying was intentional or due to their inability to decipher truth (if they were feebleminded as well) remained unclear. Indeed, Goddard seemed more worried about those who were not feebleminded: "It is the psychopath who has not deteriorated but has a normal level or even, as many of them have, a superior level of intelligence that constitutes the great social problem."[26] Given their penchant for conniving, these girls were unpredictable. Rather than acknowledging the degree of independence psychopathic girls possessed, psychologists and psychiatrists thought in terms of their emotional instability and shallowness, lack of self-control, extreme suggestibility, irritability, and other social maladjustments. Such symptoms represented a latitude of misbe-haviors for which there were no easy cures, what Dr. Richmond referred to as "psychiatric scrap baskets."[27] Although "normal" adolescent girls, too, might possess some of these qualities, it was the intensity of these traits that character-ized psychopathic girls.

Perhaps the greatest concern was the psychopathic girls' sexual proclivities, expressed in heterosexual, lesbian, or autoerotic activities. In Lunbeck's words, these women followed the "disturbing assumption of male prerogative."[28] Be-cause their defects rested in the "emotional, volitional, and orientation spheres," not the intellectual or purely physical, their diagnoses were more dif-ficult. But their treatment was not. Like low-grade feebleminded girls, psycho-pathic girls often required institutionalization to protect themselves and others from their incomprehensible actions.[29] As one professional advised, "Especially dangerous to the community were the attractive girls of high levels of intelli-gence who were nevertheless unable to protect themselves, and who were most frequently removed from the protection of the institutions by families who did not understand their weakness or who maintained a home in itself as unsafe place for them."[30] As will be discussed in chapter 8, many of these girls from Chicago were sent to the Geneva reformatory, where they continued to flaunt their sexual independence and brazenly defy rules and regulations. The psychiatrists and doctors there, concerned about their professional reputations and locus of power, used the latitude of psychopathic symptoms to label these girls as such.

Similar to their psychopathic sisters, hysterical girls exhibited aggressive be-haviors. But their associated symptoms—delusion, stupor, dream states, amne-sia, anxiety, obsessions, marked phobias, impulsivity, irritability, hypochondria, and even epilepsy—were thought to stem from unconscious or subconscious repression of desires, mostly of a sexual nature. In contrast, psychopathics will-ingly and flagrantly acted upon their conscious desires. Regardless, both types of women relied upon their reservoirs of emotional capital to manipulate men.

Dr. Abraham Myerson illustrated, for example, how, during conjugal disputes, wives sometimes displayed hysterical symptoms such as headaches, fainting spells (without impairment of consciousness), vomiting episodes, aphonia, and exaggerated paralysis simply to get their way.[31]

In addition to hysterical and psychopathic behavior, women had other aberrant behaviors for controlling men, including pathological lying. Of the nineteen cases of pathological lying in Healy's study, eighteen were female. Female pathological liars, like their psychopathic counterparts, often possessed normal and even superior levels of intelligence. The source of their illness, then, was not a mental deficiency but often defective home conditions, especially the lack of parental supervision. In only one case did Healy attribute pathological lying directly to poverty, even though many of these patients experienced it. Regardless of the symptoms and causes, one might well question how the juvenile court staff and judges were able to ascertain the truthfulness of any delinquent girls' stories. And if, as Healy admitted, some delinquent girls were highly imaginative, at what point did they become pathological liars? As noted, some court officials did acknowledge how easily some girls fabricated unlikely stories. Yet Healy never seemed to openly question the girls, though he did postulate that females by their nature were more prone to "deviate from the truth" than men.[32]

Nonheterosexual Deviances

Sexual deviance for women extended beyond the heterosexual to include lesbianism, autoeroticism, and, in some cases, frigidity.[33] Females who engaged in any of these "aberrations" transgressed the standards of "normal" female behavior and so were often characterized as masculine. Lewis Terman and Catharine Cox Miles's word-stimulus test became one means of measuring the "femininity" index of females. Women who possessed a strong female identity chose words that depicted glamour, beauty, and domesticity, not unlike prescriptive gender expectations. For example, women usually associated the word *blue* with *dress*, whereas men thought of *spectrum*. Or women, when they heard the word *powder*, thought of *room*; men, however, thought of *bullet*. Combining this index with vocational tests, ink-blot associations, and interest inventories, Terman and Miles were able to determine how gender-balanced girls were. To be sure, not all girls met the criteria for femininity. One "masculine" girl had a love of adventure, evident in her promiscuous life and "insatiable appetite for thrills." In a similar vein, her independence demonstrated a lack of emotionality that was considered characteristic of females. In another case of masculine behavior, which reached "beyond the 100th percentile," a female gang member dressed as a boy, stole cars, and even "hoboed" to Louisiana from Chicago. In some cases, however, girls were classified as masculine simply because they lacked the "instinct" of coyness.[34] That instinct theory still had some salience for psychologists in the mid-1930s was surprising given that sociologists had abandoned these ideas twenty years earlier.

The gender norms established in Terman and Miles's test were consistent with images of the "new woman," the flapper, and the vamp. Indeed, such sexualized images resonated for working-class girls, lured by the excitement of dance halls and movies, as well as for college girls who tested the sexual waters at campus petting parties. For most youth, the world shimmered with a youthfulness and excitement of its own. As one educational hygienist, Ira Wile, described it, society was in its own state of adolescence, characterized by a new morality or a "molecular redistribution" of constraints. Similar to William I. Thomas's ideas of individuation, most young people, Wile argued, were not hypersexual; rather, the traditional social controls had become "feeble."[35] Psychologist G. Stanley Hall, however, thought differently: youth were savage and needed their sexual energies bridled. In fact, youth craved excitement and adventure so much that they gravitated toward "hot and perfervid psychic states."[36]

Like other psychologists, Hall was equally disturbed by autoeroticism, largely because it led to an aversion for "normal coitus."[37] Additionally, he felt, those who engaged in autoerotic behavior might suffer other long-term negative effects, such as neurosis, psychoses, or diminished mental acuity. Despite such forewarnings, young women and girls of all social classes indulged in "the habit." Psychologist Katherine B. Davis found in her 1929 survey of young college-educated women that nearly 60 percent admitted to masturbating.[38] But autoerotic behavior was not always physical. Girls who spent their time "fantasy-weaving" or daydreaming were thought to be engaging in a psychic form of masturbation. So, too, did female patients of one doctor confess to autoerotic excitement when they sat in movie theaters or on their boyfriends' laps. Others reported becoming aroused by books, artwork, pelvic examinations, or just looking at men. (The works and authors most often listed that excited women were the Bible, William Shakespeare, Havelock Ellis, and the poetry of Alfred Lord Tennyson and Thomas Carlyle.) One girl, who had read about "self-abuse" in Hall's *Adolescence* didn't know that that was what she had been doing until someone explained it to her.[39]

Although Healy and other doctors conjectured that girls' sexual arousal resulted from their early physical maturation, they did not offer alternatives to the girls' sexual curiosity other than sublimation. Social reformers, social workers, and mothers diligently assisted girls in ridding themselves of "the habit." In his novel *Love without Money*, Floyd Dell remarked about such an older woman that "[the YWCA girls] worshipped her [a female reformer], and listened to her, and reported their moral struggles with masturbation to her, and wrote poems to her."[40] But tales of conquer were not always so successful. In one case, a girl decided to engage in sex with men to stop her habit of masturbation. She soon became pregnant, then had an abortion with complications. In later letters to her social worker, she asked for help with her depression.[41]

Clearly, the idea that masturbation turned girls away from heterosexual pleasures reflected larger social fears. Women's sexual and social independence, as well as professional aspirations, corresponded to a crisis in masculinity. Females who asserted a new form of sexual politics through self-fulfillment—be it through professional work, social reform, or communities of sisterhood—baffled the largely male medical profession.[42] As such, doctors sometimes collapsed the distinctions among female reformers, professionals, and lesbians, portraying all as masculinized. College women who chose professional careers over marriage were especially targeted. One sexologist, reinvoking Dr. Edward Clarke's refutation of women's higher education in the 1870s, postulated that intellectual women "are as a class more imaginative, romantic, poetical and amative than their less cultured sisters." But, he continued, their intellectual work consumed so much of their nervous energy that their "sexual vigor" waned considerably. Inevitably, the result was frigidity or love without affection, the latter considered another form of autoeroticism.[43]

Lurking beneath the diagnosis of frigidity were other profiles, those of adventuresses, prostitutes, café girls, and mistresses of wealthy men. Not unlike the psychopathic female, these women possessed an "overwhelming intoxication bordering on irresponsibility" even as they exhibited no evidence of mental disorders.[44] Translated differently, these women engaged in heterosexual sex physically, but remained emotionally detached from (or frigid with) their sex partners. Such psychological explanations, however, were beside the point. It was highly unlikely that psychologists and psychiatrists would have ever considered promiscuity or autoeroticism emotionally engaging or fulfilling.

Frigidity could also signal the ultimate turning away from men: lesbianism. Theories of "inversion" generally followed the paths of hereditarian, degeneracy, and evolutionary thought, with the first two being the most common. In fact, Ellis's *Studies in the Psychology of Sex*, read by many Americans, popularized the idea that sexual inversion was congenital, though Ellis did concede that homosexuality was "natural" for some persons. Degeneracy theory—clearly racist in conception—characterized primitive societies as savage and sexually promiscuous.[45] This theory took on social class dimensions in the early twentieth century. More specifically, working-class and poor persons' homosexual behavior was more often cast as immoral or perverted, whereas middle-class homosexual clients were considered "ill," thereby capable of being restored to their normal heterosexual identities.[46] Those who subscribed to the evolutionary theory did not assign class and racial privileges to homosexuals and lesbians. Instead, they thought of homosexuality as a regression to an earlier epoch, thus signaling the decline of a civilization.

Theorists with a hereditarian and degeneracy bend speculated that homosexuality could be a physical or dispositional trait. In the former case, homosexuals often engaged in unsocial sexual promiscuities. But those suffering from a dispositional ailment were potentially "good citizens" who simply suffered conflicts about their sexual identities.[47] Some of these cases were simply a matter of outgrowing particular stages of development. For example, preadolescent and adolescent girls who had crushes (or "smashes") on their female teachers, friends, and roommates usually went through a temporary stage of secondary homosexuality.[48] Single-sex schools and reformatories were especially known for these incidents. Some girls, however, did not develop beyond this stage of "libido development" but "f[e]ll into the slough of social evil."[49] In other words, they became seasoned lesbians.

As will be discussed in subsequent chapters, lesbian practices greatly distressed the superintendents and matrons of reformatories and rescue homes. Ironically, attempts to reinforce a domestic ideology through cottage life at the state reformatory at Geneva backfired. Although administrators went to great efforts to channel the girls' attention away from sexual thoughts, some inmates engaged in romantic relationships with one another. Delinquent girls were not, however, the only ones to do so. Katharine Davis's study of twelve hundred unmarried college women in the late 1920s documented that over half of her sample reported some kind of emotional relationship with other women; over 25 percent of them admitted to "overt homosexual expression[s]." Similarly, Phyllis Blanchard and Carlyn Manasses's survey of 252 teenage girls from the same period confirmed that almost 33 percent of them had "crushes" on other girls.[50] Of course, sisterly affections were not new and one can only speculate how many female social reformers and professionals themselves engaged in lesbian relationships. What was new, however, was the disclosure of such affections, encouraged in part by the abundance of professional texts and discourses about sexualities.

The proliferations of scientific discourses, genres, and texts relating to sexualities in the early twentieth century was emblematic of the "new psychology." Yet as John Burnham has persuasively argued, the narcissistic self, preoccupied with consumption and material goods, emerged alongside this new scientism. Nonetheless, romance magazines, newspaper advice columns, marital manuals, and case studies and theories excerpted for popular consumption created the illusion of shared experiences and a common understanding of these scientific theories,[51] but those who shared in this culture were limited by class and race, and they were largely heterosexual.

The emphasis on the individual further fractured a social reformist approach within the juvenile court system. Despite the fact that many delinquent girls came from homes beset with alcoholism, poverty, and crowded conditions, psychiatrists and psychologists decontextualized and stripped away their familial hardships. Instead, poverty became a variable, a single factor in a complex web of individual pathologies. Whether excavating memories, assessing the girls' social or moral capacities, or analyzing the girls' "own stories," psychiatrists and psychologists mined the recesses of the mind and emotions. The primitive, the immoral, the incomprehensible: all resided in the innermost core, the id. Much like sociologists who drafted their own abstruse maps of vice and delinquency areas, psychiatrists mapped the most interior, the most remote aspects of the girls' dreams, wishes, and sexual desires. Their charts, correlations, and case studies, however, revealed less about the delinquent girls' lives than about their own professional expansion.

3

The "Helping" Professions

Female Probation and Police Officers and African–American Social Workers

The probation system is the cord upon which the pearls of the juvenile court are strung.

—Timothy Hurley,
Juvenile Courts and What They Have Accomplished

The Chicago Woman's Club and the Juvenile Court

Like others in the "helping" professions, early female probation officers in Chicago often engaged in conflicting ideologies, discourses, and practices. This was to be expected, as their official positions were inscribed in one of the most experimental of all progressive reforms: the Juvenile Court Act of 1899. Despite Chicago reformers' insistence that the juvenile court's efficacy relied upon qualified probation officers, they did not persuade the Illinois legislature which omitted the provision for officers' salaries in the final bill.[1] Legislators may have surmised that the club women would continue their volunteer protective work with dependent and delinquent children, and further, perhaps, that prominent female clubs would financially support probation officers. Indeed, one year before the court's inception, the Chicago Woman's Club (CWC) had contributed ten dollars a month toward two officers' salaries. Additionally, CWC members assisted the officers by visiting the homes and schools of children who had been detained by the police.[2]

In essence, maternalist clubs such as the CWC—in conjunction with professional maternalists such as Julia Lathrop, Sophonisba Breckinridge, and Jane Addams—carved distinct professional and ideological niches for female employment in Chicago's juvenile court. Professional maternalists, however, placed less of an emphasis upon volunteerism and maternal qualities than maternalists, and stressed more rigorous training and commensurate salaries. Nonetheless, distinctions were often blurred as the professional and the volunteer, the scientific and the charitable, and the bureaucratic and the grassroots coexisted. Even when qualifications for probation officers did become more rigorous, women's organizations continued to exert tremendous influence on Chicago's juvenile court as they worked alongside judges, probation officers, and other professionals. Although this created a formidable "female dominion" in Chicago's juvenile court, it also contributed to the lack of prestige and professional standing in probation work.[3]

With the passage of the Juvenile Court Act in 1899, the Cook County Juvenile Court (CCJC) appointed its first probation officer, Alzina Stevens, who had already engaged voluntarily in such work through the CWC. Lathrop, speaking on behalf of Stevens and future officers, returned to the neglected provision of a salaried and, hence, qualified probation staff: "The efficacy of the law depends upon the efficiency of the probation officers, and at present these officers must be either policemen or unpaid volunteers or paid volunteers. The work in the long run must depend upon paid volunteers."[4] Lathrop's oxymoronic words, "paid volunteers," were strategic in underscoring the prodigious amount of experience and knowledge that women had already accumulated. Lucy Flower—president of the CWC as well as a trustee of the Chicago Half Orphan Asylum, the Chicago Home for the Friendless, and the St. Charles Industrial School for Boys—advanced Lathrop's recommendation. She introduced Stevens to Judge Richard Tuthill and proposed that Stevens be the first "paid volunteer." Additionally, she spearheaded the establishment of the Juvenile Court Committee (JCC), chaired by Lathrop, which coordinated the financial commitments of Chicago women's clubs and organizations.

Until the county assumed fiscal responsibility in 1905, each female group contributed ten dollars toward the salaries of mostly female probation officers, a chief probation officer, and a stenographer. Eventually, each club assumed responsibility for the salary of one probation officer, with the stipulation that he or she handle no more than sixty cases.[5] Even after the Juvenile Court Act was amended in 1905, stipulating that the county administer a civil service examination and pay for probation officers, the JCC still continued to exert tremendous influence, underwriting the salaries for five probation officers and for Emma Quinlan, supervisor for the volunteer probation officers.[6]

One of those volunteers was an African-American woman by the name of Elizabeth McDonald. The 1900 annual report of the CCJC described her as "one colored woman who devotes her entire time to the work, free of charge, and whose services are invaluable to the court as she takes charge of all colored children."[7] No club paid her a salary, although members of the Chicago Woman's Club were acquainted with her probation work as they attended most of the juvenile court sessions and discussed cases with probation officers at the Hull House weekly, and the CWC did provide her with in-kind donations of clothing and food, which she distributed to needy families. In 1905, McDonald took the first civil service examination but did not pass, due by her account to her poor schooling in Kentucky. No level of schooling had yet been stipulated for officers, however, and it was not until 1922 that a high school diploma would be required.[8] Not deterred, McDonald continued both her probationary and rescue work, exemplifying what was considered so essential for effective probation work: "the spirit of a missionary."[9]

In 1907, McDonald founded the Louise Juvenile Home for neglected and dependent children of all races. Her volunteer path thus forked from the maternalist agendas of native-born white club women, who created two auxiliaries to the juvenile court: the Juvenile Protective League, organized at the district level; and the Juvenile Protective Association (JPA), which rose from the ashes of the Juvenile Court Committee (JCC), largely dissolved by 1909. Both auxiliaries engaged in volunteer work, with members patrolling districts and neighborhoods, conducting investigative work on saloons and roadhouses, and creating boys' and girls' clubs.[10] Although these organizations functioned on a volunteer level, they greatly affected probation work, especially because of Louise de Koven Bowen's sphere of influence. Because of her affiliation with the CWC and the JPA and her formal ties with juvenile court, Bowen was able to strategically straddle both sides: she promoted volunteer work in the court, as well as better training for regular probation officers.

From "Moral" to "Social" Physicians: Professionalizing the Work of Female Probation Officers

Despite the first civil service examination in Chicago in 1905, the primary criterion for hiring probation officers was a high moral character, verified through an oral examination and three references. Although the 1911 written examination was expanded to include case studies, as well as explications of child-related laws, the application still asked whether the examinee was of "good moral character, of temperate habits, and of sound health." These qualifications would be recommended by the U.S. Children's Bureau until 1923, although the bureau would also promote a college education and casework experience.[11] Even as late as 1933, the requisites of personality, poise, appearance, and responsiveness would be listed, reflecting characteristics perceived to be female. Moral undertones persisted, even when the probation officer was depicted as a "social adjustor or straightener" and the delinquent's rehabilitation was recast into character building and habit formation.[12]

Not unlike the home visitors affiliated with the early kindergarten movement, the first probation officers were valued more for their maternal traits than professional services. Like kindergarten teachers, probation workers were often characterized as family members or tutors for the children as well as their parents, whom they instructed in child care, sanitation, and housekeeping. Because of these didactic responsibilities, some reformers advised that mothers and kindergarten teachers be hired as probation officers, as they were "devoted" and "consecrated" to child culture, attributes the civil service examination could not measure.[13] Like good mothers and "moral physicians," probation officers were to have "the personal touch" and understand "the secret byways to the child's heart," yet also be firm and resolute.[14] Herein was the rub of moral, not professional, authority: kindness and compassion peppered with the right amount of consternation and authority. As Clara Laughlin epitomized, "the tender, understanding heart in her [the probation officer] was full of sympathy for the girl's pathetic situation . . . but she was careful not to let Mary feel that sympathy too much."[15] Bowen, president of the JPA, waxed more poetically: a female probation officer should have the "strength of Samson, the delicacy of Ariel!"[16]

As a point of distinction, probation officers were initially perceived in maternal images, rather than the "old maidish" styles of dress and mannerisms associated with matrons of rescue and maternity homes. Some handbooks did, however, suggest that officers dress conservatively so as to not attract too much attention when investigating neighborhoods and homes.[17] Alternately, policewomen designated as community probation officers were to be young, modern, and stylish, especially since they patrolled department stores, amusement parks, and dance halls. Such sites of consumption and reported sexuality provided ample opportunities for policewomen to exercise their duties in moral protection and the prevention of female delinquency. Clearly, these were the prescribed duties of the fifty police probation officers hired by the city of Chicago by 1915, charged with reporting cases of "can rushing" (drinking alcohol) and youths' attendance at provocative movies, burlesque shows, and disreputable dance halls.[18] In carefully distinguishing themselves as moral guardians, policewomen allayed men's fear of loss of employment, while at the same time attempting to "purify" the corruption of predominantly male police departments.[19] Like other female probation officers, policewomen were described as public chaperones and moral protectors; they were even portrayed in maternalist language bordering on sentimental caricature: "a mother [who] smoothes out the rough places, looks after the children and gives a timely word of warning, advice or encouragement."[20]

Although both female probation and police work drew from a maternalist discourse, the conception of how to approach training varied. This difference was, in large part, a matter of timing. The first female probation officers preceded the establishment of Chicago's juvenile court. In contrast, the female police force grew out of the public concern about the increasing numbers of young women who frequented the soldiers' camps during World War I.[21] A corollary to this difference was the source of their salaries. Whereas the women's clubs subsidized those female probation officers who were not volunteers, the city or county paid for the female police force.[22] Because of the civil service examination's more stringent requirements during World War I, the city and county recruited policewomen from normal and nursing colleges. And because they specialized in investigating female delinquents, policewomen received training in hygiene, psychology, anatomy, and sociology. Such education, in Edith Abbott's estimation, closely approximated that of social work.[23] Training in patrol, observation, and social casework—the latter considering the girls' health, intelligence, "inheritance," and "training in habit formation"—was considered essential to their fieldwork.[24]

To be expected, then, policewomen observed a variety of sexually charged situations, including truant girls loitering in department store restrooms, drugstores, and confectioneries. Additionally, they kept a watchful eye on single women at train stations, vulnerable to the false promises of opportunistic men. Hotel lobbies, lounges, restaurants, rooming houses, burlesque shows, amusement parks, carnivals, and dance halls: all were frequent patrol sites for policewomen. In the case of dance halls, they often disguised themselves as patrons, particularly for halls with "no admission" or "per dance" charges, as they were considered especially dangerous for minors and unchaperoned girls.[25]

By 1916, African-American women, too, began to sign up for the police examination. Of the 27 of 265 applicants who passed the exam that year, 3 were African American. These 3 had been prominent club and church members, and like their native-born white counterparts had hoped to channel their volunteer and reformist activities into professional ones. Annie Fitts, a prominent member of the Frederick Douglass Center and Bethel Literary Club, had long been interested in wayward children. Another, Gertrude Hart, had been a schoolteacher for many years. Only Grace Wilson, though, was appointed policewoman in 1918 and assigned to the predominantly African-American third district. It was not clear why the other two were not hired, but Wilson's credentials from the Chicago School of Civics and Philanthropy (CSCP) and her welfare work with the Negro Fellowship League (an African-American social settlement in Chicago's Black Belt) and the Home for Incorrigible Girls in Glencoe (a northern Chicago suburb) more closely matched that required of trained social workers. She became the first African-American policewoman not only in Chicago, but in the entire United States.[26]

As noted, professional training for regular probation officers lagged behind policewomen's because of the volunteerism associated with the former. But there were other reasons why Chicago probation officers' training remained fairly unstandardized, at least during the court's first fifteen years. The first reason related to the state's refusal to initially subsidize probation officers. Despite the female clubs' noteworthy efforts in raising funds, they were only able to finance twenty-two officers by 1905. Fortunately, the Juvenile Court Act was amended that year to stipulate county support. But the county remained sluggish and initially paid for only twenty-three officers in 1906. (See table 1 in appendix 2.) The remaining officers were supported by women's clubs and churches, or they were volunteers.[27]

Second, problems resulted from the first civil service examination. Although the county had hoped to eliminate any form of political favoritism, as well as to screen "unqualified" applicants, Abbott's estimation of the first test was less than favorable. Among the first eight hundred applicants who "filed papers," Abbott recalled, was a mother who declared herself especially qualified because of her son's frequent run-ins with the law. Fortunately, the test became more rigorous, demanding a thorough understanding of court terminology, of laws concerning children and youth, and of reform institutions and social agencies.[28]

Third, probation work preceded training programs and schools. Before the founding of the CSCP in 1908, the Chicago juvenile court had organized monthly probation-officer meetings in an attempt to "unify" the work. Shortly thereafter, the Chicago Institute of Social Science, in cooperation with the chief probation officer, organized twenty-four lectures on the historical, legal, and practical aspects of probation work. The National Probation Association, established in 1907, similarly promoted probation training through conducting field studies of court work, developing state and local associations, and publishing bulletins and monographs on delinquency.[29] At best, these attempts were sporadic and conceptually inconsistent.

Fourth, a problem arose in 1911, when the CCJC's reputation was attacked by Peter Bartzen, then president of the Board of Commissioners of Cook County. Bartzen, in an attempt to restore his own form of political favoritism, solicited the *Chicago Examiner* to publish a series on the court's corruption. In muckraking fashion, the newspaper highlighted the mistreatment of children in reform institutions. Subsequently, the chief probation officer, John Witter, was suspended, even though he had little to do with the reformatories' administration. The case was eventually heard in the Illinois Supreme Court, which deliberated that the circuit court, not the Board of Commissioners, had the jurisdiction to remove or hire probation officers. Because the juvenile court fell under the jurisdiction of the circuit court, probation officers were to be selected by the juvenile court judge. Merritt Pinckney, then juvenile judge, deferred his authority and selected a committee of informed Chicago citizens—social-work executives, university professors, and civic-minded persons—to write a competitive examination for the selection of probation officers. Louise de Koven Bowen of the JPA chaired the Citizens' Examining Committee for its first three years.[30]

Fifth and last, the professional status of regular probation officers continued to be undermined by a cadre of volunteer officers who often worked independently of the "regulars." Nonetheless, the volunteers were essential, as the number of probation officers hired was not commensurate with the increasing numbers of delinquent and dependent children brought before the CCJC. Further, the juvenile court had expanded by 1913 to six divisions: Family Supervision, Investigation, Child Placing, Mothers' Pensions, Delinquent Boys, and Delinquent Girls. The increased casework and attendant paperwork for each division required not simply more probation officers but more competent ones. The qualifications of the nearly nine hundred volunteers in 1913 were, to say the least, questionable. A scandal in 1915, in which two male volunteers were jailed for murdering their wives, literally confirmed one researcher's assessment, that the use of volunteer officers in the courts was "dangerous." A committee, again headed by Bowen, was promptly set up to oversee the selection, supervision, and coordination of volunteers.[31]

The CSCP provided one solution to standardizing probation work in 1908 by offering the first systematic set of courses to social workers, probation officers, and the police in Chicago. Rigorous classes in history, economics, sociology, research methods, and fieldwork reflected Breckinridge's resolve to professionalize social welfare. Her strategic combination of theoretical and practical knowledge may have mitigated some of the ideological tensions between Breckinridge and cofounder Graham Taylor. The CSCP's 1909 springterm roster of lecturers, for example, featured Lathrop, Abbott, George Mead, and Breckinridge herself, as well as Judge Julian Mack and Chief Probation Officer Henry Thurston. Discussion of case records from the Illinois Children's Home and Aid Society and the juvenile court were brought to life by on-site visits to reform institutions and social facilities. With the establishment of the juvenile court's affiliate, the Juvenile Psychopathic Institute in 1909, the study of delinquency at the CSCP expanded to include the physical and psychological factors of heredity, degeneracy, venereal disease, and psychopathological conditions, perhaps precipitating the later psychiatric turn of probation and social casework.[32]

The CSCP's curricula predated National Probation Association Chair Bernard Flexner's criticism in 1915 that social work was not professional.[33] Schools of social work responded by borrowing from medical and psychiatric discourses. As trainers of "social physicians" these schools adopted a laboratory model that encompassed family casework, administrative duties, and course work in psychology, psychiatry, criminology, and penology. School administrators posited that social and probation workers' steadfast qualities of tact, discretion, and patience, combined with a knowledge of psychiatric and psychological principles, would lead to a thorough understanding of the girls' personalities,

subconscious desires, and external manifestations.[34] Correspondingly, delinquency was no longer simply an "offense"; it was now conceptualized as a
"habit of life," subject to therapeutic change.[35] Consequently, female probation
officers were to conjoin intuitive forms of understanding with scientific ones
to transform the girls' outlooks on life.

In turn, the personality of those in the helping professions assumed enormous importance. Social-work professional Miriam Van Waters, for one, advised
that social workers and others exhibit a "normal" personality—that is, one em-
anating warmth, emotional control, and restraint.[36] Additionally, she supported
the study of great literature so that probation officers and social workers could
view young girls' traumas as part of the larger universal drama of human nature.
Respectively, delinquent girls would "make good" through character building,
behavior goals, and the cultivation of social esteem.[37] Ironically, even though
these goals were purported to be scientific, they were not so different from the
traditional ones used by volunteers and club women, such as organizing girls'
clubs and chaperoning settlement dances.

Some professionals were skeptical of the emphases on personality and psychoanalysis, including Edith Abbott, who thought that character development
should be connected to social justice.[38] Others were equally dismissive but argued that probation work did not entail bookish knowledge but simply "constructive friendships," not unlike those that mothers should develop with their
daughters.[39] The most effective way to reach a girl was to take her to a restaurant or theater, where she could divulge her problems like a daughter, or, as
Franklin Chase Hoyt of the National Probation Association bluntly phrased it,
where a confession could be coaxed.[40] Even Alice Thompson, assistant to Judge
Mary Bartelme, recommended that female officers encourage the girl to express her own point of view by "say[ing] something good about the girl," such
as "how clean she looks," or "how she keeps regular work hours."[41] These sce-
narios resembled the cozy room adjoining the juvenile court, replete with the
potted plant and trimmed tablecloth, where Judge Bartelme and female probation officers engaged the delinquent girls in "frank" discussions, considered to
be the "most baffling part" of a judge's work.[42]

These confidential relationships were recommended not only for white
probation officers but also for African-American ones. Albert Beckham, psychologist with the Institute for Juvenile Research in Chicago, advised that
African-American probation officers be paired with African-American delinquents so that close relationships could be nurtured.[43] Other social-work educators agreed, arguing that probation officers' assignments should match the
race, ethnicity, and language of their clients.[44] African-American social-work
professionals concurred, pointing out that they not only better understood
conditions of discrimination but that they feared some white officers were
prejudicial.[45] One African-American social worker, in fact, commented how

white social workers often insisted that African-American families conform to white standards or else be diagnosed as "disorganized."[46] But African-American social-work educator Forrester Washington disagreed, asserting that the "scientific method" would enlarge all social and probation workers' sympathy and tolerance. In turn, clients would be diagnosed and treated appropriately, not blamed for conditions beyond their control.[47]

Probation Officers and Female Delinquents

The scientific language of delinquency expanded to encompass different diagnoses and pathologies. This held especially true for delinquent girls' deviant sexual behaviors, variously classified as psychopathic, perverted, egocentric, and neurotic. Because of the "delicate nature" of girls' cases, herein referring to the sexual nature of nearly 80 percent of most female juvenile court cases in Chicago in some years, it was recommended that delinquent girls be paired with female probation officers.[48]

Herbert Lou, for one, argued that female probation officers and judges were not qualified to work with teenage boys, especially delinquent ones. Correlating mental unsoundness with female sexuality, he spoke especially of the "hysterical" outcries of detained girls, arguing that emotional instability and sexual "non-conformity" were the primary causes for girls' delinquency.[49] Despite his purported scientific diagnoses, this behavior could only be supervised by women. Rephrasing popular novelist Floyd Dell's assertion that sex was a young girl's "capital," Lou recommended that delinquent girls be taught that sex is beautiful.[50] He was not alone in proffering such "scientific" explanations. Mary Dewson of the Lancaster School for Girls in Massachusetts pointed out that the development of decency was not simply moral but physiological: "It takes seven years for the physical tissue of the body to change throughout. The spiritual body grows as slowly. The special problem with the girl is to grow her mind and her emotional nature into a more wholesome form."[51] Using Dell's metaphor, it could be said that scientific morality became the female probation officers' "capital."

The issue of immorality was a common thread in the CCJC, from the dispositions of delinquent girls to deliberations on mothers' pensions. Females were thought to be predisposed to immoral activities because of their physical and emotional vulnerability, as well as the socially constructed categories of dispositions. Boys, as then expected, engaged in the more socially aggressive behaviors of burglary, larceny, and malicious mischief. Charges of immorality for them usually referred not to rape or assault, but to homosexual behavior. Girls' violations, on the other hand, were more broadly classified so that immorality and incorrigibility were often interchangeable.[52] Accordingly, female immorality encompassed a range of activities, such as passing suggestive notes in school, loitering on street corners, riding in automobiles with boys, or working in houses of "ill repute." Because of this latitude, "questionable" girls and young women were subject to intense public and private scrutiny.

Probation officers not only deliberated on the behavior of young girls but their parents, particularly mothers. As late as 1919, the annual reports of the CCJC cited the mothers' "immorality" as a contributing factor to female delinquency, whereas the fathers' conditions were more often cited as "cruel" or "drunken." Similarly, mothers were more often classified as "insane" than fathers. The conjoining of mental and moral unfitness of mothers was also reflected in the Mothers' Pensions Division, which held pensioners to strict standards of sound physical and mental health as well as upstanding moral character. Like delinquent girls who were often classified as feebleminded, defective, or psychopathic, pensioners were compared to psychopathic women and considered to have "conduct deviations."[53]

Given this focus on sexual behavior it should not be surprising that almost all of the probation officers in the divisions of Delinquent Girls and Mothers' Pensions were women. Similarly, most officers in the Family Supervision Division were female because of their gender specific roles as moral guardians of the home.[54] Despite problems of neglect and poverty in the children's homes, the judges and probation officers usually considered the home the salient solution. Many delinquent girls, for example, were sent back to their own homes prior to their court date or because their cases were continued generally. Juvenile court records indicated that from 1906 to 1927, 20 to 47 percent of delinquent girls were released to their parents while remaining under the supervision of a probation officer. Court records available from 1915 to 1927 also showed that 8 to 15 percent of delinquent girls were assigned a guardian rather than probated to their own homes (see table 14 in appendix 2). Most of these guardian arrangements were considered successful, as only a small percentage of delinquent girls were returned to the judge.[55]

An average of 47 percent of the girls brought before the court the first time from 1906 to 1912 (the only years that recorded number of offenses with dispositions) were placed on probation. But as will be discussed more fully in chapter 5, probation diminished proportionately with second- and third-time offenders, as more of these girls were committed to the Chicago Home for Girls, the House of the Good Shepherd, or the Geneva State Industrial School.[56] Family configurations also influenced the likelihood of probation for delinquent girls. When both the mother and father were present in the household, there was a greater likelihood of probation, as there was if the mother only was present. When a father deserted his family the girl was especially placed on probation, perhaps because commitment to an institution would have deprived the mother of her daughter's income. In families where there were stepmothers, institutional commitment was more common than probation, mostly to alleviate tensions between the girls and their stepmothers.[57]

Ethnic differences in delinquent girls' treatment emerged as well, at least from 1928 to 1929. Only 25 percent of native-born white girls (based upon both parents' nativity) were placed on probation, compared to almost 40 percent of African-American girls from 1904 to 1926. For girls of Irish, Italian, Polish, and Jewish descent (the term *Jewish* admittedly an ambiguous one), probation fell somewhere between that for native-born white and African-American girls.[58] Clearly the recommendation that children be placed with probation officers of similar ethnicity was not always carried out, given the dearth of African-American and immigrant probation officers. This may have partly contributed to some of the problems probation officers experienced in their work, although there were other contributing factors.

One factor was that the criteria of "success" for delinquent girls (or any other population) was never explicitly articulated. Although it probably meant not violating a law, many girls eluded the supervision of their probation officers by changing addresses, running away, or forging their parents' signatures on probation or parole reports. Essentially, then, it was more often a matter of evasion than of nonviolation. A second issue was that despite prescriptions of sympathy and personal warmth, probation officers' relationships with their youthful clients were compromised by their heavy caseloads. One evaluative study of probation officers in 1925 found that they were not able to be systematic in their initial and follow-up visits. Although the court had recommended that probation officers visit one week after their assignment, at least 55 percent of the delinquent girls had not met with their respective officers until two or three weeks later. In fact, the average period between the officer's assignment and her initial visit, at least in 1925, was over twenty-five days. In some cases, probation officers wrote up their investigative reports even though they had not yet visited the homes. Clearly, their average of sixty-seven cases was more taxing than the recommended fifty.[59] Third, the problem of low salaries contributed to a less qualified staff. Chicago officers' salaries were only $87 per month in 1908; by 1925, their salaries had doubled to $170 monthly. By the 1930s the salary had increased to only $180 per month because of pay reductions during the Depression. These salaries were considered by most standards to be inadequate, even though court officers' salaries were 20 percent higher than those of caseworkers employed in private agencies in Chicago.[60]

The Community Model

By the late 1920s, the U.S. Children's Bureau had become so disenchanted with the ineffectiveness of probation officers, as well as other court personnel, that it recommended a more decentralized, community approach to solving delinquency. In 1930 the bureau advocated that child guidance clinics, habit clinics, truant schools, and community facilities be used as an alternative to the cumbersome and lengthy court process.[61] Following the bureau's advice, the School of Social Service Administration (SSSA) established a Juvenile Court Probation Project in the Stockyard neighborhood of Chicago and created a creche, children's clubs, and parents' classes. Additionally, predelinquent and delinquent children were administered psychological and psychiatric tests so that their behavioral problems could be better diagnosed and treated.[62]

The combination of community-centered and individualized approaches was complementary, not contradictory. Given the lean Depression years, the community model was probably more cost effective than hiring additional probation officers. The promotion of child guidance clinics was especially popular then because of available funding for the SSSA to establish a visiting teacher program. With funding from four sources in the early 1930s—the National Association for Visiting Teachers, the National Probation Association, the Commonwealth Fund, and the Public Education Association of New York City—the SSSA decided to launch a visiting teacher training program with Chicago Normal College.[63] Although that collaboration did not flourish, the SSSA was largely responsible for the hiring of seven visiting teachers in the Chicago schools. As a member of the National Committee on Visiting Teachers, Edith Abbott was undoubtedly pivotal in procuring these funds. At the same time, she refused to compromise her position on professional rigor. As she so vigorously warned, a visiting teacher must be trained in social work or she would be "positively dangerous."[64] Despite the SSSA's and Abbott's plans, the visiting teacher program and the Juvenile Court Probation Project were short-lived, largely because of discontinued funds.

It was not entirely clear how these programs affected probation officers' work. The Juvenile Court Probation Project had collaborated with the probation department and so had never severed its ties completely with the juvenile court. Yet it conceived of itself as an alternative model to the court. In actuality, the community facilities established through the project, as well as the close cooperation it fostered with schools and social agencies, were not so different from those strategies utilized by the first probation officers, and CWC and JPA members. In short, the community model had come full circle.

To what extent, then, had probation officers' work changed since the early 1900s? And what were the enduring effects of maternalist organizations on probation work? Despite the SSSA's "experimental" programs, the work of probation officers remained fairly consistent from the 1910s through 1935. The Citizen's Examining Committee continued, at least until the mid-1930s, to administer the probation officers' examination and interview applicants. In court deliberations, the number of youth under the supervision of probation officers, at least delinquent girls, did not increase dramatically during this time period. What did change, however, was the role of the maternalist organizations. As will be discussed more fully in chapter 5, they still volunteered their services to the juvenile court, although Judge Bartelme redirected their efforts from interviewing girls and parents to the more indirect activities of donating clothes and other necessities. The club women were especially energetic in fund-raising for the Mary Clubs and other transitional homes to which the juvenile judges sent paroled delinquent and dependent girls. Similar to the earlier arguments posed by Lathrop for securing salaries for probation officers, Bartelme differentiated the professional responsibilities of probation officers from volunteers. In this way, she attempted to enhance the professional status and work of Chicago's female probation officers, while also taking advantage of a formidable esprit de corps.

Despite this differentiation, the feminization of probation work, like social work, created its own diminished professional status. The persistence of personal and social characteristics that reflected distinctly female roles contributed to probation officers' low salaries and lack of prestige. Rather than emphasizing disciplinary knowledge or professional practices, probation work continued to emphasize affective qualities and the corresponding roles of sympathetic friend, confidant, and surrogate mother, despite increased caseloads. In short, these roles reflected the legacy of moral and maternalist prescriptions which had been inscribed in the original Juvenile Court Act of 1899.

African-American Social Workers in Chicago

The employment trajectories of many African-American female social workers differed from those of their white counterparts. Many Chicago social workers had received their degrees from the SSSA, although Loyola and Northwestern Universities trained nearly 12 percent.[65] The SSSA student body included a small number of African Americans, although other African-American social workers in Chicago had received their degrees from the historically black Fisk and Atlanta Universities. Regardless, the social work programs at all three colleges were rigorous. Under the tutelage of prominent social work educators, social work students at all of these institutions engaged in historical, economic, and political inquiry as well as original social investigations.

In establishing the first African-American social-work fellowship program in 1911, the National Urban League sought to recruit a cadre of promising students who would focus on the specific economic and social conditions of urban African-American communities, and also hoped these fledgling social workers would promote cooperation—meaning nondiscriminatory practices—among social service agencies.[66] The first fellows who completed their degrees had attended Fisk University and the New York School of Social Work. The League shortly added to its list the University of Chicago, the University of Pittsburgh, Atlanta University, and other established schools. Although the fellowships stipulated that graduates engage in social work for at least one year, African-American social workers were not required to work for the League. Nonetheless,

nearly one-third of them did so, in part because of discriminatory hiring practices and in part because the League's "social uplift" ideology appealed to their
sense of community commitment.[67]

Under the tutelage of George Haynes, Fisk University's social-work program offered both certificates of training and fellowships. Regardless of the
program in which students enrolled, the course work in economics, labor, sociology, African-American history, and "the Negro Problem" was demanding.
The requisite classes in sociology included sociological principles, recreation,
practical sociology, social research, and statistical methods. Following the completion of course work, seniors engaged in a fieldwork project, often in the juvenile court or at Nashville's settlement, the Bethlehem House.[68] Insisting that
African Americans could best meet the needs in their own communities,
Haynes recruited ministers, doctors, and teachers to the program to be educated in "scientific methods" and the "new social point of view."[69] Haynes may
very well have employed this rhetoric to open doors for Fisk graduates, as well
as to remind others of Fisk's top reputation. Doors did open for Fisk graduates,
some of whom continued their studies at the University of Chicago, such as
Uxenia Scott Livingston and Irene McCoy Gaines.[70]

The reputation of the Atlanta University School of Social Work, under E.
Franklin Frazier's direction from 1922 through 1926, equaled Fisk's. The Atlanta
School, too, offered classes in social casework, fieldwork, social investigation, and
community organization, as well as requiring its students to conduct an original
investigation of African-American community life.[71] At year's end, certificates
were given, granting graduates the credentials to work as probation officers,
Urban League secretaries, or as staff members of other African-American agencies. Those who completed the two-year program specialized in techniques of
community work, survey work, and industrial, housing, and recreational issues.

In having students work directly with the immediate communities, the Atlanta School created webs of professional involvement, as well as the next
generation of social-work educators and activists. Gary Ward Moore, a former
probation officer, joined Atlanta's faculty; Forrester Washington succeeded Frazier as director of the school in 1927. Faculty member Lugenia Burns Hope, as
president of the Atlanta Neighborhood Union, nurtured a community perspective among the Atlanta students.[72] This cadre of social workers was especially
remarkable given the fact that as of 1930 only 1.5 percent of African-American
college students graduated in social work.[73]

Drawing upon sociological theory, many of the African-American social-
work educators emphasized assimilation and differentiation. But they qualified
these terms. Jesse Thomas, for one, spoke of the need for African Americans to
assimilate to urban life, not mainstream culture. Like Frazier, he and other
African-American social workers emphasized social over economic adjustment,
often difficult because of the migrants' poor education and their disposition toward "clinging" to old customs and habits.[74] But George Haynes spoke more to

economic equity, emphasizing employment and access to decent housing and health services. He ironically observed that the resources in the red light district of Chicago's "white world" were all too available to African Americans.[75]

Like sociologists, African-American social workers differentiated migrants and their families according to typologies. Jesse Thomas classified African-American migrants as "straight" or "really [*sic*]," depending upon whether they originated from the rural or urban South. Haynes, too, noted differences in patterns of adjustment between "detached" men and single women, as well as those who later joined their families.[76] In alignment with Frazier's model, some African-American social workers took note of how class stratification affected family mores, marriage patterns, and residential choices. Edith Harris's study of African-American club women corroborated Frazier's thesis that there were seven Black Belts in Chicago, not only one. She found these communities to be stratified by distinct differences in family stability, measured by home ownership, child-rearing patterns, community institutions, and rates of delinquency and dependency.[77]

Of particular concern to African-American social-work educators was family "disintegration," although the term held different meanings. Monroe Work concluded that family disintegration resulted from each family member's varied types of employment; disintegration was also compounded by divorce, desertion, crime, and housing problems. Others thought in terms of the traditional nuclear family model, what Irene Graham called "family solidarity" based upon the "modern city family." She, alongside other social workers, cited the deplorable conditions of male lodgers, who placed families "in peril."[78] As noted earlier, to offset high rents in the poorest parts of Chicago's Black Belt, many African-American families had no choice except to take in lodgers. Given the menial salaries of African-American mothers, many of whom worked as cooks and domestic maids, lodgers became a viable supplementary income. Social workers' adherence to the nuclear family model belied the strength and resilience of African-American extended families and fictive kin. Nonetheless, Graham's concern for the children who "shift[ed]" from relative to relative matched that of the juvenile court's.[79]

As might be expected, differentiation struck a professional chord: it affected where most African-American social workers worked. By and large, most African-American social workers were employed by African-American community agencies. Although segregation certainly had its negative effects, some African-American professionals may have benefited from it, at least in terms of jobs. Although African-American social workers criticized mainstream agencies that refused to employ them or to offer services to poorer African Americans, they also argued that there were distinct problems African Americans faced that could only be understood by them. Forrester Washington, for one, pointed out how there was more desertion, widowhood, illegitimacy, and underemployment in the African-American communities, resulting in greater "family disorganization."[80] But others underscored the issues of racism and segregation.

When employed in mainstream organizations, African-American social workers faced the added difficulty of representing two distinct groups: their agencies and African-American clients. Eugene Jones thought it important for African-American social workers to work with mainstream agencies so that more services could be made available to poorer communities. But Dorothy West's story "Mammy" vividly portrayed one African-American social worker's poignant experiences, as she was forced to use a separate entrance for "colored" workers while still representing the agency. How her professional affiliation was perceived by her less fortunate clients revealed another complexity. When one older domestic requested of her, "You're my own people, child. Can' you fix up a story for them white folks at the relief?" the social worker, fearful of losing her job, replied that she could not.[81]

Perhaps to avoid such conflicts, many African-American social workers preferred to work in their own community agencies, and in Chicago, many were hired through the Chicago Urban League. In fact, the League often created positions specifically for them. To illustrate, following a conference on juvenile delinquency, the League established a Children's Department and employed an African-American social worker. When community centers were established in the predominantly African-American schools of Coleman, Hayes, Douglass, and Willard, the League made sure that African-American directors were hired. They also assisted Helen Sayre, former director of one of the community centers, to secure a welfare worker position with the LaSalle Entry Division of the Montgomery Ward Company. Her assigned duties were to ensure that the six hundred African-American girls employed as temporary clerks and typists received fair treatment, as well as to organize recreational and social activities for them. Through the League's persistence, the Social Service Department of the Cook County Hospital hired an African-American caseworker who worked specifically with African-American unmarried mothers. When the Cook County Bureau of Public Welfare hired five African Americans, the League declared, "It can truly be said that the color line has practically been eliminated in social service in Chicago."[82]

The color line, to some extent, had also lifted in Chicago's municipal and juvenile courts. Despite discrimination, some African-American female social workers did work in Chicago's juvenile and domestic courts, the county and city hospitals, and welfare offices. Edith Sampson was employed in the Investigation Division and later the Mothers' Pensions Division of the CCJC. In her latter position, she worked with at least two other African-American female employees. Joanna Snowden-Porter, one of five African-American probation officers employed by the juvenile court during the 1920s, was the only African-American officer assigned to work in a predominantly Irish-American neighborhood. Her situation created much tension, which continued through 1932 when the League waged its final battle with the Cook County Bureau of Public Welfare, and a previous order stating that African-American social workers could not work with white families was revoked. Sophie Boaz and Birdye Haynes (George Haynes's sister), who had received graduate fellowships to the SSSA, worked at the Wendell Phillips Settlement, a West Side African-American facility. Boaz would later become a probation officer with the juvenile court.[83] Irene McCoy-Gaines, a graduate of Fisk, likewise attended the CSCP and the SSSA, and later accepted positions with the juvenile court, Chicago's African-American YWCA, and the Cook County Welfare Department.[84] Some African-American social workers, though, grew disenchanted with mainstream public agencies and the courts and developed their own initiatives. Social worker Bertha Perry worked at the Abraham Lincoln Center (a South Side social settlement), then moved to the northern suburb of Waukegan in 1928 and opened her own private organization, the Princitian. There, she assisted migrants in locating employment and housing, and providing them with legal advice.[85]

Professional relations established with southern migrants, however, were not so simple, as class differences sometimes prevailed. White Chicagoans did not always distinguish African Americans by class but instead judged most by their perceptions of newcomers' "maladjusted" behavior. As one African-American female social worker articulated, "When these persons come to the city, their crude manners and habits make it hard for other Negroes."[86] Nonetheless, social worker Evelyn Harris found that most African-American social workers were sympathetic to migrants' conditions, especially those of unwed mothers. As one social worker surmised, "To me, unmarried motherhood is no worse than marrying a no-good man who would seek a divorce three months after marriage." Another added, "They are a part of nature. The unmarried mother is no different from the married mother. Nature is nature." Other social workers argued that their attitudes depended on each girl's circumstances. As one social worker distinguished, "When the girl or the woman has been incorrigible I have no sympathy for her. I think she becomes a menace when she has no conception of social evaluation. But the girl who gives vent to her passions voluntarily, I think, is to be pitied."[87]

African-American club women were generally sympathetic to unwed pregnant girls and prostitutes as well. In cooperation with the League, they converted a funeral home into a shelter for homeless African-American "street walkers." Although the Sunshine Haven for Women remained open for only six months, the League further assisted by hiring Irene Graham as a caseworker. The League and club women likewise took a proactive role in caring for unmarried African-American girls. Amanda Smith, former manager of a home for dependent African-American girls, assisted the girls with hospital care. Additionally, the League worked with the Chicago Board of Education to create, at Keith School, a day school for the girls. They rented a four-room apartment for them and hired a visiting teacher to help them in their academic work. Supervised by a matron, they learned to housekeep, budget, and to shop for and prepare their dinners. Additionally, they spent one hour of each afternoon sewing for themselves and their babies.[88]

Club women engaged in other League activities as well. Alongside social workers and probation officers, members from the Chicago and Northern District Association of Colored Women's Clubs attended the League's workshops and meetings, as well as participated in "block work," dispensing advice to recent migrants in the neighborhood. One executive secretary of the St. Louis Urban League suggested that women club members who "[we]re attempting as well as they can to do social work" be given positions in the Urban League.[89] Many did, in fact, go on to become neighborhood secretaries of Urban League chapters, often training through the League's courses and institutes. Eugene Kinckle Jones's calculation that at least half of the Urban League's staff was female indicates, in part, the League's reliance upon club women.[90]

Although nearly fifteen hundred African Americans were engaged in some type of social work nationally by 1928, only five hundred were formally trained. Most of the latter were public health nurses, family welfare agents, and probation officers; comparatively few were hired for court, prison, or parole work. The others had perhaps attended the Urban League's institutes or taken college courses, but not completed degrees. They also included the large number of African-American club women who volunteered their time to social uplift activities. In a sense, this cadre of volunteers mirrored the volunteer probation officers of the juvenile court.[91]

Previous scholarship on social and probation work education has focused on increased professionalization and standardization. Although it was true that social and probation workers embraced the medical model, I have argued throughout this chapter that this reflected an intensification of professional discourse. In their actual engagements with clients, social workers and probation officers often relied upon more traditional practices. This aspect, along with the low status and prestige of their positions as well as the feminization of social work, did little to improve their salaries. By 1930 more than 70 percent of social workers and nearly 90 percent of paid caseworkers nationally were female.[92] In Chicago, where female social workers were more likely to be employed in private agencies, they received a salary 20 percent less than those who worked for public agencies.[93]

Whether women were employed by the courts or social agencies or volunteering for community organizations, these moral guardians took on a monumental task. They wrestled not only with young girls' sexual rebellion and incorrigibility but the various commercial amusements that tempted girls. As discussed in the next chapter, Chicago was saturated with vice areas, cabarets, dance halls, roadhouses, movie theaters, and saloons. After long days of work, many girls frequented these places. So did the maternalists, probation officers, and policewomen—though for entirely different reasons.

Part Two

Delinquent Girls In and Out of the Juvenile Court

4

Work and Leisure in Delinquent Girls' Lives

The dance-hall is truly a passion with working-girls. The desire to waltz is bred in the feminine bone.

—Hutchin Hapgood, *Types from City Streets*

Working–Girls' Leisure

The narratives that circumscribed female delinquency arose from multiple sources. The case studies of delinquent girls were comprised of versions told by family members, neighbors, employers, and the girls themselves. That probation officers and judges often distrusted the girls' own stories was clear. Surrounded by the popular and alluring texts of movies, romance novels, white slave narratives, and vaudeville, the girls could easily encode their stories in such melodramatic casts and language. The familiar templates of seduction and abandonment not only protected the girls' reputations but often spared boyfriends and male relatives. The girls' facility with these genres and their conventions of character, plot, and sensational descriptions equaled that of rescue workers, vice commissioners, and maternalists who profited from their own versions.

It was no small wonder that the girls embraced these images. William Marion Reedy's appraisal of America in 1913 as "sex o'clock" spoke to how sexual imagery saturated public life.[1] Be it seductive figures on movie screens, in advertisements, department store displays, or popular fiction, the lines between spectacle and spectator blurred. Working girls, with their fetishes of beaver hats, willow plumes, and silk hosiery, literally put themselves on display, conjuring up anthropological turns of the exotic, primitive, and taboo. Here was the "new woman" gone awry: the syncopated monotony of factory work relieved (or re-lived) through the latest dance gyrations, her outfit an assemblage of piecework attachments purchased with weekly wages. As such, the working-class girl's life was consumed not only by poor wages and working conditions but by com-mercial desires. In a pirouette of liminality, she was betwixt and between established social order, inverting gender relations while also reaffirming her economic and social dependence upon men.[2]

There were ample opportunities for working girls to engage in public amusements in Chicago; it was indeed a city of sites, with its world fairs, tower-ing skyline, fashionable department stores, and commercial recreations. Visitors to the 1893 World's Columbian Exposition—what John Kasson called a "colos-sal sideshow"—could behold displays of the latest inventions alongside those of primitive and exotic cultures, including Little Egypt's gyrating dance perfor-mances.[3] Such collusions of the primitive and the modern were further elaborated in the city's department store displays. The Chicago State Street Illu-mination Festival of 1926, celebrating the first electric light switch, ushered in a new "commercial aesthetic," muting differences between the natural and artifi-cial, the primitive and contemporary.[4] Some advertisers hoped that the blur-ring distinctions between artifact and artifice in museum displays could be profitably used in department stores.[5]

In turn, department stores became not just "sites" but "sights" of consump-tion. Marshall Field built grandiose courts and columns, awash in skylights, in his department stores.[6] Newly created mannequins, draped in seductive light and satin, attracted so much attention that skirmishes broke out. Fearing such occasions, Marshall Field wisely decided against lingerie displays, which many considered too "Frenchy."[7] Mirrors in department stores multiplied glamorous images of the single, slender self. In spite of these Dionysian displays, the con-cept of "public" conflated to obscure differences between spectacle and spec-tator. The illusion of engagement, critical theorists argued, masked the coercion of mass production and consumption. Instead, consumerism was veiled as democratic and American, as an investment in the public good. A per-son's worth, then, could be summed up by his or her purchases.[8]

To be expected, advertisers catered especially to women. As one salesman celebrated, "Women, indeed, [are] the shoppers of the world." Face powder was depicted as "French," despite its origin; corsets were designed to reflect a young woman's "sinuous grace," despite her physique.[9] Typical bywords—*sweet, Paris, youth, charm*, and *exquisite*—conspired to create desire not only for female con-sumers but for the men they sought to catch or keep. One chapter of a 1920s advertising book entitled "Intensifying Feminine Consciousness of Sex" recommended such whimsical phrases as "dainty enough to kiss," "'who is she?' asks the stag line," and "still the thrill of courtship."[10] But women's buying power was not restricted to beauty products alone. As heads of households, they spent more than two-thirds of their money on domestic goods. By the late 1920s, women purchased 90 percent of their households' dry goods, 67 percent of foods, and almost 68 percent of cars.[11]

The latest models of closed automobiles provided multiple opportunities for privacy, freedom, and pleasure. Those young women who frequented dance halls, movie theaters, and roadhouses, which were outside Chicago's Loop and even the city limits, relied upon cars as transportation. Attendance levels at these commercial amusements demonstrated how popular they were in Chicago. In 1925 alone, an estimated 14 million persons flocked to public dance halls, 12 million to theaters and vaudeville, and 120 million to motion pictures. Not surprisingly, attendance for these recreations far surpassed those considered more edifying and wholesome. Only an estimated five million Chicagoans attended settlements and social centers, four million public libraries, and four million athletic clubs.[12]

To be expected, social reformers were alarmed by these numbers and so advised that more wholesome recreations be organized for adolescents, especially for young women. School principals, social reformers, and social agency directors barraged teenage girls with surveys to ascertain just how many of their after-school hours were spent loitering at the corner soda fountain and riding around in automobiles with boyfriends.[13] The results of their surveys indicated, to their surprise, that most girls did not indulge in these carefree activities. Rather, most spent their time reading fiction. But their optimism waned when they discovered that most girls, especially working-class girls, did not read the classics but popular family journals or magazines, such as *True Story*, *I Confess*, and *Hot Dog*, best known for their "sizzling" romance stories.[14] However, educator Henriette Walter thought differently. Such reading, she conjectured, provided a backdrop for girls' daydreaming and fantasy weaving. Referring back to instinct theories, she surmised that the girls' instincts of sympathy and rivalry guided their reading selections. As such, their preferences for the romance and suspense novels of Ethel Dell, Zane Grey, and Kathleen Norris served a purpose.[15]

The lure of romance and suspense drew youth and children to the movie theaters as well. During the 1920s, over 33 percent of moviegoers in Chicago were nonadults, compared to 25 percent nationally.[16] But not all movie theatres in Chicago catered to the young. The "Bright Light Area" theaters in Chicago's Loop, with their palatial architecture and decor, were for wealthy clientele only. As one patron described the opulence of the Chicago Theatre, "The lobbies are decorated with brass rails, marble, and heavy upholstery. Beautiful paintings hang on the walls. A gold piano and harp adorn one end of the lobby. The theatre itself seats 3,755 people. It is lighted by the indirect method and all sorts of effects may be produced from vivid tones to soft ones. This lighting is constantly changed during musical numbers."[17]

But by and large, most Chicago movie theaters catered to neighborhood patrons and so had a smaller seating capacity. In fact, over 405 of Chicago theaters were five-and-ten-cent theaters, with a seating capacity of 300 or fewer. Similar to the ethnic theaters in New York City described by Stuart and Elizabeth Ewen, the Chicago neighborhood theaters functioned much like community centers where immigrant families congregated.[18] Once sound was added to movies, however, chain theaters moved into the ethnic neighborhoods and forced the smaller theaters to close.[19]

Melodramatic portrayals of the vamp, the gamine, the white slave, and the social butterfly in the silent films were especially salient for immigrant girls. Although Ewen and Ewen note that immigrant women negotiated their own meanings of these female representations, often making fun of them, these same women's daughters may have reacted differently.[20] Fascinated by jazzy rhythms, debonair gentlemen, and Rapunzel-haired maidens, some girls may have aspired to be like the actresses, despite the gendered and ethnic stereotypes. Indeed, even before some girls stepped into the theater, movie owners appealed to the girls' desires of becoming actresses and performers by holding singing and dancing contests.[21] These contests served to attract a potential crowd of patrons, although the owners may have had other motives as well. Sometimes they let young women and girls into the theater for free, with the tacit expectation that the owners would be paid back later with sexual favors. Or they gave girls free tickets in exchange for doing odd jobs, such as sweeping or dusting the theater. Using this sort of maneuver, one Chicago proprietor assaulted fourteen girls.[22]

Concerned about girls' vulnerability, Juvenile Protective Association (JPA) officers and volunteers visited nearly three hundred five-and-ten movie theaters. There they found evidence of demoralizing conditions such as the above, as well as over two hundred violations of fire and building codes and municipal laws. Through their advocacy work, they were able to close down many of these theaters. Other social organizations and commissions joined forces with the JPA. The Chicago Motion Picture Commission, whose prominent members included Judge Victor Arnold and Ernest Burgess, investigated policemen's issuance of "pink permits" for adult-only shows and found that many children and youth were admitted to these performances. Despite the commission's recommendations, little changed. Undaunted, the National Congress of Mothers, the Parent-Teacher Associations, and the Chicago Woman's Aid Society employed another strategy. They organized and maintained a Better Films for the Family Committee, selecting and recommending family films to movie theater owners.[23] How successful they were in persuading the owners to show these films may have been another matter. It was doubtful whether these wholesome alternatives diminished youth's preference for romantic and adventurous movies.

Given youth's high degree of suggestibility, some psychologists, along with female reformers, thought the impact of movies deleterious. But William Healy and Augusta Bronner's multivariate analysis of delinquency found that movies accounted for only 1 percent of delinquency. This was far less than other commercial recreations, especially dance halls and cabarets, which accounted for least 20 percent of delinquency. Nonetheless, movies continued to be singled out for their negative influences. They were accused of producing St. Vitus' dance, as well as restlessness, lack of sleep, and eye strain.[24] When Ernest Burgess asked teachers what physical effects movies had on their students, the teachers reported fatigue, lack of energy, and "dulled mentality."[25]

That movies did have a direct effect on delinquent girls' behavior was clear in at least one study of the girls' reformatory in Geneva. At least 25 percent of the girls interviewed there reported how movies directly influenced their emotions and activities. More exactly, nearly 50 percent of these girls stated that movies had tempted them to lead a "gay fast life"; almost 75 percent agreed that movies made them desire fancy clothes and fast cars.[26] Many inmates gave examples of how they imitated movie stars' walks, attire, the ways actresses beheld their lovers, and even their "love techniques," such as flirting, kissing, and necking. As one seventeen-year-old white inmate explained, "I like to see men and women fall in love in the movies and go out to parties, etc. It teaches me how to do the same. . . . It makes me get all stirred up in a passionate way." Another girl agreed, "I learn a lot from the movies. When I marry a man he's got to know how to make love. Did you ever see Eugene O'Brien make love? Oh how I love to go to the movies." But some expressed anger and frustration, not excitement. As one girl responded, "I can't stand the grind—same thing always over again. I just go frantic when I think that some people have everything and I have nothing. I feel this way worst of all when I go to the movies."[27]

Above and beyond movie theaters, dance halls were thought to be most rife with sexual temptations and pleasures. By 1912, Chicago had over 325 dance halls, 240 of which sold liquor. These dance halls became another site of protest for JPA volunteers who, respectably accompanied by their husbands, conducted surveys on youth drinking and dancing habits. They found that over 50 percent of the dance halls permitted "immoral" dancing and that nearly 25 percent had rooming houses adjoining or nearby, thereby encouraging sexual experimentation. Much to their dismay, the JPA members noted that the police who patrolled many of the dance halls did not break up youth who engaged in what the JPA deemed the "grossest and mostly dangerous forms of 'tough' dancing."[28] The women were not the only ones to express alarm at such vulgarity. Chief Probation Officer William Bodine, too, spoke of the degenerate dances of the "grizzly bear," which he described as the "ungraceful and unspeakable wrestling of the sexes" and the "zoological contortions" of the waltz and two-step.[29] But as Kathy Peiss has discussed, these new dances not only were expressions of sexual independence but subversions of middle-class refinement.[30] It is quite possible that some of the girls may have even exaggerated their body motions to further alarm the female reformists.

Not all dancing, though, was for amusement only. Some girls, hoping their dance hall performances would lead to a career on stage, performed in burlesque shows. Sociologist Burgess, reporting on such amusements, described the girls' "shimmy shake in song, dance, and pantomime," as well as their nudity: "Barefoot dancing with naked limbs being shown through transparent nets, abbreviated skirts with flesh colored tights emphasizing the form and contour of the body by effective colored lights . . . under the guise of art."[31] In addition to dancing at burlesques, girls participated in dance marathons at taxi-dance halls, dancing with as many as forty men per hour and up to two hundred per night. Although male partners paid the patrons twenty-five cents for a two-minute dance, the girls received just a portion of the charge. At most, the dancers made a mere four to five dollars a night, plus coins showered from the audience.[32]

Several of Burgess's male graduate students conducted investigations of taxi-dance halls. They found that most of the dancers supplemented their daytime factory wages by working at the taxi-dance halls. Many of the dancers were immigrants or daughters of immigrants, such as the young Polish and Italian women at the Chicago Dancing Academy.[33] But others were native-born white girls new to the city, such as one girl who explained that she left home after an argument with her parents. When she couldn't find a decent job, she and a girlfriend worked at the "Chicago," as well as boarded together to save money. Like other dancers there, they made only eight to nine dollars weekly but supplemented their wages by becoming "gold diggers," that is, giving men a good time in exchange for meals and movie tickets.[34]

Out of necessity these girls invested in new clothes, carefully orchestrated for the desired effect. Some saved part or all of their wages to purchase the accoutrements of silk hosiery and willow plumes. Although Jane Addams was sympathetic to working-class girls who used such measures to advance themselves socially, she and other social reformers disapproved of their outfits.[35] To be expected, some of the girls were brought before Judge Mary Bartelme on charges of immorality and incorrigibility. Their very attire alerted Bartelme to what had led them astray. For example, an Italian girl hid her effects of "silk stockings, rouge, a lavaliere, and silk underwear" from her family. Another delinquent girl, Gladys, wore "a picture hat, with jaunty rubbed fur" and "preened herself with a fat animal content." Bartelme summed up her character succinctly: "She could break both hearts and laws."[36]

Some delinquent girls presented to Chicago's juvenile court were members of girl gangs. Mostly daughters of first-generation Polish, German, Irish, Jewish, and Scandinavian immigrants, "gang girls" exchanged stories and bragged about their conquests. Often, they worked in conjunction with male gangs, such as the famous Italian-American "Forty-two Gang." While male gang members stripped cars, the girls stole pocketbooks, shoplifted, broke into stores, or wrote bad checks.[37] True to their motto, "to outwit somebody out of something," the girls also worked independently. One gang girl, who met many of her friends at Dreamland Cabaret, described her Jewish friend, Jeanette: "That girl has a line. She can take a guy's pants off in five seconds and he won't know about it." Other girls may have been less skilled than Jeanette, admired as a "con girl," but nonetheless boasted of their small successes. As one Italian girl, "the girl bandit," explained, "I'm no con girl. A con girl makes big dough. I'm just out for the price of a pair of stockings, a box of powder, a sandwich, or a package of cigarettes, or a dinner or enough to pull through for one day."[38]

Many also frequented any of the 171 roadhouses in the Chicago area. Largely for the daring and indiscreet, roadhouses offered opportunities for illegal activities, such as prostitution and drinking, or for intimate dancing. Gang girls, however, were not the only customers. In some of the Polish neighborhoods' roadhouses, police and even judges met regularly to drink and exchange news on the horse races,[39] but clientele were usually drawn along class lines. As one middle-class female character in Floyd Dell's novel *Love without Money* expressed, "A roadhouse where no questions are asked—that's possible, but I'm scared to do it. If I'm going to be caught, I'd rather it were in some place I'd not be ashamed of."[40]

Instead, middle-class customers chose black-and-tans on Chicago's South Side, whereas working-class youth gravitated toward roadhouses and saloons. Regardless of which amusements youth chose, many served liquor. In fact, in many dance halls, dancing was secondary to drinking. JPA members were shocked at the "barefoot can dances" in some dance halls where youth danced on greased floors and filled their tin cans with beer during intermissions. At one dance hall, the girl who drank the most won a $100 prize. Other saloons, like plush movie theaters, lured customers not through money but their spectacular sights, such as one built from the remains of the Chicago Fire, with a museum and "fire memorabilia." But most saloons were neighborhood places where ethnic food and camaraderie were the usual fare. Because many forms of recreation was financially or socially prohibitive to ethnic families, members often congregated at these saloons.[41]

Some scholars have discussed the masculine ethos of saloons, though women were present as well. But as Kathy Peiss has noted, working-class women were usually segregated in the back rooms where they ate their lunches, thus affirming gender distinctions. Boys, on the other hand, were groomed into saloon culture through odd jobs and through "beer cards" dispensed to them.[42] Given the saloons' neighborhood settings, girls did meet young male friends there, but they would have been under the watchful eyes of brothers and other male relatives. Regardless, these neighborhood saloons fell short of the lure and excitement of dance halls. After a long day of factory or domestic work, girls and young women did not want to return to their neighborhoods or rooms but to another world that made them forget about the next day's work shift.

Working–Girls' Wages

Many working-class girls who lived independently in Chicago could not make ends meet. It was not atypical for working girls to earn under ten dollars a week. Salesgirls in department and retail stores averaged from six to eight dollars weekly, and female shopkeepers, under the age of sixteen, four to eight dollars. Nearly half of stenographers and secretaries brought home higher salaries of twenty-five to thirty-three dollars weekly.[43] Despite their higher salaries, these girls still had to stretch their wages to pay for their room, board, clothing, and extra expenses. Some girls boarded with coworkers, remained with their families, or relied upon male friends. It was a small wonder that many single women turned to men not only for leisure but economic sustenance, as most earned less than a livable wage.

In Chicago, expenses for room and board varied, depending upon the neighborhood and type of accommodations. One housing survey conducted in 1921 noted three ways through which young working women could locate proper housing: professional or commercial lodging houses; special institutional homes and residence clubs; and classified registries of rooms in private homes. Annie Marion MacLean, an investigator-turned-saleswoman, lived in one boarding home that charged only $2.50 per week.[44] However, many of these boarding homes for working women limited their boarders to particular ethnic or employment groups. For example, the Eleanor Association opened six clubs for business girls, as well as a room registry. The Margueritte Home in Evanston likewise accepted only business girls. On the north side of the city, there were several homes for Scandinavian domestic workers.[45] Many of these had strict rules regarding male visitors and unrespectable behavior and even had curfews. Others, such as the McKinley Home, did not even permit boarders to attend public dances.[46]

Perhaps because their parlors provided little privacy for receiving male guests, boarding houses were not so popular with independent young working women; they chose instead to live in furnished rooms.[47] In actuality, however, few young girls lived in such residences. One sociological study of room registries in Chicago in 1928 concluded that only 6 percent of the female residents were eighteen years or younger, although some younger girls may have lied about their age. Additionally, the study suggested that some young working women who lived in furnished rooms made more money than the average working-class girl. Almost 40 percent made between sixteen and twenty-five dollars weekly; only 16 percent earned less than fifteen dollars.[48]

Of those delinquent girls who were employed, most were domestic servants and waitresses, followed by factory workers. Although reformists and social workers argued that criminal behavior resulted from out-of-home employment, a government investigation revealed that 80 percent of all female criminals engaged typically in housework, sewing, laundry, and other service work. Further, nearly 75 percent of those were servants and waitresses.[49] Studies of girls brought before the Chicago juvenile court or committed to Chicago's reform institutions similarly noted that most were employed in domestic service or factories. In Chicago, nearly 54 percent of delinquent girls, at least in 1918, were domestic servants in private homes, hotels, and boarding houses; nearly 13 percent were employed in textile, hosiery, and knitting factories.[50]

These percentages were significant since the percentages of girls and women employed as domestic workers declined nationally from 33 percent in 1900 to 18 percent by 1920. This meant that delinquent girls and women were overrepresented in these occupations. Ethnically, the number of immigrant and African-American women and girls in these positions was disproportionate as well. Six times more African-American than native-born white girls under the age of 16 worked as domestics.[51] As I have discussed elsewhere, African-American girls who had been trained for clerical work were denied employment in Chicago's mainstream businesses, as well as department stores and factories. Out of necessity many turned to domestic work, made "respectable" through training schools and classes.[52]

Nonetheless, they had to compete for domestic jobs, especially with young Swedish women who were also overrepresented in the trade. Like their African-American counterparts, Swedish domestic workers were paid little, an average of four dollars a week, although those with cooking duties could make up to fifteen dollars. One editor of a Chicago Swedish newspaper hastened to point out, however, that these jobs held other advantages. Compared to factory work, domestic work was not as "morally dangerous." The reason, he decried, was "not only because the former [factory worker] is too eager and hasty in seeking diversion without discretion, but also because she is less strong, and because the very nature of her work is more wearing and nerve-racking." In a private home, however, a young domestic could be persuaded to engage in "ladylike" behavior. What remained unacknowledged was the possibility of seduction by the man of the house or male servants.[53]

Domestic work at hotels, too, employed mostly immigrant and African-American women. The JPA's 1912 investigation of fifty Chicago hotels found that most maids in first-class hotels were Irish and German, whereas lower-class hotels hired mostly Polish, African-American, and "down and out" native-born white females. Many of the maids boarded in the hotels' employee sleeping rooms, described by the JPA as crowded, unsanitary, and poorly ventilated. Of equal concern to the JPA was the lack of wholesome recreation for these employees. Citing the tragedies of a fifteen-year-old Polish maid who became pregnant and of another employee who died of an abortion, the JPA recommended that hotel owners hire welfare secretaries to offer girls "friendly help and sympathetic counsel" regarding their work and recreation.[54] Implicit in this recommendation was moral supervision and guidance.

The JPA also expressed the concern that single women who worked as waitresses eventually became prostitutes. Indeed, waitresses' hours were long and the money short, as Frances Donovan revealed in her investigation of waitress life. In participant-observation fashion, she worked for nine months in the Loop's restaurants and tearooms, as well as at suburban golf clubs. She reported that the most lucrative wages were at the clubs, where a girl could earn up to forty-five dollars per month, plus room and board. Given the seasonal nature of these positions, many young women worked at the next best place: tearooms. With experience, Donovan's weekly wage at the tearoom reached nearly twelve dollars. Because of the higher wages, as well as the wealthy clientele there, many of her coemployees were actually college girls. As one graduate of an eastern college explained, "I can earn just as much money and have a great deal more freedom than I could as an ordinary teacher and I meet more interesting people."[55] For those working in less-established Loop restaurants, their wages and tips were much lower. And their hours were long, especially the "two-meal girls" working both lunch and evening shifts. Many of the latter made only eight dollars a week for a ten-hour shift; the luckier made up to twenty dollars.[56]

Although single waitresses might live in furnished rooms, they spent little time there. Instead, they accompanied friends or coworkers after work to movies, cafés, dance halls, and roadhouses. Correspondingly, they spent much of their wages on clothes, arguing that nice clothes were necessary for hiring and employment as a waitress. In sociological fashion, Donovan interpreted her coworkers' love of clothes as symptomatic of their whims, emblematic of individual disorganization and demoralization.[57] As she detailed three coworkers' off-work attire, "Marietta was tilting a ravishing hat over one eye at an irresistible angle; Lorraine, seated upon the floor, was pulling a pair of lavender silk stockings over her slender young legs; Dolly was pasting a microscopic bit of court plaster just above the dimple on her right cheek, and Irene was carefully adjusting a hair net and nose veil."[58]

As with other working girls, waitresses dressed to entice men. In one waitress's words, "I always keep two or three fellows on the string and I get all I can out of them. Sometimes they get tired out and quit but I always get others." When Donovan asked her how, she quickly replied, "It's easy, always make them think that you intend to go the limit and then when it comes to the show down, giv'em the merry ha! ha! The damn fools will stand for it over and over again. Men are easy to string."[59] Donovan, however, thought their sex pursuits bordered on prostitution, offering as evidence the number of waitresses brought before the Chicago Morals Court. Similar to William Thomas's adventuress, Donovan's waitress sought constant amusement because the pace of her work "keyed her up to a nervous pitch where she demand[ed] more stimulation."[60]

Girls who worked in department stores were also prey to the temptations of fashions, high life, and men. The JPA estimated that in 1911 nearly 15,000 women were employed in the downtown Chicago department stores and nearly 10,000 in neighborhood stores. Of the two hundred salesgirls interviewed by JPA members, almost all were American-born and under twenty years of age.[61] Like other working girls, most could not live independently for less than eight dollars a week, as their board averaged around three dollars. MacLean, an investigator who had joined the ranks of department salesgirls one Christmas season, confirmed how low the wages were. Initially offered three dollars a week for her first job, she surmised that this amounted to "starvation or shame."[62] After adding sales commissions and subtracting work expenses, she found her take-home weekly pay to be only six dollars. She estimated that, in a two-week period, she had worked about 175 hours and received twelve dollars, slightly more than six cents an hour.[63]

Associated with salesgirls' low wages were concerns about moral vulnerability. Bosses or customers often approached the girls, prompting social hygienists to describe the department store as a "school for scandal."[64] JPA President Louise de Koven Bowen pointed out how salesgirls were exposed to constant temptations, be it the lures of high fashion, the advances of her boss, or propositions from a "cadet," a recruiting officer from a prostitution house.[65] All of the girls whom MacLean had befriended told her stories of how they had been approached by such men. Low wages prompted one coworker to consider, "If I don't get more wages I'll have to go bad. But I'd hate to disgrace my family."[66] Some of her coworkers had already taken that path.

Although factory girls received higher wages than salesgirls, statistically they were more likely to become delinquent.[67] This indicated that being in dire economic straits was not the sole reason for delinquency. Family background, ethnicity, age, and neighborhood residency, discussed more fully in the following chapter, were contributing factors as well. Many factory girls were from immigrant families, whereas salesgirls were more often native-born Americans. Public-school policy indirectly encouraged immigrant girls as young as fourteen to obtain work certificates and thereby work up to eight hours daily. Polish and Bohemian girls in Chicago's Stockyard district were generally disinterested in schooling and enthusiastically took entry-level factory jobs. Although familial economic conditions might necessitate work, many girls chose this kind of employment in order to be with their friends. To be expected, the powerful sway of peer culture affected the girls' identities. Some changed their names to those of characters they had read about in romance magazines; others spun stories about their adventures based on popular plots.[68]

Yet many working-class girls' lives at home were far from different from their social lives. At home, many mothers tried to curtail their independence and free time. Some immigrant girls rebelled, withholding a portion of their wages for amusements and clothes.[69] Some ran away, hoping to escape the strict supervision of their parents or even the sexual advances of stepfathers, brothers, or neighbors. As described more fully in chapter 5, intergenerational conflicts among immigrant daughters and parents were rife in the juvenile court, making immigrant parents easy targets of blame for court officials.

5

The Cook County Juvenile Court and Delinquent Girls

The Juvenile Court maintains or strengthens the ties of the
family more frequently than it breaks them.

—David Henry Hoover,
"A Study of Juvenile Probation in Cook County"

The Founding of the First Juvenile Court

As noted, the legislation for the first juvenile court in the country was a cooperative effort between female reformers and male lawyers. Previous to the bill's passage, the Chicago Woman's Club (CWC) had launched a reform agenda that included improving conditions in police stations and jails, funding a school for boys awaiting their trials, and informally conducting probation work. Conceiving the Juvenile Court Act of 1899 as an extension of these activities, the club formed a specific committee, chaired by Julia Lathrop, to oversee and assist in the bill's progress.[1] As a member of both the CWC and the State Board of Charities, Lathrop had requested that the Chicago Bar Association appoint a committee to investigate delinquent and dependent children. Membership of this committee grew, and by 1898 included Judge Harvey Hurd, Lucy Flower, Julia Lathrop, and Hastings Hart, then superintendent of the Illinois Children's Home and Aid Society.[2] Lathrop, however, was well aware of the need for female activists to defer to the more powerful influence of males. As she advised,

"This [the creation of the juvenile court] is a legal matter. It must not go to the Legislature as a woman's measure; we must get the Bar Association to handle it."[3] Although Lathrop and Flower helped to draft the bill, the Chicago Bar Association presented the bill to the legislature. This arrangement, among others, reaffirms Kathryn Kish Sklar's contention that men and women utilized their different vantage points to contribute to state-building efforts: men, their political capital; and women, their volunteerism.[4]

The bill originally consisted of twenty-one sections detailing the court's purposes and jurisdiction, and underscoring the importance of probation work. The basic premise was that delinquent children should not be treated like adult criminals, especially through commitments to jails and penitentiaries. Instead of punishing children, juvenile court officials were to investigate the circumstances of children's lives, especially their homes and neighborhoods, in order to decide how best the children could be reformed. In essence, the state enlarged its function as *parens patriae*, determining which parents were unfit, neglectful, and immoral. The roles of probation officers as investigators and official representatives of the children were especially critical in these deliberations. As Timothy Hurley insisted, "The probation system is the cord upon which all the pearls of the juvenile court are strung."[5] As discussed earlier, however, the bill's provision for probation officers' salaries was eliminated, perhaps because the legislators reasoned that probation work would be continued voluntarily by the club women.

Although the CWC and other women's clubs funded the first probation officers, prominent club members soon joined the Juvenile Court Committee, creating the first probation officer examinations, organizing the Juvenile Protective League to prevent delinquency, and persuading the county to assume fiscal responsibility for probation officers' salaries.[6] The club women, then, used the foothold of volunteerism to ensure their continued involvement, to secure semiprofessional and professional positions for women, and to enact future reform. Indeed, the Juvenile Court Act was not an isolated endeavor, but ushered in other child-related legislation. Acts were passed to establish a home for delinquent boys (1901), to regulate state visitation of children placed in family homes (1905), to create county detention homes (1907), to create mothers' pensions (1911), and to form a boy's court (1914).[7]

Regardless of the maternalists' good intentions, some historians have interpreted these measures as intrusive to family life. Mary Odem, in noting that female reformers recommended environmental solutions while also supporting detention homes, reformatories, and parental schools, concluded, "It [protective work] entailed using the state for the purposes of surveillance, legal prosecution, detention, and institutionalization of young women and girls who engaged in suspect behavior."[8] This was, in fact, Lathrop's basic tenet: that "state action" should eliminate environmental problems such as "grinding" poverty, a large contributor to delinquency.[9] Her investigations for the State Board of Charities in the late 1880s had exposed her to conditions of the mentally ill, epileptic, and feebleminded, as well as to the impoverished, who required humane institutionalization. Her advocacy for such facilities, as well as mental hygiene clinics, favored state-building in tandem with the increased medicalization of delinquency.

However, Lathrop was not singular in these resolutions. The progressivist melding of science and reform was the alchemy upon which social reformers predicated their visions, club women donated their time, and judges deliberated on girls' commitments. In turn, the scientific models of sociologists, psychologists, and psychiatrists reified middle-class reformers' prescriptions of moral and sexual behavior. Such prescriptions were inscribed in the legal definitions of female delinquency, as well as in the criteria of moral fitness and economic dependency for mothers' pensions. The Mothers' Pensions Division and the Court of Domestic Relations, both created in 1911, undergirded the belief that families should be kept together and that children not be "invisible" through the court process.[10]

Despite this equation of family unity, professionals concluded that in some cases it was necessary for children to be removed from their homes. This might entail commitment to another family, a guardian, or an institution. Institutional life created further isolation as the children were usually separated according to their status as dependents and delinquents, as well as by gender. However, the definitions of a dependent, neglected, or delinquent child were not always clear, and the juvenile court sometimes used the terms interchangeably. In some cases, dependent children were sent to institutions for delinquents, despite concern for moral infection.[11]

Delinquent children were originally defined as those under sixteen who had violated a city or state ordinance or law. But the definition expanded to include girls up to the age of eighteen whose activities included incorrigibility, association with vicious or immoral persons, vagrancy, frequent attendance at saloons and pool halls, immoral conduct, and the use of indecent language. In the case of delinquent girls, incorrigibility often masked immorality in order to protect the young girl's and her family's reputation. When incorrigibility was broadened to include "deliberately and consistently unmanageable" children, the courts not only had more jurisdiction but gave parents another avenue for disciplining their defiant girls.[12] What officials and parents did not anticipate were the ways in which delinquent girls, too, used the courts to their own advantage.

On the other hand, many parents and girls did not anticipate an often lengthy and unwieldy court process. Some parents, using the powerful sway of a court order to coerce their daughters into submission, later regretted their swift actions and asked the judge to release their daughters. In some cases, the daughters surprised their parents, requesting that the judge appoint a guardian or, in rare cases, commit them to an institution. Parents were sometimes caught off guard when a concerned or vindictive neighbor or relative filed a petition. Regardless of the circumstances, once the parents were summoned, they were required to answer the petition or face contempt of court. Before the hearing, a probation officer interviewed the parents and investigated the home. In most Chicago cases, the girls were allowed to remain in their homes prior to the hearing, although commitments to the detention home were sometimes necessary if parents were noncompliant. The probation officer at the preliminary hearing proceeded to present the girl's case and recommend treatment to the judge. In the Chicago court's first years, the club women and matrons of delinquent girls' facilities assisted Judge Richard Tuthill in his deliberations.[13]

This maternal influence was enlarged when Mary Bartelme, former school teacher, public guardian, and court referee, became assistant to juvenile court Judge Merritt Pinckney in 1913. She decided that her hearings should be more informal, in a small room where the confidence of girl could be "easily won."[14] This setting also gave Bartelme ample opportunity to determine whether the girls were lying or telling the truth. Located on the tenth floor of the county building, this room was quaint and picturesque: "A long window-box of white birch ... filled with blooming plants and trailing vines. Seasonable wild flowers in Japanese wall-vases hang behind the judge's desk. There [is] a good rug on the floor, and one or two good pictures are on the yellow-tinted walls."[15] The private room also resolved the vexing problem of public voyeurism, especially of journalists and curiosity seekers who frequented the courtroom. Of special concern was that these sessions might "lessen [the girl's] modesty and her desire to do right." At first, the audience's benches were moved far away so that curiosity seekers could not hear the proceedings. But the better solution was a room of her own where the delinquent girl could "unburden her soul."[16]

When deliberating, juvenile court judges could choose from among five possible treatments. They could dismiss the case or petition because of insufficient evidence, or if the girl and her parents resolved their differences. Investigations by probation officers determined whether cases should be brought before the Cook County Juvenile Court (CCJC), and indeed, many were not. To illustrate, for the court year 1916, less than one-third of all cases for dependent and delinquent children resulted in court appearances. Second, judges could continue the case generally, which meant a new petition need not be filed if the girl was brought back to court. Third, a guardian might be appointed if the home environment was not suitable. In nine out of ten cases, Bartelme estimated, the problem rested with the girls' home environments, not the girls themselves. Fourth, a girl could be placed on probation, either in her own home or in another's, under the supervision of a probation officer. With the institution of the CCJC's Child Placing Division in 1913, delinquent girls began to be placed more often in foster homes. However, the court's hope was that "unfit" parents would eventually be reformed and reunited with their children. And fifth, a girl could be institutionalized. This last treatment was especially recommended for the feebleminded, psychopathic, and sexually promiscuous, although victims of incest were also sent to such facilities for their protection.[17]

Despite the choice of treatment, a female cadre of noncredentialed volunteers and semiprofessional probation officers carried out their supervisory roles. The matrons of state institutions were perhaps even more unqualified, as their appointments were often predicated upon political favors. During the 1920s, Bartelme was especially instrumental in the resignation of matrons and superintendents who failed to enact progressive reform in delinquent institutions.

In effect, then, the maternal influence remained the bedrock of the juvenile court. Female organizations, most notably the CWC and the Juvenile Protective Association (JPA), did not disappear when the county hired probation officers and social workers. Rather, they acted as interstitial agents between the juvenile court, social service bureaus, and public schools. To illustrate, prior to the founding of the JPA the Juvenile Protective League had organized auxiliary leagues, consisting of nearly three hundred female volunteers, to patrol their districts for troubled children. The JPA enlarged these efforts, engaging in preventive work, visiting the juvenile and domestic relations courts, and conducting over 15,000 "miscellaneous" visits to unwholesome recreations, as well as to 8,000 families. In the JPA's estimation, these efforts were "formative" rather than "reformative."[18]

As a corollary, the JPA conducted surveys on housing conditions, saloons, poolrooms, dance halls, carnivals, roadhouses, "baby farms," gypsy parlors, beer gardens, cabarets, stag parties, and "disorderly" houses and hotels. Although images of JPA members occasioning these places, accompanied by their husbands, now seem quaint, they performed their surveys with the utmost seriousness. In turn, the results were often impressive. In many cases, they were able to close down bars or restaurants that sold liquor to youth. They also exposed Chicago policemen's collusion with prostitution houses. But their activities were not always appreciated by those they most sought to reform. One girl, who returned to a prostitution house after working in a factory for one week, met several JPA members and retorted, "It is easy enough for you with your fine clothes and your soft food, to preach to a girl like me, but I just cannot stand working all day and going home at night to a miserable little hall bedroom where I cannot even see to read, and I am going back where at least I will have some comfort and companionship."[19]

Mary Bartelme and Chicago's Delinquent Girls

As the first female public guardian of Illinois in 1897, Mary Bartelme reported regularly to the state, as well as to the CWC, on her supervision of children boarding in institutions. Her elementary teaching experience and law degree from Northwestern University had prepared her for her appointment in 1913 as assistant to the juvenile court judge, for which her primary responsibility was hearing delinquent and dependent girls' cases.[20] Essentially, Bartelme held the legal status of a probation officer; as such, she could not render a decision but could only recommend treatments to the judge. Bartelme was well aware of this limitation as she affirmed, "I intend to devote my time not so much to passing judgment as to assist those unfortunates brought to me."[21] Nonetheless, complaints were issued that she postured as a judge and presided without a warrant of law. Bartelme was further accused of depriving children of their constitutional rights, as they were taken from their parents without consent. The charges were investigated and found to be untrue. As a matter of course, all orders were signed by the judge himself. Further, the judge declared, the children's rights were not forfeited but preserved by the court, which had only their best interest in mind.[22]

With the passage of the Nineteenth Amendment, Bartelme declared her candidacy for juvenile judge in 1923 and won. She credited her victory largely to the overwhelming support of the club women, whose connections she had nurtured. They would reelect her in 1929 and 1931 as well.[23] Despite her promotion, Bartelme continued to meet with dependent and delinquent girls and their parents in her intimate room, where she reconciled their intergenerational differences. Although she found many of the cases to be conflicts between immigrant parents and daughters, she refused to categorize their difficulties, perhaps because she herself was the daughter of Alsatian immigrants. There were many reasons, she countered, for girls going astray: parental neglect; the presence of lodgers; the lure of public amusements; the boredom of factory work; automobile larks; and recalcitrant foreign parents.[24] In true progressive fashion, she argued that "the problem is one of the individual."[25]

Accordingly, Bartelme often acted as a cultural broker with foreign-born parents and their Americanized daughters. To illustrate, "LL" was an Italian-American girl, committed to the House of the Good Shepherd for stealing her mother's pension check. Released on probation one year later, she began to frequent the dance halls, staying out until the early morning. Bartelme approached the girl pragmatically, asking her to tally up the costs of her silk stockings, hats, and dresses. She then asked the girl to total her costs for her room, board, and clothing. Bartelme proceeded to scold the girl for her selfishness. But LL refused to take the blame, complaining that the House of the Good Shepherd had made her that way. Besides, she argued, she was not a delinquent, as she had not yet lost her "virtue." At this point, LL's mother intervened and asked that her daughter be given another chance. Through mutual agreement, all three decided that the Mary Club was the best remedy. There, LL would be supervised, as well as learn to contribute to a household.[26]

At other times, Bartelme focused not only on readjusting the delinquent girls but their parents. Such was the situation of "EN," a fourteen-year-old Polish girl, who ran away from home because she wanted to attend a public, not Polish, school. Although her father had been an American citizen for twenty years, he still could not speak English and persisted in his "old ways." Bartelme chided him for limiting his daughter's ambitions to learn English, study stenography, and find work. But she also sympathized with the mother. Through negotiations, the parents finally permitted their daughter to attend public school and the mother promised to no longer scold EN.[27]

In many cases, mothers, more so than fathers, were faulted. This was one twist of the maternalist legacy that blamed immigrant mothers for not only failing to teach their daughters to become good women but to become good *American* women.[28] Most curiously, immigrant mothers were accused of not teaching their daughters how to cook, keep house, and tend young children, even though many mothers persisted in these traditional duties. What Bartelme and other professional maternalists sometimes failed to consider was how immigrant mothers themselves mediated and negotiated two cultures—especially those who worked outside of their homes. On the one hand, maternalists and professional maternalists insisted on preserving the traditional family; when immigrant families did not fit the middle-class mold, they were chastised. On the other hand, the maternalist concerns of motherhood and home life were often those expressed by many immigrant mothers, who wanted their daughters to know the quintessential joys of "wifehood and motherhood."[29] Likewise, many mothers and fathers wanted their daughters to remain virgins before marriage, evoking Bartelme's belief that "the most precious things a girl has are her good name, her maidenly delicacy, her self-respect, her love of esteem, and her hope of a happy, honorable marriage."[30] Although Bartelme's conversations with delinquent girls and the families revealed her astute understanding of these convergences, her speeches to mainstream organizations were not always so sympathetic.

This may have been because all too often she met with parents, especially mothers, who encouraged their daughters' deception. This was true of "LP," a sixteen-year-old Bohemian delinquent girl, who was not entirely sure who the father of her future baby was. Although she was GT's girlfriend and had slept with him, she also had sexual relations with another boy. When GT refused to marry her, her mother had him arrested. The mother, although claiming to have kept an eye on her daughter, admitted that she knew her daughter was sexually involved with another boy but thought that GT would marry her. She was just as angry with her daughter for telling GT about the other boy, retorting, "But I never thought she'd be such a fool." LP was temporarily taken from her mother, but not before Bartelme attempted to explain to both of them "the moral code to which they [we]re being held amendable." However, the mother was not LP's only problem as Bartelme found the daughter "sullen and slow of intelligence," as well as "brutishly passionate." Consequently, LP was sent to the Chicago Home for Girls, with the later arrangement of placement in a good country home as a domestic worker. But, Bartelme forewarned, if she did not "make good," LP would stay at the Chicago Home until she was eighteen.[31]

In Rose's case, her father was pleased that she "had one over" on Bartelme and the court. Bartelme described the fifteen-year-old German-American girl as "pretty" and "slovenly," the latter undoubtedly referring to her dress "trimmed with soiled and tawdry lace" and her woolen tam "pulled, Apache style, over one ear." Needing money to buy a georgette waist for a dance with a soldier friend, Rose stole a wristwatch. When she denied her crime, Bartelme took her alone to another room where she admitted the truth. Bartelme attributed the girl's behavior to feeblemindedness, corroborated by a report from the Juvenile Psychopathic Institute. But when she showed the report to her father, he jokingly responded that his daughter was so smart that she had tricked the court into thinking she was incapable.[32]

Indeed, the prospect that Rose had pulled one over on the court was not to be lightly dismissed. It was proverbial court knowledge that girls, better versed than boys in the art of deception, often concocted scripts from movies or romance novels.[33] Nonetheless, probation officers and judges, familiar with such melodramatic casts and characterizations, insisted that they knew when a girl was untruthful.[34] In a few cases, the girls themselves may have been purposeful in their deception. Ethyl Sturges Dummer related how when a pregnant girl was held as a witness against two boys, she exclaimed to her probation officer, "Do you think I am going to send them to jail for giving me a good time?" As promised, she lied throughout the trial and the boys were set free.[35] But lying was a complicated matter. It was sometimes used as a tool of rebellion and independence or to protect a boyfriend. Often it was done to conceal the pain of incest, the shame of a one-night stand, or to keep siblings from similar experiences. And in some cases, especially those involving feeblemindedness, girls might not always be capable of distinguishing truth from suggestion.

Without access to the Chicago juvenile court records, it is difficult to ascertain the truthfulness of the girls' stories. However, we should not presume that the records themselves were entirely factual or truthful, as they probably contained ethnic and gendered prejudices of the girls' behaviors. Equally, if not more important, one cannot dismiss the question of reliability of intelligence, psychological, and personality tests, especially considering their linguistic and cultural biases. The various filters through which the girls' stories were told and interpreted demonstrated how thickly texted the juvenile court records were. Bartelme and other court officials did not reflect on these complexities but instead placed their progressivist trust in professional knowledges and affiliated institutions. Although the judicial officers prided themselves on their ability to ferret out the truth, such affirmations masked the occasions, however numerous they might have been, when the girls or the parents were the final victors.

On the other hand, the official scripts of evaluations and reports must have been foreboding to some immigrants, especially those not literate in English. These reports obscured what may have been to them common-sense explanations for their daughters' behavior: stubbornness; ill health as a child; or foolish American ways. It must have been especially confusing to immigrant parents to be told that their daughters were not capable of keeping promises. In many of these cases, Bartelme asked ministers or community representatives to accompany families and assist her in discussing the court's findings.[36] Likewise, the frequent accusations of incest required Bartelme's utmost discretion and understanding. In one case, when a girl accused her father of having sexual relations with her, Bartelme was able to get to the bottom of the story: the girl lied to avenge a stepmother's beating.[37] But in other cases, the mother was often surprised that her new husband had molested a daughter. Bartelme defused these situations, negotiating the treatment with the girl and her mother. In one case, the girl agreed to tell the truth only if she were not committed to the detention home. Yes, she confessed, her stepfather had raped her as early as the age of twelve, even though she made up a story about a man coaxing her into his automobile. Consequently, the girl was sent to live with an aunt.[38]

Not all girls had a relative with whom they could stay. Bartelme's concern about suitable facilities in which to place girls led her to donate her West Side home as a facility for dependent girls in 1914. This was the beginning of the Mary Clubs, soon to expand to three locations. All of these clubs were essentially transitional residences for delinquent and dependent girls whose home conditions necessitated removal or whose prior commitments had not worked out.[39] Like other such girls' industrial homes, the clubs received a per diem rate for each dependent and delinquent girl received from the juvenile court; they also accepted private subscriptions and contributions from community organizations. To ensure continued financial support from the women's clubs, Bartelme carefully selected board members from the clubs.[40]

The Mary A Club, established in a "good" district of Austin, Illinois, in 1916, was in part financed by the women's clubs of Austin and Oak Park, and administered by a matron who as an orphan had been raised by Bartelme. This club home accommodated up to fifteen dependent girls who attended school during the day and helped with the household chores in the evening. Most girls stayed there an average of fourteen days, receiving medical, as well as "moral" and "spiritual" care.[41] The Mary B Club in Evanston accepted up to seven semidelinquent and delinquent girls for one to three weeks. After school, the older girls assisted with child care or housework in neighboring homes, which provided them with spending money. Some girls did not reside at the club but instead spent their Sunday afternoons or evenings there.[42] A third Mary Club for African–American girls was established by the Friendly Big Sisters' League, although its location was not disclosed.[43]

Regardless of the Mary Club affiliation, Bartelme corresponded regularly with all the girls; in turn, they expressed appreciation for these "little halfway houses of Hope."[44] More often than not, the Mary Clubs did function as halfway homes for girls until they could be placed with acceptable families or guardians. This meant that many girls' stays at the Mary Clubs were short-lived. For example, within a four-year period, one Hungarian–American girl had lived with seven different families, at the Mary B Club twice, and at the Mary A Club three times. Her stays at the Mary Clubs were for only one to three months' duration; given these short residences, it should not be surprising that the girl never adjusted to any of the settings. Violet, a fifteen-year-old girl brought in on a charge of immorality, was first placed in a club for working girls. There she took a turn for the worse, stealing other girls' possessions, staying out past curfew, and having sexual relations with the janitor. She was next placed in the Mary A Club until a family took her in. But that family found her unsatisfactory and so she lived in four different homes and two other working-girls' clubs. A German–American girl, under juvenile court supervision, had been placed in six different private homes, the Chicago Detention Home twice, the Chicago Home for Girls twice, the Cook County Hospital twice, and the Mary A Club four times.[45] How, we might ask, could there be any semblance of family or home life at the Mary Clubs or other facilities, given the short length of the girls' temporary residences?

Despite the length of the girls' tenure, whenever the girls left the Mary Clubs, Mary Bartelme and the club women provided them with suitcases filled with new clothes. This was, in fact, one of the many volunteer activities encouraged by Bartelme in her attempt to distinguish the work of professional and volunteer probation officers. During Bartelme's tenure as judge, the club women distributed over 9,000 of these suitcases, each of which contained two union suits, two pairs of knit stockings, sets of bloomers, two coverall aprons, a nightgown, a kimono, comb, toothbrush, powder, and a pretty box or creton bag filled with thread, needles, thimble, and other useful articles. Further, the club women donated money, visited the girls' families, sent holiday cards, and knitted and sewed clothing for the suitcases.[46] Many of the girls expressed gratitude for clothes the likes of which they had never been able to afford, which led to a "new belief in themselves."[47]

The Chicago Court's Delinquent Girls

Who were Chicago's delinquent girls? The CCJC kept records on the girls' ethnicity, family backgrounds, charges, and dispositions. (For a discussion on the reliability of this source data, see appendix 1.) Court records, augmented by studies of social workers and other professionals, revealed how the court and the affiliate reform organizations and institutions attempted to mediate the unique circumstances of each girl, while also considering the multiple "scientific" categories, classifications, and typologies of female delinquency. Indeed, the juvenile court was not an autonomous organization but rather a site of contestation where intersecting layers of professional, semiprofessional, public, and maternalist discourses shaped the concepts of what constituted female delinquency. As Christopher Lasch has noted, delinquency increased because of juvenile courts and their attendant probation work.[48] Enlarging upon this idea, I argue that delinquency became an "artifact," so to speak, not only of the court but of the professional literatures and the female organizations' engagement. Much like the disciplines and organizations from which it drew, the court responded to the delinquent girls in specifically gendered, raced, and classed ways.

There were fewer studies of delinquent girls than boys in Chicago (and perhaps nationally) for four reasons. As already discussed, male delinquents in Chicago outnumbered delinquent girls three to one and, in some years, four to one (see tables 2 and 3 appendix 2). Consequently, there was more data for the study of boys. Second, delinquent boys' charges constituted the more serious offenses of larceny, burglary, malicious mischief, and assault, as opposed to the leading female charges of immorality and incorrigibility.[49] Third, because most of the Chicago School's faculty were male, it may have been more logical for them to study delinquent boys. Lastly, even though professional maternalists wrote about delinquent girls, their works received less attention.[50]

Despite the differences in gendered delinquent behavior noted by Chicago court officials and professionals, there were also similarities. Like delinquent boys, most delinquent girls were fifteen to sixteen years of age. Similarly, delinquent girls were increasingly brought to the juvenile court not only once or twice but up to ten times (see table 8 in appendix 2). And German-American, Irish-American, Polish-American, and African-American delinquent boys and girls, when compared to their respective ethnic Chicago populations, were overrepresented in the juvenile court.[51]

However, a fuller portrait of delinquent girls can be drawn if we compare them not only to delinquent boys but to all children brought before the juvenile court. From 1904 through 1927, delinquent girls constituted the smallest population brought before the CCJC. Not only did delinquent boys outnumber delinquent girls during those years but so did dependent boys and girls, the latter two groups often by two to one (see tables 2 and 3 in appendix 2). Despite the smaller number of delinquent girls, they were more often committed to reform institutions and associations than delinquent boys, at least until 1920 (see tables 4 and 5 in appendix 2). Given the moral and social imperatives of protecting young girls' sexuality, as well as providing care for those who had "fallen," rescue homes, homes for unwed mothers, and girls' reformatories served the dual functions of reforming girls, as well as providing prenatal and natal care. As some scholars have noted, these sites of seclusion likewise contained the girls' sexuality and the spread of venereal disease.[52] However, the influence of representatives from the Chicago Home for Girls, the House of the Good Shepherd, the Geneva Industrial School, and other reform institutions who attended the early court sessions should not be dismissed, as they assisted the judge in his deliberations. They certainly advocated for institutional commitments, in part to take advantage of per diem monies and in part because there were no county probation officers until 1906.

For most of the years between 1904 and 1927, delinquent girls were more likely not to be under the supervision of a probation officer than other dispositions (see tables 6, 7, and 13 in appendix 2), but this was not true for African-American girls. This pattern was somewhat paradoxical because most court officials and social workers recommended that children be paired with probation officers from the same ethnic group. Because there was a dearth of African-American probation officers in the CCJC, such pairing was not always possible. But there was another reason why African-American girls were more often sent back to their homes than to reform institutions: discrimination. Although most Chicago reform institutions admitted African-American delinquent girls, the Chicago Home for Girls and the House of the Good Shepherd admitted mostly immigrant girls. As will be discussed more fully in chapter 9, when the Sisters of the Good Shepherd opened the Illinois Technical School for Colored Girls in 1909 to accommodate dependent African-American girls, they also admitted some African-American delinquent and semidelinquent girls.[53] To be sure, the Sisters had noted the need for such a facility. But they and others seemed to tacitly agree that segregation was the best policy. Some social reformers and sociologists criticized the lack of available, as well as segregated, reform institutions for African-American delinquent girls. But their concerns obscured what I believe was a more troubling feature: the preponderance of African-American girls arrested and charged with delinquency in the CCJC.

African-American delinquent boys, too, were more often sent back home than placed in reform institutions.[54] But this reflected a more general trend, at least until 1919, with delinquent boys. This pattern may well have been due to the large numbers of delinquent boys, as well as the paucity of institutions to accommodate them, but I believe it also reflects deep-seated beliefs about appropriate gender behavior. Given the prevailing concerns with boys' emasculated behavior, some court officials may have tolerated certain types of aggression or at least believed that it could be channeled through sports and other physical recreations.[55] Not necessarily so with delinquent girls. Their dilemma revealed two sides of a coin. On the one hand, delinquent girls were considered sources of sexual contamination, especially those who were well developed physically and sexually curious. On the other hand, given the presumed female predilection for feeblemindedness and suggestibility, girls were thought to be vulnerable to preying men. Accordingly, institutions protected delinquent girls, as well as those they attempted to seduce. Additionally, reform institutions taught delinquent girls domestic skills, uplifting moral attitudes, and religious devotion, all important lessons that reformers thought had been neglected in their homes. Elaborated in another of the juvenile court's departments, the Mothers' Pensions Division, "bad mothers" were often held responsible for their daughters' delinquent behavior.

Of all the groups brought before the CCJC, dependent boys and girls were most often placed in institutions and associations (see tables 4 and 5 in appendix 2). Given their younger ages and, thus, the greater possibility for shaping their moral and social behavior, such placements were probably considered the best measure against parental neglect, abuse, and even death or desertion. There was also the expressed concern that younger children be isolated from the more seasoned delinquents who would lead them astray. As a result, more institutions for dependent than delinquent children were established in Chicago: orphanages, industrial schools and homes, and home-finding societies, many of which served specific ethnic and religious groups. Nonetheless, dependent girls sometimes "rubbed elbows" with delinquent girls in jails, in Chicago's Detention Home, and in reform institutions such as the State Industrial School for Delinquent Girls in Geneva. Because of overcrowded conditions in many of the reform institutions, the rhetoric of segregation could not always be practiced.

Whether delinquent girls were placed in institutions or under probation, roughly 60 to 70 percent of them from 1904 to 1927 were first-time offenders (see table 8 in appendix 2). To be expected, most first-time offenders were brought in on charges of immorality and incorrigibility (see tables 11 and 12 in appendix 2, for charges of all delinquent girls). Following the Vice Commission's 1910 report on prostitution, the JPA surveys on dance halls and places of ill repute, and the public's concern with white slave traffic, the number of immorality charges for delinquent girls increased from 1909 to 1912. The founding of the Juvenile Psychopathic Institute (JPI), which correlated feeblemindedness and psychopathic behavior with sexual misbehaviors, also probably influenced the charges of immorality for delinquent girls. In short, it was not necessarily that girls engaged in more sexual activity as much as the heightened public awareness of such matters. Accordingly, the court responded to this "thicket" of sexual discourses by classifying more girls as immoral than incorrigible.

Second-time appearances of delinquent girls averaged slightly over 20 percent, with third- and fourth-time appearances less than 7 percent and 4 percent, respectively. Recidivism did increase during the war years, but did not dramatically decrease thereafter. Margueritte Elowson's 1930 study of seven hundred Chicago delinquent girls from 1928 to 1929 indicated that 80 percent of the female repeat offenders did not commit the same offense, although most did commit acts of incorrigibility.[56] However, given the interchangeability of incorrigibility and immorality, her conclusions should be questioned. Even though the charge of incorrigibility might mask immorality, it often presumed its presence. How, it was asked, could a girl stay out late at night and not commit a sexual act? Ironically, girls may have sought to protect themselves by going to dance halls with peers. Nonetheless, the social construction of female adolescence prompted court officials to think in terms of their sexual misconduct.

To elaborate, a three-year study by Sophonisba Breckinridge and Edith Abbott in 1912 noted how 80 percent of the girls were brought in on the charge of immorality, as opposed to only 2 percent for boys.[57] Boys were, in fact, rarely charged with sexual offenses, and when charged with such conduct, it was usually for homosexuality. Even when girls were held as material witnesses in sex cases, it was often presumed that they had serious conduct—hence moral— problems even if they were not declared delinquent. Similarly, girls were more often detained for venereal disease than boys, perhaps because boys were not as medically scrutinized as girls and because of the gravity of female sterility if left untreated.[58] Such examples corroborated how the thread of immorality in the juvenile court was distinctly gendered.

Although the CCJC did not correlate specific charges with ethnicity, it did do so for ethnicity and recidivism, at least from 1906 to 1912. The ethnicity of second- and third-time offenders, based upon the fathers' nativity, were similar to first-time offenders: most were German, native-born white American, Bohemian, Irish, Polish, and African American.[59] (See tables 9 and 10, appendix 2, for ethnicities of all delinquent girls from 1904 to 1927.) African-American sociologists had expressed alarm at the rise in African-American female delinquency, thought to be exacerbated by discrimination. Indeed, African-American girls comprised less than 7 percent of delinquent girls in 1903 but by 1927 that had increased to 25 percent. These percentages far exceeded the general African-American population in Chicago, which in 1923 was nearly 4 percent.[60]

Sociological theories of family disorganization, especially of African-American families, certainly informed the juvenile court's concepts of female delinquency. Although more delinquent girls lived in two-parent than single-parent households, their backgrounds revealed aspects of "broken" families: poverty, neglect, lack of parental supervision, early exposure to immoral conduct, alcoholism, remarriage, and parents' death. These problems were sometimes compounded by hereditary aspects of feeblemindedness, venereal disease, alcoholism, and epilepsy.[61] One court annual report estimated that 67 percent of all female and male delinquency could be traced to negative home conditions, particularly immorality, alcoholism, desertion, poverty, and broken families.[62]

A closer examination of the court records, however, point to the father's death as one of the primary contributing factors in female delinquency. Most delinquent girls' fathers were working-class men employed as laborers, machinists, carpenters, and tailors. The loss of their incomes must have dealt severe economic blows to their families.[63] In turn, this may have affected the court's deliberations of mothers' pensions, which mandated that children over the age of fourteen contribute economically to the household. Certainly the youths' work obligations affected their school attendance, which in turn exacerbated truancy. The very organization of the juvenile court's divisions, while attempting to attend to the unique needs of children and single mothers, was problematic. The reasons were not just bureaucratic but ideological: economic viability remained secondary to adherence to moral fitness. As such, a young girl's school attrition was less important than ascertaining the mother's criteria for entitlement.[64]

But how, social reformers asked, could single mothers provide stability for their families in the midst of poverty? As early as 1909, court officials and social workers had deliberated on whether poverty itself constituted neglect. The resounding conclusion was that poor homes need not be neglectful ones.[65] Parents could still offer moral and psychological, if not economic, support to their children. Parents, then, were responsible for their children's bad behavior. The juvenile court sought to rectify this dilemma, becoming a school of sorts for mothers, to whom advice on character building was offered.[66] When Judge Merritt Pinckney characterized parents as "either dishonest, intemperate, shiftless, or immoral," he most offered as evidence the character of the bad mother. In one of his court tales, two girls were brought in from a chop suey restaurant (often a front for a prostitute house), their painted faces and vulgar slang symptomatic of their moral demise. When Pinckney asked one of the mothers what she thought of her girl's behavior, the mother replied that at least her daughter had paid nothing for her dinner. As Pinckney sadly informed her, "It seems to me that your price, a mother's price, for that dinner was a human soul."[67]

As Carolyn Strange has noted, despite problems of neglect, immorality, or poverty, the home was considered the logical solution.[68] This was often the case in the CCJC. A number of delinquent girls were sent back to their homes, often under the supervision of a probation officer. But in cases where their homes were thought unfit, girls were sent to others' homes. In fact, of 290 delinquent girls placed on probation in 1913, one-third were assigned to families other than their own.[69] Prior to these placements, probation officers investigated these homes and familiarized the guardians with the girls' histories. These new mothers were encouraged to call the probation officer anytime there were problems. If probation was not successful, the girls were then brought back to court. This was not common, though, as only twenty-six girls returned to the court in 1913.[70] In these instances, problems may have stemmed from misunderstandings about the girls' employment as domestic workers.[71]

To be expected, family configurations influenced the likelihood of delinquent girls' probation to their own or others' homes. According to Elowson's 1930 study, when the mother and father resided together or when the mother was present in the household, there was a greater chance that the girl would be returned to her own home. But a delinquent girl was usually placed on probation when a father deserted his family as well; this may have been because commitment to an institution would have deprived the mother of her daughter's income. In families where there were stepmothers, however, Elowson found that, at least from 1928 to 1929, institutional commitment was more common than probation, perhaps to alleviate the tension between the girl and the stepmother.[72]

The nature of girls' sex offenses also influenced the judges' deliberations. Because girls' sex delinquency was considered more "dangerous," court officials more often recommended institutionalization of girls than boys.[73] Embedded in these deliberations were the images of victims, good girls whose paths had forked, and sexualized demons who were a danger not just to themselves but to society. Returning to Elowson's study, if it was the girl's first sex offense or if she had engaged in sexual relations with only one man, she was generally placed on probation. Here, the assumption (and hope) may have been that the relationship would culminate in marriage. But if a delinquent girl recommitted a sexual offense with more than one man or if she engaged in "promiscuous" sex (which was never defined), she was more often institutionalized. In cases of statutory rape, girls were more often placed on probation or had their cases dismissed. But girls who were victims of incest, at least 70 percent of them, were placed in institutions, most likely for their protection. Feebleminded girls, too, were more often institutionalized, although "high grade defectives" were often placed under the close supervision of probation officers or relatives.[74]

The number of delinquent girls' cases dismissed or continued generally, as well as the number appointed guardians, increased significantly during the war and thereafter. This may have been the influence of Mary Bartelme, then assis-

tant to the juvenile judge. As detailed, Bartelme spent a great deal of time negotiating shared understandings with the girls and their parents. Given the
amount of attention to each family, she became quite skilled in teasing out
cases where parents used the court to reestablish parental authority, and cases
where the girls concocted scripts to rebel or protect themselves. But there may
have been another reason that Bartelme relied more upon these deliberations.
As examined in the later chapters, Bartelme became increasingly disenchanted
with reformatory institutions that did not embrace progressive reformatory
measures, such as student governments, commercial education, and curricula
tailored to the girls' individual interests and aptitudes. As assistant to the juvenile court judge, Bartelme responded by recommending that fewer girls be sent
to institutions, thus reducing their juvenile court monies. This was apparent
with the Chicago Home for Girls, whose commitments from the CCJC decreased by 6 percent from 1913 to 1919. When Cynthia H. Embree established a
more progressive curriculum in the early 1920s, the number of commitments
to the Home slowly increased.[75]

The juvenile court's choice of institutions, though, was not always clear-
cut. There were a number of institutions to which delinquent girls could be
sent. But by and large, most girls were sent to three: the Chicago Home for
Girls; the House of the Good Shepherd; and the State Industrial School for
Delinquent Girls in Geneva. Specific events and attendant publicity, such as a
scandal at the delinquent girls' state reformatory in 1910 (detailed late in chapter 8), certainly influenced a judge's deliberations. That year, court commitments to the Geneva school decreased by 3 percent. But other significant
events or developments did not necessarily seem to affect the delinquent girls'
dispositions. In 1908, the House of the Good Shepherd organized a separate
industrial class for delinquent girls. However, that arrangement did not significantly increase the percentage of all delinquent girls sent to the House of the
Good Shepherd.[76] Likewise, neither Peter Bartzen's attack on industrial
schools in 1911 nor the *Dunn v. Chicago Industrial School* lawsuit filed in 1917
(detailed in chapter 9) appear to have greatly affected the number of commitments to any of the three institutions.

Despite Bartelme's concern with progressive reform in juvenile institutions,
she most often sent girls to the institution that enacted the least reforms: the
House of the Good Shepherd. This may have been in part because the previous
judge had committed a large number of girls there. Indeed, from 1906 to 1912,
the House of the Good Shepherd had accepted at least twice as many commitments from the juvenile court as the state reformatory. Of course, it could be
argued that the state school served delinquent girls from all Illinois counties
and so could not accommodate as many girls from Chicago. But for many of
the same years, the House of the Good Shepherd had twice as many commitments as the Chicago Home for Girls. If the percentages of delinquent girls

committed to the House of the Good Shepherd from 1913 to 1927 are totaled, generally twice as many delinquent girls were committed to a Catholic institution than the Chicago Home for Girls (see tables 13 and 14 in appendix 2).[77] This did not happen because there was a preponderance of Catholic delinquent girls; the percentages of Protestant and Catholic delinquent girls brought before the CCJC were roughly equal. Further, the House of the Good Shepherd did not restrict admission to Catholic girls, although many Catholic parents wanted their daughters committed there.

The higher number of commitments with the House of the Good Shepherd was true not only for first-time, but second- and third-time offenders as well. Given the institution's reported high rate of failure (65 percent), why did Bartelme continue to send girls there?[78] As will be discussed more fully in chapter 9, there were a number of reasons. First, the Catholic diocese was powerful not only in Chicago politics but in the juvenile court. More specifically, the archdiocese donated large amounts of money for Catholic orphanages, homes for dependent children, and even contributed to the Mothers' Pensions Division's fund when the juvenile court lagged behind in payments. The juvenile court could not afford to alienate the cardinal by decreasing its commitments to the House of the Good Shepherd, much less other Catholic institutions. Second, honoring children's religious affiliation through institutional commitments was a long battle over which Cardinal George Mundelein and other Catholic leaders fought.[79] Needless to say, they were successful in their efforts. Third, because the House of the Good Shepherd was the largest facility for delinquent girls, more girls could be accommodated there. And fourth, the institution established a wage fund in 1918 that ensured each delinquent girl at the House of the Good Shepherd a start-up fund for her parole. Bartelme and other court officials were favorably impressed with this initiative and responded by sending more girls to the Sisters of the Good Shepherd.

Regardless of the girls' commitments, the success of these reform institutions was difficult to measure. To be discussed in subsequent chapters, the flow of admissions and competition for juvenile court funds certainly influenced the number of girls who "made good." Thus, the administrators of these facilities probably inflated their success stories. Second, the criteria of success was ambiguous; it usually meant not violating a law. But many girls eluded the supervision of probation officers, changing their addresses or forging their parents' signatures on reports. Often it was more a matter of evasion than nonviolation. Nonetheless, the juvenile court was congratulatory in its records, stating that at least 85 percent of boys and girls released from probation lived "good, industrious lives."[80] They were less vocal about success rates at reform institutions.

Given the above criteria for success, the conclusions in Healy and Bronner's study of delinquent girls' outcomes were likewise questionable. They found that German-American, Italian-American, and Russian Jewish girls most often "failed" to be reformed, whereas Slavic Americans, African Americans, and native-born whites were most "successful." They also noted that family configurations influenced the likelihood of reform. Girls committed to institutions showed a slightly higher failure rate than those placed on probation. However, given the questions raised about the effectiveness of probation, these rates of "success" and "failure" should, again, be questioned. Delinquent girls' reform was least successful when one of their parents was absent. But when both parents were deceased, the rate of success was much higher, at 80 percent. One can only surmise that such girls were grateful for the care given them.[81]

What are we to make of the CCJC's deliberations? Because the juvenile court was such an ambitious social experiment, the conjunction of ideology and practice was often inconsistent. But the court was generally faithful to a maternalist ideology in its vision of the girls' futures: motherhood, marriage, and home. Indeed, the entire court process, from intake to commitment, bespoke these prescriptions, be it Bartelme's coaxing an immigrant girl to truth, the policewoman masking immorality charges to protect a girl's reputation, or the sympathetic wisdom of a female probation officer. As "professional" mothers, female court officials offered themselves as role models to delinquent girls and their mothers, as well. Of course, they neglected, like other progressive reformers, to fully account for class and ethnic differences.

Additionally, women were able to secure paid positions for themselves and others by bridging their maternalist beliefs to social work practices. The juvenile court owed much of its expansion to its female staff. In turn, professional organizations, university departments of social work, and social service agencies fed the fires of professionalization. But as I have argued in chapter 3, despite the inflated professional discourse, probation and social work remained "unscientific." One cannot help wonder to what extent the women's clubs and organizations were handmaidens to the juvenile court and whether the reverse was true as well.

Although historians have discussed the coercive elements of the court, there was a kinder, gentler side as well. In many ways, the court functioned as a welfare institution, especially through its provisions of medical and dental care, and hospital and social agency referrals. Many girls would not have otherwise received treatment for venereal disease, or the removal of their adenoids, tonsils, or rotten teeth. In the reform institutions to which they were committed, many received room, board, and schooling, as well as medical services for themselves and their newborns. In fact, the girls and their parents sometimes used the court and these affiliate institutions for these very services. Although one could argue that these services stemmed from psychomedical and efficiency models, outcomes of better health and living conditions often resulted.

The next chapter examines some of these services offered in the Chicago Detention Home and the Juvenile Psychopathic Institute. Similar to other aspects of the juvenile court, the Home expanded to accommodate medical and psychiatric facilities. Again the maternal and scientific not only coexisted but had much to gain from one another.

Edith Abbott, professor and later dean of the School of Social Service Administration at the University of Chicago, contributed significantly to the professional development of social work and public welfare administration.

Courtesy of Special Collections, University of Chicago.

Sophonisba Breckinridge, professor in the School of Social Service Administration at the University of Chicago, whose numerous publications on social work and public welfare included *The Delinquent Child and the Home* and *Truancy and Non-Attendance in the Chicago Schools*, both coauthored with Edith Abbott.

Courtesy of Special Collections, University of Chicago.

Robert E. Park, one of the "first wave" professors of Sociology at the University of Chicago, most known for his work on human ecology and ethnic minority groups.

Courtesy of Special Collections, University of Chicago.

William I. Thomas, a sociologist of the "Chicago School," who published on the social adjustment of immigrants, particularly immigrant girls, in the United States.

Courtesy of Special Collections, University of Chicago.

Lucy Flower was instrumental in drafting the bill to create the first juvenile court in America, the Cook County Juvenile Court, as well as in professionalizing probation work.

Chicago Historical Society Photo, ICHi-29968.

Affiliated with the Probation Department of the Cook County Juvenile Court, policewomen patrolled department stores, dance halls, train stations, and saloons to safeguard young women.

Chicago Daily News, August 15, 1913, Chicago Historical Society.

Hull House resident Julia Lathrop was a prominent leader in child welfare reform as a member of the Illinois State Board of Charities and later as the first head of the federal Children's Bureau.

University of Illinois at Chicago Library, Jane Addams Memorial Collection, folder 267, negative 476.

As president of the Juvenile Protective Association and the Juvenile Court Committee, Louise de Koven Bowen contributed her time and financial resources to the prevention of juvenile delinquency and the development of Chicago's juvenile court.

University of Illinois at Chicago Library, Jane Addams Memorial Collection, folder 239, negative 392.

Hull House,
335 S. Halsted Street
Chicago   March 18th.

My dear Mr. Thurston:

We have visited ten 5 cent theaters on Halsted between Forquer and Madison and on Madison St.

Practically all visiting was done in the evening between 7 and 11 o'clock.

Character of shows generally harmless, sometimes silly, frequently poor – One case was reported of pictures showing a "hanging" (Borosini) No really indecent ~~indecent~~ pictures were shown.

All shows were well patronized during the hours visited. Audience consisted of people from babies to grand-fathers. Large numbers of children but usually accompanied by some older person. Several unaccompanied women about the Madison street places but nothing to show character of women.

A young boy about 10 or 12 was found singing on Halsted between Taylor and Forquer.

The fact that women are allowed in practically all saloons probably accounts for the fact that they do not make use of the 5 cent places. If there is some restriction of the saloons it would probably be advisable to keep a closer watch on the 5 cent places.

Yours truly,

(Signed) J. A. Britton.

Letter from J. A. Britton to one Mr. Thurston.

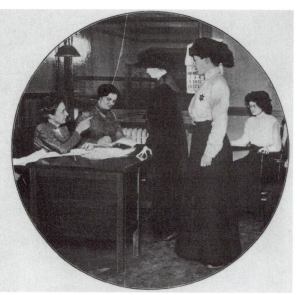

A Court for Girls with a Woman Judge

NEWS of the deliberations of women jurors in the courts of Kansas and of the Pacific Coast will not seem so novel, perhaps, after a new judicial institution that is being tried in Chicago becomes better advertised. Judge Pinckney of the Chicago Juvenile Court has organized a court that will not admit men to its sessions even as spectators. The judge, the bailiff, the probation officers, and the clerk of the court are women. The prisoners are wayward girls or girls who, as the Judge, Miss Mary M. Bartelme, says, "have never had a chance."

The sound idea that led to the formation of this feminine tribunal is that an erring girl ought to find it less difficult to tell a true, frank story to a woman than to a man. The court has been in session since the first week in March. It tried fifteen cases on the first day; and apparently has proved itself a success since the beginning.

Our photograph shows Judge Bartelme at her desk in the court room questioning a girl who has just been brought before her by a woman probation officer. The clerk of the court sits at the Judge's left.

Judge Mary Bartelme, the first female juvenile court judge, deliberated with delinquent girls, as well as their parents.

University of Illinois at Chicago Library, Mary Bartelme Papers [92-15], negative 2a. (Chapter 5)

The new Juvenile Court Building in Chicago in 1907, which included the juvenile court and the juvenile detention home.

University of Illinois at Chicago Library, Jane Addams Memorial Collection, Survey (circa 1909–1910), negative 1214. (Chapter 6)

6

The Chicago Detention Home and Juvenile Psychopathic Institute

"I read the stories in the newspapers and the jokes and she [the guardian] said these were frivolous. She said I ought to be mending my clothes. Out in the country I had lots of fun climbing trees and things like that."

—One girl's "own story" from William Healy,
Case Studies of Mentally and Morally Abnormal Types

The Chicago Detention Home

Prior to 1899, delinquent and even dependent children in Chicago were treated much like adult criminals. That is, if their bail could not be posted, they were thrown into jail; if found guilty by the police justice system, they were sentenced to Bridewell Penitentiary.[1] This inhumane mistreatment greatly concerned the Chicago Woman's Club, which as early as 1892 recommended a school in the Chicago jail for delinquent and neglected boys. The following year, the club established a school there, as well as hired a female teacher for fifty dollars a month. In suggesting that a female teacher could replace a male guard at a much lower salary, the club women laid the groundwork for future female employment in the Chicago Detention Home, most notably a superintendent, matron, head and assistant teachers, and attendants. Indeed, Florence

E. Scully, the teacher at the jail school would later become superintendent of
the Chicago Detention Home in 1906.[2]

Based upon their success with the jail school, the club women requested in
1897 that the county assume responsibility for the teacher's salary. The sheriff
agreed, and the women proceeded to advocate full force for the passage of the
Juvenile Court Act. The establishment of the jail school and the women's supervisory work with the boys undoubtedly helped to convince many legislators of the need for a juvenile court, as well as an affiliate detention home.
Consequently, a stipulation inscribed within the Juvenile Court Act of 1899
was that detained children should be cared for "as in a family home."[3] Although
earlier reformatories had intimated a familial setting, as noted by David
Rothman, the concepts of family and home now resonated with maternalist
impulses.[4] Who better to care for troubled children, especially girls, than sympathetic women? Who better to create a homelike setting than, once again,
nurturing women?

Fittingly, the club women established the first detention home in 1903 in a
two-story house, where delinquent girls and dependent children resided; they
also "fitted up" a stable in the back for delinquent boys. The all-female Juvenile
Court Committee maintained this detention home until 1907 when the city
and county gave provisional support, respectively a per diem food allowance of
eleven cents per child and transportation to and from the juvenile court. In
Louise de Koven Bowen's estimation, however, the county's commitment was
next to nothing. Its carriage frequently broke down and the chief of police disregarded her repeated requests to replace it. Finally, the Juvenile Court Committee relented and bought its own carriage. But a new problem arose: the
county horse was too small to pull it. The fire department accommodated by
donating a larger horse but it was too lame to walk, much less pull a vehicle.[5]

Despite the county's meager assistance, the women managed the Home
until 1907. Another committee, comprised of delegates from Chicago's various
women's clubs, assisted them by inspecting the Home's conditions. They
pulled down the bedcovers to see if they were laundered, tasted the food, and
looked for dust under beds. When committee members found only one sheet
on some boys' beds, they expressed disapproval. But the Juvenile Court Committee had a ready rejoinder: the boys removed the top sheets, purportedly to
not dirty them with their shoes, which they wore while sleeping. But the boys
had another motive. They didn't want the matrons to smell them smoking
their shoestrings, the only available substitute for cigarettes. When the women
tasted the soup and found worms in it, the committee assured them it was
only vermicelli. Whether it was edible was another matter: one boy, who had
escaped and returned with several stolen chickens, had probably grown tired
of the institutional food, although he claimed to have felt sorry for the women
in charge.[6]

In 1906, officials drew up plans for a building that would house both the juvenile court and detention home. This new facility, hailed as part of a "children's block," was strategically adjacent to the Hull House, the Dante Public School, and a large playground. A new park was proposed, along with a compulsory education center and child study department. In the fall of 1907, the detention home relocated to the Hull House neighborhood, although plans for the new park, education center, and child study department never materialized. The new location marked a changing of hands from the club women to the county, as the Illinois General Assembly gave the board of county commissioners the authority to create and maintain the detention home.[7] But the new facility's proximity to the Hull House ensured the maternalist influence, although their roles would become secondary through the promotion of female employment.

This new detention home certainly fulfilled its custodial role as a place of shelter for children awaiting trial. But whether the institution was "safe" or like "a family home," as prescribed by law, was questionable. Needless to say, the impact of the women's clubs had already diminished. The building's architecture, a far cry from the former two-story home, reflected its judicial and custodial character. On the first floor were the juvenile courtrooms. The dormitories for delinquent boys and dependent children were housed on the second floor. Delinquent girls were intentionally segregated from dependent girls on the third floor as officials feared that the latter would be influenced by the older girls' "seasoned" stories, as well as infected by outbreaks of venereal disease.[8] Some officials, however, countered that some dependent children could also be a "menace" to other dependent children. Judge Mary Bartelme agreed: "Oh, how we need segregation in the Juvenile Detention Home. Hardened little criminals rubbing elbows with children who have committed their first offense thru total ignorance!"[9] William Healy and Augusta Bronner of Chicago's Juvenile Psychopathic Institute (JPI), too, would later acknowledge the problems of "moral contamination," as well as youths' cultivation of rebellious attitudes toward the law and the court while detained at the Chicago Detention Home. The Home's segregated arrangements were later amended so that "trustworthy" delinquent girls could assist dependent children with sweeping and scrubbing floors, dusting furniture, and washing their clothes. It was not clear whether the girls also helped to care for the babies, some only three months old, as the Home provided accommodations for the infants' mothers to receive temporary care.[10] In all likelihood, these mothers were delinquents themselves awaiting trial, and perhaps adoption of their infants.

Segregation, as a rule, could not always be practiced, especially given the increased numbers of detained children and subsequent overcrowding at the Home. Overcrowding, though, was a complicated problem and occurred for a variety of reasons, including the stipulation that parents had to be notified of their children's detention. The juvenile court typically published these notices in Chicago newspapers, even though some parents had deserted their families and resided in other states. Regardless, parents had twenty days to respond to the petitions, after which the court issued its decrees. Unfortunately, public notices prompted another sort of crowd. Curious neighbors, bystanders, and journalists often gathered to stare at the children. This was an especially unfortunate outcome when the court relocated to the county building in 1913, which required transporting the children to and from the Home.[11] Officials considered this situation especially detrimental for delinquent girls, who suffered humiliation and whose "modesty and desire to do right" might be diminished. In response to the girls' instant notoriety, as well as to prevent their escapes, the county hired a female juvenile officer to escort them. Reasoning much like maternalists, officials considered it improper for the girls to be accompanied by a male officer.[12]

Overcrowding and perhaps concern with escapes prompted another change in accommodations. In 1915, officials dedicated a new school building, connected to the Home by two bridges. Although the intent of the bridges was to segregate the boys from the girls, delinquent girls were also separated according to charges of immorality and incorrigibility. Given the latitude of incorrigible behavior, as well as the interchangeability of the two charges, this separation may have been more official than pragmatic. Regardless of these distinctions, all of the girls' schedules were similar. Academic classes were supplemented by industrial activities in the manual training room and sewing room. After school, the girls returned to their dormitories on the second floor. Although most had roommates in dormitory rooms, girls with contagious diseases or "inverted" (lesbian) inclinations were assigned to single bedrooms. Adjacent to the girls' sleeping quarters was the Home's hospital, which had then expanded to three examination rooms, medical and dental offices, and a branch office of the JPI.[13] The proximity of medical and mental facilities to the girls' residence was not unintentional. Although all children received medical care, delinquent girls demanded more attention because of the higher number of incidents of venereal diseases, pregnancies, stillbirths, and abortions.

Despite attempts to keep the girls segregated, the staff could not isolate them completely from the outside world. Boys and men often shouted to the girls from the windows and passed tobacco or other forbidden items to them. The situation had become more serious when the Home separated from court. Consequently, the superintendent recommended that a fence be built around the Home and a police officer be hired to patrol the premises. Better window bars, locks, and gates, she declared, would deter any plans for escape.[14] To be expected, delinquent girls had been persistent in such attempts: as early as 1908, sixteen of them had escaped, and by 1917 that number had increased to sixty-seven. Although the windows were barred, the girls still smashed them or filed away at the iron grills. Security issues were resolved to the staff's satisfaction when the Home relocated next to the juvenile court in 1920 and the county built a fifteen-foot wall around it.[15] Although some decried these prison-like conditions, officials described the Home as "convenient, sure and safe."[16]

The officials' language had apparently shifted. They no longer praised the "family-like" atmosphere of the Home; instead, they attempted to reconcile family life with social efficiency. The concept of family accordingly became interiorized as the Home created a community room where delinquent boys and girls spent their evenings in "family sing." There they learned to appreciate good music, especially ballads and folk songs, and to change their mental attitudes. The Home also expanded its gymnasium to include a track, basketball courts, and boxing facilities. A trained athletic director was hired to coordinate sports activities, as well as to teach "scientific" boxing.[17] These additions were evidently designed to curb the boys', not the girls', physical energies. Instead, the girls could amble about on the three-acre grounds, enclosed by the fifteen-foot stone wall, or they could swing or listen to "lantern talks" in the evening.[18] The expansion of facilities did not contradict the wall's containment. Rather, the spacious interior mirrored the changing concepts of reforming character. Educators no longer sought to be punitive but instead tried to change the very interior of the girl—her motives, her inner thoughts, her desires, and her habits. Even girls with the most calculating and hardened features could be reeducated.

Notwithstanding, some citizens still expressed concerned about the near-prison experiences for children and youth. This was a painful criticism for the staff, as the Home had originally been founded to protect children from the more debilitating effects of jails and workhouses. Others took a more pragmatic perspective, however, calculating the Home's efficiency in terms of space, time, and dollars. Not unlike the Gary, Indiana, school model, which prided itself on its social efficiency and cost-effectiveness, the Home was referred to as a "million dollar plant." Even its window bars were touted as "very efficient looking."[19] Per diem costs reflected fiscal efficiency as well: daily rates per dependent child in 1917 were seventeen cents, only six cents more than in 1903; delinquent boys were more costly, at twenty-four cents.[20] The costs for delinquent girls, although not stated, were probably higher yet, given their mandatory pelvic examinations, and higher rates of pregnancy and venereal disease. The last matter was, in part, exacerbated by intense medical scrutiny and, in part, by the Chicago Vice Commission's rallying cries against the evils of prostitution. In retrospect, the inordinate amount of attention paid to the girls may have come at the boys' expense, as many of them remained undiagnosed and thus untreated.

Despite the above criticisms, an appropriate appraisal of the Home demands an examination of the entire detention process, from police arrests to court commitments. Because the Home functioned as an intermediary facility, its overcrowded conditions resulted from many factors: delayed court hearings; the need for psychiatric evaluations; the children's medical conditions; over-crowded reform institutions; and uncooperative parents. Regarding the last aspect, many children were detained at the Home simply because their parents refused to ensure that their children would attend the court hearings. In contrast, many parents brought their daughters to the Home to be committed because of immorality, despite the girls' protests and pelvic examinations, which sometimes indicated the contrary.

Such was the case with Mary M., who had run away from home when she heard her father speak disparagingly of her dead mother to her stepmother. After having worked as a domestic for two years, Mary stole ten dollars from her live-in family so she could live independently in a hotel. Her father, "frantic" to know her whereabouts, finally found her and took her immediately to the Home. Although a medical examination was procedural, the report's conclusion that Mary M. was "morally o.k." allayed one of the father's fears. But Mary's virginity presented a problem for her stepmother, who upon realizing Mary would not be institutionalized, threatened to leave her husband unless Mary was locked up. Mary was kept in the Chicago Detention Home for one month while a probation officer arranged for placement with her grandmother.[21] Given Mary's longing for independence, it was doubtful she would remain at her grandmother's house for long, however. This case, among others, illustrates how parents used the juvenile court and detention home to resolve family conflicts.

In a similar fashion, it also illustrates how judges and probation officers mediated family conflicts. As Judge Mary Bartelme's negotiations with delinquent girls confirmed, court officials were quite familiar with various family turmoil, be it neglect, poverty, physical violence, or incest. Often girls were committed to the Home or to other institutions for protection from male family members. This was true for Ellen T., a fourteen-year-old brought to the Home by her father for "running out nights." The investigation, however, revealed a curious twist: she had been a victim of incest committed by an older brother; a warrant was promptly issued for his arrest. Rather than prosecute him, however, the court committed him to the Lincoln School for the Feebleminded. In turn, Ellen, classified as a high-grade mental defective, was released to an aunt.[22] Even with access to complete records, it would be difficult to ascertain all the innuendo of this case. Was Ellen actually a victim of incest or had she concocted the story about her brother? Was the brother truly feebleminded or was his commitment a viable alternative used to protect Ellen and even younger sisters? Ellen's brother did satisfy one definition of feebleminded in his lack of "ordinary prudence" in managing himself. Ellen's diagnosis, alternately termed "subnormal," was more hopeful: she could live a productive life if placed under appropriate adult supervision.[23] Despite the court's adherence to mental classifications, Ellen's father was probably not prepared for the final outcome of this case. His intention to use the court for disciplining Ellen had taken an unexpected turn.

Nonetheless, the father's concern for Ellen's late hours reflected that of many parents. Although the patrol wagon brought children to the Home throughout the day, more girls were taken into custody in the late evening hours. If the Home was too crowded, they remained at the police station or were returned to their own homes. Although jail detention was illegal, it was not unusual for children to be detained there or at the police annex for a week.[24] Some girls even requested to stay there because it was safer than their homes. Given that police stations were described as "unfit" for children as well as adult prisoners, this was a surprising request. In fact, the police station at Central Station was considered so vile that children were transferred to the "safer" stations on West Chicago or Shakespeare Avenues.[25]

In situations where it was a first (and minor) offense, parents usually picked their children up after the police officers' customary warnings. But police reports indicated ethnic and gender disparities in detention decisions. Over two-thirds of the detainees in the Chicago jails were boys; nearly half of those were African American. The rates for African-American girls were disparate as well. Over half were held in jails or police stations, compared to approximately three-fourths of the native- and foreign-born white girls, who returned home.[26] Whether these practices reflected the prevailing sociological notion of "disorganized" African-American families, the dearth of African-American probation and police officers, or a combination of factors, these disproportionate rates remained constant through 1935.

Police also exercised discretion about detention depending upon the children's ages. Children under the age of ten caught begging or panhandling were usually sent home with a warning; those under fourteen were sent home with a letter to the parents. But those over fourteen were the ones most often detained and brought before the court. This may, of course, have reflected not simply age but recidivism or the severity of the offenses. For delinquent females, detention was also touted as a form of protection, as well as an indication of how vigilant the policewomen and volunteer female patrols were.[27]

For those children and youth admitted to the Home, the first order of business was to record vital information in the official ledger: their names, birth dates, times of admission, parents' names and addresses, siblings' names and ages, the grades and schools last attended, their wages, the dates of hearing, their charges, the names of their probation officers and precincts, and assigned court numbers. The children were then taken to the nurse's office for a "green soap shampoo" and an "antiseptic bath."[28] The Home's annual reports were replete with descriptions of the "filthy" conditions of delinquent boys and girls brought to the Home. Heads and bodies were infested with vermin, so their hair was shaved. Many of the girls wore clothes that alerted the nurse to questionable moral behavior: silk stockings, willow plumes, and low-cut dresses. Some wore no underwear. Whatever attire they wore was usually banished to the fumigating room in the basement.[29]

The children then lined up for their physical examinations. A nurse took their temperature, pulse, and respiration rate, as well as nose and throat cultures. Vaginal cultures and pelvic examinations were routine for delinquent girls, not only to detect venereal disease but to determine whether they had engaged in any sexual activity. As Mary Odem has noted, such evidence was often necessary for the judge to determine cases of rape or incest. In many cases, pelvic examinations also confirmed the need for extended care, especially because of pregnancies. In 1917 alone, twenty-three girls were found to be pregnant. This condition, along with any "deficiencies," were recorded by the nurse and doctor and sent to the judge.[30] To be expected, many children's "deficiencies" reflected the poor and unsanitary conditions of crowded tenements and flats where many lived. They also spoke to the lack of adequate medical care. The physician's reports noted a prevalence of malnutrition, anemia, undernourishment, scabies, pediculosis, rhinitis, enlarged cervical glands, and venereal disease.[31] When the Home began to provide dental services in 1907, cavities, infected gums, and abscessed teeth were commonly reported. This prompted one dentist to correlate delinquency with poor dental care, citing as anecdotal evidence how one young boy's behavior fits ceased after his impacted teeth were removed. Despite this unscientific conclusion, the expansion of health services did corroborate the increased medicalization of delinquency and the judge's concern with correlations between physical and mental defects.[32]

Some parents may have committed their children to the Home so they would receive medical attention. Relatives of Anna M., a sixteen-year-old white girl, brought her to the detention home because they could not care for her. The expenses for weekly clinic visits to treat her congenital skin condition were financially prohibitive for the family. After three months, her condition improved but she could not be placed anywhere, given the crowded conditions of other facilities. Soon thereafter, she was diagnosed with Vincent's infection. Although not contagious, this condition required further medical treatment. Such a long detention eventually took its toll on Anna, who pleaded to be placed with a family. As she wrote to her probation officer, "Please get me out of here because I am feeling lonesome when my girl friends are going out. You ought to see how I was crying this week because all my best friends are gone and I wish I would go, too. If you'll take me out, I'll try my best and go myself to the hospital." After 180 days at the detention home, Anna was placed in another institution and not sent back home.[33]

Although Anna's situation reflected the perennial problems of overcrowded institutions, it also pointed to indispensable medical provisions for children who might have otherwise remained untreated. But not everyone was pleased with the quality of the detention home's medical services. The Illinois Association of Criminal Justice, for one, was critical of the children's group examinations and the attendant lack of privacy. Indeed, more than one child was usually present in the examining room as they were inspected in rapid succession. During one day, the association tallied twenty-five children's medical examinations in thirteen minutes; on another day, twenty-seven in seventeen minutes. This prompted the association to further question the accuracy of the physician's reports, which they found to be brief and disorganized.[34] Because the girls' medical reports were sent to the judge, along with reports from the probation officers and psychiatrist, this information could have some bearing on the judge's final deliberations.

In large part, the children's length of detention, too, depended upon these medical investigations. Prior to medical and psychiatric services, the average stay for delinquent girls in the Home was rather short: only six days. The average detention period of twenty-seven days for delinquent boys did not always reflect the severity of their charges as much as the cumbersome detention process, which was unable to handle the large number of boys arrested and detained. As enumerated (in table 2 of appendix 2), there were three to four times more delinquent boys than girls in the juvenile court, at least until 1935.[35] By 1917, however, delinquent girls on the average spent eight days in the Home, two days longer than delinquent boys. By 1924, the girls average residence was thirteen days, five days longer than the boys. This disparity increased until the average length of stay for girls was between twenty-eight and forty-one days by 1930 while for boys it was only one to twenty days.[36] Clearly the length of detention for delinquent girls was complicated by quarantines, overcrowded conditions at the reform institutions, and the increased medicalization of their behavior.

But ethnic differences emerged as well. Delinquent African-American girls were frequently held for up to six months, far longer than for any other ethnic group.[37] There were, of course, native-born white and immigrant girls who also slipped through the cracks and remained at the Home for an inordinate length of time. Fourteen-year-old Ruth W. was one such unfortunate person. She was detained for 210 days as a witness against several men with whom she had sexual relations. The men, on the other hand, were freed on bond. Although one could quickly surmise a case of gender injustice, it is possible that Rose was kept at the Home for her own protection, for treatment of venereal disease, or because her home life was untenable. The fact that she was eventually tested as a high-grade mental defective and sent to the House of the Good Shepherd indicated that she was, indeed, capable of reform.[38]

Seventeen-year-old Rose B. was also detained as a witness against a man charged with raping her. Perhaps the judge distrusted Rose's story or her emotional state, as he ordered a complete mental examination, while the felony court released the man on a fine of $100. That he was released before Rose's examination might appear precipitous. On the other hand, the Home continued to provide protection for Rose while ascertaining the reliability of Rose's story. Rose was not detained as long as Ruth W. After fifty days, she was released to a probation officer. Clearly she was not inordinately feebleminded or immoral, or she would not have been placed under such supervision. In one of many strange twists of the juvenile court, the judge ordered that the $100 fine be given to Rose's probation officer for her care.[39]

Rose's and Ruth's situations reflect how the juvenile court attempted to address each case individually while at the same time working under institutional constraints. This was, in fact, considered one of the hallmarks of the juvenile court and the detention home. Despite the large numbers of children who moved in and out of the Home, the staff portrayed themselves as attending to each child's needs. In actuality, this would have been impossible. The Home had accommodations for approximately 325 children, yet 8,000 to 9,000 children were detained there annually. They could accommodate so many children because more than 40 percent of them were detained for only one or two days during some years.[40] At best, these children received minimal medical care while awaiting release.

But the progressive rhetoric of tending to each child's individual circumstances may have reflected a more medicalized model of delinquency due to a shift in the Home's population. During the court's first ten years, there were more dependent than delinquent children in the Home. But thereafter delinquent children constituted the larger group. In fact, by 1913, delinquent children comprised 79 percent of the Home's population; of this group, delinquent girls constituted 20 percent.[41] The delinquent girls' behavioral problems, sexual curiosity, and medical complications probably necessitated more attention and longer detention periods. Thus, the term *individual* most likely referred to those delinquent girls who required further medical and psychiatric testing.

Despite the lengthier stays of delinquent girls, the impact of the Home's educational programs on them was questionable. Like other institutions for delinquent girls, the Home emphasized character building and moral reform. This entailed a schedule of industrial activities, the kind of activities many of them abhorred. The girls awoke at five each morning to scrub the entire department before breakfast. They then cleared the tables and washed the dishes, tables, and tea towels. Afterward, they made their beds, prepared the vegetables for dinner, and scrubbed the dining room floor. Delinquent boys, although required to scrub the main hall of the dependent section and kitchen, did not have to prepare food or wash the dishes.[42]

The girls also attended domestic science classes in sewing, crocheting, needlework, and fancywork to help them readjust "mentally and morally." Since each girl's stay varied in length, a particular piece of embroidery might be worked on by five different girls. Nonetheless, such instruction was thought "creditable," as the teachers believed that most girls, especially immigrant ones, had never been taught these useful skills by their mothers.[43] In the teacher's estimation, the girls seemed to enjoy sewing their own hats or dresses, or "freshen[ing] up a soiled ribbon."[44] Undoubtedly the teachers encouraged a middle-class style of fashion and code of respectability. Similarly, in their cooking classes the girls learned the "correct methods" of housekeeping, table manners, and family serving. Such knowledge led to good habits and neatness, thought to be lacking in their "European peasant style" homes. After-school hours were spent, once again, scrubbing, sweeping, dusting, and washing and mending their own clothes.[45] The director of domestic arts insisted the girls be constantly occupied, especially during those evening hours when "idleness [wa]s particularly offensive and dangerous."[46]

As might be expected, the concern here was sexual activity—autoerotic or lesbian. Recreational activity would discourage what one annual report referred to as "bad sex thinking and dangerous habits." Music was one such sexual outlet or sublimation. Although the superintendent emphasized the need for self-expression, her own words confirmed its true purpose: "A household that sings generally indicates a condition of good mental hygiene and these opportunities for singing are therefore to be freely encouraged."[47] Accordingly, the Home purchased two new pianos for the assembly room, where the girls and boys alternately performed songs and dances. Although both groups were respectively supervised by female and male attendants, the male attendant was characterized as a "disciplinarian," whereas the female was a "housekeeper."[48]

Even literacy lessons, although purportedly individualized, were linked to the girls' reform. One assignment was to write an account of their cases in letters that the teacher then submitted to the court. Whether the judge took the girls' accounts seriously is another question, although the girls, through demonstrable expressions of contriteness and shame, had perhaps hoped to persuade the judge. The girls were also allowed the privilege of writing letters to their friends, which were read out loud, perhaps to ensure their wholesome content or to garner further information about their cases and social lives. Whether these letters were ever mailed was not clear. Letters written to the girls' parents were read by the teacher as well, as were letters from the parents. This was, once again, to curtail negative influences.[49]

Although these assignments were designed to "bring out" each girl's individuality, they served other purposes: monitoring communication; assessing character; and providing information for the judge. If anything, the teachers' schedules were so taxed because of the varying abilities and temperaments of their students that they could not attend to individual needs in their literacy lessons or any other activity. The only pragmatic way in which instruction was ever individualized was when children were found to be "clever" at some craft and so were allowed to spend more time doing that. Some educators cautioned, however, that activities should not be too enjoyable or the children would not want to leave the detention home.[50]

As the children's activities were monitored, so too were the parents' visits with their children during the two designated hours per day. Before 1918, parents could speak to their children only through iron bars. But the following year the Home furnished a large family room with books, pictures, and a phonograph for family visits.[51] Once again the Home attempted to reconcile the contradictions between its familial and custodial duties. Additionally, it may have tried to model its own version of middle-class family life for immigrant parents. The staff was also probably concerned that the children would tell their parents negative stories about the Home. Clearly, children who were punished did have such stories to tell, although some may have embellished with details.

The Home staff did not use corporal punishment, but it did restrict some children to a diet of bread and milk. Other children were detained in isolation cells. This plan worked especially well for delinquent girls, who after one hour of confinement often showed "a change of heart."[52] But sometimes younger girls were subjected to this treatment. Juanita, a ten-year-old African-American girl, was placed in the Home after her visiting teacher and principal found her teaching other children "acts of sex perversion." Apparently, her rebellious behavior did not desist as she spent five months of her yearlong commitment in an isolation cell. Eventually the Home abolished this practice and converted the isolation cells into conference and interview rooms.[53]

Although such methods may seem extreme, some parents approved of these forms of discipline. As noted, some brought their children to the Home as a last resort when their own threats or beatings were ineffectual. Children were sent, then, to the Home for various reasons: detention; discipline; their safety; and medical treatment. Some were also sent to receive psychiatric and psychological evaluations from the JPI.

Chicago's Juvenile Psychopathic Institute

It was not a coincidence that the JPI was founded in 1909, the same year as the National Committee for Mental Hygiene. Nor was it unusual that Julia Lathrop was a charter member of the national organization, as well as a trustee of the JPI. Lathrop's hope that the juvenile court would ameliorate the "wastage of human life" of dependent and delinquent children extended to the institute's diagnostic services for troubled children.[54] For Lathrop, scientific investigation and treatment for children most incapable and vulnerable—those with mental defects—was reasonable, as well as compassionate. Jane Addams would join Lathrop as a board member of the JPI, perhaps persuaded by Hull House resident Alice Hamilton, who recommended psychopathic training for medical students. Ethyl Sturges Dummer was another likely influence on Addams. Concerned about child labor, she had joined the National Child Labor Committee in 1905. Her amateur studies of psychopathology and psychoanalysis demonstrated her keen interest in mental hygiene. Accordingly, she underwrote the costs of the JPI, including William Healy's directorship.[55]

These female social reformers had conceived of the JPI as an extension of the Chicago Detention Home. The impulse for child study had originated with women's clubs, then expanded to detention homes where children could be closely observed during their school and recreation hours. Observational reports, accompanied by psychological and psychiatric test results, were then given to the judge so that the children would be appropriately placed.[56] Given the large number of children detained at the Home, however, the JPI increasingly narrowed its focus to "exceptional" or "baffling" children—that is, those who required intensive and long-term study. These included the psychopathic, neurotic, egocentric, epileptic, feebleminded, and "perverted."[57]

William Healy's initial training had not prepared him for the psychiatric study of troubled children. Although he had studied psychology with William James at Harvard University and had attended several of Sigmund Freud's lectures in Vienna, his medical specialty was gynecology. This background, as well as his first professional position at a state hospital in Wisconsin, may have predisposed him to think in terms of female pathologies. As will be discussed later, Healy sometimes held less than scientific preconceptions about delinquent girls' behaviors despite his multivariable approach to delinquency.[58]

Conceivably, Healy argued, there were "a thousand and one influences" for delinquency. Results from his longitudinal study of young male and female recidivists from Chicago's juvenile court documented at least fifteen causative factors, among them mental abnormalities, bad companionship, abnormal physical conditions, and defective home conditions. (The last referred to alcoholism, immorality, parental neglect, divorce or death of a parent, and poverty.)[59] Despite much evidence of impoverished households, Healy never recommended economic amelioration. Instead, he focused on other environmental and hereditary influences. As such, family medical histories verified predispositions toward epilepsy, feeblemindedness, and mental instability. The children's medical examinations substantiated physical defects and differentiated etiologies of inherited traits, such as excess energy, an irritable temper, and hypersexual tendencies. And, as noted in chapter 2, the anthropometry of the children was correlated to their developmental histories.[60]

Healy and his psychologist, Augusta Bronner, used a series of tests to assess the children's various abilities: spatial discrimination; ability to sustain attention; motor coordination; associative processes; perception of form and color relationships; language and math; mental representation and analysis; ability to follow instructions; and vocational aptitudes. Healy and Bronner, in fact, had devised many of these tests. For example, their form–board test, which evaluated children's perceptions of form and color relationships, consisted of puzzle pieces of farm animals. But many urban children who had never seen farm animals had difficulty matching body parts. Their construction tests, which required placing differently shaped pieces within a prescribed area, measured the ability to "profit by experience." But how could these repeated trials represent what girls had gained from real-life experience? Healy and Bronner also measured visual perception and analysis by a person's ability to figure out how to open a puzzle box locked by a series of chains and links. They believed that such clinical tests would reveal defects in mental functionings, often caused by childhood or adolescent conflicts, or might indicate feeblemindedness.[61]

One drawback to this extensive battery of tests was that it was time-consuming. Like the Chicago Detention Home's staff, the JPI was overwhelmed by the large numbers of children who required examinations. Healy was especially concerned about detecting feebleminded children before they were brought to court. Yet, as noted, feeblemindedness was not always ascertained through the Binet test. In fact, a person could "pass" the Binet test and still be subnormal in intelligence if there were deficiencies in attention, mental analysis, judgment, or apperception. Beyond results from intelligence tests, Healy and Bronner looked for other mental "aberrations," including the inability to give accurate testimony, to remain attentive, to demonstrate willpower, to "profit" from experience, to morally discriminate, and to use language responsibly. The last was especially useful for diagnosing pathological liars and feeblemindedness.[62]

Despite the court's preoccupation with feeblemindedness, statistics from its 1909 annual report revealed that only 10 percent of delinquent girls and boys definitively fit that description. Beyond that, 8 percent were classified as mentally subnormal, 8 percent as mentally dull, and 9 percent as possessing poor mental capacity. These percentages remained fairly constant, at least for the next five years. Although delinquent girls, more often than boys, were classified as feebleminded, they constituted less than 20 percent of all female delinquent cases. Nonetheless, by 1920 the court had become so concerned with feebleminded girls that plans were made to study them more intensely.[63] The JPI created a discrimination scale to distinguish "normal" children from those with more serious behavioral problems. This examination was expedient and could be accomplished in only a few minutes, thus accommodating a large number of children in the Home. Each week, they examined the children in groups of sixty; of those, nearly one-third were given additional tests for feeblemindedness. By 1920, nearly seventy children per week fit the clinical description of "feebleminded."[64]

As discussed, feeblemindedness in delinquent girls was closely associated with illicit sexual practices, including autoerotic behavior. Healy did not subscribe to the earlier belief that masturbation led to madness, but he did argue that such indulgences were antisocial and led to further types of misbehavior. Accordingly, he advised parents to curtail these activities. Some mothers took Healy's words to heart. One girl, brought in for stealing and running away, was classified as mentally dull. Her outstanding problem, however, was not one of self-support or of intelligence but her excessive masturbation. The concerned mother, following Healy's advice, treated the girl's behavior "in a most vigorous fashion" and ultimately succeeded.[65] Although the mother's course of reform was not disclosed, Healy did describe another mother's. Her sixteen-year-old admitted to indulging in the "bad habit" since she was seven years old. Healy's diagnosis was summative on this matter: "It is plain to see why this girl seems so dull in her ordinary reactions." The mother, a "vigorous woman" who was eager to cooperate, was extremely vigilant, even to the point of sleeping with her daughter. In this way, the mother claimed to have "built up" her daughter's resistance to autoerotic temptations.[66]

Some girls may have been tempted because of early physical maturation, which awoke their incipient sexual desires. Healy found that nearly 13 percent of the children he studied had experienced some type of early sexual experience, and not all were consensual.[67] In correlating the girls' physical and emotional development, however, he was sometimes less than objective. To illustrate, he characterized one patient as a "lazy and easy-going, over-developed girl, either frank in sex desires or perhaps indulging in glib talk about religion and personal reformation." Occasionally, his appraisals even bordered on a kind of professional voyeurism. For example, he described one client as follows: "Physically she was splendidly developed, possessed a finely-shaped head with broad, high forehead, and intelligent strong face."[68]

In addition to the girls' beauty or physical endowment, Healy oftentimes attributed their highly charged sexuality to "mental peculiarities." These might include adolescent instabilities, impulses, or extreme suggestibility. To illustrate, one girl thought to be especially clever at her "orgies of stealing" remained undetected in her petty thievery. Healy attributed her stealing impulses to awakened sex impulses. As further evidence, he noted how her impulsive activity ceased once she married.[69] In yet another case of stealing, an eighteen-year-old girl living in extreme poverty wore luxurious clothes and stayed in cheap hotels. Healy suspected her of immorality, although a pelvic examination confirmed that she was still a virgin. Despite her high moral ground, as well as her correct responses to the moral discrimination tests, Healy still focused on her "orgy of misbehavior." His recommendations were not so different from those of matrons at rescue homes: "light" amusement, close companionship, and "repressive control."[70]

Some delinquent girls' cases of mental conflicts and adolescent instability resulted from their menstrual cycles. Several earlier psychiatric studies had confirmed the antisocial and neuropathic tendencies of females resulting from "auto-intoxification" during certain stages in their menstrual cycle. Referred to as "menstrual mental aberration," symptoms included diminished self-control, as well as increased impulsivity, irritability, dizziness, and "temporary stupefaction."[71] Because these catchall symptoms might indicate any number of emotional or mental pathologies, Healy found a differential diagnosis sometimes tenuous. For example, one seventeen-year-old was described as restless, obstinate, and willful by her mother and other "good" women. But Healy found her to be a "splendid specimen" and to possess a "distinctly good-looking [and] rather sensuous type of face," extraordinary mental abilities, and the "keenest perception." Although he admitted his evidence was circumstantial, his final diagnosis was menstrual mental aberration. Here he relied upon others' observations in concluding that premenstrual days could send some girls "over into the border."[72]

Given these states of "temporary stupefaction," how could Healy or others even trust the girls' stories? Here Healy relied upon the Aussage test to measure their ability to give truthful testimony. Essentially, this test assessed the ability to recall accurately. But some girls—especially those with exceptional language abilities—may have intentionally confused or misled psychologists and psychiatrists. These girls were successful with the court's audiences as well. To illustrate, one girl described to the juvenile court judge how she was sold to a white slaver who had assaulted and cut her with a razor. Later examined by the JPI, she was found to be lying, as she had cut herself to get attention. Consequently, she was deported back to her country of origin.[73] But not everyone trusted Healy's diagnoses or the judge's deliberations. At another hearing, the public crowd found the girl's story more persuasive than her medical report. As Healy recollected, "We were informed later that much indignation at our report to the judge was expressed by the crowd in attendance at the trial. The girl's first story was so well told that many had been irrevocably convinced of the utter guilt of the father."[74]

Although Healy acknowledged that youth might "put one over" on the judge, he never suspected that the same would happen to him. Swayed by the psychiatric persuasion, he believed that the institute's examinations could establish evidence of truth or falsification. But Healy wanted to delve deeper than testimony, to try to understand the delinquent's inner world. In creating another research tool, the youth's "own story," Healy turned the tables on his patients, asking them why they were predisposed toward certain misbehaviors. He asked them to dig deep into their early memories and excavate buried traumas and emotional conflicts. Not unlike the probation officers who coaxed children into their confidence, Healy approached his clients in a sympathetic manner. He encouraged them to talk about their interests, motivations, day-dreams, and activities.[75] These stories, he hoped, would lead to more scientific treatment plans, what he described as "properly developing along the lines of forward-looking, right-minded, human engineering."[76]

Of course, the delinquent's "own story" gave the girls opportunities to con-trive, to outwit, or to confess. As noted, their versions sometimes contradicted those of family members, probation officers, and teachers. These variations like-wise revealed other differences: whereas adults emphasized sexual misbehav-iors, the girls more often complained about their monotonous lives. Family members of a twelve-year-old French-Canadian girl spoke adamantly of her immorality, especially her "sex habit." But her "own story" revealed another source of conflict. She disliked housework intensely and told Healy she wanted to live in the country where things would be "different" and "freer."[77] (For her own assessment of the situation, see the epigraph that begins this chapter.) She was eventually placed in a country home where she spent her time "unprofitably" reading Shakespeare. Placed in yet another home, the girl was accused by her housemother of being "stupid" and "feeble-minded," again because of her autoerotic habits. Placed once again, she narrated how she would repeatedly forget about her cooking duties and instead read a book or flirt with boys. The housemother, quite dissatisfied with the girl, said that she was "crazy about nickel shows, careless about her dress," that she "forgot easily, and had a "happy, don't care attitude." Transferred yet again, the girl repeated how much she disliked housework. In fact, she reiterated, the only time she was truly happy was when she was reading a book, especially a romance novel. In her last and final placement, the family complained that she would not tend to her household chores but instead would "stand at night in the pasture for an hour or two looking up in the air."[78] Apparently, no one took the girl's consis-tent statements about her intense dislike of housework seriously. Instead, the housemothers attempted to bend her will to conform to prescriptive models of domesticity and sexuality.

Healy supplemented such girls' "own stories" with the moral discrimination test. One scenario in the test presented a poor Russian man whose neighbors were a sick widow and her small starving children. The man eventually stole bread from a baker's shop and gave it to the widow to feed her children. The test asked whether the man's decision to steal was right or wrong. To be sure, the only correct response was "wrong." But some girls, although giving the wrong answer, were thoughtful. Clara, a recent Russian immigrant, had perhaps observed such occasions in her mother country. As she carefully reasoned about the situation, "You bet he do right. He did not steal money. He stole bread. If he steal money to get clothes or anything like that it's different. You bet I do the same. That girl in the Mission Homes she steal $2 from me. I did not tell no one."[79] Despite Clara's fairly sophisticated reasoning, Healy and Bronner found her to be "clearly feebleminded," a "moron with special language ability." But how could Clara, who was fluent in Russian, German, and French and was quickly learning English, be feebleminded? Once again, the shadow of immorality hovered. Her passion for the singing of Enrico Caruso and fashionable clothing and her vivacious character confirmed her predilection for vice. Perhaps Healy also distrusted her theatrical persona when she spoke of her noble ancestry and her refusal to seek assistance from a Chicago dispensary. Comparing herself to the "poor dirty people" there, she proudly told him, "I am clean and proud. I don't want you to tell any of those society women where I am—I don't want them giving me anything at all—I am able to earn my own living. You ought to see me on the street. I have a pretty dress and a long black plume, and if those women would see me they would ask me how much it cost and where I got it and everything. They did make trouble for me at one place, and when I got home my landlady said, 'You little liar.' They told her I was a Russian Jew. You know they are dirty and ignorant, and I am not a Russian Jew at all. My right father and mother were French."[80]

In the case of another immigrant girl diagnosed as hypomanic, Healy and Bronner dismissed not only her answers to the moral discrimination test but her discussion of a real ethical situation. Complaining about one of her teachers, she argued how wrong it was that the teacher refused to give poor students books for their classes. After all, she reasoned, the books did not belong to the teacher but the board of education. Instead of considering her interpretation of an actual experience, Healy and Bronner focused on the girl's "most ignorant" immigrant family, especially her mother, who lived with a "low-grade foreigner." Diagnosing her problem as one of excitability, the girl was committed to two years at a reform institution.[81]

In 1914, Healy and Bronner left the JPI for the Judge Baker Foundation in Boston. In their later reflections, they criticized the detention process, which confounded children's rehabilitation because it was used for punitive reasons. Further, they argued, in mixing innocent girls with the more seasoned ones, detention actually encouraged future delinquency.[82] Like social work professionals Grace Abbott and Miriam Van Waters, Healy and Bronner believed that deinstitutionalization held more promise than detention. All four hoped that changes in the girls' home environments, and more individualized and "elastic" treatment plans, could better build the girls' characters. Drawing from John Dewey, they proposed that the school curriculum be more purposeful and practical, not simply academic. In favoring a decentralized and community approach, they especially promoted child guidance clinics that treated not only children and youth but their families. However, as Kathleen Jones has noted, mothers more than fathers participated in these clinical sessions, and sometimes for problems related to their marriages, not their children's behaviors. Unwittingly perhaps, the child-guidance clinic staff continued the juvenile courts' practice of blaming mothers for their children's behavior problems.[83]

Following Healy and Bronner's departure, the JPI officially became a part of the juvenile court and a Cook County agency. As such, the institute not only served the Chicago juvenile court but the metropolitan area of Chicago through its two observation wards at the Cook County Psychopathic Hospital. The institute also worked with child guidance clinics in Chicago, including one on the South Side, where African-American psychologist Albert Beckham examined African-American children. Although Beckham alluded to the problems of "deteriorating" homes and the lack of wholesome recreation, he nonetheless followed the psychiatric model of rehabilitation as he focused upon the children's psychological "equipment," not poverty or discrimination. In his examination of fifty delinquent African-American boys and girls from Chicago's juvenile court, he concluded that early diagnoses, as well as correct "social and scientific therapy," had saved most of them. The therapy to which he referred essentially entailed "round[ing] out" the children's "inadequate" personalities and reeducating them so they would not feel socially inadequate. Like E. Franklin Frazier, with his concept of accommodation, Beckham believed that African-American delinquent children could assume the full "trappings" of Western culture; that is, they could transform their personalities and characters in order to become Americans.[84]

In addition to working with child-guidance clinics, the JPI conducted testing on an outpatient basis, though some children were admitted on a short-term basis to the hospital wards through the juvenile court or the Juvenile Detention Home. Under the direction of Dr. Herman Adler, who replaced Healy, the state's Division of Criminology assumed the duties of the JPI in 1917 and expanded its services to the state reformatories and child-guidance clinics throughout Illinois. However, 1920 signaled a change in focus from court services to research. Correspondingly, the JPI changed its name to the Institute for Juvenile Research (IJR). Still, through a cooperative agreement with the IJR and Cook County, an IJR psychiatrist continued to spend three afternoons a week at the Juvenile Detention Home to test problem children.[85] Given the continued large numbers of admissions to the Juvenile Detention Home, the institute was unable to accommodate all of the children. Consequently, one of its divisions focused only on feebleminded petitions.[86]

The Juvenile Detention Home and the JPI (and later IJR) extended the *parens patriae* of the juvenile court. As with other developments in the court system, there was the kinder, gentler side next to a more invasive one. Like Chicago's juvenile court, both the detention home and the JPI had their origins in the work of female reformers. But with the increased medicalization of delinquency and the growth of affiliate professions, the maternalist influence waned. The reform institutions for delinquent girls examined in the following three chapters followed a similar progression. Administered by matrons, rescue workers, and nuns, these facilities increasingly relied upon psychiatric and medical services for the diagnosis, placement, and treatment of their inmates. The shift from moral reform to rehabilitation was not simply a progressive one, however. Like a double helix, moral prescriptions and psychiatric categories were inseparable.

Part Three

Reform Institutions for Delinquent Girls

7

The Chicago Home for Girls

It [the Home] is like a gathering and a weaving together of the stitches taken by many different hands in the interests of this institution. The garment is charity.

—Chicago Home for Girls, Annual Report,
Erring Women's Refuge of Chicago
Thirty-third Annual Report

Historian Michael Sedlak has suggested that social welfare agencies, maternity homes, and benevolent organizations in the Progressive Era competed for public funds in a market of social services for delinquent and "wayward" girls.[1] Undoubtedly, the per diem rate granted to institutions for each committed inmate often tempted institutions to accept more commitments than their facilities could accommodate. There is more evidence, however, that representatives from the girls' corrective institutions cooperated, rather than competed, especially when they assisted the juvenile court judges in their deliberations. This is because the women and their affiliate institutions shared a common maternalist ideology, one that advocated the triad of motherhood, homemaking, and marriage as the most effective program of reform for delinquent girls. Professional maternalists—including Julia Lathrop, Sophonisba Breckinridge, and Mary Bartelme—likewise emphasized the primacy of motherhood and home for reforming delinquent girls. They, like the maternalists, predicated their authority upon gender, arguing that only women should deliberate on the delicate issues of delinquent girls' sexuality.

Tensions sometimes arose between the two groups, however, when professional maternalists sought to enact progressive education reform measures in corrective institutions, such as forming student government, eradicating corporal punishment, and individualizing the girls' reform programs. Correspondingly, professional maternalists believed that the female staff of reform institutions should be trained professionally in order to maximize delinquent girls' opportunities for reform.

Even before Mary Bartelme became juvenile judge in 1923, she exerted pressure on the maternalist administrators of delinquent girls' reform institutions to modernize their educational programs. One of her strategies was to curtail court funding to the institutions by decreasing the number of girls committed. She also insisted that the institutions utilize the more scientific services of psychological and psychiatric testing, especially for more difficult girls. What Bartelme and the juvenile court did not anticipate was resistance from some administrators, such as those of the Chicago Home for Girls, who deliberately attempted to maintain their own institutions' autonomy while also taking advantage of the court's financial windfall.

The Chicago Home for Girls' Administration, Finances, and Facilities

The story of the Chicago Home for Girls' founding was a familiar script, one told later by Kate Waller Barrett, cofounder of the national Florence Crittenton Mission, and by other maternity home administrators.[2] A small-town girl, unmarried and pregnant, requested help from a minister in Chicago in 1863. He turned to his wife who, along with other church women, found shelter for the girl. Soon thereafter, a girl from Chicago, whose circumstances were similar, joined the first. Perceiving a greater need to care for "erring women," the church women rented a house and hired a woman with a "missionary spirit" as matron in 1863.[3] Incorporated under the name Erring Woman's Refuge for Reform two years later, the facility received most of its initial funding from donors. Through legislation enacted in 1869, the Refuge became the recipient of additional monies from fines the city of Chicago levied against prostitution houses.[4] This enabled the Refuge to accommodate an increasing number of young women and wayward girls who sought admission.

By 1890, the Refuge was able to accommodate young women who entered as voluntarily inmates, as well as those who were committed by the police court or by their parents. With the inception of the juvenile court in 1899, the Refuge began to admit delinquent girls, necessitating a change in the institution's name to the Chicago Refuge for Girls in 1906 and later to the Chicago

Home for Girls in 1915. Pecuniary motives prompted the name changes as well, as the trustees worried that the original name could be "detrimental to [the Home's] popularity."[5]

Similar to the duties of the first minister and church women, the administration of the Home was distinctly gendered. Prominent Chicago businessmen and ministers comprised the board of trustees, and oversaw the Home's finances. Members of the board of managers and the Home's various committees—auditing, cooking school, dry goods, educational, fuel, groceries, industrial, inventory, kitchen garden, library, medical, missionary, postal supplies, publishing, and receiving—were older married women, most of whom resided in the wealthier neighborhoods of Chicago and the northern suburbs.[6] In some cases, husbands and wives participated respectively as trustees and committee members, as was the case of University of Chicago sociologist and Baptist minister Charles Henderson and his wife, Ella Levering Henderson. The Home's physicians, teachers, and superintendents were female as well. As with the Home's committee members, these staff members remained with the Home for many years. Elizabeth Stone, assistant superintendent and later superintendent, administered the Home for over thirty years; her successor, Cynthia H. Embree, continued for over fifteen years.[7]

These gendered divisions of labor, which persisted through the 1930s, reflected deliberate ideological and financial spheres of influences. Despite the Home's prosperity secured through the trustees' real estate and bond investments, the women's committees diligently raised funds through charity bazaars, calendar sales, and letter-writing campaigns. Annual contributions from the volunteer and charitable organizations of the Friendly Aid Society, the Service Club, the Flower Mission, the Chicago branches of the Needlework Guild of America, and the Young Ladies of the Hyde Park High School attested to the powerful sway of the Home's domestic and industrial curricula. Religious organizations, including the Young Ladies' Bible Class of Woodlawn Presbyterian Church, Kenwood Evangelical Church, Plymouth Congregational Church, the Presbyterian Board of Publishers, and the Bible Society provided a steady supply of Bibles, religious literature, and vesper services. Chicago companies donated monies, food, household items, and tickets for edifying recreations such as museums and concerts. The deaconesses, club women, and female volunteers from the Moody Bible Institute, the Columbia School of Expression, and the Armour Institute Dramatic Club who visited the Home complemented the staff's abiding maternal influence.[8]

Until 1916, the Home had four stable sources of income. First, the board of trustees contributed an average of 25 percent of the Home's revenue through bond investments, mortgages, rental fees, and interest. Second, the city of Chicago provided nearly 15 percent through fines from prostitution, levied mostly on those houses' visitors and owners. Because the city did not always pay these monies in full to the Home, the Home was forced eventually to hire a collections agent.[9] Third, the Home received additional monies from the city of Chicago after 1903, when the Home was designated as a shelter for female offenders, as was the city's House of Correction.[10] By the early 1900s, the Cook County Juvenile Court became the fourth monetary mainstay for the Home, providing in some years nearly half of its revenue. Initially the Home received thirty cents per day for each girl committed; by 1922, the sum had increased to forty cents. Although records are not entirely clear, it appears that the juvenile court granted this per diem rate for babies born to committed girls as well.[11] Compared to the cost of caring for the girls, however, the per diem rates were inadequate, as the annual costs for the girls' provisions by 1921 was estimated at $360. By 1931, the annual costs had risen to almost $500, or the per diem rate of $1.29.[12]

Calendar sales, bazaars, and rummage sales provided other steady, although minimal, sources of support. Until 1918, calendar sales brought in an average of 14 percent of the Home's revenue. The Industrial and Arts Department, which sold rugs and clothing made by the girls, contributed nearly 3 percent until 1920, when public sales were discontinued. Sales of the girls' canned fruits, jellies, pickles, mincemeats, invalids' baskets, and embroidery raised 2 to 7 percent. During some years, the girls' labor paid for over 25 percent of the Home's expenses, not counting the clothing and food they made for themselves. The girls contributed much more than their parents or guardians, who before the juvenile court's involvement had paid only 8 percent but after the juvenile court's commitments paid less than 2 percent.[13]

Because of the Home's diverse funds, especially its property investments, the Home remained clear of debt through the 1930s. Yet the Home's female administration continually drew another picture, not only to shield the Home's wealth from the public but also to prompt more philanthropic support. Referring to the Home's rising costs, the women lamented the postponement of their dream to relocate to the country in 1912. For the girls' sake, the staff thought it best to move from the "detrimental" influences of their predominantly African-American neighborhood on Chicago's South Side. The female staff repeatedly expressed alarm at the men and boys who jumped over the Home's fences, climbed the fire escape balconies beneath the girls' bedrooms, and peered into their windows. They considered the situation particularly dreadful in the summer when there was "constant calling and jeering" from the alleys and tenement porches.[14] Resigned to the Home's present location at 5024 Indiana Avenue, the house committee decided in 1921 to renovate the thirty-year-old Home into a "livable, sanitary, bright and cheerful home." They remodeled the industrial wing and enlarged the baby welfare room. They also purchased a new gas stove for the domestic science kitchen and equipped the laundry room with a new washing machine. The girls painted, whitewashed, and redecorated their own rooms.[15]

The need for expansion was especially critical for the Home's medical and nursery services. Unlike some of the female reform institutions in Chicago, the Chicago Home for Girls provided prenatal, natal, and maternal care. It was even likely that some unmarried women voluntarily sought admissions to the Home to take advantage of these provisions. The first medical report in 1900 had, in fact, enumerated mostly obstetrical and gynecological cases. Of the referred gynecological cases, there were no reported cases of venereal diseases, as the Home generally refused to accept infected girls. By 1923, however, Wasserman tests were administered, indicating the need for isolation rooms for such girls. By 1930, 38 percent of the thirteen hundred girls admitted since 1923 had been infected with venereal disease.[16] Such statistics were not unique to the Home, as the House of the Good Shepherd and the Illinois State Industrial School in Geneva reported similar numbers. Regardless, the possibility of contagion must have been of special concern for the pregnant girls and their newborns.

The nursery had long been the Home's pride and joy, and the board members watched over it as diligently as they did the newborns cared for there. They also nurtured affiliations with other child welfare facilities, health care agencies, and hospitals to ensure proper medical care for the babies and their mothers. As early as 1903, the Home renovated the nursery to keep it as "modern" and yet as "sunny" as possible. Likewise, they hired a head nurse for this "well-equipped" facility. By 1909, the nursery committee recommended a larger nursery, especially given the younger ages of unwed mothers and the need to teach them proper natal care. Similarly, they employed a children's specialist to teach breast-feeding methods. Her lessons were apparently successful as subsequent nursery medical reports noted an increase in the number of babies breastfed.[17] The use of ultraviolet lamps to prevent the loss of mother's milk, may have contributed to this, as well the efforts of an Infant Welfare Society nurse hired from the Mary Crane Nursery of Hull House. Through her, the Home established its own infant welfare station to examine mothers and babies, and to teach the mothers how to manage the diet kitchen and their babies' food.[18] The Home also had the distinction of having the first set of Little Mothers' Club graduates in Chicago. Sponsored by the Public Health Department, this "very thorough" course included nursing and home care for babies. Although twelve mothers had graduated in 1920, the club was short-lived, perhaps because the Home hired a new department matron.[19] Nonetheless, the nursery committee continued to improve the facilities. They renovated the day nursery and converted a room into an emergency room to care for mothers during their confinement, even though they were usually taken to Wesley Hospital for prenatal care and to the maternity wards at Wesley and Lying-in Hospitals for their deliveries.[20]

The Home cared for both white and African-American mothers and their babies, as indicated by reports, although it admitted fewer African-American girls. Pregnant African-American girls, however, were taken to the African-American Provident Hospital for their deliveries or to Cook County Hospital, where the Chicago Urban League had hired an African-American social worker to assist them.[21] There seemed to be no differences, though, in the maternal and natal care provided at the Home for white and African-American mothers. The babies slept next to their mothers, although in their cribs. At seven each morning, the babies went to the nursery, while the mothers continued their school, work, and recreational schedules, or took their turns at supervising the babies.[22]

Like other maternity homes, the Home thought that the girls' reform would be more enduring if they raised their babies; indeed, most of the mothers did keep their babies after leaving the Home. But when the girls had problems supporting themselves, the Home assisted them with other arrangements, be it marriage, adoption, or caring for the babies at the Home.[23] Records showed that the Home cared for at least three babies without their mothers, although they were probably placed for adoption later. The Home was well connected to orphanages and home-finding agencies in Chicago, and mediations often occurred without the juvenile court's intervention. As early as 1906, ten infants had been adopted, one under the auspices of the Hebrew Society. By the 1920s, the Illinois Children's Home and Aid Society arranged for many of the Home's adoptions at the mothers' requests. In some cases, the Illinois Children's Home and Aid Society and the Lutheran Home Finding Society cared for the babies until their mothers could secure suitable employment. However, this arrangement was sometimes humiliating for those mothers as other inmates in the Home spread rumors that their babies had been taken away from them.[24]

In addition to expanding its nursery facilities, the Home converted one of its rental properties into the Melissa Evans Home and Club for working girls. For some of the girls released from the Chicago Home for Girls, this club provided transitional homelike accommodations and supervision. The girls paid one to five dollars for room and board; if unemployed, they paid nothing. For some girls in the latter circumstance, the Home also secured jobs in neighborhood shops.[25] Regardless of their situations, the girls helped with the Club's upkeep under the watchful eye of a housemother. Not unlike the Chicago Home for Girls, the Melissa Evans Home and Club described itself as "a well regulated family" with an "incorruptible felicity" and an "infallible religion." Initially, in 1914, the Melissa Evans Home and Club accommodated four girls from the Chicago Home for Girls, as well as dependent girls sent from the Chicago juvenile court by then Assistant Judge Mary Bartelme. One year later, the number of girls averaged seventeen; within a year, the number increased to twenty-four, beyond the Melissa Evans Home's capacity.[26]

Because the girls worked all day and were tired at night, the committee members found it difficult to befriend them. Still, the housemother planned recreational activities and domestic instruction to keep them busy and distracted from outside amusements. Such efforts were successful, at least from the committee's perspective. On one occasion, when the girls served supper to Judge Mary Bartelme, their probation officers, and the Home's committee members, all the guests commented on the girls' transformations, especially one who had been refused by two other institutions because of her "unkempt" appearance. As they concurred, "You wouldn't recognize her now!"[27]

By 1919, the Melissa Evans Home and Club had moved to a larger building to take in more girls, although one year later Bartelme ordered that only dependent girls from the juvenile court reside there. Three years later, the Melissa Evans Home and Club closed, despite financial support from the juvenile court. Although it is not clear why the facility closed, records showed that court monies were insufficient to sustain it; in fact, the Chicago Home for Girls had provided much of its funding.[28] With the court's decision to no longer admit Chicago Home girls, the Home's administration may well have decided to break all financial ties with its "sister" home. As examined below, there were sometimes ideological tensions between the juvenile court and Chicago Home administration, and power struggles consequently ensued.

Court Involvement and the Chicago Home for Girls

The Home's administration had initially welcomed the juvenile court girls, not only because of court monies but because the women thought their moral persuasions would have a greater impact on the younger girls than if they returned to their own homes under the supervision of a probation officer. In the early 1900s, most of the Home's girls were fifteen to seventeen years of age, although some were over twenty and some infrequently younger than ten. With increased juvenile court involvement, however, the average age remained fifteen through the 1930s.[29] Many of these girls were first- and second-generation immigrants. As early as 1906, the receiving committee had admitted 104 girls of fifteen nationalities. Until 1935, however, most of these girls were native-born white Americans (35 percent) and German Americans (23 percent). Irish-American, Swedish-American, and African-American girls constituted the next largest groups through 1935, although the number of "Hebrew" or "Jewish" girls (admittedly vague designators) increased as of 1908.[30] Alarmed by the number of first- and second-generation immigrants committed through the juvenile court, the staff modified the Home's curricula to incorporate Americanization and citizenship programs, especially during World War I. Appropriating the juvenile court's language, the staff justified this by enumerating the cases of immigrant girls who had come from homes "broken" by alcoholism, immorality, desertion, neglect, and divorce.[31]

The receiving committee expressed concern not only about the girls' foreign parentage but also about their low levels of education, menial occupations, and impoverished home backgrounds. The primary causes of their delinquency, the committee concluded, were "dissolute parents" and the "demoralizing influences" of their homes. Curtailing parental influences, then, was necessary so that the Home could carry out its program of reform. The Home accomplished this in two ways. First, it enforced the juvenile court's full sentence of one to two years, despite parents' constant petitions that daughters be sent home after two to three months. Second, the staff restricted family visits and written correspondence from relatives.[32] To illustrate, the juvenile court sent "MM," a sixteen-year-old native-born white girl, to the Home because she had crossed the state border to elope with a young Filipino. Her mother, although ashamed of her daughter's escapades, requested that the girl be sent home. She told the judge that her daughter never got into any trouble, although neighbors told the probation officer otherwise. Because of the Home staff's persistence, MM remained at the Home for the full term of two years.[33]

Before the Home hired its first probation officer in May of 1900, its receiving committee had interviewed all incoming girls, including those seeking voluntary admission to the Home. In their matronly words, the committee listened to the "heart-breaking stories" of the "poor waifs," although they later acknowledged that sometimes the stories were contrived "with no resemblance to the truth and entirely different from the one told in Court."[34] Until 1902, the receiving committee and board members also attended juvenile court sessions for delinquent girls and assisted the judge in his deliberations, along with representatives from the Illinois State Industrial School for Delinquent Girls at Geneva, the Evanston Industrial Home, and the House of the Good Shepherd. When Jennie Ratcliff became the Home's first probation officer, she represented the Home at each court session, although the receiving committee continued to interview girls before admitting them.[35] It is not clear whether there was always agreement between the receiving committee and the probation officer as to which girls should be admitted. Regardless, by 1901 almost 33 percent of the girls were committed from the juvenile court. By 1908, almost 80 percent were. Not surprisingly, parental and self-referrals declined, accounting for less than an average of 10 percent of the Home's inmates from 1908 to 1935.[36]

Prior to the creation of the municipal court in 1905, nearly one-third of the Home's inmates had been referred by Chicago's police court. Jennie Ratcliff visited the district police stations and helped to determine which of those young women should be committed to the Home.[37] As of 1902, most of the girls from the police court were committed for only three to six months, a sentence the receiving committee thought too short for a change of heart and character. The municipal court judge resolved this dilemma later in 1905 when he committed older girls from the police courts for up to one year.[38] Chicago's

Mayor Carter Harrison Jr. assisted in enforcing these commitments by refusing to grant pardons for early releases. The receiving committee expressed gratitude to the judge and mayor, as they contended that a "certain class" of girls from the police court were more difficult to reform than others.[39]

In 1906, the Chicago Home for Girls began to accept young women from the municipal court. According to the Home's records, however, this practice was short-lived. From 1906 through 1908, the population of inmates from the municipal court ranged from 15 to 22 percent of the Home's incoming group.[40] Later in 1913, a special branch of the municipal court, the morals court, was established with the express purpose of eradicating Chicago's prostitution problem. As such, its jurisdiction expanded to include not only cases from disorderly houses but those involving adultery, pandering, soliciting, and vagrancy. Given this latitude, most young women brought before the morals court were arrested for violations of minor city ordinances, not prostitution. As such, they were more often fined, not committed to institutions. However, the Chicago Home for Girls did accept some young women from the morals court, at least from 1913 through 1917. (In 1913, only 17 percent of the Home's population was from the morals court but that percentage had increased to 38 by 1917). The increase in admissions was probably due to the vigilance of police officers who arrested young women at the war camps. In all likelihood, the Home took in only those they considered redeemable, thus excluding the more seasoned prostitutes. Clearly, the staff was concerned about the deleterious effects of young women from the municipal and morals courts upon the juvenile court girls because they segregated their sleeping quarters and cooking classes according to court commitments.[41]

Even though the juvenile court became the primary mechanism for channeling commitments to the Home, relations between the Home's staff and the juvenile court were often strained. Despite the hiring of a probation officer, the receiving committee still insisted on interviewing juvenile court girls and keeping records on them. These activities to some extent undermined the position of the probation officer and the juvenile court. The staff, however, may have felt differently since it was the Home that initially paid the probation officer's salary, not the juvenile court. It was not clear whether the Home continued to pay her salary after 1905, when the Illinois Juvenile Court Act of 1899 was amended to include county support for probation officers' salaries. As noted earlier, the county was sluggish in accepting that responsibility and many probation officers continued to be paid through women's organizations and churches. So it is very possible that Jennie Ratcliff continued to receive her salary from the Home, not Cook County, especially since that gave the Home the final say in the girls' releases.[42]

Similar to many maternity homes, the Home did not keep systematic or complete records. This was, in part, intentional, as it kept the locus of control in the board of managers' and superintendent's hands. In fact, prior to 1909, the Home's annual reports excluded the probation officer's reports. Thereafter, only the probation officer's reports were published, perhaps because of the small number of women committed from the municipal and police courts. Regardless, all records—considered "meagre and inadequate" by a later social worker—consisted of card files listing only the girls' names, addresses, religions, nationalities, ages, delinquent history sheets, commitment papers, and relatives' letters.[43]

That the Home's staff was distrustful of the court's ability to monitor the girls during their probation is unquestionable. Superintendent Elizabeth Wood refused to delegate responsibility to the court regarding the releases of the girls. This was consistent with Judge Richard Tuthill's ruling in 1907 that children in institutions were to be released by the institutions, not probation officers, because the inmates were wards of the institutions. Even so, the Home's receiving committee still consulted with the probation officer's reports on conditions in the girls' homes and neighborhoods, and their prospective places of employment. Based upon this information, the committee then approved which girls should be returned to the juvenile court.[44] In short, the receiving committee held the trump card in terms of the girls' releases, not the court.

Once the girls were paroled, the probation officer visited them monthly and required them to write weekly reports on their behavior. If their reports were questionable or negative (which was dubious, given self-reporting opportunities), the girls might be returned to the Home or, in rare situations, to other institutions.[45] From 70 to nearly 90 percent of the girls returned to their own homes, even though those homes had been considered "dissolute" and "broken" and often the source of their delinquency. No more than 25 percent of the girls were reported as self-supporting, although one should question what that description meant. The fact that only 25 percent of the Home's girls became employed in domestic, chambermaid, or millinery work indicated that the Home's rhetoric on economic independence rang hollow.[46]

In terms of the girls' outcomes, it is difficult to determine how many actually "made good." There are four reasons for this. First, the absence of a social worker at the Home until 1933 gave the superintendent a great deal of leeway in reporting the girls' outcomes. This was true even though a probation officer worked with the Home through 1935, with the exception of one year. As noted, during some years the superintendent excluded the probation officer's reports from the annual reports, calling into question the high percentages of reformed girls. During other years, the receiving committee's and superintendent's reports overlapped or contradicted those of the probation officer. Sometimes the committee's reports emphasized different aspects of the girls' lives, particularly their home conditions or foreign ancestry. Although the latter preoccupation dovetailed with the Home's Americanization programs, it also diverted attention away from the Home's internal problems.[47]

A second complication in determining outcomes was that the crowded conditions necessitated a constant movement of inmates in and out of the Home. Although the Home could ideally accommodate only seventy-five girls, plus ten mothers and their babies at a single time, it usually housed more. The recorded daily average, as well as the greatest and least numbers of girls, usually exceeded the Home's capacity. In some years, when at least half the girls had been committed for two to three years, the Home accommodated a total of 242 girls.[48] One cannot wonder to what extent overcrowding may have undermined the intentions of reforming the girls, as individualized attention was improbable. With a steady number of releases, the Home attempted to maintain a more reasonable number of girls.

Third, letters published in the superintendent's reports tell us little about how many girls were actually reformed, as they were selected for evidence of exemplary outcomes. Letters from the "old girls" followed the familiar scripts of redemption and gratitude, similar to the Crittenton Home inmates described by Regina Kunzel.[49] As one Home girl expressed, "I do not know in what way I can show the ladies that I appreciated what they did for me while at the refuge, unless by my good behavior in the future."[50] In some cases, the girls carried on the proselytizing of the Home: "You just wait! I'll show you I will do good work in the world. I will be a respectable woman. . . . I can help my sisters now. They shall never go to dance houses or associate with bad companions. I will watch over them."[51] Others, too, embraced a righteous and narrow path, including one woman's daughter, born in the home, who became an assistant superintendent of a Sabbath school.[52]

Many girls did express genuine gratitude for the superintendent's and probation officer's care, although such letters were probably singled out for publication. One girl, who remained at the Home for six years, wrote that she was now a "happy and respected wife." Another inmate later contributed financially to the home. Yet another was not only married to a professional man and had two sons, but was nearing completion of her medical studies through a university scholarship.[53] Additionally, some girls expressed gratitude for a second chance, as was the case with one girl who claimed to not be ashamed to have been at the Home but was "proud" to have had "the chance to rise above my former mistakes, for which I was not responsible, and I am now going to make good."[54] Undoubtedly, the Home did provide a homelike environment with ample food, medical care, and schooling—provisions that may not have been as available to the girls in their own homes.

These exuberant displays of praise, though, did not quite match the probation officer's reports from 1910 through 1922. Her numbers showed that of those girls released, only half who returned to the city were "doing well." Nearly 14 percent left for other Midwestern states and their outcomes remained unknown. Less than 10 percent married, and even fewer transferred to other institutions. By her account, an average of 20 percent returned to the Home or were classified as having "doubtful" conduct. The unknown conditions of many parolees reflected not simply inadequate record keeping but ambiguous results of the Home's reform program.[55] Further, some "successes" were deemed so only because of lack of follow-up visits. To illustrate, the juvenile court judge sent "DO," a Swedish-American girl, to the Chicago Home for Girls after she confessed to several affairs with her neighborhood boys. Reports indicated that she adjusted remarkably well at the Home and so was sent to live with a relative. The next year she was pregnant and unwed. A later investigation revealed that she had not been living with her relative, as the probation officer had noted, but instead with an older man.[56] The example of DO exemplified one of many cases found in the superintendent's reports from 1926 to 1935 designated as "unknowns."

Allusions to girls under "mental care" from the same time period coincided with the more frequent use of psychological and psychiatric services through the Chicago branch's Institute of Juvenile Research (IJR) and the South Side Child Guidance Clinic in the 1920s. The Home referred girls to the clinic mostly for pregnancy or venereal disease tests. Girls brought before the juvenile court a second time were generally referred to the IJR for psychological and psychiatric tests.[57] The Home proudly proclaimed this new psychomedical path during the 1920s and 1930s, declaring that it was now "an institution for the hospitalization of delinquents."[58] Accordingly, of fifteen of the Home's girls who received psychopathic examinations in 1935, six were reported to have psychopathic tendencies; eleven other girls were classified as "dull normal" the same year.[59] As of 1932, the staff also required girls to undergo psychiatric or psychological evaluation before allowing them to share sleeping rooms. The Home staff worried that some girls might become too friendly with one another and learn about "unhealthy" sex practices. They were especially concerned with the more vulnerable girls who might not be able to distinguish another girl's concocted stories from the truth and thus be subject to manipulation.[60] Similar to concerns expressed by Margaret Reeves, who had conducted a national survey of female reform institutions, the staff considered roommates "a serious moral problem" and double rooms the least desirable of all sleeping arrangements.[61]

From 1933 to 1934, Helen Haseltine, a social worker from the School of Social Service Administration (SSSA), provided casework services, as well as supervised graduate students' work for the Home. They spent much of their time referring the girls to social service agencies, such as the Central Free Dispensary, Cook County Hospital and Clinics, the Illinois Social Hygiene League, and St. Luke's General Clinic. They also worked closely with the high schools, as well as signed up the girls for recreational activities at the South Chicago Community Center, the YWCAs, and the Eleanor Clubs. Some girls, however, needed more serious attention and so received psychiatric and psychometric testing through the arrangements of Edith Abbott. For unusually difficult girls—again, those mostly from the juvenile court—a female psychologist from the University of Chicago (whose name was not given) and Dr. Chamberlain of the IJR developed constructive treatment plans.[62]

Finally, the girls' outcomes were questionable because of the Home's domestic curricula. As detailed in the next section, the girls engaged in mostly housework and little academic or commercial education. To what extent, then, could they become self-supporting? Although the staff forwarded the rhetoric of viable self-support, the true intent of their domestic, religious, and recreational curricula was containment through marriage, motherhood, and homemaking.

The Home's Reeducation Programs

As early as 1896, the Home's schoolroom had been described in the annual reports as "systematic," similar to those found in public schools.[63] However, because of the Home's crowded conditions, the older and younger girls attended classes alternately in morning and evening shifts. Nearly 60 percent of the girls, some of whom were older, were initially placed in the grammar school because of their low educational attainment. These classes emphasized more basic literacy skills because many girls did not know how to read or even write their own names in English. Once they progressed in their writing abilities, they were assigned poems with "fine ennobling thought[s]" to copy and study.[64] They were also required to write letters home to practice their writing and grammar, although the teachers probably read them to ensure that no negative remarks were made about the Home. Similarly, the girls were encouraged to acquire the "reading habit," which entailed patiently reading the opening book chapters of a book rather than rushing to the more exciting episodes. As one report "rephrased" a young African-American girl's progress, "I guess I kin 'onderstann' dat book jes es well as de white folks kin" [*sic*].[65]

The library committee complemented the teachers' efforts. As early as 1898, members of the committee had read to the younger girls; later they hired an invalid woman to do so. The older girls were given lectures on grand literature, including one by University of Chicago Professor Martha Foote Crowe on Harriet Beecher Stowe. The library housed donated books, religious newspapers, and women's magazines, including the *Ladies Home Journal,* the *Medical Missionary Journal, Young Christian Soldier,* and *Youth's Companion.* Such literature was morally fortifying because it kept the girls busy on the "long rosary of days," especially Sundays, the designated library day. (Even medically quarantined girls were given magazines to read, which were later destroyed.) When the girls checked out their minimum one book per week, their usual choices, however, were not so edifying. Rather than selecting novels by Charles Dickens,

Henry Wadsworth Longfellow, or Louisa May Alcott they chose the popular fictions and romances of Gilbert Parker, Hall Caine, and E. P. Roe.[66]

The curricula remained fairly constant until the 1920s when commercial education, considered a progressive measure by the juvenile court, was introduced. By the 1920s, most girls began to attend junior high and high school classes, indicating perhaps the positive effects of compulsory schooling and the Home's curricula.[67] The Home proudly published the girls' academic progress, even though the staff noted that the girls' "impulse to mental labor [was] generally lacking."[68] As the staff imagined, many girls came from "irregular" or "broken homes" and so had not attended school beyond third or fourth grade. For incentives, the teachers dispensed prizes to the best students and instituted honor rolls. Not all girls were thought capable of excelling, though; the 1914 report noted that many girls were subnormal in intelligence.[69] Similar to the mental hygiene efforts of other female reform facilities, the Home began to stress the importance of teachers developing "insight" into these girls' "innermost thoughts."[70]

Despite the attention given to some academic learning, the Home's emphasis was primarily domestic. The annual reports lauded the benefits of such a curriculum: it taught character-building skills; prepared the girls for employment; and socialized them into their future roles as wives and mothers. Accordingly, the girls' schedules were rigorous. The younger girls' schooling consisted of four hours of academics per day, plus sewing, embroidering, cooking, laundry, and housework. Upon completion of sixth grade, each girl was expected to spend at least two hours a week in the laundry room. The managers surmised that the girls almost delighted in this "colorless" routine, although if the girls were asked, they may have given a different reply. The managers lamented how unskilled the girls were in sewing, laundry, and household skills, which they had not been taught in their homes. The board justified all such work on the grounds that it would contribute to the girls' understanding of the dignity of labor.[71]

Domestic work also taught the girls thrift. Referring in particular to the immigrant girls' lack of assimilation, the board declared, "They were not brought up to frugal ways in this land of plenty." Especially during the lean war years, the managers chastised the girls for not being sympathetic to the concept of sacrifice.[72] In attempts to conserve food, the girls tried different menus from the government bulletins. Initially, the staff observed, the girls became upset when sugar was rationed but they eventually showed a "spirit of helpfulness." The Home, too, practiced its own cost measures, although these were not limited to war efforts. The reports, for example, estimated the cost of materials for each girl's cooking lesson at only two cents.[73]

As early as 1896, the cooking school had claimed to teach the girls "self-support," considered an indispensable part of housework. The teacher gave instructions two hours a week "in simple, practical chemistry," during which the girls learned about the physiology of food, and how it "nourish[ed] the brain or nerve tissues."[74] The girls also pickled fruits and jellies for their own consumption and for public sale, as well as learned to bake bread and make meals from cheap cuts of meat. In the advanced cooking class, they canned vegetables and fruits, and preserved pickles, jellies, and mincemeat as Christmas presents for their families.[75] As noted earlier, many of these goods were also sold at bazaars and thereby contributed to the Home's finances.

To train for cooking and service positions, the Home purchased tables from restaurants used at the Columbian Exposition of 1893. The girls prepared menus of four to five courses served by others, although the lessons were sometimes mere gestures because no food had been prepared. Even so, the girls were expected to be graceful when serving. As the board members acknowledged, "It is something of an ordeal to sit at the table and pretend to partake of a meal when nothing is served, and visitors are present."[76] Through these simulations, the Home's kitchen garden department hoped to raise "domestic service" to its "true dignity." The staff also hoped that many girls would later be hired as domestics for private families. Some girls did later become cooks or maids for families but most domestic jobs could not economically sustain them. The Home's true concern was not employment so much as the girls' eventual marriages; the Home's staff hoped "that each one of our girls will find her true place in a home of her own, where the cooking and washing and even housecleaning will take on new interest for her because of her training here."[77]

For similar reasons, sewing was another useful skill. Again, the staff forwarded the arguments of "dignity of service" and a "useful, independent and respected" livelihood, although in truth sewing was a "considerable income" for the Home.[78] The board of managers nonetheless argued that some girls could later earn as much as ten to twelve dollars weekly as seamstresses. More importantly, it stressed that learning to sew their own clothes would counter the girls' temptation to procure "pretty" clothes through improper means. Accordingly, the girls sewed their own clothing, as well as shirtwaists, skirts, suits, comforters, table linen, dress bags, and fancywork, and even a wedding trousseau for sale. The annual reports enumerated their productivity. In one year alone, the girls had sewn or woven a total of 525 undergarments, 150 dresses, 5 graduating outfits, 68 miscellaneous articles, 10 Halloween costumes, 70 handkerchiefs for Valentine's Day, and 50 rugs.[79]

In their sewing classes, the girls not only learned basic stitches but more elaborate designs. They started with mending and simple hemming, then progressed to pattern making and alterations. During one four-month period, they made over 158 dresses, as well as undergarments, infants' clothes, and household supplies. The girls also learned art needlework, Irish crochet, and how to sew with Japanese crepe. Elaborate pieces made by the girls included two "rose" quilts, nine luncheon sets, embroidered towels, embroidered centerpieces, drawn work, nine crepe shirtwaists, and jabots.[80] These pieces were most likely sold at the Home's bazaars.

In 1905, the industrial department purchased three looms for rug weaving. Although the staff acknowledged that such lessons did not seem practical for purposes of employment, they insisted that the loom "develop[ed] character" and taught patience. Espousing the recapitulation theory, the staff argued that weaving was important as "the education of the hand comes first in the Culture Historic Period of the race and should come before academic work."[81] Taught by women affiliated with the Arts and Crafts Department of the University of Chicago, the girls designed and dyed rugs for their own rooms and for rummage sales. In addition to weaving, the girls learned woodworking and built invalids' baskets, bookends, and footstools, as well as learning simple home repairs. Basket making and chair caning were also taught as managers thought that the girls would be pleased to contribute their time and skills to their own comfort while at the Home.[82]

For other lessons in character building, as well as in physical culture, the girls were given laundry duties. To be expected, they found this work "a drudgery" even after modern steam equipment was installed, Indeed it was time-consuming, as the staff calculated that if each girl was responsible for eight pieces, eighty-seven girls would wash at least 688 pieces, plus bedding. By 1930, each girl not only spent six to eight hours weekly in the laundry room but was required to take daily classes in laundry since the staff insisted they could then later be employed in commercial laundries.[83]

In total, then, the girls not only did the laundry but sewed, mended, cooked, wove rugs and scarves, and made pottery. Additionally, they sewed curtains and draperies, dresses, and underwear, as well as planned lunches, preserved food for winter, baked and served meals, and scrubbed the stoves and utensils. Despite the institutional nature of this work, the managers stressed the importance of making such tasks as home-like as possible. But in reality, the girls subsidized their own keep, thereby contributing to the Home's low costs.

In addition to domestic and industrial work, the staff touted religious fortification. Because the girls' "passport" to the home had been one of "shame, sorrow, and disgrace," religious devotion became the path to the girls' "true freedom" and salvation.[84] Many elder Christian women assisted the girls through their "refining influence" in assisting them in prayers and devotion. The Home's Missionary Committee, comprised of forty such women, guided the girls in their prayers, temperance meetings, and Bible readings. Female visitors from the Moody Institute and the Christian Endeavor Society led the girls in their Sunday-school lessons, Friday and Sunday afternoon services, evening meetings, and vesper services, which included three hours of silence. Although the last was not compulsory, the staff reported that many girls participated, perhaps hoping to shorten the length of their stays at the Howe.[85]

The Home acknowledged the many female volunteers who unselfishly gave of their time and wisdom. Imaging the Home as a tightly-woven fabric, the superintendent elaborated, "It is like a gathering and a weaving together of the stitches taken by many different hands in the interests of this institution. The garment is charity."[86] Letters from girls were published that attested to the Home's refining influence of the volunteers and staff members. Many of these girls married and had children, having learned "the right path." Several wrote that the Home was responsible for the "foundation of their present prosperity."[87]

Wholesome recreation, too, was morally edifying, as well as a much-needed respite from school and domestic work. On Saturday night, the girls' "own night," they usually played games and entertained in the chapel. A new gymnasium built in 1905 provided the girls with more space for exercise. By 1921, the Home hired a playground worker for directed play, especially in gymnastics, physical culture exercises, and sports. Her efforts were complemented by an instructor from the recreation center at the Hull House, who taught the girls folk dancing.[88]

Folk dancing dovetailed with the creation of Americanization clubs for immigrant girls. Several clubs were organized by the Daughters of the American Revolution, who also donated patriotic books, sponsored speakers and contests, and celebrated patriotic holidays. By 1919, the Home had created its own Americanization committee to assist in supervising these club activities. As committee members surmised, most inmates from European countries stood "in direct need of Americanization."[89] As such, the girls memorized the Pledge of Allegiance and learned about American heroes and the flag's symbolism. They also practiced "correct" American speech through poetry, speech making, and essay contests. Such lessons were considered essential for molding the right thoughts and actions, especially as the English language was deemed "not only the best language but the real currency of thought, and too, that even the right to vote means the duty to vote right."[90]

Also tied to citizenship education was a progressive form of student government instituted in 1921 by Superintendent Cynthia H. Embree. Modeled on a city commissioner plan, each of the three halls constituted a city unit. Each hall's government was comprised of four groups: the council girls, citizens, unnaturalized citizens, and aliens. All girls were unnaturalized citizens until they proved themselves worthy of citizenship—that is, when they demonstrated proper conduct and attitudes. A student council of five girls assisted the matrons in enforcing the Home's rules by discussing modes of discipline and studying each girl's weak points.[91] Based upon their assessments, the council granted privileges to well-behaved girls, some of which reinforced prescriptions from beauty culture: wearing silk stockings on Saturday night, attending movies, buying candies and toiletries from the Home's store, or visiting families on weekends. The staff heralded the positive effects of this peer government, citing it as a "real factor in creating a spirit of contentment and good will in the Home."[92] One cannot help but wonder, though, to what extent this system created favoritism and division among the girls.

The Chicago Home for Girls' straight and narrow path of reform through salvation eventually forked with the professional services of social workers, psychologists, and psychiatrists. Similarly, the previous recreational activities of temperance meetings, Bible readings, and vesper services became more secular. In truth, the Home could not continue to shroud its image to the public, especially to the juvenile court judges. The Home's shift from redemption to rehabilitation, in fact, began with Judge Mary Bartelme's discontent with the Home's administration in the early 1920s. Her recommendation of Cynthia H. Embree as the Home's superintendent signaled a move toward progressive reform in reformatories, even though Bartelme later had problems with Embree.

Whether or not the staff conceded to the wishes of Bartelme and the juvenile court, the Home was able to prosper for three reasons. First, the volunteer efforts of the committee members, as well as the cooperative services of hospitals, social service agencies, and the University of Chicago enabled the Home to keep the costs of salaries and its overhead low. The financial shrewdness of the trustees, often masked by the evangelical and maternalist rhetoric of the female staff, was one reason. Second, there were few institutions to which delinquent girls in Chicago could be sent. The state reformatory remained overcrowded, as it took in girls from all of Illinois. The House of the Good Shepherd, although admitting girls of all faiths, especially welcomed Catholic girls. As a nonsectarian Protestant facility, the Chicago Home for Girls conceived of itself as offering Protestant girls the best religious and moral guidance. The Home, however, did not limit itself to Protestant girls but also accepted Jewish girls, soliciting assistance from rabbis and the Jewish Women's Aid Societies.[93]

Third, the maternalist ideologies of the Home and the court coalesced to support the Home's moral and domestic model of reform. Despite the juvenile court's later psychomedical model of rehabilitation, the impetus for the formation and early administration of the juvenile court had been maternalist. Bartelme, as an active member of the Chicago Woman's Club, worked within this maternalist ideology, as she created a distinct female sphere in the juvenile court for dependent and delinquent girls, and for its female staff. Similar to the Home's staff, she recommended reforms based upon a domestic and industrial curricula, a homelike and familial setting, and supervision by sympathetic women.

Thus, it was not only Mary Bartelme who mediated her power; the Home staff did so as well. The fact that the Home was able to adapt to changes mandated by the court while also maintaining some degree of autonomy attested to the multiple strategies of the Home and other women's organizations in their state-building activities. These women crafted, conjoined, and sometimes contested ideologies and practices in the arena of female delinquency. The language and the noticeable silences in the Chicago Home for Girls' annual reports provide us with examples of one organization's attempts to maintain ideological control and financial independence.

8

The State Industrial School for Delinquent Girls in Geneva, Illinois

They revel in smutty talk, delight in reading obscene literature,
and enlarge, in most salacious style, upon their conquests of
the unaware male, their sex attraction and physical makeup.
—Dr. Esther Stone, "A Plea for Early Commitment"

Lack of financial remuneration, as well as a love of adventure, prompted Nellie to escape from the farm family to whom she had been paroled by the Illinois State Industrial School for Delinquent Girls' staff. Described by Superintendent Ophelia Amigh as so ordinary in features that she would "hardly attract a white slave trafficker," Nellie had fooled her new family into thinking she was trustworthy. Eventually they allowed her to attend church alone, after which she hopped a train and befriended a male stranger who gave her money and a friend's address. This "friend" happened to run a prostitution house, where she met two other girls from the school at Geneva.[1] Although Nellie's episode illustrated the "traffic of shame" condemned in reformist tracts and white slave narratives, Amigh had other reasons for writing about such a troublesome girl. Criticized severely by several Chicago journalists for her inhumane punishment of Geneva's inmates, Amigh sought to vindicate her reputation. How could she reform Nellie and her likes when dens of prostitution coaxed them into shame and ruin?

Unwittingly, Amigh's attempt to displace her culpability backfired, for such accounts as Nellie's only served to confirm how troubling conditions were at Geneva. Not only did Amigh subject recalcitrant girls to handcuffs and whips,

but after years of commitment and parole, many remained unruly and unre-
formed. Through their acts of rebellion and subversion, many Geneva girls
overrode the staff's and the juvenile court's authority. Their resistance to rehabilitation, evidenced in the number of returned parolees and escapees to the
school, further called into question the effectiveness of the school's organization, staff, and curricula.

Despite pronouncements of preparing girls for a livelihood, the domestic
curricula, extracurricular activities, and employment during parole indicated
otherwise. Instead, girls were instructed to become good mothers, wives, and
Christian women. Many of the girls appeared to follow these prescriptions. But
a closer analysis of their letters and in-school and parole activities demonstrated
that they often employed particular scripts to their advantage, for example, to be
given permission to visit their families or male friends, or to plan escapes. Likewise, the school relied upon its own scientific prescriptions of young women's
behavior, especially those of a psychopathic or "inverted" (lesbian) nature, to
mask the girls' resistance to rehabilitation. Yet their tabulations of attempted and
successful escapes, feigned hysteria and insanity, and open acts of sexual defiance
pointed to the various ways in which the girls kept a culture of resistance intact.

Diagnosis and Defiance: The Geneva Girls' Transgressions

Despite the school's preoccupation with an influx of a "foreign population," most
Geneva girls were native-born Americans. In fact, the ethnic population at
Geneva reflected that of delinquent girls brought before Chicago's juvenile
court; most were of American parentage, the next most common were girls of
Polish, then German, heritage.[2] Many of the native-born white inmates were
poor Southern migrants from various Illinois counties, including Cook County.
Another set of Southern migrants, African-American girls, constituted the sec-
ond largest group from the early 1900s through 1935.[3] The large number of
African-American inmates at Geneva, nearly one-fourth of the school's population of approximately four hundred, resulted from the overrepresentation of
African-American girls in the juvenile courts, as well as the paucity of reform institutions that admitted them. As has been noted, the Chicago Home for Girls accepted disproportionately fewer African Americans and the House of the Good
Shepherd accommodated mostly first- and second-generation immigrants.[4]

When the Sisters of the Good Shepherd opened a school for dependent
African-American girls on Chicago's South Side in 1911, the juvenile court
began to send fewer semidelinquent and dependent African-American girls to
Geneva.[5] Even though the Illinois statutes had defined delinquency to include
ages ten to eighteen, the juvenile courts still sent underaged African-American
and some white girls there, a shocking situation for many, including Sophon-

isba Breckinridge's interns. School Superintendent Ophelia Amigh acknowledged how unfair it was to place younger girls with the older, more seasoned ones but she did not have the heart to turn them away. In actuality, she did not have the authority to transfer them to institutions for dependent children.[6] The placement of dependent girls in institutions for delinquents persisted through the early 1930s, a practice that then-Superintendent Florence Monahan thought reflected the judges' "lack of imagination."[7]

Despite the girls' age, ethnicity, and social classes their most frequent dispositions were "immorality" and "incorrigibility," the latter often masking sexual misbehavior. However, a number of Geneva girls similar to those described by Mary Odem and Carolyn Strange, had been sexually assaulted by relatives or brought to court by parents for disciplinary or economic reasons.[8] In one case, neighbors brought a young girl who had been assaulted by her brother-in-law to the Chicago juvenile court. Accordingly, the judge sent her to Geneva for protection. In other cases, parents insisted that their daughters be sent to Geneva on charges of immorality, even though medical examinations revealed no sexual activity.[9] On the other hand, some parents and their pregnant daughters requested commitments to receive adequate maternity care. Unlike middle-class girls whom social workers referred to private maternity homes or whose parents whisked them away to distant relatives, poor girls had little choice except a state institution.[10]

Despite the vulnerability of delinquent girls who had been seduced or raped, the judicial, psychiatric, and medical literature focused on their "waywardness." But many of Geneva's girls, formerly employed as domestic or factory workers, simply sought excitement after their long hours of work. Undoubtedly, the commercialized amusements of dance halls, cabarets, and saloons, as well as seductive movie romances, promised adventure. Despite this saturation of sexual imagery, most professionals and reformers continued to conceive of young women's proper behavior in terms of modesty, sexual restraint, and innocence.[11] Girls not fitting those standards, especially those of the working class and poor, were "problem" women, subject to the moral and scientific categories of defective delinquents, psychopaths, adventuresses, speiler (or dance) girls, women adrift, charity girls, or fallen, feebleminded, or "inverted" women.[12] The proliferation of psychological, medical, and psychiatric tests reified these categories, replete with symptoms of hysteria, self-mutilation, egocentric behavior, and sexual aggression. Elizabeth Lunbeck has already noted the medical profession's preoccupation with female sexual independence.[13] At Geneva, the doctors not only diagnosed the girls' sexual independence and transgressions as psychopathic and hysterical but sometimes masked the girls' resistance to disciplinary codes in their diagnoses to maintain their professional reputations.

Psychologists and psychiatrists sometimes relied upon invasive tests and interviews when questioning females about their daydreams, autoerotic activities, "inverted" inclinations, and heterosexual involvements.[14] As was noted in chapter 2,

their studies confirmed the historicoanthropological concepts that primitive societies engaged in promiscuous hetero- and homosexual behaviors. Medical experts contended that many lower-class immigrants' and African Americans' sexual
behaviors were "primitive" and thus "congenital." Yet they diagnosed middle-
class clients differently. Whereas working-class girls' dances indicated overactive
libidos, middle-class girls' petting parties were simply "a natural sexual expression." The popular texts of Havelock Ellis and Floyd Dell, in fact, celebrated middle-class girls' premarital adventures. Regardless, such heterosexual prescriptions
were regulatory, especially for girls who discovered the pleasures of lesbianism
and autoeroticism, and would thereby revoke "normal" coitus.[15]

In a similar vein, the professional staff at Geneva often categorized poor and
working-class heterosexual girls as feebleminded. In actuality, the median IQ of
the Geneva girls was "dull normal" or "borderline feebleminded" (the 80 to 90
range). Many of these girls were thought to have intractable behavioral problems or, expressed differently, sexual disturbances.[16] One nationally renowned
psychologist distinguishing between two grades of feeblemindedness, low and
high, thought that women in the lower grade could not comprehend right
from wrong. Females in the higher grade, he warned, knew right from wrong
but could not understand the dangerous consequences of their actions. Such
consequences included prostitution, illegitimacy, and "criminal tendencies."[17]

Superintendent Ophelia Amigh, a former Civil War nurse, openly discussed
the problems of inmates with low mentality who had "no greater aim in life
than to produce their kind." Although she initially argued that they could be
reformed "to become good wives and mothers and take pride in establishing
good American homes," she later recommended sterilization of those who
would "continue to increase the population in these undesirable numbers."[18]
Referring to the problem as one of "race and color," she pleaded, "I hope no
sickly sentimentality will keep our law makers from passing a bill if it is presented again, making the operation of sterilization legal on all who are pro-
nounced by a competent physician and psychologists as unfit to bear children
or to procreate their kind."[19] The administration of psychiatric and psychological examinations provided an alternative solution for some of these girls: institutionalization in the state mental asylum.

Psychopathic girls, on the other hand, constituted another sort of problem;
indeed, their intelligence quotients were not only normal but often above
normal. As will be discussed later, Geneva girls classified as psychopathic and hysterical often exhibited certain symptoms, but in many instances, I argue, the girls
contrived these behaviors to resist the matrons' disciplinary measures or to cam-
ouflage plans to escape. Nonetheless, the *psychopathic* diagnosis became a catchall
for girls who did not conform to disciplinary codes or whose behavior was
brazenly defiant. In arguing that the disease originated from various sources—
physical maladies, childhood traumas, or social or personal disorganization—
doctors accounted for many of the girls' baffling behaviors.

Other doctors, however, stressed psychopathology as a conduct disorder, thereby hoping to rehabilitate their patients. Anne Bingham, in her study of female inmates of the Waverly House in New York City, for one, conceived of psychopathic behavior as "marked emotional instability, difficulty in dealing with new situations, and the tendency to blur situations rather than to deal with them head-on." The usual symptoms were impulsiveness, hyperaffectivity, and "shallow" recklessness (prompting the question of whether it could be otherwise). But others distrusted such easy diagnoses, evident in one's remark about a Massachusetts reformatory: "It does not seem possible that everyone who goes to Lancaster can be surly, sullen, have outbursts of temper, etc. Certainly we never see a case whose description doesn't have nearly all those adjectives."[20]

Before undergoing psychiatric and psychological tests, the Geneva girls had their bodies scrutinized for diseases, pregnancy, and evidence of virginity. Following pelvic examinations, the girls received vaccinations in rapid succession. As one report described, each inmate was "Schicked for diphtheria, Dicked for scarlet fever, and vaccinated for small pox."[21] Tonsils and adenoids were frequently removed; gastrointestinal problems, attributed to the girls' abuse of cocaine, opium, and alcohol, were treated. By and large, though, the medical department's "greatest task" was venereal disease; as early as 1898, nearly 50 percent of the girls had some form of it. By 1916, the department enumerated over 4,515 treatment visits, and this increased to 18,852 by 1930. Superintendent Amigh's response to this problem had followed the psychomedical model already in vogue: "A good psychologist in every court ought to be considered a necessity, and a good physician also."[22]

Although Geneva admitted no pregnant girls during its first years, by 1900 two new girls and three returned parolees were pregnant. The 1908 annual report listed only twenty-five girls as virgins; in contrast, sixteen of the inmates had already given birth at least once.[23] By 1916, twenty-one admissions and twenty-two readmissions were prospective mothers. The juvenile judges had previously referred most of Geneva's pregnant girls to the Chicago Refuge for Girls (later the Chicago Home for Girls) or the Elgin State Hospital for the Mentally Diseased for their deliveries. But as early as 1910, the school had recommended to the state legislature a hospital on the school grounds so that the young women could deliver their babies there. The state did not comply until 1924. Following recommendations of Illinois club women, the state eventually added an on-campus nursery, complete with its own pediatrician.[24]

Regina Kunzel has discussed how maternity homes encouraged "fallen women" to marry and to keep their babies so that they might develop maternal feelings; this was initially true of Geneva's staff.[25] Many of Geneva's parolees were hired by families to care for their young children, continuing the school curricula's emphasis on domesticity. As one report underscored, "We try to teach them what the three words mother, home and heaven mean."[26] By the 1930s, however, Geneva administrators encouraged the young mothers to give up their babies for adoption through the Illinois Children's Home and Aid Society. Given the high numbers of reparolees, the administration probably concluded that "fallen" women would be "bad" mothers.[27]

Although the Geneva staff did not condone pregnancies and heterosexual activities, they were more accepting of these behaviors than autoeroticism or sexual inversion. As was noted earlier in chapter 2, doctors influenced by Freudian thought believed that dream states (especially daydreams), hysteria, delusions, and worrying were manifestations of autosexuality; ever vulnerable to suggestibility, women could be aroused in a number of ways,[28] but the most abhorrent of sexual activities was *inversion*, meaning lesbianism. Given the perceived economic and social independence of young women in the early twentieth century, lesbianism became one ready explanation for young women who smoked, drank, cursed, or who proudly asserted their wage-earning capacities. Defying the "former self-arrogated masculine level," psychiatrists accused these women of "swap[ping] colorful stories and imitat[ing] old Adam."[29] As described later, some Geneva girls boldly narrated and enacted their independence and defiance through lesbian behaviors.

Despite the girls' sexual pasts or pathologies, once diagnosed, classified, and treated medically, they embarked on their reeducational journeys. Domestic, moral, and industrial education were the cornerstones of their reform. Declaring its aim "to build them [the girls] up, and in every way to help them to become good, self-supporting women," the Geneva School initially hired matrons to train the girls in sewing, knitting, cooking, and housework.[30] Not only did the girls learn "habits of economy"; they literally supported themselves and the school. The girls not only sewed their own dresses, underskirts, nightgowns, drawers, aprons, and stockings but their own sanitary napkins. Additionally, they sewed and embroidered sheets, pillowcases, towels, tablecloths, and curtains for their cottages.[31]

By 1908, the school hired a manual training teacher and equipped a basement room for sewing, drawing, basketry, crocheting, knitting, and weaving. Two years later, they added embroidery, stenciling, and stamping to the curriculum. By 1918, with a new industrial department, the girls became responsible for all of their clothing except shoes, sweaters, and hosiery. By 1920, girls learned to wash, card, and make yarn from the sheep raised at the Geneva School so that they would each have their own wool blanket.[32] Additionally, the girls raised their own garden produce, as well as canned, pickled, and stored vegetables and fruits for the winter months. And they assisted with milking cows, mowing hay, and painting the outbuildings. At one point, there was talk of building a cannery, as the total annual value of garden produce was estimated to be $18,000.[33] Such activities clearly had little vocational relevance for girls who would return to Chicago or other cities. Instead, their activities instilled habits of industry, as well as kept the costs of the school low.

Likewise, the intent of reform was not one of a viable income or employment for the girls, but sexual containment. Court officials had already noted the large number of delinquent girls who had previously been employed as domestic workers. In 1918, almost 54 percent of delinquent girls in Chicago had been full-time domestic servants; 32 percent of these had engaged in some form of domestic work and 16 percent performed "home work."[34] Even though reformer Miriam Van Waters had voiced her concerns that domestic work was especially "dangerous" for girls, most reform schools persisted in teaching domestic skills, as well as in paroling girls to families as domestics.[35] Clearly, the superintendents and staff knew that domestic work could not sustain young women economically.

In addition to the industrial and domestic curricula, 130 girls crowded into a one-room school where lower primary classes were held in the morning and the more advanced classes in the afternoon. Beginning with one teacher in 1898, the staff increased to thirteen by 1914. Likewise, the original staff of fourteen managing matrons, housekeepers, and laundry matrons who supervised individual cottage work grew to over ninety-four by 1916. By 1917, Geneva boasted of its first-year high-school courses in stenography, typewriting, bookkeeping, business English, business spelling, and penmanship. Girls who performed well in these classes assisted the principal with general office work, thus providing another source of unpaid labor. But by and large, the staff thought most girls incapable of completing commercial courses and so taught them to wait on tables and assist in the tearooms. By the 1930s, they offered beautician classes as an alternative commercial course as well as a means of rewarding good behavior.[36]

In addition to their academic and industrial courses, girls were expected to attend religious services and engage in benevolent work. Each cottage, in fact, had its own hymn, each denomination its own choir and glee club. By 1924, the school organized its own units of the Junior Red Cross and Girl Scouts, which sent boxes of homemade dolls, toys, and clothing to tornado victims and American Indian children.[37] The club women from Chicago and Illinois towns regularly visited the school, offering their own models of maternalism and benevolence. To illustrate, the prominent Chicago Woman's Club formed a committee to visit the girls monthly.[38] Young women from the North Shore Congregational Church in Evanston frequently held prayer services at Geneva, especially for one of the African-American cottages, Faith Cottage. The Chicago YWCA and Big Sisters organizations sent Christmas gifts as well. The African-American Chicago community likewise offered encouragement to their girls: the West Chicago Woman's Club, the Metropolitan Community Center, and the Golden Circle of King's Daughters and Sons visited the nearly one hundred African-American girls crowded into two segregated cottages to exhort them to obey their matrons so that they would develop into "noble" women.[39] Even Juvenile Judge Mary Bartelme gave an inspirational talk to the girls at the chapel, presenting each girl with a rose at the end.[40]

Pilgrims of Parole: Geneva's Unlikely Candidates

Like the club women, the women to whose homes the girls were paroled were expected to provide exemplary models of womanhood. Nonetheless, paroling or placing girls with these families served other functions. Not only was placement necessary because of the school's overcrowded conditions; it was a true test of the girl's rehabilitation. To ensure success, the staff interviewed the families to whom they sent the girls. They provided the new families with a list of their responsibilities in their "Suggestions to Employers" pamphlet: to oversee the girl's domestic work; to teach her neatness; to insist that she be respectful and ladylike; to supervise her social life; and to ensure that she correspond only with school staff.[41]

One social service worker for the Institute for Juvenile Research who examined the Geneva girls' parole experiences in 1917, found that the staff did not use consistent methods for investigating families for parole purposes. Instead, the euphemism of "good Christian homes" usually sufficed. In some cases, the Geneva staff put the girls on trains and their new families met them at the other end. Such lack of supervision prompted attempts to escape. Of six girls who escaped one year, four were never found. Of two who later returned, one was pregnant and the other infected with venereal disease. In eight other parole cases, girls became pregnant through members of their "good Christian homes." Of these, only three of the men were prosecuted; the others settled out of court.[42] Nonetheless, psychiatrists often blamed the girls for these predicaments: "They are liable without provocation to accuse the male member of the home of improper conduct, and of such accusations are usually believed by the public who do not understand the behavior of some or these girls, especially the ones afflicted with hysteria or nervous tendencies."[43]

Acknowledging the injustices of the juvenile court system, Van Waters argued how some girls would end up being reparoled for minor offenses, be it attending dance halls or smoking, while others would "get by." Other reformers agreed, pointing to the shortcomings of the parole system. For these and other reasons, it was difficult to determine the success of Geneva's parolees despite the school's prodigious record keeping of those who were reparoled, discharged, or escaped, or voluntarily returned. First of all, the criteria for parole were a deportment grade of 85 and and an "efficiency" grade for twelve months. Yet these standards were inconsistently applied. Some girls remained at Geneva for four years, others far less.[44] The implicit expectations were that a ladylike deportment would lead to a later marriage, a respectful but menial job, or involvement in church or charitable activities. Second, because many girls returned to their own families, parents could exert tremendous authority and control. The daughters' compliance could be obtained through threats of negative monthly reports or complaints to their parole officers. In many cases, the school never heard from the paroled girls or their parents again. In other cases, the girls forged their parents' signatures. Consequently, reports that announced that many girls had "permanently benefited" or were "doing well" tell us little.

Third, it was not clear what influence the parole agents themselves had, as they worked under heavy caseloads. As of 1928, there were only two female parole officers for Geneva. Nonetheless, these two often went beyond the call of duty, treating some girls as their own daughters. One officer, for example, bought graduation dresses for her girls. Some of the girls also resided with the same officer's grandmother while the officer investigated suitable homes.[45] Nonetheless, the parole officers were able to offer only so much of their time and resources.

Finally, a word needs to be said about which girls the Chicago judges sent to Geneva and their prospects for reform. Chicago court officials claimed that Geneva had the most "difficult" girls. But if we define *difficult* in terms of recidivism, this was not true. Instead, the House of the Good Shepherd admitted most second- and third-time delinquent female offenders. The term *difficult*, then, referred to others: girls who exhibited personalities and sexualities that required extensive rehabilitation, as well as the large number of African-American girls sent there. Although the Chicago Home for Girls had admitted some girls with "egocentric" personalities, its administration refused too many girls with behavior problems because of lack of on-site psychiatric facilities. Not so with Geneva, which had its own medical services and its own resident psychologist as of 1926, and regular visits from the state-employed psychiatrists.[46] Still, the larger number of girls at Geneva who required psychiatric services probably overtaxed the capabilities of its staff, especially the matrons.

Despite the school's proclamation that nearly two-thirds of its inmates "made good," Bertha Corman's 1923 report from the Institute of Juvenile Research (IJR) indicated that less than one-third adjusted to their parole experiences. Many were reparoled or transferred to new jobs; others escaped, only to be charged later with prostitution, forgery, and in one case, murder. Such was the case of Mary, paroled to a Chicago suburb. She did not commit any crime but within three weeks had accomplished a string of feats: a parole violation, marriage, surgery, a cross-country trip, and a reparole. Bored with her domestic job, she met an ex-soldier in downtown Chicago and married him the same day. The next day, he rushed her to the hospital for an appendectomy. Shortly thereafter, the hospital staff returned her to her assigned suburban family but within twenty-four hours she left again for downtown. There she met an old friend who agreed to hitchhike to Los Angeles with her. Returning to Chicago three weeks later, the police apprehended her and she was homeward bound—to Geneva.[47]

Reparolees such as Mary contributed to the school's overcrowded conditions. To alleviate this problem, Geneva sent many girls back to their own homes, even though school officials acknowledged their neighborhoods and homes were the original sources of their delinquency. Helen, for example, had been reparoled to a second employer, then sent home after six months of good behavior, only to run away. A community social worker in another state, apparently assigned to Helen, wrote back to Geneva, "Helen is with some kind of show in Missouri." Paroled back to her own home the following year, Helen's future was dubious as there she "keeps bad company, is immoral, claims to be married, which is doubtful." Some of the other girls' relatives also expressed dismay about the girls' lack of reform. One grandmother wrote that the school "had not benefitted her [granddaughter]. She is still causing us trouble but we won't let her out nights." One mother requested that her daughter be recommitted as "the officers don't see after her at all." A husband, too, requested that Geneva take his wife back as she frequently visited a "disreputable house" and neglected their child.[48]

The increased number of girls who were reparoled, returned pregnant, or escaped clearly indicated that many girls were not rehabilitated. Again, it can be argued that the inadequate and irrelevant school curricula did not prepare girls for decent employment. Clearly, agricultural work was not suitable for girls who would return to Chicago, although several of the girls' letters mentioned their joy of the rural landscape. Certainly the domestic classes prepared girls for the duties of homemaking or for domestic work. In fact, most paroled girls worked as domestics in homes, averaging at first a salary of three to five dollars a week, which later increased to seven dollars. But the estimated weekly cost of living in 1907 in Chicago, at slightly less than ten dollars, suggested that most girls would not have been able to support themselves.[49] Further, because Geneva so tightly controlled their earnings—which paid for their medical expenses, clothing, and so forth—the girls never learned to budget on their own. The school's recommendation of a boarding house in Chicago for paroled Geneva girls in the 1930s pointed to the school's awareness of the need for a transitional support system. Once again, though, their concern was monitoring the girls' sexuality, not necessarily assisting them in finding viable jobs.[50]

An analysis of the nearly 100 letters sent by the girls to Superintendent Amigh from 1900 to 1910 revealed some of the ways in which the girls understood their reformed roles and scripts during parole. It also demonstrated how cleverly the girls used the language of domesticity, religiosity, and morality for their own purposes. That many of the girls did not respond to Amigh's frequent letters of encouragement was evident in their profuse apologies for not writing earlier or more often. The apologies frequently followed with statements of appreciation for the school's staff, as well as for their present positions with their new families. Knowing full well that church service, domestic work, and upstanding moral behavior were expected, the girls provided descriptions of how well they fared. One girl wrote what "a real pleasure" it was to do housework. Another detailed how she washed clothes, scrubbed the floors, ironed, made dinner, and attended church on Sunday. Still others spoke of their straightened paths: one's thoughts were always in "fervent prayer"; another was "associating with the right class of people"; and another attended meetings of the Christian Endeavor Society and recited the Psalms. One even enclosed a religious poem that she was committing to memory.[51]

In many cases, the girls predicated requests upon these demonstrations of good behavior. Often they would ask to visit family members, friends from Geneva, or interested males. In one case, a girl asked first for the Bible she had left behind, then her perfume. Sometimes, they asked for dresses or money from their savings accounts. The more surprising request was to return to Geneva, either for a visit or permanently.[52] Although many wrote how much they missed their school friends, a few also wished to return because they could not adjust to the outside world. One girl, who had been at Geneva for six years, reminisced how she always had enough to eat at the school, something she wished for now. In another case, a girl left her new home assignment after a boy accosted her. Returning to her father's house, she faced her stepmother's rejection; Geneva seemed to be her only home. In yet another situation, a young girl asked to return to Geneva because she was "homesick" and "lonesome."[53]

Many of the girls' letters of appreciation had been written in response to a Chicago newspaper article in 1910 in which several discharged girls accused the school of inhumane punishment. Many girls came to Superintendent Amigh's defense, including those on parole who perhaps thought that a show of support might lessen their time. By and large, though, Amigh's supporters were former delinquent girls who had "made good." Most were married to "good men," had children, and considered their deeds emblematic of noble womanhood. They spoke of their prayers, their faith, and their church work. A few even engaged in temperance or settlement work, hoping to work directly with the likes of their former selves.[54] It was not surprising, then, that those who succeeded according to Geneva's standards embraced these models. For example, one woman, who had returned to factory work and gone astray, later declared, "'I don't care what anyone says to me about work, give me house work above all other kinds. . . . When they [girls] work in shops and factories, they get in with all kinds of people and go to the bad if they are not careful and are always looked down upon as tough.'"[55]

Most interestingly, a number of letters were from Chicago girls who expressed their dismay at city life. One girl wrote how tired she was of Chicago and asked to return to Geneva. Another noted how Chicago had "lost its beauty." She forewarned that "a girl can't be good in Chicago, there is too much wrong going on." Although she pledged not to go to dances, the theater, or saloons, she did admit to attending at least one dance. A more poignant letter was of a girl's visit to Chicago, where upon observing the poor, she wondered about her own family's welfare. She wrote that she felt guilty because she was well-fed whereas they were not. Her letter ended with a request to send part of her savings home.[56]

Because most of these letters contained requests or favors, the girls' expressions of gratitude or support should be suspect. The prescriptive overuse of motifs of "noble womanhood," domestic tranquility, and following the "straight path of life," as well as the formulaic structure of most letters, pointed not just to the girls' keen knowledge of such scripts but their manipulation of them. Regina Kunzel, too, has questioned the sincerity of young girls who thanked the matrons of maternity homes.[57] Like the narratives she examined, the Geneva girls' letters revealed their covert intentions. However, their forms of subversion were not always so nuanced.

Rebellion and Resistance Revisited

The girls' periodic spells of hysteria, their attempted and often successful escapes, and the charges of stealing, insubordination, and sexual misconduct were sometimes demonstrations of resistance and independence. Escapes had always been a problem at Geneva, especially because the school was next to a railroad track. Men were known to place ladders near the girls' bedroom windows, then help the girls hop the trains with them. To prevent such attempts, the school hired a night watchman. Nonetheless, records indicated that many girls were successful in their escapes.[58] Such was the case of one girl described as "incurable of wanderlust": "she could no more resist its promptings than the meteor can retrace its course in the skies."[59] She was not alone in her efforts. In one month of 1918 alone, fourteen girls escaped and were absent for more than two hours. The staff, however, conjectured that these girls would not travel far as they would "stop to have sexual intercourse with the first man who is willing."[60]

Those caught planning escapes were punished in various ways: they were transferred to other cottages; they conferenced with staff members; or they had privileges withheld. Those who actually escaped but were caught were sent to the disciplinary cottage, where they received "intensive training." The nature of such training was not disclosed, although leather handcuffs and whips had been found during Amigh's tenure. Florence Monahan, superintendent during the early 1930s, was much more understanding of the girls who attempted escapes. As she pointed out, "Some women get a facial. When things get too bad, I usually go out and buy a hat. Geneva girls had none of these outlets; their only means of escape was in the literal act of running away."[61]

The psychiatrists' reports, however, were less sympathetic. This may have been, in part, because their professional status was at stake. As a matter of course, their classifications of psychopathic or hysterical oftentimes masked the girls' efforts to escape, to resist the school's discipline, or to put one over on the staff. As early as 1896, the school had reported the misconduct of ten girls who, after being disciplined, exhibited "freedom from hysterical affections." This description is particularly interesting because there were no psychological or psychiatric evaluations yet in place. Subsequent biennial reports likewise enumerated increased incidents of "hysterical manifestations," some with no relapses, as well as cases of insanity. It is quite likely that some of the girls were mentally unstable, but the later reports of several girls who had "periodical spells bordering on insanity" but who then became rational a short time later suggested feigned emotional outbursts. Whether the girls' behavior was compulsive or pretend, the matrons isolated most of them in the Wallace Cottage where they underwent hydrotherapy, then considered the most modern and scientific method for quieting female inmates.[62]

Such methods were used for Florence, characterized by the school psychologist as "extremely incorrigible, [an] inveterate liar, [a] menace to discipline and morals." Eventually the school expelled her for temper tantrums and excessive masturbation. A physical examination "confirmed" her unstable personality as willful and tempestuous, as she stiffened her body and screamed at top of voice at the slightest provocation. The report concluded: "Has always been so." Although the psychologist did not discuss the etiology of Florence's instability, she might have suggested one of many popular theories: a glandular disturbance; exaggerated or overdeveloped traits, such as stubbornness, curiosity, suggestibility, or eroticism; or mental conflicts.[63] While at Geneva, Florence fought constantly with the other girls, disobeyed the matrons, and had attacks during which she would "break the cottage windows, use vile language, scream, kick and fight." Disciplinary measures only seemed to increase her violence. The doctor recommended ice packs and other treatments unavailable at Geneva. Although the latter treatment was never stated, it could well have been institutionalization for the insane.[64]

Institutionalization was the eventual treatment for Sylvia, committed to Geneva at the age of eleven in 1907. She, too, threw temper tantrums and uttered profanities at the matrons and other girls. Eight years later, she was paroled as a domestic worker but was returned to Geneva at least ten times for being quarrelsome with her surrogate families. Tested at the mental age of nine and a half years, as well as positive for syphilis, she was transferred to the Lincoln State School for the Feeble-Minded, where she was reported to be "happy and doing well." In Sylvia's case, the classification of feebleminded twelve years after her admission to Geneva seemed to be a last resort, perhaps another diagnosis made out of exasperation.[65]

One medical doctor's examination of over one hundred Geneva girls in 1912 substantiated psychopathic symptoms such as those demonstrated by Florence. Dr. Anne Burnet found the girls' faculty for lying "fully developed" and most often used "to suit a passing whim." Her greatest concerns, though, were the girls' hysteria and self-mutilation. In her study she highlighted the cases of four girls whom she classified as psychotic and very hysterical. One had attacks of hysterical blindness. Another experienced hysteria-like spells, considered by some psychiatrists to be "the ultimate expression of feminine wiles." The third had progressive dementia but unfortunately, Burnet noted, had been released to the city where she would "probably get into further trouble." The last, too, had spells associated with autohypnotism. Because some of the girls thought her clairvoyant, the staff secluded her and shortly thereafter, she recovered. But such medical scripts, I argue, need to be read for alternative diagnoses. Although it is not improbable that the girls exhibited symptoms of hysteria, this does not necessarily substantiate the diagnoses of "psychopathic" or "hysterical." Rather, their behavior may have been scripted and motivated by attempts to escape, by power struggles with the staff, or by a desire to relieve the tedium of institutional life. Although we can only surmise what their motives were, the subtext of Dr. Burnet's accounts indicated her preoccupation with the girls' deception and the possibility of their putting one over on her.[66]

Some girls' aggression was more difficult and protracted, although perhaps uncommon. Despite cold packs, hydrotherapy, sedatives, and talks, Freda and Rose persisted in their disruptive behavior for nine days. According to Monahan, they were "berserk psychopathic personalities" who not only tested as high-grade and promiscuous mental defectives but suffered from advanced venereal disease. Rose initiated the tirade by barricading her door, then breaking chairs and windows, even bending the windows' bars. Hurling insults at the girls below, she threatened to jump out the window. Freda followed suit in the adjoining room, screaming until she developed laryngitis. Without access to their case records, it is difficult to ascertain actual medical and mental conditions. But in one of the juvenile court's many paradoxical commitments, the judge sent the two girls to the Chicago Detention Home, a temporary residence for those awaiting trial or placement in another institution. Ironically, Freda had turned twenty-one, the legal age for release, and so was free to go. Rose's circumstances were more tragic: she eventually died in a hospital for the insane.[67]

Another medical doctor at Geneva, too, wrote about the girls' psychopathic behaviors. In recounting her Geneva experiences from 1914 to 1916, Esther Stone expressed concern for girls who tested with normal IQs but whose character and moods were unstable. These girls, she conjectured, were the most difficult, as they "possess[ed] just enough mentality and superficial education and ability to be a continued source of annoyance to themselves and the community." Elaborating on their mood swings, Dr. Stone described how they were "either exuberantly happy, furiously angry, or mildly sad, easily moved to tears or joy; some are spiteful, cunning and untrustworthy." At the same time she acknowledged how adept they were at deception, often used to plan escapes or engage in some "willfull" acts.[68] Not unlike the psychopathic cases described by Elizabeth Lunbeck at the Boston Psychopathic Hospital, these Geneva girls were independent, clever, and skilled at disrupting the order and monotony of the school.[69] Once again, the staff's concern seemed to be not so much reform as containing the young girls' aggression and resistance.

But Stone did not reserve her suspicions for "normal" girls alone. She was also skeptical of those girls who adjusted too quickly to the school's environment. Tagging them as "goody-goody girls," she estimated that they would return to their old "haunts" during parole and engage in even more immoral acts, especially given their recent confinements. In her presence, these girls remained quiet and submissive. But others bragged to one another about their sexual conquests. As it was reported, "They revel in smutty talk, delight in reading obscene literature, and enlarge, in most salacious style, upon their conquests of the unwary male, their sex attraction and physical makeup."[70] Curiously, Stone did not question the truth of their frank discussions, even though she observed their "feigned adjustments."

The Geneva girls' physical feats, however, far surpassed this bravado. Stone's records revealed the girls' penchant for high drama, as well as their attempts to put one over on the staff. For example, they "show[ed] little resistance to disease, readily become delirious, [when] temperatures [were] unusually high in the slightest illness, they faint and become fatigued easily." In one case, a girl went into a trance and registered a high temperature on a thermometer, even though her body temperature seemed normal. None of the staff quite understood how she accomplished this.[71] Another girl acted delirious in order to eventually escape, even though her temperature was normal. Recognizing the failure of her scheme, she became well two days later. In yet another case, Stone wryly noted the extreme calm with which a young girl cut her boyfriend's initials into her flesh," then "pretend[ed] to suffer intensely when her wounds were dressed."[72] To some degree, these ploys resembled those used to avoid household duties. The doctors coined the girls' feigned sickness, which miraculously disappeared right before recreation time, as "laundry illness."[73] Despite this common knowledge, the medical and psychiatric staff were under professional pressure to account for the girls' aberrant behaviors. "Psychopathic," in some cases, became the diagnosis of perplexity and exasperation, succinctly expressed in Stone's assessment of the school: "It must be apparent that our methods of dealing with defectives is comparable to that situation where the farmer locks his stable door after the horse is stolen." Accordingly, she recommended a school for psychopathics, a permanent home or boarding school where they could be studied, as well as taught domestic or industrial work.[74]

Social worker Charlotte Ruth Klein, like Stone, noted a number of serious personality disorders, including psychopathology, neurosis, psychoneurosis, hysteria, and schizoid reactions in her 1935 study of Geneva girls. Some of the girls, she noted, had exhibited such behaviors before commitment, with the most common symptoms being nail biting, spasms, fainting, convulsions, eye tics, masturbation, and stuttering.[75] She was, however, more concerned with symptoms that suggested egocentric or introverted personalities. As she noted, "The delinquent girl is an ego-centric, strongly emotional individual with a tendency toward a shut-in type of personality. She is restless, impatient and easily thrown out of balance. Although she craves strong emotions, excitement and noise, the tendency toward morbid reactions, paranoid trends and escape into or actual physical pain, fatigue, or ennui is characteristic of a pattern of melancholia."[76]

Curiously, Klein did acknowledge various forms of resistance by the girls, yet did not fully consider the above behaviors as such. Instead, she described the more traditional misbehaviors of impudence, disobedience, "shirking," note writing, lying, and stealing, as well as the more serious ones of not wearing underwear, talking loud, smoking, damaging books, and planning escapes. (The most frequent charge, however, was damaging school property.) Following progressive reforms, the school established an elaborate system of credits and demerits to discourage these activities, as well as incentives such as wearing one's own clothes (versus a uniform) or training in the staff dining room or beauty-culture facility. These incentives dovetailed with the schools' domestic curricula, as well as reinforced traditional models of femininity.[77]

It appears as if some of the staff members, especially the matrons, instigated the girls' misbehaviors. Reformatory criticism had generally focused on the lack of systematic training for matrons who persisted in their old-fashioned rules and mannerisms. Many of these matrons had received their appointments through political favors and so were unqualified. Some of the "aunties," attired in high-buttoned shoes and "rusty" turn-of-the-century dresses, had been hired during the superintendency of Ophelia Amigh, who reportedly ruled Geneva with an iron fist until politics forced her out.[78] Until 1904, Amigh had managed the Chicago Home for Girls, the Protestant home for delinquent girls and single young mothers. Working with an administrative board of prominent older, married women, Amigh conceived of wayward girls' reform through evangelistic and rescue work. Her steadfast concerns with salvation and true womanhood, then, were consonant with the Home's staff.[79]

At Geneva, Amigh's path to salvation took a cruel turn. She instituted her own peculiar punishment for difficult girls: the strong chair, a combination of a ducking stool and New England stocks. When a former matron blew the whistle on Amigh and the state launched an investigation in 1910, Mary Bartelme of Chicago's juvenile court attempted to divert public attention, especially from a chest full of leather handcuffs and whips worn down from overuse. Instead, Bartelme recommended a night watchman to detect fires and petty thefts, as well as more practical vocational course work. Superintendent Carrie O'Connor, who succeeded Amigh, concurred with Bartelme, and promptly instituted commercial classes and new forms of disciplines, including a system of privileges. But intractable girls still continued to be isolated and confined.[80]

Despite Amigh's resignation, the matrons' antagonistic behavior toward the girls, including African-American girls, did not desist. The two African-American cottages, Faith and Lincoln, had established reputations for their "mob rule and violence." In one situation, the girls had attacked a white matron, leaving her so badly injured that she could not work for several months.[81] The overcrowded conditions of the two cottages, which housed twice as many girls as other cottages, undoubtedly added fuel to the fires of discrimination. In one case, a light-skinned African-American girl, assigned to the white girls' cottage, asked to be transferred to an African-American cottage because she could not get along with her white roommates. Rather than sympathizing with her, a white matron reprimanded her, then proceeded to criticize her mixed ancestry; it is hardly surprising that shortly after the incident, the girl ran away.[82] In another situation, a white matron, upon observing the friendly behavior of white girls with a group of African-American girls, called them "white trash" and "nigger lovers." In protest, the white girls moved into the cottage with the African-American girls, causing a "minor scandal." To alleviate these problems, the school eventually hired African-American matrons and housemothers for the two African-American cottages.[83]

However, the white matrons did not abuse their authority solely with African-American girls. Because they were responsible for handling all girls' "thousand and one" minor misbehaviors, they had a good deal of latitude in disciplinary procedures. They sometimes locked the girls in their rooms for weeks for small indiscretions or acts of disobedience. The kitchen matrons barked orders to the girls who were not locked up. The house matrons, as well, insisted that the girls memorize and recite dull, lengthy poems.[84] Whether these exercises were for moral edification, for punishment, or both, they probably aggravated the girls.

There is more direct evidence that the matrons deliberately upset the girls. In one case, a matron lied to them in order to incite a riot. In another case, a matron was more successful when she convinced the girls that they had been wrongly treated. Two girls ran to the kitchen, stole butcher knives, and began to smash windows. Monahan eventually calmed them, only to discover that the matron herself had been stealing from both the school and the girls themselves. Then the scandal grew larger, with the involvement of Geneva's farmhands. One had stolen from the girls' savings accounts and was eventually convicted. Four others had reportedly seduced a female inmate, who became pregnant.[85]

But the matrons not only fought with the girls. Because of ideological tensions and power struggles, they disagreed with the professional staff. A hierarchy of disciplinary authority had developed, through which the matrons were to refer the girls with aggressive and sexual behaviors to the resident physicians. In turn, the physicians were to send the most difficult girls to the psychologist and psychiatrist. What most upset the matrons were those matters relating to the girls' sexual behavior. For example, they disapproved of one doctor's lectures on sex and sex hygiene, and contradicted her advice. Accordingly, the managing officer, who found that she could not trust the matrons with information about the girls' social histories, especially the details of their sex lives, kept the girls' records safe in her office.[86]

This is not to say that the managing officer and professional staff tolerated the girls' sexual behaviors. All of the staff expressed great consternation about the most common ways the girls relieved their sexual urges: through autoeroticism, escaping in order to have sex, and the "honey girl" or same-sex phenomenon.[87] They thought that if the girls had too much free time, they would indulge in fantasies, masturbation, and other "unhealthy habits," so they kept the girls' schedules regimented into shifts of industrial, recreational, religious, and educational activities. The matrons also recommended that the girls spend their spare time wisely, for example, "sew[ing] for their dolls or mak[ing] the numerous gadgets with which [to] fill their rooms."[88] However, these diversions held little excitement, much less significance, for the girls who sought sexual partnerships.

Of the 176 girls Klein studied in 1935, over 38 percent reported to have engaged in lesbian relationships. Whenever the staff discovered these affairs, the girls were taken out of school and isolated from their peers. The girls then embarked on a steadfast schedule of conferences with the staff, vigorous physical exercise, and extraneous activities such as sewing and reading. Their diets were also modified to exclude starchy and richer foods, purported to make the girls more self-indulgent and sluggish.[89] Deterrents aside, the professional staff tried to account for why girls turned to each other for sexual pleasure. Characterizing these relationships in heterosexual terms, Klein and other professionals described the male and female counterparts of the couples, postulating that in interracial relationships African-American girls assumed the masculine traits and white girls the feminine ones.[90] Dr. Edith R. Spaulding postulated as well that white girls "readily supplied through [their] racial characteristics a feminine substitute for the masculine companionship they were temporarily denied."[91]

The interracial "honey girl" phenomenon, the taboo par excellence, became the subject of intense psychiatric analysis, often bordering on voyeurism. Margaret Otis, for one, accounted for reformatory girls' desire for "forbidden fruit" as a cure-all for the tedium of institutional life. She conjectured that white girls often taunted African-American girls, simply to "see the coons get excited." Like other doctors, she had noted the exchange of love notes, kisses, and locks of hair, the last used as tokens of affection or as charms to punish infidelities. Edith Stone expressed her revulsion at the "nauseating love scenes" at Geneva, which included "vulgar pantomime and suggestive acts, even in broad daylight, and at school under the desks." One inmate carried her girlfriend's "soiled napkin" in her brassiere for a week as a "mark of devotion." On a daily basis, Dr. Stone observed a constant exchange of love notes, trinkets, hugs and kisses. Her reaction was not unlike that of one African-American matron, who characterized the exchange of "honey" notes as "the filthiest, nastiest stuff you can imagine."[92]

In some cases, groups of African-American and white girls formed their own families of nephews, uncles, and so forth, although the white girls had their own African-American "daddies" or "uncles." Ironically, the girls had subverted the school's and court's visions of familial cottage life with their own "violent attachment" for one another, their intrigues and jealousies, and their "self-styled [roles of] 'husband' and 'wife.'"[93] Klein and others held out little hope of reform for these white girls, much less their African-American counterparts. Even if a white girl discontinued her interracial lesbian relationship, they posited, she would later become involved with an African-American man. As one eminent psychologist contended, interracial lesbian relationships "may make it easier for white girls to have intercourse or live with colored men after they are paroled."[94] Transgressions of race, then, were beyond redemption or repair.

Some of the school's recreational activities unintentionally fostered the girls' attraction for each other. University of Chicago sociologist Philip Hauser's study of the effects of movies on delinquent girls indicated that moviegoing, a reward for good deportment, may have been counterproductive. Many of the girls commented on how excited the love scenes made them. One adolescent white girl reminisced about her former days, " 'I like to see real love pictures here and outside too. I like to see them because it makes me think of the good times I had outside.' " Another sex delinquent agreed, " 'Another picture which caused some of the matrons to get flustered over [*sic*] was Joan Crawford in "Montana Moon." Gee, but that picture had an effect, and How! I would have given anything to have been with my boy friend again.' " The girls found in the actresses ready role models. In one girl's words, " 'The kind of life such a woman leads in the movies makes me want to be like them. . . . No!! the bad endings these women get don't make me feel like keeping out of trouble after I get out.' "[95]

The inmates sometimes turned to each other to try new lovemaking strategies. As one sixteen-year-old sex delinquent explained, " 'I have sexual feelings when I see passionate love. When I go to the cottage after I see a good movie I try to practice love-making on my girl sweetheart in the cottage. We do all sorts of stuff. We act like William Haines and Ramon Navarro and Joan Crawford, Anita Page, Janet Gaynor, Betty Compson, Colleen Moore, Clara Bow.' "[96] Given the absence of men at Geneva, one girl admitted, " 'All we can do here is to take some Negro girl . . . at the Chapel or somewhere else. Kiss them for all we are worth. That is all the thrill we get.' " Another girl expressed the same view: " 'I try to learn how to make love from the movies that I see here. But that's just since I've been up here. I usually let the men do the love-making on the outside. But when you're making love to a girl it's different; they expect you to.' "[97]

Other inmates had reservations about engaging in lesbian affairs for fear of reprisal. One girl explained the usual course of events: "'When the girls here see a love scene, they get all stirred up and they go and get into trouble. They write notes to the colored girls; after you see a love picture you feel like being loved.'"[98] One girl, acknowledging the punitive aftermath of emotive and physical expressions, voiced this concern: "'Movies here worry me, for you haven't got one to make love to you. The girl next to you is all, and if you were to give her a kiss, put your arm around her, pinch her, or something, you wouldn't be counted decent. We would be here three years or more before our papers would be passed to go out or put "in punishment" for months. If I can't kiss, make love, I don't want to live. Movies here get me all aroused, make me crave.'"[99]

Although most girls confessed that the movies made them think about sex, clothes, and adventure, others felt a keen sense of injustice about their commitment to Geneva. One twenty-seven-year-old complained, "I have not had a square deal because I know a lot girls that have got away with a lot more than I did. When I see pictures that show where a girl gets away with a lot, it makes me feel bitter." A sixteen-year-old, too, expressed her bitterness at getting caught, while other girls remained free: "'When I see movies like "Modern Maidens" where young boys and girls are kissing, lying down on sofas, telling each other how much they really love, I don't think then that I am getting a fair deal. I know young girls on the outside who are doing just as we have done, went out with young boys, go with everyone that comes along.'"[100]

Paradoxically, the staff used popular movies to promote heterosexual gender roles and activities. Yet the images of dashing and sultry divas draped in satin and furs contradicted the domestic and benevolent curricula in place at Geneva. The female portrayals on the screen also represented privileges of class and of race most Geneva girls would never experience. Nonetheless, the girls created their own scripts of sexual behavior, adventure, and romance. And it is possible that they contrived their good behavior to reap the rewards of a little adventure and naughtiness.

What, then, are we to make of the Geneva girls' school and parole experiences? On the one hand, the proliferation of texts within the school's biennial reports—psychomedical charts, case study records, test results, letters, and the various department reports—indicate a preoccupation with medical models of rehabilitation, as well as attempts to diagnose as well as mask the girls' aggression and defiance.[101] At the same time, vestiges of maternalism lingered as matrons and other female staff sought to instill the virtues of domesticity, motherhood, and Christianity. The girls' responses to their reeducation varied. Some embraced the template of homemaking but others resisted. Some adopted or feigned adoption of certain elements of reform, while dismissing or embodying other lessons. The Geneva girls' expressions of resistance in and out of school suggest that the authority of the state and juvenile courts was not always more powerful. Within the spaces of official discourse, the Geneva girls boldly told their own stories.

9

The House of the Good Shepherd

They were at times nearly starving and freezing, but great loads of flour and coal came in God's good time and no one knew who sent them.

—John Patrick Walsh, "The Catholic Church in Chicago"

In 1859, a branch of the Sisters of the Good Shepherd arrived in Chicago to provide shelter and care for fallen women. The religious order's work with penitents had been an enduring commitment, alongside their vows of poverty, chastity, and obedience. Given the hardships they initially faced, their spiritual resolve placed them in good stead. Even before they moved into their first convent on Market and Hill Streets, it burned down. The Sisters immediately had another convent built, then added an industrial school in 1866 so the inmates could learn sewing, embroidery, and laundry work. Five years later, the Great Chicago Fire destroyed that school. Fortunately, the Daughters of Charity and the Religious of the Sacred Heart generously assisted the Sisters in caring for the inmates until another industrial school could be built. The Sisters also received financial support from individual donors and from fines which the city of Chicago had levied against the owners and visitors of prostitution houses. Unfortunately for the House of the Good Shepherd, as well as the Chicago Refuge for Erring Women, the city soon fell behind in its payments.[1]

Despite the House's financial instability, the Sisters persisted in their work with fallen women. Hoping to also shield young girls "before they have fallen or have been stained by serious crime," the Sisters established an industrial school for dependent and neglected girls on Chicago's South Side in 1885. The Chicago Industrial School for Girls accepted girls from the police court, as well as those brought by mothers destitute from their husbands' desertion or death, and those referred by parish priests. Because the Sisters accepted all young girls in need, the school became overcrowded in its first year. Once again, the Sisters immediately arranged to have a larger facility built.[2]

The new facility accommodated over five hundred inmates, including dependent girls from the juvenile court as of 1901. But juvenile court girls represented only a portion of the school's population. In 1908, for example, only 20 percent of the 564 inmates were committed by the juvenile court judge. As such, per diem court monies, along with minimal tuition fees and funds raised by a women's auxiliary, were insufficient. By 1911, the school's overcrowded conditions and rising debts prompted Archbishop James Quigley to close the school temporarily and transfer the inmates to St. Mary's Training School in Des Plaines, northwest of Chicago. But Archbishop Quigley had another motive as well: hoping that "brother and sister [would] grow up in the same environments," he combined St. Mary's and St. Joseph's Orphanages to reunite siblings.[3]

Even with the closing of the Chicago Industrial School for Girls, the Sisters did not desist in caring for young girls. Observing the unusually large numbers of African-American dependent girls appearing before the juvenile court, the Sisters decided to convert the South Side school to one for dependent and predelinquent African-American girls. Accordingly, the Illinois Technical School for Colored Girls opened in the fall of 1911, with one hundred girls committed either through the juvenile court or referred by parents and guardians. Depending upon their home circumstances, some students attended school only during the week; others resided at the school the entire academic year. In a few cases, girls were long-term residents. In fact, the Sisters encouraged lengthier boarding arrangements which, they argued, prevented truancy and alleviated the crowded tenements where many African-American girls lived.[4]

Despite the Sisters' good intentions, their work with the African-American girls did not please everyone. State Inspector Charles Virden had recommended that the school be established as an industrial school for dependent girls, only to discover that the Sisters had also accepted delinquent girls. Responding to a letter from a lawyer representing the Hyde Park Protective Association, a restrictive covenant association, Virden decided to visit the school so that he could later inform the association of their "good work." But the association was not interested; rather, their concern was the deleterious effect an African-American school would have upon their property values. Prominent men from the association met with Archbishop Quigley and demanded that he close the school. He tried to placate them, informing them the inmates were dependents, not delinquents. He was apparently unaware that the Sisters had taken in four delinquent girls in 1912, who, the Sisters later assured him, were so well behaved that they did not have to be isolated. To appease the archbishop and thereby the association, the Sisters reserved the second floor for delinquent girls, but thereafter the juvenile court sent only dependent girls to the school.[5]

In fact, it had been the archbishop's intentions to accommodate delinquent girls at the House of the Good Shepherd on the city's North Side. Apparently the archbishop had not followed the advice of his lawyer, who had suggested that the South Side school remain segregated so that the North Side facility could then refuse African-American girls. According to the lawyer, the Sisters could then request larger stipends from the juvenile court by arguing that African-American girls required more time and effort to reform. Even if the archbishop and the Sisters had agreed to this, the court would probably not have honored this arrangement.[6]

The Hyde Park Protective Association was not the only group that disapproved of the South Side school; a group of African-American club women did as well, though for entirely different reasons. Alarmed by the paucity and segregation of institutions for their children, they protested the school's "Jim Crow" practices. As one *Broad Ax* editorial declared, "Our people insist that if our girls are to be 'Jim Crowed' at all we prefer to have them sent to an institution organized, maintained, and controlled by our people, who are directly interested in the welfare of these unfortunates. If we must be segregated, we want to segregate ourselves; we do not want to be 'Jim Crowed' by white people and then pay them for doing it."[7] Further, the women were concerned because they thought the school did not respect the girls' religious affiliation. Ironically, this very issue had been one over which Catholic leaders and court officials had continually struggled. While it was not clear to what extent the Sisters proselytized, their enumerations of baptisms and communions of young converts probably alarmed the club women.

When the African-American club women met with juvenile court representatives, community leaders, and concerned white club women in 1913, they resolved their differences. Thereafter, a group of African-American club women and probation officers regularly visited the school and expressed "great satisfaction" with it. In fact, a leading African-American club woman, Mrs. George Cleveland Hall, roused other club women's interest in the school by forming a fund-raising guild that provided mostly in-kind goods of toys, food, clothing, sewing machines and cloth, as well as contributed money to the coal fund. Perhaps following the club women's example, high school girls from the nearby ethnic parishes established a junior auxiliary to entertain the African-American girls during holidays.[8]

The African-American club women also offered their support by attending the school's musical and oratory performances. Although no African-American newspaper covered these events, journalists from the Chicago Catholic newspaper, the *New World*, reported how the older girls read poetry without a trace of "sing-song" or "Negro accent" and how the younger "ebony lambs" danced gracefully in "slippered feet."[9] These appraisals, although not intentionally denigrating, were far different from those published in the Chicago African-American newspapers. Other school activities—such as when the domestic science department students displayed their hand-embroidered towels, pillow covers, and dresses at an exhibition commemorating the fiftieth anniversary of emancipation—probably received more favorable comments from the African-American press.[10]

The Illinois Technical School for Colored Girls was only one institution established by the Sisters for girls and young women; as has been noted, the Sisters had cared for fallen women since 1859. With the inception of the juvenile court, the Sisters expanded their North Side facility to counsel, shelter, and teach industrial skills and moral fortitude to dependent and delinquent girls while also continuing to take in older indigent women.

Building a Caring Institution: The House of the Good Shepherd

Similar to Chicago's rescue homes, the House of the Good Shepherd taught wayward girls and women religious values as well as domestic and industrial skills. Unlike most of the rescue homes' matrons, who were of middle- or upper-class backgrounds, the Sisters' origins were in the working class. As such, they understood the necessity of girls and women contributing to their households. Accordingly, the Sisters provided economic alternatives to the inmates by teaching them laundry and trade skills, not simply offering lessons in domesticity. Nonetheless, like other reform institutions, the House of the Good Shepherd relied upon the girls' industrial and domestic work to contain its rising costs.[11]

Most reform institutions typically limited their services to dependent or delinquent children, such as the State Industrial School for Delinquent Girls (in Geneva) or the Chicago Home for Girls. Not so with the House of the Good Shepherd. The North Side facility accommodated five groups of inmates. The youngest group, which attended the St. Anne's class, was comprised of dependent and truant girls. Although the juvenile court had committed many of them, parents too brought them to the Sisters for temporary care. Delinquent girls, penitents who constituted the Sacred Heart Class, were the second group. Some of them, attired completely in black, became "consecrates," whose prime responsibility was to set a high standard of behavior for the other girls to emulate. Consecrates were required to live at the House for only one year, although some repeated their commitments yearly and thereby became long-term residents. The fourth group consisted of slightly older women, some of them mothers or wives committed by relatives or through the morals or police courts. A small portion of these women became "Magdalens," known for their cloistered life of penance and prayers. Although they remained life-long residents, Magdalens were not permitted to join the order of the Sisters of Good Shepherd.[12]

Regardless of the girls' or women's religious affiliation, the Sisters accepted all in need of assistance. The House's ledgers, however, indicated that most of the dependent girls were Catholic, especially those who came via the juvenile court. Although the reliability of these records should be questioned, the high number of Catholic girls listed did correspond to the juvenile court's practice of honoring children's religious affiliation. Catholic leaders had fiercely protected Catholic children's access to Catholic institutions, as well as to Catholic homes for parole or foster care. As early as 1891, Catholic lawyer Timothy Hurley had introduced legislation to the Illinois Assembly to safeguard children's religious affiliations. Although the bill was defeated that year, it eventually passed seven years later. Given the anti-Catholic and anti-immigrant sentiments that prevailed in Chicago and in Illinois at that time, Hurley's persistence was admirable. The passage of the Edwards Act in 1889 had made it illegal for Catholic children to attend Catholic schools in Illinois. Further, the law required public school teachers to teach students in English only, not their native languages. Parents who sent their children to foreign-language schools were subject to fines for each day of attendance. Clearly, the law discriminated against Catholics, although Lutherans and other religious minorities were likewise affected. When John Altgeld ran for governor of Illinois in 1892, one of his key campaign issues was repealing the act. Catholics and Lutherans formed a voting bloc to elect Altgeld, who, true to his promise, rescinded the act.[13]

Hurley also protected Catholic children in the juvenile court by creating a volunteer Catholic probation officer program through the Visitation and Aid Society (VAS). Incorporated the same year as the passage of the Edwards Act, the VAS carried out a number of services, including placing poor children with respectable Catholic families, visiting impoverished homes, and procuring employment for "deserving" persons. Within two years, its membership grew to 350 volunteers, perhaps because Hurley had convinced court officials that children should be placed with persons of the same religion.[14]

The VAS's membership may have also increased because of competition from secular institutions, especially the Hull House. Catholic leaders worried that social settlements and other nonreligious facilities would neglect the spiritual needs of Catholic children and women. The Catholic weeklies were especially critical of Jane Addams and her female dominion, whom they called "busybodies." The editors of the *New World* questioned not only how single women could care for children but how they could possibly understand the difficult circumstances that immigrant mothers faced. Quite to the contrary, the editors suggested, God may have sent "the Irish Marys, Italian Marias and Polish Hildas" to "[save] the country from women graduates of our great universities."[15]

The hostility against Addams and her female dominion was also fueled by rumors that the Hull House was a hotbed of socialism. Perhaps some journalists misinterpreted the Hull House commitment to labor reform, especially for working women and children, as such. But there were other reasons for the Catholic weekly's criticism. As has been discussed in chapter 1, the Hull House was a well-endowed and powerful institution. And its leaders were predominantly female. The likes of independent-minded, unmarried young women such as Jane Addams, Ellen Gate Starr, and Julia Lathrop ran contrary to the traditional roles of immigrant Catholic mothers with large families. Additionally, the Hull House's agenda of professionalizing the juvenile court's probation officer staff and promoting the expansion of state institutions may have been perceived as antireligious and antifamily by Catholics. Although most social reformers and leaders subscribed to the idea of keeping families intact, they often disagreed on the means for doing so.

The rise of anti-Catholic sentiments and some Catholics' distrust of secular institutions, however, did not seem to affect the Sisters. Considering the financial problems they experienced during the 1880s and 1890s, the Sisters' benevolence was quite remarkable. They felt otherwise, trusting that God would provide. It was, in fact, with this deep faith that the Sisters decided to purchase eleven acres at Graceland and Racine Streets in 1892 for a larger facility. To protect the inmates, they also had a ten-foot wall built around the property so that "the stricken soul may walk unmolested through green lawns and garden paths."[16]

This was not a sound financial investment, as the House's expenditures were in excess of $37,000 by 1893. Although laundry work had been a steady source of support during the 1880s, when the Sisters had contracted with the famous Kingsley's Restaurant and Chicago's "fashionable" hotels, it was not sufficient to offset their debts. Monies obtained from the sales of the inmates' hand-sewn and cooked goods, from donations, and from provisional tuition fees were even less secure. In an effort to lessen their debts, the Sisters opened a retail store in 1894 to sell the girls' plain and fancy needlework, satin underwear, and infants' outfits.[17] But the retail store may have provoked the Illinois Women's Alliance, a Protestant woman's group, to claim that the Sisters confined the girls and were "depriving them of their liberty." Both the mayor of Chicago and the city council visited the House and found these accusations to be untrue. To the contrary, they praised the Sisters for their work.[18] Still facing debts two years later, the Sisters decided to open their doors to the public one afternoon. This was unusual, as the Sisters themselves had little contact with the outside world and had always safeguarded the privacy of the girls and women. Calling the occasion a "donation party," the Sisters received over two thousand visitors, who in turn left money, clothes, and other provisions.[19]

The commencement of juvenile court commitments in 1900 alleviated the House of the Good Shepherd's financial duress. By 1901, nearly 80 percent of the delinquent and dependent girls at the House were committed through the juvenile court. The remaining 15 percent were referred by social agencies, and 5 percent through private arrangements. House records from 1900 to 1903 indicated that mothers were two to three times more likely to commit their daughters to the House of the Good Shepherd than were fathers. Mothers, especially those who faced desertion, widowhood, or impoverishment, perhaps relied upon the institution for temporary financial relief.[20]

The first juvenile court judge, Richard Tuthill, was largely responsible for the large number of delinquent girls committed to the House of the Good Shepherd during his tenure. He remained a strong supporter of the Sisters who, he exclaimed, did their fine work "without [the] blare of trumpets."[21] Although a non-Catholic, Tuthill also supported the House by joining a fund-raising committee formed in 1904 by prominent businessmen, the Citizens' Committee to Aid the Sisters of the Good Shepherd in the Erecting of Adequate Buildings for the Performance of Their Chosen Work of Saving Women and Girls.[22] The professional and volunteer roles of Tuthill were not conflicted, just as Timothy Hurley's duties as head of the organization's press committee, as president of the VAS, and as the juvenile court's first chief probation officer were not indicative of divided allegiances. Quite the reverse: as Maureen Flanagan has discussed, Chicago businessmen and professionals were very much engaged in reformist politics, often through their private clubs and organizations, which were quite different from women's.[23]

Such formal and nonformal networks were undoubtedly at work when Tuthill persuaded city officials to designate the House of the Good Shepherd as a house of shelter in 1903. This meant that women from the police and municipal courts could then be committed to the Sisters' care. In 1905 alone, seventy-one inmates committed to the House from the police court. In turn, these numbers translated into financial remuneration. From 1904 to 1908, the city paid the House over $15,000, and nearly the same amount over the next two four-year periods. In later years, however, the city would fall behind in its payments.[24]

Judge Tuthill assisted Hurley and the Sisters of the Good Shepherd again in 1908 when Chief Probation Officer John Witter decreed that juvenile court children could only be released by probation officers, not the staff of reform institutions. With the county assuming fiscal responsibility for probation officers in 1906, Witter perhaps sought to unify and standardize probation work by limiting such decisions to court staff. The Sisters did not necessarily disagree with Witter or the court officials; in fact, they concurred with the usual court commitments of eighteen months to two years for delinquent girls, acknowledging that a shorter stay could not "sow the seeds of virtue and industry in gardens so choked with weeds."[25] But the Sisters were often badgered by parents who requested their daughters' early releases because they missed their daughters or needed the girls' wages.

Hurley, as president of the VAS, had additional concerns. Witter's order would complicate dependent and delinquent girls' placements with Catholic families who preferred to negotiate privately with Catholic institutions and volunteer agencies, not court officials. Accordingly, Hurley appealed to Tuthill to use his influence to override Witter's decision. Subsequently, the court declared that girls committed to the House of the Good Shepherd and other reform institutions were wards of the institutions and so could not be released by the juvenile court's staff.[26]

Contestations such as these were not just ideological but financial. Commitments from the juvenile, municipal, and police courts provided much-needed monies to rescue homes and reformatories. Court commitments, however, also often resulted in overcrowding, as was the case with the House of the Good Shepherd. In September of 1904, the Sisters broke ground for a new building, replete with laundry facilities and a power plant on the site purchased in 1892. In 1906 and 1907 respectively, they added a brick stable and a dependent children's wing with its own dormitory, dining room, dish room, music room, arts and crafts room, library, kitchen, infirmary, and shower and sewing room. Even separate playgrounds, spacious lawns, and gardens were landscaped for dependent and delinquent girls. Finding the new accommodations so polished and clean, one journalist remarked that the institution resembled "an exclusive girls' college," not a reform school.[27]

Despite enlarged facilities, the House of the Good Shepherd still remained overcrowded. Although the state had licensed the school for 350 girls, nearly 500 resided there at any given time.[28] This was, in large part, because of the juvenile court. In 1908, the year the new facility opened, the court committed nearly twice as many delinquent girls as the year before. According to juvenile court records, the judge committed nearly twice as many delinquent girls to the House of the Good Shepherd as to the Illinois State Industrial School for Girls from 1910 to 1914. (The 1910 scandal at Geneva undoubtedly affected the number of delinquent girls committed from Chicago.) Similarly, delinquent girls committed to the House of the Good Shepherd far outnumbered those at the Chicago Home for Girls.[29] The larger accommodations at the House of the Good Shepherd were one reason for more commitments. A second reason was the creation of an industrial class for delinquent girls in 1909. Although no court or institutional reports discussed criteria for deciding which delinquent girls were committed to the industrial class, it appears as if most were older girls who specifically worked in the commercial laundry.[30]

The Sisters had always considered the commercial laundry an investment and, as noted, in 1908 had a stable built with twelve stalls for wagons and horses for transporting the laundry. They estimated that the income from the laundry, as well as from the girls' sewing and the court stipends, would be sufficient "to defray our expenses and take care of interest."[31] Yet as the epigraph that opens this chapter suggests, this wasn't always enough—though somehow they managed to survive.[32]

Like other social welfare institutions, the House relied upon the goodwill of individuals, charity organizations, and businesses to assist them with daily provisions for the inmates. Marshall Fields, Richardson Coal Company, Armour Company, Ogden Gas Company, America Radiator Company, Sears, Commonwealth Edison, Thiel Detective Service, even the Chicago Police Commission gave monetary and in-kind gifts such as furniture, food, altar flowers, and medicine. One Knights of Columbus council contributed soap, toothbrushes, pens, pencils, and Christmas gifts for the girls. By 1907, six doctors volunteered their time giving medical examinations; by 1916, fourteen did so. Even Juvenile Court Judge Merritt Pinckney gave financial donations to the House.[33]

In 1907, a group of Catholic women formed a ladies' auxiliary to "furnish material support to the Religious of the institutions in the arduous and charitable labor of reclaiming unfortunate sinful women and of preserving those in danger of falling into evil ways."[34] With a membership of nearly four hundred by 1910, the auxiliary drew mostly from the city's Irish parishes, although some members, including Tuthill's wife, were not Catholic.[35] One of auxiliary's first activities was to sponsor a lecture by Reverend John Glennon of St. Louis, who fittingly spoke on "the philosophy of charity." This event alone raised $4,000 for the House, nearly as much as was raised by the charity baseball game at Comiskey Park organized that year by the Chicago mayor and judges from the various courts. The auxiliary's card parties, field-day benefits, raffles, tag days, and Christmas sales of the girls' needlework and homemade foods contributed significantly as well.[36]

Despite the generosity of the women's auxiliary, businesses, and monies committed from the city and the juvenile court through the war years, the Sisters continually worried about finances. Indeed, they had good reason to be concerned: after 1916, the city had not honored its commitment to the House of the Good Shepherd as a house of shelter, resulting in a substantial loss of income. Monies from the juvenile court wards, then thirty cents per diem per inmate, totaled almost $13,000, only one-seventh of the House's required income. Fortunately, the commercial laundry was a success. Receipts from 1917 indicated that it netted more than $33,000, over one-third of the House's budget. Sewing sales contributed almost half of that amount.[37] The House was also fortunate because the Sisters did not receive salaries, which were the largest expenditure for most reform institutions.

In 1917, Cardinal George Mundelein alleviated some of the Sisters' worries by establishing the Associated Catholic Charities (ACC). A centralized agency which distributed monies to various Catholic organizations, the ACC demonstrated Mundelein's financial prowess as a businessman. Prior to Mundelein's leadership, Chicago's Catholic parishes had functioned largely as separate ethnic enclaves. There were three reasons for this. First, former Archbishops Patrick Feehan and James Quigley were Irish, as were most of Chicago's parishes. As such, they fostered Irish nationalism through parish organizations such as the resurgent Gaelic societies. Second, the Irish parishes were the wealthiest of all ethnic parishes, as measured by per capita donations. This undoubtedly fueled each parish's social solidarity rather than a collective spirit at the diocesan level. Third, Archbishop Quigley's belief that the ideal parish was a place where the priest knew every church member, including the children, reflected and reinforced his idea of closely knit ethnic neighborhoods and institutions.[38]

Cardinal Mundelein thought differently than his predecessors. He realized that as the largest diocese in the country, Chicago was extremely powerful and wealthy. As of 1916, the Chicago diocese's assets were estimated to be nearly $50 million, although most were unliquidated assets such as school and church properties. Only the Marshall Field family of Chicago held larger holdings in the city. It was, in fact, this financial stronghold that permitted the ACC to assist the Cook County Juvenile Court with its payments of mothers' pensions and the per diem costs for dependent and neglected children at Catholic institutions when the juvenile court lagged behind during the war years.[39] This assistance undoubtedly strengthened alliances between the Church and court as well as indicated the extent to which the Church functioned as a social welfare institution.

Mundelein's efforts to centralize Chicago's diocesan power occurred not only through the ACC but through the Catholic schools and parishes. Unlike the former archbishops who nurtured ethnic allegiances, Mundelein promoted the Americanization of Catholic school children. He did this in part by standardizing the parochial school curricula and requiring teachers to use English, not the immigrant students' native languages. Mundelein also penetrated the largely Protestant stronghold of Chicago's board of education by advocating for Catholic representation, one that would reflect the city's nearly 50 percent Catholic population. In a similar vein, he recommended that the public schools hire more Catholic teachers, especially Catholic women to serve as role models for the increasing number of Catholic girls who transferred to public schools.[40]

A second site where Mundelein consolidated diocesan power was in the parish. During the war years, he unified the parishes' patriotism by having them purchase war bonds. He also appealed to the parishioners' collective support in 1917 when the circuit court ruled in the case of *William H. Dunn v. the Chicago Industrial School for Girls* that state support for Catholic institutions had violated the separation of church and state. Dunn had accused the juvenile court and specifically probation officers of violating parents' rights when they committed children to institutions. Consequently, a court injunction prevented probation officers from receiving salaries for at least a month. Mundelein was less concerned about probation officers' pay than the lack of state support for neglected and dependent children in Catholic institutions. Accordingly, he distributed over a million copies of a letter he had written and translated into seven languages in order to stir the parishioners' indignation.[41] This collective effort paid off, along with Mundelein's financial contributions to the mothers' pensions fund and to dependent and delinquent children. The Illinois Supreme Court overturned the circuit court, thereby restoring funding to the Chicago Industrial School for Girls and other Catholic institutions. As has been noted by Edward Kantowicz, this court case mobilized Mundelein to establish a more centralized and autonomous organization (the ACC) for funding Catholic institutions, rather than rely upon the state and county.[42] Mundelein demonstrated his adeptness at courting businessmen and politicians by meeting with twenty-eight prominent

Chicago leaders, described by one scholar as the "who's who of Chicago Catholics." The mostly Irish group of Democratic machine bosses, prominent businessmen, bankers, lawyers, doctors, and judges was enthusiastic and pledged its support for the organization. During the ACC's first year alone, these men helped raise over $430,000 from 52,000 contributors.[43]

Alongside these efforts, Mundelein consolidated monies from the individual ethnic parishes in several ways. First, he decreed that each church take up a collection for the ACC on designated Sundays. Second, he asked parish volunteers to collect donations door-to-door. During the 1920s, the parishes collectively contributed almost $750,000 to the Catholic charities through church and neighborhood collections, and their benevolent societies.[44] In turn, the ACC distributed these monies through the Central Charity Bureau, which Mundelein created after the parishes' first collection drive.[45]

The ACC monies allowed Mundelein to expand the number of Catholic welfare agencies in the Chicago area, many of which were for girls and women. To illustrate, he built a maternity hospital for mothers on the city's South Side, similar to St. Vincent's on the North Side. He established clubs for working girls in downtown Chicago that offered meals at reasonable costs and provided wholesome recreation. His request for boarding homes for girls and women in different parts of the city resulted in the three YWCA-like "Rita Clubs," plus the Jeanne d'Arc Hotel, a hotel for women working in the downtown area.[46] This expansion of facilities was consistent with his priority of safeguarding children and youth, as well as keeping families intact. As he told the parish priests and their congregations, "Please remember, I shall insist on the children being cared for first, the older people can wait."[47]

Concerned about delayed provisions from the court and the city, the Sisters requested money from the ACC in 1919. Accounts from that year indicated that the House of the Good Shepherd received only a small amount from the ACC, less than 1 percent of the ACC's expenditures. The following year, however, the ACC increased the amount to almost $10,000 because Mundelein preferred that the Sisters solicit monies from the ACC, not the United Charities. Skeptical of secular organizations whose administrative costs absorbed much of their funds, he argued that the low overhead of the ACC permitted more monies to go directly to Catholic children's welfare.[48]

Mundelein's interest in decreasing Catholic institutions' reliance upon private philanthropies was one of necessity. By the early 1920s, the Wieboldt Foundation had reduced funding to various Catholic agencies, preferring instead to support the United Charities. In 1925, when St. Hedwig Orphanage and the House of the Good Shepherd requested funds from the Wieboldt Foundation, their requests were denied, the reason being that the institutions did not sufficiently disclose the necessary financial information.[49] This was not an uncommon complaint of many Catholic charities, whose reports were considered incomplete and "unscientific." Yet as one scholar has suggested, there were good reasons why the Sisters of the Good Shepherd did not keep accurate accounts. The first was their humility: the Sisters did not want to enunciate their successes; they simply wanted to carry out their vows. Second, the Sisters wanted to protect the reputations and privacy of the girls and women at the House. And third, the Sisters were more concerned with doing good deeds than documenting them.[50] But charity from the heart was a far cry from the accountability of philanthropy. By 1935, however, the House finally received support from the Community Fund, indicating that the Sisters' accounting at last conformed to standard reporting procedures.[51]

Reforming Delinquent Girls:
The Work of the Sisters and Catholic Women

The House of the Good Shepherd's program of reform for delinquent girls, in many ways, resembled that of other institutions. To be sure, moral rejuvenation of each girl was imperative. Upon entrance to the House, each girl assumed a new name and thereby a new identity. Nothing from her past was to be disclosed but instead "laid aside as a garment worn."[52] To assist the girls in building their new lives, the Sisters were instructed to be vigilant: "watch them [the girls] in your chapel, watch them at work; redouble your vigilance; watch them particularly during the hours of recreation."[53] Some girls quickly learned the religious script required of them, even if they did not personally embrace it. As one observer noted, "It did not take them long to learn, however, that dangling rosary beads in the hand and a demure and affected penitent mien could release them from eagle eyes and mopping pails."[54]

Even though there were separate departments for dependent and delinquent girls, they all learned some type of useful trade in order to become "good women and useful members of society." Each morning the girls arose at five to attend mass—even those who were not Catholic. Industrial and school work filled the remainder of the day. Those under the age of sixteen attended school for half a day; those under eighteen only three hours. When not in their classes, the younger delinquent girls worked on hand stitching garters and wristlets, crocheting, and embroidering table runners, luncheons sets, and handkerchiefs. They also did piecework for factories, such as making artificial flowers and ornaments for coat collars, or tying strings for small tags. The older delinquent girls worked in the commercial laundry and the millinery department. Some also sewed skirts, shirtwaists, wrappers, or put finishing touches on silk underwear for department stores.[55]

The Sisters used no form of corporal punishment, but whenever the girls rebelled against the Sisters' authority, encouraged "revolts," or acted immorally (although such activities were never specified), they were required to engage in some form of penance.[56] In 1918, Mundelein added a pecuniary motive for good behavior: he created savings accounts for the delinquent girls. In turn, the Sisters instituted a demerit system, subtracting a penny from the girls' accounts for each misbehavior. The girls could not earn back their money through good deeds but were instead granted special privileges, such as taking voice lessons or playing in the orchestra.[57]

The savings fund, however, served a larger purpose: it was connected to the girls' future livelihoods. Whereas the matrons of rescue homes and female reformatories touted domesticity and noble womanhood as eminent goals, the Sisters and Cardinal Mundelein emphasized industrial and commercial work as viable forms of employment. The mother superior's expressed goal for the inmates to learn the "real beauty" of homemaking was not only so they could cook their own food or make their own clothes but also so that they could earn a living. She thought it far more productive for the girls to learn skills, such as sewing or laundering, than to simply dust and mop.[58]

The wage fund served other functions as well. First, the fund compensated for the "pittance" of court monies.[59] As mentioned, the per diem rate of thirty cents was so woefully inadequate that it did not even cover a girl's room and board. Contributing nearly as much as the court monies, the wage fund alleviated some of the House's rising debts. Second, the saving accounts acted as a deterrent for early releases. Mundelein conjectured that if the girls' wages were secured in their savings accounts, they would not want to leave the House before they had completed their two-year commitment.[60] Translated differently, the longer the girls remained in the House, the larger their savings and the greater the likelihood of their reform. Third, in providing start-up funds for parole, Mundelein hoped to reduce the chances of recidivism. In short, girls would not fall victim to men's pecuniary incentives if they could support themselves.[61] Mundelein did not consider the possibility, however, that some girls desired adventure, excitement, and sexual companionship, regardless of their financial security.

Finally, Mundelein argued, the girls worked for themselves. This statement, however, requires some qualification. In 1918, 250 girls had accumulated a total of $6,000 in their savings, an average of only $24 per girl.[62] What "working for themselves" meant, then, was that the girls paid for their own room, board, clothing, and other necessities, and had a little left over in savings. To ensure some measure of accumulation, Mundelein decided to contribute over $5,000 annually to their accounts. Consequently, most girls' savings increased from an average of $35 to $150.[63]

Expecting criticism of his wage fund, Mundelein acknowledged that some reformers might instead recommend a boarding house for working girls. His thinking, though, was careful and steadfast: he was not averse to a boarding house and hoped that someone would eventually establish one. But, he stated, the Sisters' work with "spiritual convalescents" came first. Working girls who had already withstood the temptations of the outside world did not need as much help as the House's inmates, who required economic and moral fortification.[64]

The story of thirteen-year-old "L." illustrates how her savings allowed her to reestablish herself economically during her parole. L.'s father had her committed to the House of the Good Shepherd because he could not control her. Within a short time, she was released without supervision but then later recommitted. She had, in fact, requested to be sent back, telling the judge it was too difficult for her to say no to the neighborhood boys and to obey her strict father. After two years, she left the House with forty-eight dollars from her savings account. When the Sisters placed her in a girls' club until a suitable home could be found for her, L. ran away, declaring that she did not want to be treated like a child. The next day she took matters into her own hands; she visited a former inmate from the House, whose mother gave L. permission to live with them. Following an investigation of the home, L. took up residence there and started working at a nearby lampshade factory. Because she had learned this work at the House, her beginning weekly salary was twenty-five dollars.[65]

Court officials praised the wage fund, although at least one person was initially suspicious. In May of 1918, Mary Bartelme visited the House to discuss eliminating the Catholic Big Sisters court attendant's services; but she also wanted to find out if there was actually money in the girls' accounts.[66] When the mother superior showed her the bundles of bank books, Bartelme "fairly gasped." The mother superior wrote jokingly to Mundelein that he had the "court guessing" and may have even frightened the officers, "as Bartelme is trying very hard to please the sisters."[67] Apparently convinced by the wage plan, Bartelme committed nine girls to the House two days after her visit, and promised more. She was true to her word, as indicated by the number of commitments in 1918.

The other purpose of Bartelme's visit, to eliminate the Catholic Big Sisters' work in the courtroom, was consonant with her vision of separating professional responsibilities from volunteer activities. The House of the Good Shepherd had few trained staff to supervise the girls during their paroles and so had to rely upon Catholic social welfare organizations.[68] As early as 1901, the VAS had assisted the Sisters by employing three probation officers and two police officers to represent Catholic children in the court and supervise them during parole. The society also paid for truant officers in parochial schools, as well as helped to place Catholic children temporarily in private Catholic homes. Increasingly, it became more difficult for the society to recruit new members and to raise the funds necessary for the officers' salaries, despite the generosity of two wealthy Catholic meatpackers, Michael and John Cudahy. When the society disbanded in 1911, the House of the Good Shepherd and other Catholic child welfare agencies lost this cadre of trained and volunteer probation officers.[69]

However, the VAS was only one of many Catholic societies that assisted the House of the Good Shepherd. Founded in 1893, the Catholic Women's League (CWL) engaged in rescue and probation work, as well as supported Catholic girls' clubs, circulating libraries, temperance societies, nurseries, and settlements. Their most organized activity, however, was the protection of girls new to the city. Concerned especially with white slave traffic, the CWL published pamphlets, circulars, and cards that forewarned newcomers of the city's dangers. In 1917 alone, CWL members had written over eighteen hundred letters to that effect, which they distributed to parish priests; in turn, the priests sent these letters to priests in Poland, Ireland, Italy, and other European Catholic countries. When a newly arrived foreign girl presented a copy of such a letter to a league member at the railroad station, she was assured a safe haven and moral protection.[70]

The CWL assisted immigrant girls in other ways as well. The 1917 annual report enumerated that the league had found jobs for over 434 girls, represented 72 girls in the juvenile court, returned 27 girls to their out-of-state homes, placed 20 girls in private homes, arranged for 21 girls' adoptions, and placed 14 girls in boarding homes. Working as volunteer probation and parole officers, league members also visited over 508 girls' homes that year. Lastly, they referred 3 girls to the House of the Good Shepherd.[71]

In 1917, Cardinal Mundelein asked these already active women to begin yet another organization: the Catholic Big Sisters. He was prompted by a Catholic publicist who had written of his recent visit to the Chicago Detention Home, where he met at least thirty Catholic girls. The home's matron pointed out to the publicist how many of these girls were repeat offenders who simply needed sympathetic friends. The publicist advised the cardinal, "If each of them had some Catholic woman to take care of her and take an interest in her that would save her. Nothing else will."[72] Accordingly, a group of women formed the Catholic Big Sisters "to sponsor, counsel, and help spiritually or materially all girls and women in need of such assistance."[73] Although they formed various committees, including a clothing committee that made first-communion dresses and layettes for funeral shrouds, their most visible committee was the court committee. Members of this committee attended the court proceedings of the juvenile and domestic relations courts to ensure that Catholic girls and women be committed to Catholic institutions and placed in Catholic private homes.[74] Eventually, Bartelme's recommendation that members of volunteer organizations leave the matter of court representation to trained probation officers diminished the maternalist influence of this committee.

Shortly thereafter, the work of the Catholic Big Sisters became mostly "constructive." Many girls, they argued, simply needed wholesome recreation, school scholarships, or "kindly advice."[75] In encouraging women from different parishes to join the organization, members argued, "The girl often returns to the very environment in which she met her downfall, and many of the old associates are only too ready to test her strength to resist evil." As a "sympathetic friend of high ideals" ready to help a girl, a practical Catholic woman might assist by opening up her home, or meeting with her parents or parish priest.[76]

In addition to offering their emotional resources to delinquent girls, the Catholic Big Sisters and other women's organizations provided financial assistance to the House of the Good Shepherd. Recognizing the need for domestic training, they paid the salaries of the House's domestic science teachers. To meet the expenses for the House's new chapel, 2,500 members of the Illinois Club for Catholic Women contributed at least $10,000 as of 1923 to the chapel fund. The ladies auxiliary assisted by selling individual bricks, thereby netting $5,000 in one year alone. The Ladies of Isabella contributed an equal amount. Through these fund-raising activities, the House of the Good Shepherd's chapel was completed in 1926.[77]

Despite the goodwill and prodigious work of volunteer women's organizations and the Sisters, some delinquent girls resisted their help. Some, for example, did not wish to return to their families and so claimed not to know their whereabouts. One sixteen-year-old from Germany claimed she did not know "anything about her parents," that she was "raised in a German orphan asylum." Another sixteen-year-old declared that she knew "nothing about her parents, " that she was "raised in a New York orphan asylum." Although some girls were probably estranged from their families, it is quite possible that others did not want to adjust to their parents' nightly curfews, or to have to hand over their weekly wages. Exasperated, the sister superior wrote about one seventeen-year-old delinquent girl that she was "real foolish," did not know anything about her parents, and "would not give any information about herself."[78]

To be expected, House records indicated other forms of noncompliance or misbehavior. As early as 1905, there were six escapes while delinquent girls were being transported to the juvenile court.[79] (Clearly, the ten-foot wall would have been to difficult for them to scale.) Although the Sisters' comments about these and other girls were minimal, the words "pregnant," "venereal disease," and "feebleminded" increasingly appeared in the margins of the ledgers, as well as requests that such troubled girls be transferred to the state reformatory, the Chicago Home for Girls, the Chicago Detention Home, or the city's psychopathic hospital.[80]

As did the staff of the Chicago Home for Girls, the Sisters found some delinquent girls' emotional outbursts difficult to control. One girl in 1913 had to be turned away from the House because of an "ungovernable temper" that "imperiled" her companions. Another girl, "MA," was administered a psychopathic test because of her stubbornness, sullenness, and bad temper, the last two characteristics attributed to being in an institution for too long. The Sisters, perhaps not wanting to criticize or admit to failure, simply called her a "conundrum."[81] Although MA was compliant during school hours and sometimes even timid, the Sisters discovered that underneath lurked a "determined stubborn will." On one occasion she stayed in bed for three days rather than wear a kitchen apron. At other times she stood still, as if a statue. She finally became so "unreliable" that she wandered for hours and then lied about her whereabouts. The Sisters finally asked that she be transferred. The Chicago Psychopathic Hospital staff then gave her another test and found that she was apathetic and catatonic. Consequently, she stayed at the hospital for two months, during which time she exhibited no acute symptoms. The staff could not account for her compliance, although they acknowl-edged that the hospital's policy "to not cross the patients" may have mitigated her misbehavior. They did not consider the possibility that MA may have scripted her emotional outbursts, catatonic posture, or compliance. Her later placement with fifteen different families should have raised questions about MA's compliance.[82]

It was not clear to what extent the Sisters accepted the psychomedical model of reform, but some Catholic leaders were openly critical of the juvenile court's reliance upon IQ tests and psychopathic examinations. Loyola Univer-sity's dean of sociology, Father Frederic Siedenburg, thought the Binet test was biased and questioned why so many children were classified as feebleminded. His criticism of the psychopathic examination was even harsher: "The judges of the courts could not themselves in many instances pass the examination under the same circumstances and in the environment of the poor victim." He countered that lack of moral integrity was as much to blame for delinquents' misbehavior as physiological or mental defects. Correspondingly, he recom-mended that they learn to take responsibility for their "sins and crimes."[83]

For these reasons, he would not have been so sympathetic with "BO," a fif-teen-year-old Polish girl whose father worked in the steel mills. BO's mother brought her to court because she had run away from home and admitted to stealing clothing and having sex with multiple partners. We cannot know BO's side of the story, although she was probably upset because her mother de-manded all of her weekly paycheck. IQ tests revealed that BO had the mental age of an eleven-year-old, yet the court committed her to the House of the Good Shepherd, not an institution for the feebleminded, perhaps because the latter was overcrowded. Two years later, BO was released to her parents but ran away again because her father refused to let her go out at night; she was sent back to the court. Placed with a family as a domestic worker, she began to fre-quent a man's apartment nearby, where she received money for sex. She be-came pregnant and was then placed in St. Mary's Home, from which she ran away. Soon thereafter she became ill and was sent to Cook County Hospital for postabortion care. Placed again with several families, each time without success, she eventually found a job in a downtown bindery where she earned eighteen dollars per week and remained out of court.[84]

It is not clear why the court did not return BO to the Sisters, as the House of the Good Shepherd accepted more second-, third-, and even fourth-time of-fenders than any other institution, at least from 1906 to 1912.[85] Although this practice was consistent with the Sisters' ethic of not turning away anyone in need, it may have accounted for the increased number of difficult girls at the House. The case of thirteen-year-old Norwegian-American Florence illustrates that the Sisters' difficulty with her may have stemmed, in part, from her failure at other institutions. Florence was first placed in the Chicago Home for the Friendless, along with her siblings, when a neighbor reported that her mother was immoral and her father intemperate. After Florence's release to her parents, her mother soon deserted Florence's father but took her children with her. For a while, the court could not find the family but then discovered that two of the children had been placed in a Danish home for dependents. Florence was later brought to the juvenile court on a delinquent petition because her mother suspected her of immorality. Florence admitted to living with two different men and so was placed in the Mary A Club.[86]

Florence did not remain there for long. Disobedient and truant, she was asked to leave. The court then sent her back to her mother, who, in turn, enrolled her in a Catholic school. Florence did better for a while, then left school so she could work. She was soon arrested in a rooming house for Filipino men but the case was dismissed because of insufficient evidence. Although her mother had requested that Florence be placed with a stable family, Florence still continued to socialize with her Filipino friends and was again arrested. When the judge threatened to send her to the State Industrial School for Delinquent Girls in Geneva, she ran away from home, only to be found again in a "disorderly" house with Filipino men. Florence's mother retained a lawyer and so Florence was not held at the Chicago Detention Home but sent back home upon the mother's promise that she would bring Florence to court. Her mother did not honor that agreement and Florence's case was continued. When Florence was found again, she admitted to visiting her Filipino friends. In exasperation, the judge finally sent her to the House of the Good Shepherd. Five months later, the Sisters discovered she was pregnant. Following her child's birth, Florence was dismissed from the House and her baby placed in an orphanage. When the court located her several years later, she had at last married the baby's father.[87] Given Florence's home environment, her varying dispositions, and both her and her mother's refusal to cooperate with the juvenile court, the Sisters must have known that she would be difficult to reform. Yet they willingly took her in.

How do we evaluate the Sisters of the Good Shepherd's work with delinquent girls? Unlike other reform institutions' administrators, the Sisters did not publish reports about their successes or failures with delinquent girls. As mentioned, there are plausible reasons for their silence: the Sisters' humility; their avoidance of public attention; their submission and obedience to the archbishops and cardinal; and their focus on doing good deeds, not recording them. Far more is known about Mundelein's or Hurley's contributions to the House of the Good Shepherd than the Sisters'. And yet, beneath the nuns' invisibility was their enduring sense of commitment, evident in the numerous times they rebuilt or enlarged their facilities because of disasters or overcrowding. The Sisters remained steadfast in their care of delinquent girls, regardless of the girls' religion, age, family background, number of offenses, and ethnicity. How steadfast the girls were in embracing reform was another matter.

Conclusion

In July of 1999, Chicago celebrated the centennial of the Cook County Juvenile Court. However, this cause for celebration also gave rise to a reevaluation and, in a number of instances, harsh criticism of the court's trajectory. With the recent cases of several young children accused of homicide in Chicago, some court and public officials had reverted back to the idea that these offenders be tried as adults in criminal courts. Others, however, have questioned the extent to which young children can understand the serious consequences of their crimes or understand the waiving of their Miranda rights. On a larger scale, scholars and practitioners have questioned to what extent the juvenile court has strayed from its original mission as a kindlier, gentler alternative to the adult criminal court of 1899 in its attempts to rehabilitate, not punish, youthful offenders.

Sadly, there are persistent patterns in Chicago's juvenile court one-hundred-year history. Many of these patterns reflect nationwide trends as well. For one, there are still disproportionate numbers of children of color, especially African American, in the juvenile court system. According to Steve Drizan of Northwestern University School of Law's Children and Family Justice Center, African-American children comprise only 15 percent of the population nationally. Yet they constitute 26 percent of arrests, 32 percent of court referrals, 36 percent of those charged, 41 percent of those detained before trial, 46 percent incarcerated, and 52 percent of juvenile delinquents transferred to the adult court. At the Cook County Juvenile Detention Center, 80 percent of those detained are African-American.[1] Second, this detention center, like the first Chicago Detention Home, remains overcrowded, as many children and youth await trial in one of the sixteen delinquent courts or sixteen neglect and abuse courts.[2]

Third, we still lack professional consensus on what types of rehabilitative programs lead to "success," or even what constitutes "success." Understandably, nonrecidivism does not necessarily mean that children and youth are thriving. Indeed, many children and youth return to their homes where they continue to suffer physical, sexual, or verbal abuse. They return to neighborhoods where there are crumbling school facilities, few opportunities for future employment, and pressure to join gangs (if they have not already). In terms of reform facilities, although deinstitutionalization has decreased in many states, the effectiveness of public and private institutions is still questionable. Charles H. Shireman and Frederic G. Reamer, in their discussion of the problems of net widening, have noted that many facilities take in children and youth who need not be in any. But because continued funding relies upon "success" stories, the juvenile courts continue to commit children and youth to private programs and facilities.[3] Fourth, many of these commitments to public and private institutions continue to be based upon race and gender. In Cook County, for example, African Americans and girls are more likely to be placed in foster care, whereas white boys are more often placed in group homes and shelters.[4]

Not surprisingly, other historical patterns persist, especially for delinquent girls. As in the early twentieth century, many girls today are status offenders; that is, they are not arrested for serious offenses but those for which they can be taken into custody such as truancy, running away from home, and incorrigibility. In 1991, for example, of all youth who had been brought to juvenile courts for running away from home, 61 percent were girls. Similarly, most girls under eighteen in 1995 were arrested for status offenses, respectively 24 percent for larceny and 21 percent for running away.[5] Many of these girls, like their earlier counterparts, were brought to juvenile courts by their parents. As Meda Chesney-Lind and Randall Shelden have conjectured, daughters may be referred more often than sons by parents today because of concerns with female sexuality. Sadly, many of these girls, victims of physical and sexual abuse, are returned to their troubled homes.[6]

Restoring, much less building, caring parental-child relations in such damaging circumstances is certainly a problem, and one that the juvenile court is not prepared to fully undertake. As the Institute of Judicial Administration- American Bar Association Juvenile Justice Standards Project group has emphasized, "Using legal compulsion to restore (or provide) parent-child understanding and tolerance and to build up mechanisms for conflict resolution within the family unit is akin to doing surgery with a spade."[7] Despite the ambitious undertaking of the first juvenile court to reform both children and parents, it could not ameliorate the very source of many home problems: poverty. Barry Feld has criticized the absence of systemic social and economic reform; arguing further, he has postulated that "[t]he existence of a juvenile court provides an alibi to avoid fundamental improvement."[8] For this reason, he recommends abolishing the juvenile court.

In all fairness, the founders of the juvenile court could not anticipate how the nature of delinquency would change, especially in terms of the more violent charges of offenders. This is true not only for delinquent boys but for girls. Perhaps because of gang affiliation, delinquent girls have become more involved in violent crimes, especially aggravated assaults. According to the Chicago Crime Commission, an estimated one in five members of Chicago gangs in 1999 was female.[9] Many of the young members of "girl gangs," such as the Black Women United in Chicago, have been lured into drug traffic and corresponding activity.[10] Given the lack of economic alternatives in public housing and other inner-city locations, the salience of illegal drug activity should not surprise us.

What, then, can juvenile courts do to assist delinquent girls in turning their lives around? Returning to the community model, I would advocate that juvenile courts continue to work in conjunction with other social and educative institutions to ensure the well-being of all youth, especially delinquent youth. Schools should teach meaningful curricula that connects school-based learning to community forms of knowledge. Schools and employment sites should provide viable forms of vocational training that would translate into livable incomes. On a psychological level, family and group counseling services can provide young girls and their families with opportunities for dialogue and mediated resolutions. Rather than policing young girls' social and sexual behavior, health clinics could provide sound advice on birth control, sexually transmitted diseases, and for those who choose to keep their infants, mothering skills and health care.

We have much to learn from the first juvenile court's mistakes and solutions. Chicago's juvenile court is still an ambitious social experiment in the making. The fact that there is so much controversy, contestation, and change occurring within the institution attests to its potential. As with its predecessor, today's Chicago juvenile court represents a confluence of voices: judges, lawyers, probation and parole officers, social workers, psychiatrists and psychologists, administrators of corrrective and community-based facilities, advocacy groups, community spokespersons, and politicians. Delinquent girls, too, navigate the juvenile court system and continue to contribute to this confluence.

Appendix One:
Notes on Primary Sources

As noted in chapter 1, Ernest Burgess and other sociologists criticized social workers and probation officers for the paucity of useful information in their reports. What should and should not be detailed, much less included, in social case records were clearly topics of frequent debate for those in the helping professions, as well as administrators of reform institutions. After all, such types of data supported claims of scientific objectivity and professionalization, as well as measures of success in reforming those who had gone astray.

Yet Emil Frankel of the New Jersey Department of Institutions and Agencies, writing in 1930, thought otherwise. In his study of the statistical contents of annual reports of twenty-eight reform institutions for delinquents, he found that there was little agreement on what units were used for tabulating data. Although all of the institutions he studied included financial information, their selection of data varied. The same was true for the nativity, ethnicity, previous school attendance, offenses, and home backgrounds of delinquent youth at these institutions.[1] How, he asked, could any conclusions be made from such a hodgepodge of information?

Historians who study the reform institutions of the nineteenth and twentieth centuries share Frankel's frustrations. Veritable historical scholarship relies heavily upon the reliability and trustworthiness of primary sources. One should necessarily question the accuracy of the institutional records of the reform institutions, as well as juvenile court records such as those I have examined herein. I have already discussed how a poststructuralist approach accommodates the inflated language found within the literatures of fledgling professions and affiliate reform institutions. Nonetheless, a discussion of the nonavailability and veritability of primary sources, and how my own theoretical framework added to the puzzlement and elucidation of such a complex subject as female delinquency, is in order.

Let me begin with the nonavailability of primary sources. There are no Cook County Juvenile Court (CCJC) case records from the years 1899 to 1935. There are, however, CCJC case files from 1899 to 1936, with gaps. These juvenile case files are closed and accessible only through the permission of the presiding judge of the Cook County Circuit Court. In my effort to locate them and be granted permission, I was informed by administrators in charge that there were neither case files nor records available for the time period I requested. My persistence did not pay off. To my knowledge, only one historian,

David Tanenhaus, has been granted permission to look at what case files exist. Much of the collective demographic information about family backgrounds found in the CCJC annual reports does draw from these case files and so these annual reports were an invaluable source. However, information about individual delinquent female cases from the case files would have been highly useful in "fleshing out" how the girls, their families, and professionals negotiated the processes of the juvenile court.

Probation and parole officers' reports from the Chicago Home for Girls, the House of the Good Shepherd, and the State Industrial School for Delinquent Girls in Geneva, Illinois not only were not available but destroyed. At the Geneva school, the records had been stored for decades in one of the barns, whose roof had finally collapsed during a violent rain storm. As such, the annual and biennial reports of the Geneva School and the Chicago Home for Girls were the primary sources used for those two institutions. The House of the Good Shepherd's records were even more problematic. The Sisters of the Good Shepherd in Chicago were very gracious in bringing out boxes of ledgers and other materials, some dating back to the 1860s, for me to examine. However, the ledgers contained minimal information: a girl's name, date of birth, ethnicity, age, religion, level of education, and how she came to be committed (i.e., through the courts, self-referral, or parents). I have used material from these ledgers sparingly, as many of the entries were incomplete, illegible, or questionable in terms of veracity. Only when the ledgers' figures (numbers, ages, or ethnicity of inmates) corresponded with the CCJC annual reports' records did I make use of them.

In order to ascertain how internally consistent the data of the CCJC annual reports were, I checked all numbers within each table for a given year, as well as across all the years. (An annual report frequently contained a compilation of data for five years to indicate changes, say, in the types of charges or dispositions.) I also checked the data across all the annual reports (1904 to 1927) for consistency. To be expected, I found some anomalies, though by and large there were fewer than expected. In almost all instances, I could account for these inconsistencies (i.e., typographical errors, such as reversing numbers, or mislabeling columns, i.e., "delinquent boys" instead of "delinquent girls"). Not only did I check data within and across the CCJC annual reports, but also against the data in the annual reports of the Chicago Home for Girls and the Geneva School. If I could not ascertain the reliability of the annual reports' data I did not use it.

As with many institutional records, the classifications of data in the CCJC annual reports changed over time. For example, "nativity" was usually defined by the fathers' nativity but in some years by both parents' nativity. In these cases, I used only the data on the fathers' nativity for all years. For some years, certain types of data were recorded, only to be omitted in other years. For example, from 1906 to 1912, the numbers, ethnicity, charges, and dispositions of recidivists were recorded, but not in the years thereafter. Fortunately, some forms of data were classified consistently throughout and so constitute the information found in the tables in appendix 2.

Many graduate students of the University of Chicago's School of Social Service Administration and the School of Sociology wrote theses and dissertations that utilized the case files and records of the CCJC and probation and parole officers from the female reform institutions. Some of the graduate students, such as Helen Haseltine, worked in reform institutions and so were able to observe the daily lives of the delinquent girls, as well as talk with them. These were rich sources for contextualizing institutional life. As noted, these sources, in their multilayered narratives, lend themselves to a poststructuralist analysis.

Similarly, there were many dissertations and theses that examined Chicago's immigrant communities, public amusements, and social welfare agencies. These, along with the annual reports of maternalist organizations, especially the Chicago Woman's Club and the Juvenile Protective Association, were invaluable sources. The task of teasing out the rhetoric (professional, reformist, or otherwise) from professional practices, volunteer engagement, and the lived conditions of delinquent girls' lives is, of course, the ongoing task of the historian. To be sure, there were many examples of class, gender, and racial bias.

Across these diverse sources I found persistent patterns in the ideologies, professional practices, and public perceptions about delinquent girls in Chicago, which had led me to several conclusions. First, female delinquency was larger than the CCJC, the affiliate professions, the women's organizations, and even the girls themselves. The beliefs and practices surrounding female delinquency reflected a confluence of special interest groups, all of whom I have discussed. Secondly, this confluence demonstrated, to some degree, how flexible and expansive the CCJC was. That it could accommodate so many professional and nonprofessional constituencies not only illustrated its incipient bureaucracy but its willingness to respond to social change and influences. Despite the CCJC's good intentions, many of its constituents' responses focused on policing the sexuality of working-class immigrant, African-American, and native-born white girls. In attempts to reach into the girls' homes and thus reform the parents, probation officers and maternalists were often intrusive and condemning. And, as noted, they were not always successful in their efforts.

Like the institutions the Chicago School of Sociology studied, the CCJC was in a state of flux, as it accommodated to varying social, cultural, and political circumstances, as well as professional influences. Accordingly, the CCJC reflected the social processes of immigration, urbanization, and industrialization that then so fascinated the Chicago School. The CCJC was not only an urban laboratory for sociologists but a training school for fledgling professionals, a social welfare institution where the middle-class and poor mingled, and an acculturating institution where immigrant parents and children learned what it meant to be both "American" and "other." For delinquent girls it was many places as well: a place of containment, perhaps imprisonment; a place of refuge or protection; a place to "put one over" or to make amends; and a place of camaraderie and peer support.

Appendix Two:
Tables

Table 1. Number of Probation Officers Assigned to Cook Country Juvenile Court, 1904 to 1927

Year	Police Probation Officers*	County Probation Officers
1904	21	0
1905	n.a.	n.a.
1906	23	23
1907	22	23
1908	26	31
1909	30	35
1910	30	35
1911	30	35
1912	34	37
1913	35	53
1914	35	76
1915	50	77
1916	53	79
1917	49	81
1918	44	86
1919	25	86
1920	30	101**
1921	27	101
1922	28	102
1923	28	106
1924	29	106
1925	28	111
1926	28	113
1927	29	117

*   Assigned by the chief of police and commissioned as probation officers.
**   Beginning in 1919, all persons who were classified on the payroll as "probation officers" are included. Figures for previous years include only those assigned fieldwork.

Source: CCJCAR 1927, 41.

Table 2. Number of Delinquent and Dependent Boys and Girls Brought to Cook County Juvenile Court, 1904 to 1927

Year	Delinquent Boys	Delinquent Girls	Dependent Boys	Dependent Girls	Total
1904	1545	354	898	730	3527
1905	2018	455	1212	1088	4773
1906	2131	432	1237	957	4757
1907	1973	539	896	791	4199
1908	1651	517	876	707	3751
1909	1352	464	852	677	3345
1910	1161	475	961	699	3296
1911	1320	483	1076	920	3799
1912	1105	537	1363	1255	4260
1913	1363	592	1089	1022	4066
1914	2258	659	1227	1065	5209
1915	2326	586	1212	1117	5241
1916	2191	594	1116	1194	5095
1917	2328	679	1023	1050	5080
1918	2306	730	1054	1029	5119
1919	2647	755	935	901	5238
1920	1912	638	682	580	3812
1921	1754	661	658	634	3707
1922	1330	576	722	700	3328
1923	1283	532	801	734	3350
1924	2079	628	953	867	4527
1925	1963	550	1054	959	4526
1926	1671	594	1106	998	4369
1927	1588	609	1147	971	4315

Source: CCJCAR, 1906 to 1927.

Table 3. Percentages* of Delinquent and Dependent Boys and Girls Brought to Cook County Juvenile Court, 1904 to 1927

Year	Delinquent Boys	Delinquent Girls	Dependent Boys	Dependent Girls
1904	44	10	25	21
1905	42	10	25	23
1906	44	10	26	20
1907	47	11	21	19
1908	44	14	23	19
1909	40	14	25	20
1910	35	14	29	21
1911	35	13	28	24
1912	26	13	32	29
1913	34	15	27	25
1914	43	13	24	20
1915	44	11	23	21
1916	43	12	22	23
1917	46	13	20	21
1918	45	14	21	20
1919	51	14	18	17
1920	50	17	18	15
1921	47	18	18	17
1922	40	17	18	21
1923	38	16	22	22
1924	46	14	24	19
1925	43	12	21	21
1926	38	14	23	23
1927	37	14	25	23

*   Percentages are rounded to the nearest whole number.

Source: CCJCAR, 1906 to 1927.

Table 4. Number of Delinquent and Dependent Boys and Girls Placed in Institutions and Associations,*
1904 to 1927

Year	Delinquent Boys	Delinquent Girls	Dependent Boys	Dependent Girls
1904	630	229	639	493
1905	770	304	764	624
1906	541	258	820	564
1907	547	300	557	401
1908	497	275	604	421
1909	437	236	609	404
1910	487	254	676	399
1911	608	239	636	432
1912	379	232	794	628
1913	468	217	690	510
1914	522	288	692	462
1915	463	263	594	450
1916	410	210	540	435
1917	469	279	471	381
1918	495	286	549	422
1919	854	301	529	425
1920	641	215	373	271
1921	638	236	378	274
1922	445	152	442	333
1923	436	168	453	323
1924	702	156	561	370
1925	700	201	409	442
1926	724	211	406	445
1927	747	237	725	500

* Associations include ethnic and religious orphanages and societies, among them the Catholic Home Bureau, the Catholic Home Finding Society, the Jewish Home Finding Society, the Illinois Children's Home and Aid Society, the Evangelical Lutheran Home Finding Society, the Norwegian Lutheran Home Finding Society, and the National Protestant Woman's Association.

Source: CCJCAR, 1906 to 1927.

Table 5   Percentages* of Delinquent and Dependent Boys and Girls Placed in Institutions and Associations,** 1904 to 1927

Year	Delinquent Boys	Delinquent Girls	Dependent Boys	Dependent Girls
1904	41	65	71	68
1905	38	67	63	57
1906	25	56	66	59
1907	28	56	62	51
1908	30	53	69	60
1909	32	51	71	60
1910	42	53	70	57
1911	46	49	59	47
1912	34	43	58	50
1913	34	37	63	50
1914	23	44	56	43
1915	20	45	49	40
1916	19	35	48	36
1917	20	41	46	36
1918	21	39	52	41
1919	32	40	57	47
1920	34	34	55	47
1921	36	36	57	43
1922	33	27	61	48
1923	34	32	57	44
1924	34	25	59	43
1925	36	37	39	46
1926	43	36	37	45
1927	47	39	63	51

*   Percentages for each group are calculated from the total number within each group who were brought before the Cook County Juvenile Court, and are rounded to the nearest whole number.

** Associations include ethnic and religious orphanages and societies, among them the Catholic Home Bureau, the Catholic Home Finding Society, the Jewish Home Finding Society, the Illinois Children's Home and Aid Society, the Evangelical Lutheran Home Finding Society, the Norwegian Lutheran Home Finding Society, and the National Protestant Woman's Association.

Source: CCJCAR, 1906 to 1927.

Table 6.   Number of Delinquent and Dependent Children Placed on Probation, 1904 to 1927

Year	Delinquent Boys	Delinquent Girls	Dependent Boys	Dependent Girls
1904	764	121	243	229
1905	1064	136	431	440
1906	1163	168	376	370
1907	1195	205	316	359
1908	928	222	252	277
1909	740	189	186	229
1910	521	188	205	247
1911	520	205	270	336
1912	554	264	276	323
1913	689	290	299	379
1914	808	299	309	362
1915	926	282	445	472
1916	931	196	293	414
1917	1021	229	237	299
1918	690	240	221	270
1919	735	191	169	161
1920	564	153	103	111
1921	427	182	112	132
1922	337	122	111	140
1923	336	145	182	170
1924	592	201	173	248
1925	549	138	255	290
1926	463	148	260	234
1927	352	130	226	216

Source: CCJCAR, 1906 to 1927.

Table 7. Percentages* of Delinquent and Dependent Children Placed on Probation, 1904 to 1927

Year	Delinquent Boys	Delinquent Girls	Dependent Boys	Dependent Girls
1904	49	34	27	31
1905	53	30	36	40
1906	55	36	30	39
1907	61	38	35	45
1908	56	43	29	39
1909	55	41	22	39
1910	45	40	21	35
1911	39	42	25	37
1912	50	50	20	26
1913	51	49	27	37
1914	36	45	25	34
1915	40	39	37	42
1916	42	33	26	35
1917	44	34	23	28
1918	30	33	21	26
1919	28	25	18	18
1920	29	24	15	19
1921	24	28	17	21
1922	25	21	15	20
1923	26	27	23	23
1924	28	32	18	29
1925	28	25	24	30
1926	28	25	24	23
1927	22	21	20	22

*   Percentages for each group are calculated from the total number within each group who were brought before the Cook County Juvenile Court, and are rounded to the nearest whole number.

Source: CCJCAR, 1906 to 1927.

Table 8. Number of Delinquent Girls per Times Brought to Cook County Juvenile Court, 1904 to 1927

Year	1st Time	2nd Time	3rd Time	4th Time	5th Time	6th Time	7th Time
1904	275	79	0	0	0	0	0
1905	345	81	20	8	1	0	0
1906	326	85	14	7	0	0	0
1907	379	114	29	12	2	2	1
1908	363	116	30	8	0	0	0
1909	332	96	26	5	4	1	0
1910	346	95	27	7	0	0	0
1911	339	109	31	4	0	0	0
1912	376	114	37	6	2	2	0
1913	392	141	40	16	3	0	0
1914	407	144	70	24	10	2	2
1915	367	145	47	21	3	2	1
1916	385	128	45	25	8	2	1
1917	435	155	57	18	7	4	2
1918	459	169	67	23	9	2	0
1919	490	154	59	27	13	10	1
1920	433	131	44	17	9	4	0
1921	433	132	56	22	13	1	2
1922	381	111	49	22	7	3	2
1923	341	91	51	23	16	4	2
1924	407	141	40	21	9	4	3
1925	333	117	54	29	10	1	5
1926	372	123	48	28	12	6	4
1927	367	123	70	30	14	5	0

Note: Numbers for a given year do not necessarily equal the total numbers of girls brought before the juvenile court that year because, in some years, girls returned as many as ten times.

Source: CCJCAR, 1906 to 1927.

Table 9. Number of Delinquent Girls Brought to Cook County Juvenile Court according to Ethnicity,* 1906 to 1927

Year	German	Irish	American	French	Polish	Bohemian
1906	90	48	80	19	49	16
1907	n.a.	n.a.	n.a.	n.a.	n.a.	n.a.
1908	114	46	90	7	93	20
1909	72	37	84	3	77	22
1910	90	34	87	20	82	19
1911	96	43	79	11	65	14
1912	114	53	65	7	84	26
1913	122	54	90	7	84	20
1914	n.a.	n.a.	n.a.	n.a.	n.a.	n.a.
1915	99	36	95	7	107	18
1916	n.a.	n.a.	n.a.	n.a.	n.a.	n.a.
1917	107	44	112	11	112	28
1918	79	52	152	4	128	23
1919	70	42	182	7	157	15
1920	59	37	142	2	99	13
1921	45	31	175	5	136	13
1922	41	21	270	3	117	13
1923	42	25	99	7	105	18
1924	38	31	134	0	107	0
1925	42	11	125	2	102	0
1926	36	10	142	6	91	0
1927	42	14	133	1	91	0

Year	Swedish	African-American	English	Italian	Norwegian	Russian[+]
1906	15	30	14	11	14	13
1907	n.a.	n.a.	n.a.	n.a.	n.a.	n.a.
1908	8	52	15	12	15	17
1909	18	41	7	16	4	22
1910	8	37	20	12	10	19
1911	9	46	5	20	6	18
1912	15	35	14	22	10	21
1913	20	61	7	30	11	15
1914	n.a.	n.a.	n.a.	n.a.	n.a.	n.a.
1915	21	78	13	27	6	18
1916	n.a.	n.a.	n.a.	n.a.	n.a.	n.a.

Table 9 (continued)

Year	Swedish	African-American	English	Italian	Norwegian	Russian[+]
1917	17	80	7	38	7	29
1918	19	121	2	45	6	23
1919	7	112	10	44	3	28
1920	10	128	8	33	1	12
1921	7	100	1	43	3	24
1922	12	116	2	28	2	20
1923	13	108	2	39	4	12
1924	10	107	3	39	4	26
1925	7	97	8	23	4	14
1926	4	115	5	27	0	19
1927	2	154	3	32	10	16

*   Ethnicity or nationality is based upon parents' nativity, usually the father's, as well as by geographic location or county. *American* refers to native-born white girls. Number includes all girls brought to the Cook County Juvenile Court, regardless of the number of times they appeared in a given year.
+   Russian also includes designation of Russian Jew.

Source: CCJCAR, 1906 to 1927.

Table 10. Percentages* of Delinquent Girls Brought to Cook County Juvenile Court according to Ethnicity,**
1906 to 1927

Year	German	Irish	American	French	Polish	Bohemian
1906	21	11	19	4	11	4
1907	n.a.	n.a.	n.a.	n.a.	n.a.	n.a.
1908	22	9	17	1	18	4
1909	16	8	18	1	17	5
1910	19	7	18	4	17	4
1911	20	9	16	2	13	3
1912	21	10	12	1	16	5
1913	21	9	15	1	14	3
1914	n.a.	n.a.	n.a.	n.a.	n.a.	n.a.
1915	17	6	16	1	18	3
1916	n.a.	n.a.	n.a.	n.a.	n.a.	n.a.
1917	16	6	16	2	16	4
1918	11	7	21	.5	18	3
1919	9	6	24	1	21	2
1920	9	6	22	.3	16	2
1921	7	5	26	1	21	2
1922	7	4	23	.5	20	2
1923	8	5	19	1	20	2
1924	6	5	21	0	17	0
1925	8	2	23	.3	19	0
1926	6	2	24	1	15	0
1927	7	2	22	.1	15	0

Year	Swedish	African–American	English	Italian	Norwegian	Russian[+]
1906	3	7	3	3	3	3
1907	n.a.	n.a.	n.a.	n.a.	n.a.	n.a.
1908	2	10	3	2	3	3
1909	4	9	2	3	1	5
1910	2	8	4	3	2	4
1911	2	10	1	4	1	4
1912	3	7	3	4	2	4
1913	3	10	1	5	2	3
1914	n.a.	n.a.	n.a.	n.a.	n.a.	n.a.
1915	4	13	2	5	1	3

Table 10 (continued)

Year	Swedish	African-American	English	Italian	Norwegian	Russian[+]
1916	n.a.	n.a.	n.a.	n.a.	n.a.	n.a.
1917	3	12	1	6	1	4
1918	3	17	.2	6	1	3
1919	1	15	1	6	.4	4
1920	2	20	1	5	.1	2
1921	1	15	.1	7	.4	4
1922	2	20	.3	5	.3	3
1923	2	20	.4	7	1	2
1924	2	17	.5	6	1	4
1925	1	18	2	4	1	3
1926	1	19	1	5	0	3
1927	.3	25	.5	5	2	3

★ Percentages are rounded to the nearest whole number or, in cases where percentages are less than 1, to the nearest tenth.

★★ Ethnicity or nationality is based upon parents' nativity, usually the father's, as well as by geographic location or county. *American* refers to native-born white girls.

+ Russian also includes designation of Russian Jew.

Source: CCJCAR, 1906 to 1927.

Table 11. Number of Delinquent Girls Brought to Cook County Juvenile Court according to Their Specific Charges, 1906 to 1927

Year	Immorality	Incorrigibility	Larceny	Forgery	Burglary	Robbery	Disorderly Conduct	Assault
1906	86	266	54	0	0	0	26	0
1907	n.a.	n.a.	n.a.	n.a.	n.a.	n.a.	n.a	n.a.
1908	76	379	55	0	3	0	4	0
1909	162	202	77	8	0	1	7	2
1910	205	158	73	4	1	3	5	11
1911	191	181	70	7	0	0	3	9
1912	246	191	70	6	0	0	3	4
1913	269	220	74	2	1	2	11	3
1914	223	327	87	5	1	0	10	4
1915	259	257	52	1	5	1	4	1
1916	264	251	63	3	0	1	4	0
1917	312	262	80	0	2	0	9	2
1918	311	324	73	0	0	1	1	5
1919	321	293	103	0	3	2	5	8
1920	348	211	65	8	1	4	1	0
1921	311	261	66	11	1	3	1	2
1922	247	224	77	1	1	1	4	2
1923	179	277	46	13	6	3	1	2
1924	176	379	39	13	1	5	1	3
1925	149	334	34	5	9	6	0	4
1926	139	393	48	4	2	0	0	5
1927	119	431	34	3	11	4	0	3

Year	Malicious Mischief	Concealed Weapons	Obtaining Money under False Pretenses	Stealing from Railroad Cars or Automobiles	Attempted Suicide	Arson	Embezzlement	Drunkenness
1906	0	0	0	0	0	0	0	0
1907	n.a.	n.a.	n.a.	n.a.	n.a.	n.a.	n.a.	n.a.
1908	0	0	0	0	0	0	0	0
1909	0	0	0	0	0	1	0	3
1910	0	0	2	0	0	0	0	10
1911	1	0	0	0	0	0	0	11
1912	1	0	3	0	0	0	1	11

Appendix Two: Tables

Table 11 (continued)

Year	Malicious Mischief	Concealed Weapons	Obtaining Money under False Pretenses	Stealing from Railroad Cars or Automobiles	Attempted Suicide	Arson	Embezzlement	Drunkenness
1913	0	0	0	0	0	0	0	7
1914	0	0	0	0	0	0	0	5
1915	2	0	0	0	0	0	0	1
1916	0	0	0	0	0	0	0	8
1917	3	0	0	0	4	0	0	5
1918	0	0	0	11	3	0	0	2
1919	0	1	1	0	3	0	0	6
1920	0	0	0	0	0	0	0	0
1921	0	1	0	0	2	0	0	2
1922	0	1	1	0	2	0	0	4
1923	0	1	1	0	1	0	0	2
1924	2	1	1	2	0	1	0	3
1925	0	1	4	0	3	0	0	0
1926	0	1	0	2	0	0	0	0
1927	1	0	0	3	1	0	0	0

Source: CCJCAR, 1906 to 1927.

Table 12. Percentages* of the Three Leading Charges of Delinquent Girls Brought to Cook County Juvenile Court, 1906 to 1927

Year	Immorality	Incorrigibility	Larceny
1906	20	62	13
1907	n.a.	n.a.	n.a.
1908	15	73	11
1909	35	44	17
1910	43	33	15
1911	40	37	14
1912	46	36	13
1913	45	37	13
1914	34	50	13
1915	44	44	9
1916	44	42	11
1917	46	39	12
1918	43	44	10
1919	43	39	14
1920	55	33	10
1921	47	39	10
1922	43	39	13
1923	34	52	9
1924	28	60	6
1925	27	61	6
1926	23	66	8
1927	20	71	6

*   Percentages are rounded to the nearest whole number.

Source: CCJCAR, 1906 to 1927.

Table 13. Number of Delinquent Girls Brought to the Cook County Juvenile Court according to Their Dispositions, 1906 to 1927

Year	PR/H	PR/O	DIS	LG	CG	GE	HG	HIN	CH
1906	161	——	33	0	0	52	121	0	59
1907	205	——	31	0	0	n.a.	n.a.	n.a.	n.a.
1908	221	1	20	0	0	57	143	0	70
1909	168	21	32	0	0	47	99	16	60
1910	151	33	29	0	0	35	118	13	77
1911	183	22	24	0	0	53	103	22	58
1912	241	23	31	0	0	49	105	34	43
1913	277	13	51	0	0	54	99	17	66
1914	n.a.	n.a.	n.a.	n.a.	n.a.	n.a.	n.a.	n.a.	n.a.
1915	144	39	74	45	7	81	82	40	54
1916	164	32	72	90	11	61	76	33	40
1917	202	27	64	61	26	85	75	62	57
1918	192	48	92	69	21	97	102	43	44
1919	176	15	123	62	46	115	99	48	39
1920	129	24	92	56	101	84	79	21	31
1921	153	29	97	57	77	50	95	37	54
1922	127	15	133	64	69	48	57	19	28
1923	127	18	102	43	67	27	71	17	53
1924	182	19	132	73	57	26	69	17	44
1925	121	17	71	80	39	48	79	20	54
1926	134	14	94	86	43	59	80	20	52
1927	124	6	97	61	65	58	97	23	59

PR/H = Probation at Girls' Home; PR/O = Probation under Supervision of Probation Officer; DIS = Dismissed; LG = Legal Guardian; CG = Continued Generally; GE = Geneva; HG = House of the Good Shepherd; HIN = House of the Good Shepherd's Industrial Class; CH = Chicago Home for Girls.
—— = Reports did not distinguish between PR/H and PR/O.

Note: Numbers do not equal total number of girls brought to the Cook County Juvenile Court, as there were other dispositions, including deportation, parole to county agents, and commitments to other reform institutions or hospitals.

Source: CCJCAR, 1906 to 1927.

Table 14. Percentages★ of Delinquent Girls Brought to Cook County Juvenile Court according to Their Dispositions, 1906 to 1927

Year	PR/H	PR/O	DIS	LG	CG	GE	HG	HIN	CH
1906	37	——	8	0	0	12	28	——	14
1907	38	——	6	0	0	n.a.	n.a.	——	n.a.
1908	43	.2	4	0	0	11	28	——	14
1909	36	5	7	0	0	10	21	3	13
1910	32	7	6	0	0	7	25	3	16
1911	38	5	5	0	0	11	21	5	12
1912	45	4	6	0	0	9	20	6	8
1913	47	2	9	0	0	9	17	3	11
1914	n.a.	n.a.	n.a.	n.a.	n.a.	n.a.	n.a.	n.a.	n.a.
1915	25	7	13	8	1	14	14	7	9
1916	28	5	12	15	2	10	13	6	7
1917	30	4	9	9	4	13	11	9	8
1918	26	7	13	10	3	13	14	6	6
1919	23	2	16	8	6	15	13	6	5
1920	20	4	14	8	16	13	12	3	5
1921	23	4	15	9	12	8	14	6	8
1922	22	3	23	11	12	8	10	3	5
1923	24	3	19	8	13	5	13	3	10
1924	29	3	21	12	9	4	11	3	7
1925	22	3	13	15	7	9	14	4	10
1926	23	2	16	15	7	10	13	3	9
1927	20	1	16	10	11	10	16	4	10

PR/H = Probation at Girls' Home; PR/O = Probation under Supervision of Probation Officer; DIS = Dismissed; LG = Legal Guardian; CG = Continued Generally; GE = Geneva; HG = House of the Good Shepherd; HIN = House of the Good Shepherd's Industrial Class; CH = Chicago Home for Girls.
—— = Reports did not distinguish between PR/H and PR/O.

★ Percentages are rounded to the nearest whole number, or in the cases where percentages are less that 1, to the nearest tenth.

Note: Numbers do not equal total number of girls brought to the Cook County Juvenile Court, nor do total of percentages equal 100, as there were other dispositions, including deportation, parole to county agents, and commitments to other reform institutions or hospitals.

Source: CCJCAR, 1906 to 1927.

Notes

Abbreviations

Locations
Chicago Historical Society (CHS)
Harold Washington Library, Chicago, Municipal Reference
   Collection (HWL)
House of the Good Shepherd Convent (HGSC)
Joseph Cardinal Bernadin Archival Research Center (JCBRC)
Northwestern University (NU)
University of Chicago Special Collections (UCSC)
University of Chicago Regenstein Library (UCRL)
University of Illinois at Chicago Special Collections (UICSC)

Archive Collections
Abbott, Edith and Grace Papers (EGA)
Bartelme, Mary Papers (MB)
Bubasz, Steven S. Papers (SB)
Burgess, Ernest Collection (EB)
Chicago Council of Social Agencies (CCSA)
Chicago Home for Girls Annual Reports (CHGAR)
Chicago Municipal Court Annual Reports (CMCAR)
Chicago Refuge for Girls Annual Reports (CRGAR)
Chicago School of Civics and Philanthropy (CSCP)
Chicago Urban League Annual Reports (CUL)
Chicago Woman's Club Meeting Records (CWCMR)
Community Funds Records (CFR)
Cook County Juvenile Court Annual Reports (CCJCAR)
Illinois Department of Public Welfare Annual Reports (DPWAR)
Erring Women's Refuge of Chicago Annual Reports (EWRCAR)
Illinois Children's Home and Aid Society (ICHAS)
Illinois State Training School for Girls at Geneva (formerly the State Home for Juvenile Fe-
   male Offenders at Geneva) Biennial Reports (GBR)
Juvenile Protective Association of Chicago Annual Reports (JPAAR)
Juvenile Protective Association Papers (JPAP)
Madaj Collection (MC) (Joseph Cardinal Bernadin Archival Research Center)
McCoy-Gaines, Irene Collection (IMG)
Police Reports of the City of Chicago to the City Council (PRCC)
Report of the General Superintendent of Police of the City of Chicago to the City, 1899 to
   1930 (RGSP)
Welfare Council of Metropolitan Chicago Records (WCMC)
YWCA of Metropolitan Chicago (YWCA)

Introduction

1. See, for example, Mary Lynn McCree Bryan and Allen F. Davis, eds., *Years at Hull-House* (Bloomington: Indiana University Press, 1990); Allen F. Davis, *Spearheads for Reform: The Social Settlements and the Progressive Movement, 1890–1914*, 2nd ed. (New Brunswick, NJ: Rutgers University Press, 1984); Anne Meis Knupfer, *Toward a Tenderer Humanity and a Nobler Woman-hood: African American Women's Clubs in Turn-of-the-Century Chicago* (New York: New York University Press, 1996); Andrew Abbott, *Department and Discipline: Chicago Sociology at One Hundred* (Chicago: University of Chicago Press, 1999); Martin Bulmer, *The Chicago School of Sociology: Institutionalization, Diversity, and the Rise of Sociological Research* (Chicago: University of Chicago Press, 1984); and Steven J. Diner, *A City and Its Universities: Public Policy in Chicago, 1892–1919* (Chapel Hill: University of North Carolina Press, 1980).

2. Elaborating on Molly Ladd-Taylor's framework, I use the terms *maternalism* and *professional maternalism* to refer respectively to nonprofessional and professional women and their organizations, which circumscribed their activities around motherhood and children's welfare. Molly Ladd-Taylor, *Mother-Work: Women, Child Welfare, and the State, 1890–1930* (Urbana: University of Illinois Press, 1994). See also Seth Koven and Sonya Michel, eds., *Mothers of a New World: Maternalist Politics and the Origins of Welfare States* (New York: Routledge, 1993); and Lynn Y. Weiner, "Maternalism as Paradigm: Defining the Issues," *Journal of Women's History* 5 (Fall 1993): 96–115.

3. Sophonisba Breckinridge and Edith Abbott, *The Delinquent Child and the Home* (New York: Russell Sage Foundation, 1912), 37.

4. Mary E. Odem, *Delinquent Daughters: Protecting and Policing Adolescent Female Sexuality in the United States, 1885–1920* (Chapel Hill: University of North Carolina Press, 1995).

5. Kathryn Kish Sklar, "The Historical Foundation of Women's Power in the Creation of the American Welfare State, 1830–1930," in *Mothers of a New World: Maternalist Politics and the Origins of Welfare States*, ed. Seth Koven and Sonya Michel (New York: Routledge, 1993), 43–93.

6. Elizabeth Lunbeck, *The Psychiatric Persuasion: Knowledge, Gender, and Power in Modern America* (Princeton, NJ: Princeton University Press, 1994).

7. Lunbeck, *The Psychiatric Persuasian*, 523.

8. Knupfer, *Toward a Tender Humanity and a Nobler Womanhood*, 4–6.

Chapter 1

1. The term *female dominion* is taken from Robyn Muncy's book, *Creating a Female Dominion in American Reform 1890–1935* (New York: Oxford University Press). Mary Jo Deegan, *Jane Addams and the Men of the Chicago School, 1892–1918* (New Brunswick, NJ: Transaction, 1988), 34–35. I do not intend to necessarily polarize the female reformers' work from that of male sociologists but rather to point to differences in their theories, methodologies, and goals. Some scholars have questioned whether the University of Chicago sociology department was indeed, a "school." See, for example, Andrew Abbott, *Department and Discipline: Chicago Sociology at One Hundred* (Chicago: University of Chicago Press, 1999); Lee Harvey, *Myths of the Chicago School of Sociology* (Avebury, England: Gower, 1987); and essays in Gary Alan Fine, *A Second Chicago School? The Development of a Postwar American Sociology* (Chicago: University of Chicago Press, 1995). So, too, does Dorothy Ross caution that the Hull House was not just a woman's sphere but a "heterosocial world"; Dorothy Ross, "Gendered Social Knowledge: Domestic Discourse, Jane Addams, and the Possibilities of Social Science," in *Gender and American Social Science: The Formative Years*, ed. Helene Silverberg (Princeton: Princeton University Press, 1998), 235–64.

2. Kathryn Kish Sklar, "Hull-House Maps and Papers: Social Science as Women's Work in the 1890s," in *Gender and American Social Science: The Formative Years*, ed. Helene Silverberg (Princeton: Princeton University Press, 1998), 127, 142. The definitive biography of Florence Kelley is Kathryn Kish Sklar, *Florence Kelley and the Nation's Work: The Rise of Women's Political Culture, 1830–1900* (New Haven: Yale University Press, 1995). See also Mary Jo Deegan, ed., *Women in Sociology: A Bio-Bibliographical Sourcebook* (Westport, CT: Greenwood Press, 1991), which appropriately includes entries on Edith Abbott, Jane Addams, Sophonisba Breckinridge, and Florence Kelley. Jennifer Platt argued for the inclusion of Ethel Sturges Dummer. Although not trained as a sociologist, Dummer did publish sociological articles, as well as participated in sociology conferences, probably because of her generous funding of sociological studies. Jennifer Platt, *A History of Sociological Research Methods in America 1920–1960* (Cambridge: Cambridge University Press, 1996), 260–61.

3. Nancy Folbre, "The 'Sphere of Women' in Early-Twentieth-Century Economics," in *Gender and American Social Science: The Formative Years*, ed. Helene Silverberg (Princeton: Princeton University Press, 1998), 36. Estelle Freedman, using the example of Miriam Van Waters, has discussed how professional women sustained their networks with maternalist organizations. Estelle B. Freedman, "Separatism Revisited: Women's Institutions, Social Reform, and the Career of Miriam Van Waters," in *U.S. History as Women's History: New Feminist Essays*, ed. Linda Kerber, Alice Kessler-Harris, and Kathryn Kish Sklar (Chapel Hill: University of North Carolina Press, 1995), 170–88.

4. Edith Abbott, *The One Hundred and One County Jails of Illinois and Why They Ought to Be Abolished* (Chicago: Juvenile Protective Association, 1916), 20, 22; Edith Abbott, *Statistics Relating to Crime in Chicago* (Chicago: Chicago School of Civics and Philanthropy, 1915), 37–38, 43.

5. Edith Abbott, *The Experimental Period of Widows' Pension Legislation* (Chicago: University of Chicago Press, 1917), 9. See also Sophonisba Breckinridge, *The Illinois Poor Law and Its Administration* (Chicago: University of Chicago Press, 1939).

6. Edith Abbott and Sophonisba Breckinridge, *Truancy and Non-Attendance in the Chicago Schools* (Chicago: University of Chicago Press, 1917), 179, 184, 206, 226–27.

7. Sophonisba Breckinridge and Edith Abbott, *The Delinquent Child and the Home* (New York: Charities Publication Committee, 1912), 150–51. See also Sophonisba P. Breckinridge, "Chicago Housing Problem: Families in Furnished Rooms," *American Journal of Sociology* 16 (November 1910): 289–308.

8. See, for example, Clifford Shaw with Frederick M. Zorbaugh, Henry D. McKay, and Leonard S. Cottrell, *Delinquency Areas: Study of the Geographic Distribution of School Truants, Juvenile Delinquents, and Adults Offenders in Chicago* (Chicago: University of Chicago Press, 1929); T. V. Smith and Leonard D. White. eds., *Chicago: An Experiment in Social Science Research* (Chicago: University of Chicago Press, 1929); University of Chicago Local Community Research Committee, *Social Research Base Map of the City of Chicago* (Chicago: University of Chicago Press, 1926). Charlene Haddock Seigfried situates the Hull House model of social democracy within the philosophical school of pragmatism. See "Socializing Democracy: Jane Addams and John Dewey," *Philosophy of the Social Sciences* 29 (June 1999): 207–30. Mary Jo Deegan, conjoining the frameworks of "critical pragmatism" and "cultural feminism," speaks of the Hull House women's "feminist pragmatism"; Mary Jo Deegan, "The Second Sex and the Chicago School: Women's Accounts, Knowledge, and Work, 1945–1960," in *A Second Chicago School? The Development of a Postwar American Sociology*, ed. Gary Alan Fine (Chicago: University of Chicago Press, 1995), 336.

9. University of Chicago Local Community Research Committee, *Social Research Base Map*; Ernest W. Burgess, "The Determination of Gradients in the Growth of the City," *Proceedings of the American Sociologist* 21 (1927): 178–84; Robert E. Park, Ernest W. Burgess, and Roderick D. McKenzie, *The City* (Chicago: University of Chicago Press, 1925; reprt., 1967);

Robert E. Park and Ernest W. Burgess, *Introduction to the Science of Sociology* (Chicago: University of Chicago Press, 1924).

10. Allen F. Davis has discussed social reformers' class biases in *Spearheads for Reform: The Social Settlements and the Progressive Movement, 1890–1914*, 2nd ed. (New Brunswick, NJ: Rutgers University Press, 1984). Five of the ten papers published with the Hull House Maps and Papers in 1895 focused on female-related issues, including child labor and sweatshop labor. Sklar, "Hull-House Maps and Papers," 128–29.

11. William Isaac Thomas, *The Unadjusted Girl: With Cases and Standpoint for Behavioral Analysis* (Boston: Little, Brown, 1937).

12. Lela B. Costin, *Two Sisters for Social Justice: A Biography of Grace and Edith Abbott* (Urbana: University of Illinois Press, 1983), 71, 87, 89.

13. Kathryn Kish Sklar, "Who Funded Hull House?" In *Lady Bountiful Revisited: Women, Philanthropy, and Power*, ed. Kathleen D. McCarthy (New Brunswick, NJ: Rutgers University Press, 1990), 95, 97, 105, 106, 109.

14. Robert M. Mennel, "Ethel Sturges Dummer," in *Notable American Women: The Modern Period*, ed. Barbara Sicherman and Carol Hurd Green with Ilene Kantrov and Harriette Walker (Cambridge, MA: Belknap Press of Harvard University Press, 1980), 208–10.

15. State of Illinois, *Laws of the State of Illinois Enacted by the Forty-First Assembly* (Springfield, IL: Phillips Brothers, 1899), 137.

16. See, for example, Louise de Koven Bowen, *Our Most Popular Recreation Controlled by the Liquor Interests: A Study of Public Dance Halls* (Chicago: Juvenile Protective Association, 1912); and Louise de Koven Bowen, *Five and Ten Cent Theatres: Two Investigations* (Chicago: Juvenile Protective Association, 1909 and 1911). Between 1897 and 1927, over 120 surveys were conducted in Chicago. See Allen Eaton, *A Bibliography of Social Surveys: Reports of Fact-Finding Studies Made as a Basis for Social Action; Arranged by Subjects and Localities* (New York: Russell Sage Foundation, 1930); Frederick Warren Jenkins and Bertha Fairfield, comps., *Bulletin of The Russell Sage Foundation Library, No. 14: The Social Survey* (New York: The Russell Sage Foundation Library, 1915). Although sociologists did not usually conduct surveys, they often made use of their findings. See Martin Bulmer, Kevin Bales, and Kathryn Kish Sklar, "The Social Survey in Historical Perspective," in *The Social Survey in Historical Perspective, 1880–1940*, ed. Martin Bulmer, Kevin Bales, and Kathryn Kish Sklar (Cambridge: Cambridge University Press, 1991), 1–48.

17. Evans Ames Thomas, "The Sociology of William I. Thomas in Relation to the Polish Peasant" (Ph.D. diss., University of Iowa, 1986), 33, 35, 37; Fred R. Wacker, *Ethnicity, Pluralism, and Race: Race Relations Theory in America before Myrdal* (Westport, CT: Greenwood Press, 1983), 22; Martin Bulmer, "The Methodology of the Taxi-Dance Hall: An Early Account of Chicago Ethnography from the 1920s," *Urban Life* 12 (April 1983): 99; Paul Goalby Cressey, "The Closed Dance Hall in Chicago" (Master's thesis, University of Chicago, 1929); Martin Bulmer, *The Chicago School of Sociology: Institutionalization, Diversity, and the Rise of Sociological Research* (Chicago: University of Chicago Press, 1984), 47; Victoria Lynn Getis, "A Disciplined Society: The Juvenile Court, Reform, and the Social Sciences in Chicago, 1890–1930" (Ph.D. diss., University of Michigan, 1994), 25–26, 162, 167–68, 223–24; Ernest W. Burgess, "The Moral Decay of the Modern Stage," in *The 1919 National Conference of Social Work* (Chicago: Rogers and Hall, 1920), 502; Harvey, *Myths of the Chicago School of Sociology*, 36. William Thomas, as a member of the Chicago Vice Commission in 1911, also worked with club woman Ellen Henrotin, Charles Henderson, and judges. See the Vice Commission of Chicago, *The Social Evil in Chicago: A Study of Existing Conditions* (Chicago: Gunthorp-Warren, 1911).

18. Smith and White, *Chicago*, 35–36; Bulmer, *The Chicago School of Sociology*, 99.

19. Steven J. Diner, *A City and Its Universities: Public Policy in Chicago, 1892–1919* (Chapel Hill: University of North Carolina Press, 1980), 534.

20. 1920–1921 DPWAR, NU, 53. The CSCP and the SSSA are discussed more fully in chapter 3.

21. Robert E. L. Faris, *Chicago Sociology, 1920–1932* (San Francisco: Chandler, 1967), 10; Ross, "Gendered Social Knowledge," 243. Charles Zeublin, a member of the Chicago Sociology School from 1894 to 1908, was a resident of the Hull House. Virginia Kemp Fish, "Hull House: Pioneer in Urban Research During Its Creative Years," *History of Sociology* 6 (Fall 1985): 43. Dorothy Ross has argued that the early Chicago School faculty were "inspired" by the Hull House; Dorothy Ross, *The Origins of American Social Science* (Cambridge: Cambridge University Press, 1991), 226.

22. Faris, *Chicago Sociology*, 12.

23. Ibid., 52. Park was so known for his "crustiness" that some students refused to enroll in his classes; Ibid., 30. The most complete study of Park to date is Fred H. Matthews, *Quest for an American Sociology: Robert E. Park and the Chicago School* (Montreal: McGill-Queen's University Press, 1977).

24. Anthony Oberschall, cited in Barbara Ballis Lal, *The Romance of Culture in an Urban Civilization: Robert E. Park on Race and Ethnic Relations in Cities* (New York: Routledge, 1990), 17.

25. Diner, *A City and Its Universities*, 531, 536; Rolf Lindner, *The Reportage of Urban Culture: Robert Park and the Chicago School*, trans. Adrian Morris (Cambridge: Cambridge University Press, 1990), 9. The tensions of Park versus Breckinridge and Edith Abbott reflected interprofessional competition, as articulated by Andrew Abbott, *The System of Professions: An Essay on the Division of Expert Labor* (Chicago: University of Chicago Press, 1988).

26. Bulmer, *The Chicago School of Sociology*, 68.

27. Paul Goalby Cressey, "A Comparison of the Roles of the 'Sociological Stranger' and the 'Anonymous Stranger' in Field Research," *Urban Life* 12 (April 1983): 103; Bulmer, "The Methodology of the Taxi-Dance Hall": 99. Park hired Charles Johnson as a part-time researcher for the Chicago Urban League to gather information on the African-American communities of Chicago; Arvarh E. Strickland, *History of the Chicago Urban League* (Urbana: University of Illinois Press, 1966), 42. One outcome was a study following the Chicago Race Riot of 1919; see the Chicago Commission on Race Relations, *The Negro in Chicago: A Study of Race Relations and a Race Riot in 1919* (Chicago: University of Chicago Press, 1922). But Park was disillusioned by professionals who dabbled in reform, perhaps because of his involvement with the Community Center Association. From 1922 to 1924, he was president of the association, whose goal was to enact change from within the neighborhoods, not Chicago's political machinery, but Park found the social reformers in the organization ineffectual. Wacker, *Ethnicity, Pluralism, and Race*, 66.

28. Ruth Shonle Cavan, "The Chicago School of Sociology, 1918–1933," *Urban Life* 11 (January 1983): 409; James Bennett, *Oral History and Delinquency: The Rhetoric of Criminology* (Chicago: University of Chicago Press, 1981), 146. See also Platt, *A History of Sociological Research Methods*; Jennifer Platt, "The Chicago School and Firsthand Data," *History of the Human Sciences* 7 (1994): 57–80.

29. Lindner, *The Reportage of Urban Culture*, 92.

30. Ibid., 100, 62.

31. Ibid., 70.

32. Paul Goalby Cressey, cited in Steven C. Dubin, "The Moral Continuum of Deviancy Research: Chicago Sociologists and the Dance Hall," *Urban Life* 12 (April 1983): 86, 89; see also Paul Goalby Cressey, *The Taxi-Dance Hall: A Sociological Study in Commercialized Recreation and City Life* (Montclair, NJ: Patterson Smith, 1969; University of Chicago, 1932; reprt.) Thomas, *The Unadjusted Girl*, 231.

33. Dubin, "The Moral Continuum of Deviance Research": 79, 80.

34. Platt, *A History of Sociological Research Methods*, 44, 262.

35. Thomas, "The Sociology of William I. Thomas," 37; Shaw, Zorbaugh, McKay, and Cottrell, *Delinquency Areas*, x; Thomas, *The Unadjusted Girl*, 105–16, 158–92; E. Franklin Frazier, "The Negro Family in Chicago" (Ph.D. diss., University of Chicago, 1931); Platt, "The Chicago School and Firsthand Data": 57; James T. Carey, *Sociology and Public Affairs: The Chicago School* (Beverly Hills: Sage, 1975), 103.

36. Dorothy M. Brown, *American Women in the 1920s: Setting a Course* (Boston: Twayne, 1987), 36; Faris, *Chicago Sociology*, appendices A and B, 135–50. Deegan has called the time period from 1892 to 1920 the "golden era" for female sociologists, followed by the "dark era of patriarchal ascendancy." But if one examines dissertations and theses from 1920 to 1935, female sociologists articulated social welfare concerns, even if they did not act upon them. Deegan, "The Second Sex and the Chicago School," 333.

37. Faris, *Chicago Sociology*, 135–50. Some students took courses that focused on children's and women's welfare from Breckinridge and Abbott. Faris, *Chicago Sociology*, 260. To date, scholars are still recovering the contributions of early female sociologists. See, for one, Linda J. Rynbrandt, *Caroline Bartlett Crane and Progressive Reform: Social Housekeeping as Sociology* (New York: Garland, 1999).

38. Ruth Shonle Cavan, *Business Girls: A Study of Their Interests and Problems* (Chicago: Religious Education Association, 1929), 16, 21.

39. Frances R. Donovan, *The Saleslady* (Chicago: University of Chicago Press, 1929); and *The Woman Who Waits* (Boston: Gorham Press, 1920). In the preface of the latter book, Park's assessment of Donovan's work reflected his concern with methodological rigor as well as social amelioration. Although he hoped that her work would contribute to an understanding of female employment, he thought her research unsystematic and informal.

40. Thomas D. Eliot, "Objectivity and Subjectivity in the Case Record," *Social Forces* 6 (June 1928): 543. Eliot was field secretary for the American Social Hygiene Association, an organization concerned with prostitution, venereal disease, and eugenics. For further information on social work and the dilemma of professionalism, see Karen W. Tice, *Tales of Wayward Girls and Immoral Women: Case Records and the Professionalization of Social Work* (Urbana: University of Illinois Press, 1998).

41. Eliot, "Objectivity and Subjectivity in the Case Record": 542.

42. Erle Fiske Young, "The Scientific Study of Social Case Records," *Journal of Applied Sociology* 9 (January 1925): 285, 286; Eliot, "Objectivity and Subjectivity in the Case Record": 543. Mowrer considered social case records in social agencies of poor quality and thus questionable in analyzing family disorganization; Ernest W. Mowrer, *Family Disorganization: Introduction to a Sociological Analysis* (Chicago: University of Chicago Press, 1927), 187.

43. Ernest Burgess, "What Social Case Records Should Contain to Be Useful for Sociological Interpretation," *Social Forces* 6 (June 1928): 526; Ernest Burgess, "The Study of the Delinquent as a Person," *American Journal of Sociology* 28 (May 1923): 662; Maurice J. Karpf, "Sociologists and Social Workers Meet," *The Family* 9 (April 1927): 39–40; Frank J. Bruno, "Some Case Work Recording Limitations of Verbatim Reporting," *Social Forces* 6 (June 1928): 532–34.

44. Burgess, "What Social Case Records Should Contain": 526; Eliot, "Objectivity and Subjectivity in the Case Record": 541–42.

45. Eliot, "Objectivity and Subjectivity in the Case Record": 540, 543. See also Karpf, "Sociologists and Social Workers Meet": 40.

46. Burgess, "What Social Case Records Should Contain": 526.

47. Ibid.: 528.

48. Ibid.

49. See chapter 3 on probation officers' concerns with ascertaining the truth of delinquent girls' stories. The category of pathological liars, a largely female aberration, is discussed in chap-

ters 2 and 6. F. Stuart Chapin, director of the Smith College Training School for Social Work, thought that by interviewing members outside of the family, a social worker could avoid subjectivity based upon their observations. But he did not consider the subjectivities of those interviewees. F. Stuart Chapin, "The Relations of Sociology and Social Case Work," in *Proceedings of the National Probation Association* (New York: National Probation Association, 1920), 360.

50. Reed Bain, "The Impersonal Confessions and Social Research," *Journal of Applied Sociology* 9 (July 1925): 357, 358. Bain did, however, question how authentic one's "confession" could be because people often sublimated situations to present themselves in a more positive light.

51. Thomas D. Eliot, "What Social Workers Think of Sociology." *Welfare Magazine* 17 (May 1926): 38–47; Maurice J. Karpf, "Sociology and Social Work: A Retrospect," *Social Forces* 6 (June 1928): 512, 513, 515.

52. Ibid.: 516. I examined the table of contents of the issues of *Social Service Review* from 1928 to 1935 for authors' contributions.

53. Lindner, *The Reportage of Urban Culture*, 71; Erle Fisk Young, "The Social Map Base," *Journal of Applied Sociology* 9 (December 1924): 202. Park contended that there was a moral, as well as physical, organization to cities. Robert Park, "The City: Suggestions for the Investigation of Human Behavior in the Urban Environment," in Park, Burgess, and McKenzie, *The City*, 4. See also R. D. McKenzie, "The Ecological Approach to the Study of the Human Community," in *The Urban Community: Selected Papers from the Proceedings of the American Sociological Society*, 1925, ed. Ernest Burgess (Chicago: University of Chicago Press, 1926), 63–79.

54. Young, "The Social Map Base": 205; Cavan, "The Chicago School of Sociology": 412; Shaw, Zorbaugh, McKay, and Cottrell, *Delinquency Areas*; Mowrer, *Family Disorganization*; Frazier, "The Negro Family in Chicago." Drake and Cayton divided African-American neighborhoods in Chicago into four types: mixed and unadjusted, mixed and adjusted, contested areas, and segregated areas; see St. Clair Drake and Horace Cayton, *Black Metropolis* (New York: Harcourt, Brace, 1945), 180. See also R. D. McKenzie, "The Scope of Human Biology," in *The Urban Community: Selected Papers from the Proceedings of the American Sociological Society, 1925*, ed. Ernest Burgess (Chicago: University of Chicago Press, 1926), 167–82.

55. Robert Ezra Park, *The Collected Papers of Robert Ezra Park*, ed. Everett Hughes, Charles Johnson, Jitsuichi Masuoka, Robert Redfield, and Louis Wirth (Glencoe, IL: The Free Press, 1950), 359.

56. Carey, *Sociology and Public Affairs*, 104; Stow Persons, *Ethnic Studies at Chicago, 1905–1945* (Urbana: University of Illinois Press, 1987), 101. See also James B. McKee, *Sociology and the Race Problem: The Failure of a Perspective* (Urbana: University of Illinois Press, 1993), 109–11.

57. Thomas, *The Unadjusted Girl*, 4. In some cases, the strife resulted in physical violence. Elizabeth Pleck found that 94 percent of the Illinois Humane Society's case records in 1930 contained evidence of family violence. Many of the parents of these families were foreign-born; Elizabeth Pleck, "Challenge to Traditional Authority in Immigrant Families," in *The American Family in Social–Historical Perspective*, 3rd ed., ed. Michael Gordon (New York: St. Martin's Press, 1983), 505. Jane Addams's elaboration of young girl's desire for adventure and recognition, the latter vivified through her clothing, especially the "huge hat, with its wilderness of bedraggled feathers," preceded Thomas's articulation of the adolescent girl's four wishes. See Jane Addams, *The Spirit of Youth and the City Streets* (New York: Macmillan, 1909; reprt., Urbana: University of Illinois Press, 1972), 8, and chap. 3.

58. William I. Thomas, "Race Psychology: Standpoint and Questionnaire, with Particular Reference to the Immigrant and the Negro," *American Journal of Sociology* 17 (May 1912): 767.

59. Park, *The Collected Papers*, 267. John Stanfield argues that Park transplanted Booker T. Washington's ideology to the Chicago School model but that perspective does not do justice to the complexity of Park's theories. John H. Stanfield, *Philanthropy and Jim Crow in American Social Science* (Westport, CT: Greenwood Press, 1985). Of course, one could well ask why the sociologists did not question whether Appalachian whites had their own homeland.

60. Wacker, *Ethnicity, Pluralism, and Race*, 42, 45; Benjamin P. Bowser, "The Contributions of Blacks to Sociological Knowledge: A Problem of Theory and Role to 1950," *Phylon* 42 (Summer 1981): 180–93; Stanfield, *Philanthropy and Jim Crow*, 24; W. E. B. Du Bois, *Dusk of Dawn: As Essay toward an Autobiography of a Race Concept* (New York: Schocken Books, 1968), 64–65.

61. E. Franklin Frazier, *The Negro Family in Chicago* (Chicago: University of Chicago Press, 1932), 30; E. Franklin Frazier, "Family Disorganization among Negroes," *Opportunity* 9 (July 1931): 205; Elliott Ruddick, "W. E. B. DuBois as Sociologist," in *Black Sociologists: Historical and Contemporary Perspectives*, ed. James E. Blackwell and Morris Janowitz (Chicago: University of Chicago Press, 1974), 31, 33. Franklin referred to the economic aspects that affected African-American families' integration in "Is the Negro Family a Unique Sociological Unit?" *Opportunity* 5 (June 1927): 165–66. Here he also refuted the notion of instincts, especially those pertaining to sexual behaviors. See also Gail Bederman, *Manliness and Civilization: A Cultural History of Gender and Race in the United States, 1880–1917* (Chicago: University of Chicago Press, 1995), 31–41. One reason why African Americans could not assimilate was because of the inferior education promoted by philanthropists and missionaries in the South. See E. Franklin Frazier, "A Note on Negro Education," *Opportunity* 2 (March 1924): 77. Frazier also examined the pathology of race prejudice in "The Pathology of Race Prejudice," *Forum* 77 (June 1927): 856–61.

62. Edward Reuter believed that antipathy was natural, whereas prejudice was socially acquired; Reuter, cited in W. O. Brown, "Race Prejudice: A Sociological Study" (Ph.D. diss., University of Chicago, 1930), 10–11; W. O. Brown, "The Negro Problem: A Sociological Interpretation," *Opportunity* 8 (November 1930): 330–31. See also W. O. Brown, "Culture Contact and Race Conflict," in *Race and Culture Contacts*, ed. Edward B. Reuter (New York: McGraw-Hill, 1934), 34–47. Frazier was less concerned with assimilation than with integration. See G. Franklin Edwards, "E. Franklin Frazier," In *Black Sociologists: Historical and Contemporary Perspectives*, ed. James E. Blackwell and Morris Janowitz (Chicago: University of Chicago Press, 1974), 101–2; Anthony M. Platt, *E. Franklin Frazier Reconsidered* (New Brunswick, NJ: Rutgers University Press, 1991). Park, too, was aware that African Americans could not assimilate because of differences in skin color. He did not think of assimilation in terms of equality as much as ethnic groups working toward common "American" goals. Ross, *The Origins of American Social Science*, 360–361.

63. Jules Karlan, *Chicago: Backgrounds of Education* (Chicago: Werkman's Book House, 1940), 160–61; Stuart Alfred Queen, Walter Blaine Bodenhafer, and Ernest Bouldin Harper, *Social Organization and Disorganization* (New York: Thomas Y. Crowell, 1935), 538–39.

64. Karlan, *Chicago*, 160, 256–57; Queen, Bodenhafer, and Harper, *Social Organization and Disorganization*, 160–61.

65. Karlan, *Chicago*, 100–105, 155; Queen, Bodenhafer, and Harper, *Social Organization and Disorganization*, 235. See Kimball Young, "A Sociological Study of a Disintegrated Neighborhood" (Master's thesis, University of Chicago, 1918), 42; and Norman S. Hayner, "Hotel Life and Personality," *American Journal of Sociology* 33 (March 1928): 784–95. Nearly 60 percent of couples living together in one Lower North Side neighborhood in zone 2 were not married. Harvey W. Zorbaugh, "The Dweller in Furnished Rooms: An Urban Type," in *The Urban Community: Selected Papers from the Proceedings of the American Sociological Society, 1925*, ed. Ernest Burgess (Chicago: University of Chicago Press, 1926), 100–101. See also Harvey W. Zorbaugh's classic sociological work, *The Gold Coast and the Slum* (Chicago: University of Chicago Press, 1929).

66. Smith and White, *Chicago*, 114–15; Breckinridge, "Chicago Housing Problem": 293.

67. Shaw, Zorbaugh, McKay, and Cottrell, *Delinquency Areas*, 23–32. The researchers did acknowledge that differences in male delinquency rates could have been skewed by wealthier parents who paid off police. But they argued that the more serious crimes of burglary and

arson were not committed by boys in wealthier neighborhoods but poorer ones. Faris, *Chicago School*, 75.

68. Shaw, Zorbaugh, McKay, and Cottrell, *Delinquency Areas*, 204, 205. Park thought that delinquency resulted, to some degree, from community organizations' dysfunctionality. Robert Park, "Community Organization and Juvenile Delinquency," in *The City*, eds. Robert E. Park, Ernest W. Burgess, and Roderick D. McKenzie (Chicago: University of Chicago Press, 1925), 106.

69. Shaw, Zorbaugh, McKay, and Cottrell, *Delinquency Areas*, 23–32; Betty Marwood Hill, "A Comparative Study of Delinquency in Four National Groups in Cook County Juvenile Court of 1930" (Master's thesis, University of Chicago, 1932), 71, 74, 79, 80. Elaborating on the "old world traits" theory, Hill discussed how cultural aspects influenced delinquent behaviors. For example, Italian-American male gangs and their affiliations with the mafia encouraged trouble with the police. On the other hand, Italian-American girls, closely protected at home, had lower delinquency rates than their male counterparts. Hill, "A Comparative Study of Delinquency," 80–81. Sociologist Mabel Agnes Elliott noted that most male and female delinquents lived in heterogeneous immigrant neighborhoods, but she did not examine dispersion as Hill did. See Mabel Agnes Elliott, "A Correlation between Rate of Juvenile Delinquency and Racial Heterogeneity," *Welfare Magazine* 17 (July 1926): 5–15.

70. E. Franklin Frazier, "Chicago: A Cross-Section of Negro Life," *Opportunity* 7 (March 1929): 71; Earl R. Moses, *The Negro Delinquent in Chicago* (Washington, DC,: Washington Public Schools, 1936), 47. See also Earl R. Moses, "Delinquency in the Negro Community," *Opportunity* 11 (October 1933): 304–307.

71. Queen, Bodenhafer, and Harper, *Social Organization and Disorganization*, 244; Frazier, "The Negro Family in Chicago," 100, 111, 124, 130; Karlan, *Chicago*, 99. To be discussed more fully in chapter 5, African-American male and female delinquent youth were overrepresented in Chicago's juvenile court. By 1929, 25 percent of all female delinquents brought to the juvenile court in Chicago were African American. Moses, *The Negro Delinquent in Chicago*, 77; Frazier, "The Negro Family in Chicago," 243.

71. Frazier, "The Negro Family in Chicago," 115, 124, 130, 206; Ethel Ramsey Harris, "A Study of Voluntary Social Activity Among the Professional Negroes in Chicago" (Master's thesis, University of Chicago, 1937), 37.

72. Ernest R. Groves, *The American Family* (Chicago: J. B. Lippincott, 1934); Ronald L. Howard, "Sociology and the Family in the Progressive Era, 1890–1920," in *A Sociology History of American Family Sociology, 1865–1940*, ed. John Mogey (Westport, CT: Greenwood Press, 1981), 42; Paula S. Fass, *The Damned and the Beautiful: American Youth in the 1920s* (New York: Oxford University Press, 1977), 108.

73. Burgess, quoted in White and Smith, Chicago, 185.

74. Ronald L. Howard, "From Ecology to Interaction: Family Sociology in the 1920s and 1930s," in *A Sociology History of American Family Sociology, 1865–1940*, ed. John Mogey (Westport, CT: Greenwood Press, 1981), 68; Howard, "Sociology and the Family," 44–45.

75. Christopher Lasch, "Social Pathologists and the Socialization of Reproduction," in *The American Family in Social-Historical Perspective*, 3rd ed., ed. Michael Gordon (New York: St. Martin's Press, 1983), 83. University of Chicago sociologist William Ogburn noted that in 1922, of every 76 marriages, 10 ended in divorce; by 1928, it was 10 in 60. William F. Ogburn, "The Changing Family with Regard to the Child," *Annals of the American Academy* 151 (September 1930): 22.

76. Ernest Burgess, "The Moral Decay of the Modern Stage," in *The 1919 National Conference of Social Work* (Chicago: Rogers and Hall Company, 1920), 503.

77. Moses, *The Negro Delinquent in Chicago*, 36, 369, 372. Moses may have been influenced by Frazier, who spoke of the close bonds between mothers and their children. See E.

Franklin Frazier, "Traditions and Patterns of Negro Family Life in the United States," in *Race and Culture Contacts*, ed. Edward B. Reuter (New York: McGraw-Hill, 1934), 195. One popular idea in family sociology and social work was the "democratic" family. One sociologist, for example, asked whether it was democratic for daughters or sons to give their wages to their parents. Day Monroe, *Chicago Families: A Study of Unpublished Census Data* (Chicago: University of Chicago Press, 1932), 172–73.

78. Margaret Hogkiss, "The Influence of Broken Homes and Working Mothers," *Smith College Studies in Social Work* 13 (March 1933): 265. According to her, 75 percent of delinquent girls, most of them of African-American and foreign parentage, came from broken homes.

79. Monroe, *Chicago Families*, 45, 81; Gertrude Eileen Sager, "Immigration: Based upon a Study of the Italian Women and Girls of Chicago" (Master's thesis, University of Chicago, 1914), 26; Alice Quan Rood, "Social Conditions Among the Negroes on Federal Street between Forty-Fifth Street and Fifty-Third Street" (Master's thesis, University of Chicago, 1924), 36–37; Frazier, "Chicago: A Cross-Section": 71.

80. Irene Graham, "Family Support and Dependency among Chicago Negroes: A Study of Unpublished Census Data," *Social Service Review* 3 (December 1929): 547, 551. Graham was a research assistant and graduate student with the SSSA. Sociologist Gertrude Eileen Sager, too, spoke of how the presence of lodgers led to immorality and broken families; Sager, "Immigration," 26. Graham preferred the term *household* to *family*, a more accurate term for describing many African Americans' residential arrangements; see Irene Graham, "The Negro Family in a Northern City," *Opportunity* 8 (February 1930): 48. Frazier noted how many African-American domestic workers at hotels watched white people "on parade" and so acquired their bad habits. See E. Franklin Frazier, "Three Scourges of the Negro Family," *Opportunity* 4 (July 1926): 212.

81. In her analysis, Hill found that the Swedish, followed by the German and Irish, scored highest in family disorganization, even when they lived in low-delinquency communities; Hill, "A Comparative Study of Delinquency," 6, 43, 86.

82. Faris, *Chicago Sociology*, 74; Shaw, Zorbaugh, McKay, and Cottrell, *Delinquency Areas*, 139–42.

83. Thomas, *The Unadjusted Girl*, 231. See also Morris Janowitz, ed., *W. I. Thomas on Social Organization and Social Personality: Selected Papers* (Chicago: University of Chicago Press, 1966). On the interactive nature of individual personalities and society, see Charles Johnson, "Negro Personality Changes in a Southern Community," in *Race and Culture Contacts*, ed. Edward B. Reuter (New York: McGraw-Hill, 1934), 208; Queen, Bodenhafer, and Harper, *Social Organization and Disorganization*, 455; Thomas, *The Unadjusted Girl*, xvii. Robert E. Farris and Warren Dunham, in their structural analysis of mental disorders, found schizophrenia more prevalent in the poor and disorganized areas of the city; see their *Mental Disorders in Urban Areas: An Ecological Study of Schizophrenia and Other Psychoses* (New York: Hafner, 1960), 76.

84. Bennett, *Oral History and Delinquency*, 133; Thomas, *The Unadjusted Girl*, 244, 250–51, 253.

85. One volume of *The Polish Peasant in Europe and America* was devoted to a full autobiography of a Polish immigrant in the United States.

86. William I. Thomas and Florian Znaniecki, *The Polish Peasant in Europe and America*, ed. Eli Zaretsky (Urbana: University of Illinois Press, 1996); Thomas, "The Sociology of W. I. Thomas," 112; Thomas, *The Unadjusted Girl*, 86; Robert M. Mennel, *Thorns and Thistles: Juvenile Delinquents in the United States, 1825–1940* (Hanover, NH: University Press of New England, 1973), 185.

87. William I. Thomas, *Sex and Society: Studies in the Social Psychology of Sex* (Chicago: University of Chicago, 1907), 215–16.

88. Havelock Ellis, *Studies in the Psychology of Sex*, 3rd ed. (Philadelphia: F. A. Davis, 1929), 41; W. I. Thomas, "Adventitious Character of Woman," *American Journal of Sociology* 12 (July 1906): 40; Thomas, *Sex and Society*, 112, 208–9, 233, 234; Thomas, *The Unadjusted Girl*, 109.

89. The only reason that more girls did not become adventuresses was the "inhibitive effects" of their upbringing. Thomas, "The Adventitious Character of Woman": 41; Thomas, *Sex and Society*, 101−2, 244, 243.

90. Elizabeth Lunbeck, *The Psychiatric Persuasion: Knowledge, Gender, and Power in Modern America* (Princeton: Princeton University Press, 1994).

91. Thomas, *Sex and Society*, 241; Thomas, "The Adventitious Character of Woman": 42.

92. Mennel, *Thorns and Thistles*, 186; Faris, *Chicago Sociology*, 14.

93. Thomas, *The Unadjusted Girl*, 8−9.

94. Evelyn Buchan, "The Delinquency of Girls" (Master's thesis, University of Chicago, 1922), 13, 15, 24.

95. Zorbaugh, "The Dweller in Furnished Rooms," 102.

Chapter 2

1. Carrol Smith-Rosenberg, "Discourse of Sexuality and Subjectivity: The New Woman, 1870−1936," in *Hidden from History: Reclaiming the Gay and Lesbian Past*, ed. Martin Bauml Duberman, Martha Vicinus, and George Chauncey Jr., (New York: New American Library, 1981), 269.

2. Michel Foucault, *Power/Knowledge: Selected Interviews and Other Writings, 1972−1977,* ed. Colin Gordon (New York: Pantheon Books, 1977), 37. See also Foucault's *The History of Sexuality: An Introduction*, vol 1. (New York: Vintage Books, 1990).

3. One doctor, influenced by Ethel Dummer's hypothesis about feeblemindedness, suggested that delinquent girls' low intelligence may have resulted from "inhibited mental activity" produced by profound emotional shock in childhood. Ethel S. Dummer, *Why I Think So: The Autobiography of an Hypothesis* (Chicago: Clarke-McElroy, n.d.), 151. For how narratives about the past are shaped through psychoanalysis, see Donald E. Polkinghorne, *Narrative Knowing and the Human Science* (Albany: State University of New York Press, 1988); and Donald Spence, *Narrative Truth and Historical Truth: Meaning and Interpretation in Psychoanalysis* (New York: W. W. Norton, 1982). Regarding the history of psychoanalysis in the United States, see Mary Jo Buhle, *Feminism and Its Discontents: A Century of Struggle with Psychoanalysis* (Cambridge, MA: Harvard University Press, 1988).

4. Healy, *The Individual Delinquent: A Textbook of Diagnosis and Prognosis for All Concerned in Understanding Offenders* (Boston: Little, Brown, 1929).

5. Foucault, *Power/Knowledge*, 110, 126; Foucault, *The History of Sexuality*, 29, 41−47.

6. Albert Ellis Webster, "The Relation of the Saloon to Juvenile Delinquency" (Master's thesis, University of Chicago, 1912), 11.

7. Ibid.

8. White House Conference on Child Health and Protection, *The Delinquent Child* (New York: The Century Company, 1932), 28; Mabel Carter Rhoades, *A Case Study of Delinquent Boys in the Juvenile Court of Chicago* (Chicago: University of Chicago Press, 1907), 15, 16−17.

9. Following a Boasian turn, anthropometry was used by a number of anthropologists, including Melville Herskovits and Margaret Mead. Some anthropometric studies did acknowledge correlations among children's heights and weights and their home conditions. Not surprisingly, those children living in overcrowded and impoverished conditions had the smallest weights and heights. See Franz Boas, "Growth and Development, Bodily and Mental, As Determined by Heredity and by Social Environment," in *The Child, the Clinic and the Court* (New York: New Republic, 1925), 178−88; Lee D. Baker, *From Savage to Negro: Anthropology and the Construction of Race, 1896−1954* (Berkeley and Los Angeles: University of California Press, 1998), 182.

10. William Healy and Augusta F. Bronner, *New Light on Delinquency and Its Treatment* (New Haven: Yale University Press, 1936), 7, 38. See also Healy, *The Individual Delinquent*; Augusta F. Bronner, William Healy, Gladys M. Lowe, and Myra E. Shimberg, *A Manual of Individual Mental Tests and Testing* (Boston: Little, Brown, 1938). Healy's examinations closely followed Walter Fernald's ten-point scale in its inclusion of developmental, family, medical, school progress histories and psychological tests. Ransom A. Greene, M.D., "Progress in Understanding and Control of the Feeble-Minded," *Annals of the American Academy* 151 (September 1930): 131.

11. Henry Goddard's study cited in Truman Lee Kelley, *Mental Aspects of Delinquency* (Austin: University of Texas Press, 1917), 59, 95; Peter Tylor, "Denied the Power to Choose the Good: Sexuality and Mental Defect in American Medical Practice 1850–1920," *Journal of Social History* 10 (June 1977): 481. See Augusta F. Bronner, *A Comparative Study of the Intelligence of Delinquent Girls* (New York: Teachers College, Columbia University, 1914).

12. Studies by Margaret Otis and C. S. Bluemel cited in Kelley, *Mental Aspects of Delinquency*, 61, 87–88. Even Truman Kelley, who created standardized achievement tests, thought delinquent girls were more mentally backward than delinquent boys; Kelley, *Mental Aspects of Delinquency*, 60.

13. Healy and Bronner, *New Light on Delinquency and Its Treatment*, 52; Victoria Lynn Getis, "A Disciplined Society," 189.

14. Henry Goddard, cited in Stuart Alfred Queen, Walter Blaine Bodenhafer, and Ernest Boudlin Harper, *Social Organization and Disorganization* (New York: Thomas Y. Crowell, 1935), 509; Paul Hanly Furfey, *Social Problems of Childhood* (New York: Macmillan, 1929), 95–96.

15. Herman M. Adler, M.D., "Our Responsibility for the Future," in *The Child, the Clinic and the Court* (New York: New Republic, 1925), 68.

16. James W. Trent, Jr., *Inventing the Feeble Mind: A History of Mental Retardation in the United States* (Berkeley and Los Angeles: University of California Press, 1994); Steven Noll, *Feeble-Minded in Our Midst: Institutions for the Mentally Retarded in the South, 1900–1940* (Chapel Hill: University of North Carolina Press, 1995); Philip R. Reilly, *The Surgical Solution: A History of Involuntary Sterilization in the United States* (Baltimore: Johns Hopkins University Press, 1991).

17. Henry Goddard, cited in Trent, *Inventing the Feeble Mind*, 168. Some persons recommended sterilization not only for feebleminded women but for nymphomaniacs. Knight Dunlap, *Personal Beauty and Racial Betterment* (St. Louis: C. V. Mosby, 1920), 62, 66. Chicago professional maternalists were noticeably silent on the issue of sterilization. Julia Lathrop argued only that segregated institutions were critical for certain populations. Edith Abbott spoke of how sterilization resulted in more extreme physical effects for females than males, especially "artificial menopause"; but she did not necessarily voice disapproval. Julia C. Lathrop, "The Defective Child and the Juvenile Court," in *The Child in the City: A Series of Papers Presented at the Conferences Held during the Chicago Child Welfare Exhibit*, ed. Sophonisba Breckinridge (Chicago: Department of Social Investigation, Chicago School of Civics and Philanthropy, 1925), 224. Edith Abbott, "Sterilization of Mental Defectives," box 25, folder 11, EGA, UCSC.

18. John Edward Ransom, *A Study of Mentally Defective Children in Chicago* (Chicago: Juvenile Protective Association, 1914), 48. The juvenile court could not commit a person to the colony but could only recommend that parents or guardians do so.

19. David H. Orro, "Judge Exposes Mistake; Dixon Heads Blamed," *Chicago Defender*, October 5, 1940.

20. Augusta Bronner cited in James Bennett, *Oral History and Delinquency: The Rhetoric of Criminology* (Chicago: University of Chicago Press, 1981), 115.

21. William Healy and Mary Tenney Healy, *Pathological Lying, Accusation, and Swindling* (Boston: Little, Brown, 1926), 266.

22. See The Illinois Revised Statutes 1925, chap. 23, section 346, cited in Elizabeth Caroline Davis, "State Institutional Care of the Feebleminded in Illinois," (Master's thesis, University of Chicago, 1926), 110; Arthur B. Spingarn, *Laws Relating to Sex Morality in New York City* (New York: The Century Company, 1926), 115; Howard Becker, "Mental Subnormality and the Local Community: An Outline of a Practical Program," *Social Service Review* 6 (June 1932): 256–59; Arnold Gesell, "Handicapped School Children," in *Guidance of Childhood and Youth*, ed. Benjamin C. Gruenberg (New York: Macmillan, 1927), 298.

23. Harrison A. Dobbs, "Institutional Care for Delinquent Children: A New Appraisal," *Annals of the American Academy* 151 (September 1930): 174–75; Gertrude Louise Runyon, "State Institutional Care of the Epileptic in Illinois" (Master's thesis, University of Chicago, 1931), 59. Nonetheless, this did not rule out the advisability of legal sterilization. Greene, "Progress in Understanding and Control of the Feeble-Minded": 136.

24. Davis, "State Institutional Care of the Feebleminded in Illinois," 123; Herman M. Adler, "Prevention of Delinquency and Criminality by Psychiatry," *Welfare Magazine* 17 (January 1926): 200–1.

25. Elizabeth Lunbeck, *The Psychiatric Persuasion: Knowledge, Gender, and Power in Modern America* (Princeton: Princeton University Press, 1994), 302, 517, 524. That most of the female patients in the Boston Psychopathic Hospital were native-born whites employed as domestic or factory workers suggests class biases. Winifred Richmond, Ph.D., *The Adolescent Girl: A Book for Parents and Teachers* (New York: Macmillan, 1925), 89.

26. Henry Herbert Goddard, *Juvenile Delinquency* (New York: Dodd, Mead, 1921), 27, 32, 41, 44–46; Henry Goddard and Helen F. Hill, "Delinquent Girls Tested by the Binet Scale," *Training School Bulletin* 8 (1911): 50–56; Henry Herbert Goddard, *Feeble Mindedness: Its Causes and Consequences* (New York: Macmillan, 1914).

27. Ernest R. Groves, "Juvenile Delinquency," in *Guidance of Childhood and Youth*, ed. Benjamin C. Gruenberg (New York: Macmillan, 1927), 309; Richmond, *The Adolescent Girl*, 87–88.

28. Lunbeck, *The Psychiatric Persuasion*, 523.

29. Phyllis Blanchard and Carlyn Manasses, *New Girls for Old* (New York: Macaulay, 1930), 514. Blanchard, a former student of G. Stanley Hall, lectured at the Pennsylvania School of Social and Health Work and was a psychologist for the Philadelphia Child Guidance Clinic. Like sociologists, she utilized historical and anthropological literature in her discussion of female sexuality.

30. Davis, "State Institutional Care of the Feebleminded in Illinois," 103–4.

31. William I. Thomas and Dorothy Swaine Thomas, *A Child in America: Behavior Problems and Programs* (New York: Alfred A. Knopf, 1928), 443; Runyon, "State Institutional Care of the Epileptic in Illinois," 121–22; A. Myerson, M.D., "Hysteria as a Weapon in Marital Conflicts," *Journal of Abnormal and Social Psychology* 10 (1915–1916): 4. See also L. E. Emerson, "A Psychoanalytic Study of a Severe Case of Hysteria," *Journal of Abnormal and Social Psychology* 7 (February–March 1913): 385–406.

32. Healy and Healy, *Pathological Lying, Accusation, and Swindling*, 114, 117, 126, 134, 214, 244, 249, 268, 262.

33. Histories of homosexuality and lesbianism include Jeffrey Weeks, "Movements of Affirmation: Sexual Meanings and Homosexual Identities," in *Passion and Power: Sexuality in History*, eds. Kathy Peiss and Christina Simmons with Robert A. Padgug (Philadelphia: Temple University Press, 1989); George Chauncey Jr., "From Sexual Inversion to Homosexuality: The Changing Medical Conceptualization of Female 'Deviance,'" in *Passion and Power: Sexuality in History*, eds. Kathy Peiss and Christina Simmons with Robert A. Padgug (Philadelphia: Temple University Press, 1989); John D'Emilio and Estelle Freedman, *Intimate Matters: A History of Sexuality in America* (New York: Harper and Row, 1988); George Chauncey Jr., *Gay New York: Gender, Urban Culture, and the Making of the Gay Male World, 1890–1940* (New York: Basic Books, 1994).

34. Lewis M. Terman and Catharine Cox Miles, *Sex and Personality: Studies in Masculinity and Femininity* (New York: McGraw-Hill, 1936), 23, 35, 40, 322–25, 344. G. Stanley Hall, too, agreed that coyness and modesty were age-old female traits; G. Stanley Hall, *Adolescence: Its Psychology and Its Relations to Physiology, Anthropology, Sex, Crime, Religion and Education*, vol. 2 (New York: D. Appleton, 1904), 116.

35. Blanchard and Manasses, in their survey of college and working girls, found that only 20 percent approved of petting. But one must be skeptical of such self-reporting. Many of the girls did acknowledge that they engaged in "exploratory activity," although they did not specify what that included. Petting was one way "to be safe and yet not sorry." Blanchard and Manasses, *New Girls for Old*, 69–70. Ira S. Wile, "The Sex Problems of Youth," *Journal of Social Hygiene* 16 (October 1930): 426, 427. Wile was a lecturer on educational hygiene at New York University and Columbia University.

36. Hall, *Adolescence*, 73.

37. This idea was expressed by Ellis as well. See Ellis, *Studies in the Psychology of Sex*, 261.

38. R. P. Neuman, "Masturbation, Madness, and the Modern Concepts of Childhood and Adolescence," *Journal of Social History* 8 (Spring 1975): 14. In advocating for abstinence, G. Stanley Hall argued that masturbation required more energy than sexual intercourse to produce the same amount of pleasure, hence the source of neurosis; Neuman, "Masturbation, Madness, and the Modern Concepts of Childhood and Adolescence": 16. Katharine Davis sent questionnaires to ten thousand women, most of whom were members of the General Federation of Women's Clubs and graduates of women's colleges. She appealed to their intelligence in requesting that they answer questions about their sex experiences. In her words, "Norms based upon the experiences of large numbers of intelligent individuals have never been established, yet they are fundamental to any sound educational program." Katharine Bement Davis, Ph.D., *Factors in the Sex Life of Twenty-Two Hundred Women* (New York: Harper and Brothers, 1929), chap. 6, 95.

39. Blanchard and Manasses, *New Girls for Old*, 33, 35; Walter M. Gallichan, *Sexual Apathy and Coldness in Women* (Boston: Stratford, 1930), 96; Robert Latou Dickinson and Lura Beam, *The Single Woman: A Medical Study in Sex Education* (Baltimore: Williams and Wilkins, 1934), 179, 192, 238, 239, 121.

40. Floyd Dell, *Love without Money*, (New York: Farrar and Rinehart, 1931), 7. Gallichan noted that "cold-natured" women were those most often involved in social reform, including "female emancipation crusades, purity campaigns, and societies for the suppression of vice." Gallichan, *Sexual Apathy and Coldness in Women*, 12–13.

41. Mrs. M. M. Pierce, "The Study of A Delinquent Girl," box 79, folder 7, EB, UCSC.

42. Chauncey, "From Sexual Inversion to Homosexuality," 104; Smith-Rosenberg, "Discourse of Sexuality and Subjectivity," 267–68.

43. Gallichan, *Sexual Apathy and Coldness in Women*, 32, 33, 138. Havelock Ellis believed that in the cases of married women, especially those who were highly intellectual, excessive masturbation often led to frigidity and the subsequent demise of their marriages; Ellis, *Studies in the Psychology of Sex*, 261.

44. Edith Livingston Smith and Hugh Cabot, M.D., "A Study in Sexual Morality," *Journal of Social Hygiene* 2 (October 1916): 529, 530, 538. Hugh Cabot was a doctor at the Massachusetts General Hospital and Harvard Medical School.

45. David F. Greenberg, *The Constructions of Homosexuality* (Chicago: University of Chicago Press, 1988); D'Emilio and Freedman, *Intimate Matters*, 224; Judith Staiger, *Bad Women: Regulating Sexuality in Early American Cinema* (Minneapolis: University of Minnesota Press, 1995), 43; Weeks, "Movements of Affirmation," 99. See also Siobhan Somerville, "Scientific Racism and the Emergence of the Homosexual Body," *Journal of the History of Sexuality* 5 (Summer 1994): 243–66.

46. Chauncey, "From Sexual Inversion to Homosexuality," 100, 101.

47. Helen T. Woolley, "Personality Trends in Children," in *The Child, the Clinic and the Court* (New York: New Republic, 1925), 59; Douglas A. Thom, M. D., *Normal Youth and Its Everyday Problems* (New York: D. Appleton-Century Company, 1932), 64.

48. Wile, "The Sex Problem of Youth": 416, 417; Lillian Faderman, *Odd Girls and Twilight Lovers: A History of Lesbian Life in Twentieth-Century America* (New York: Columbia University Press, 1991), 89; Greenberg, *The Constructions of Homosexuality*, 424; Blanchard and Manasses, *New Girls for Old*, 104; Richmond, *The Adolescent Girl*, 124–25; Ira S. Wile, "Sex and Normal Human Nature," in *Sex in Civilization*, ed. V. F. Calverton and S. D. Schmalhausen (New York: Macaulay, 1929), 608–9.

49. Wile, "The Sex Problem of Youth": 415; William A. McKeever, *Training the Girl* (New York: Macmillan, 1916), 160.

50. Davis, *Factors in the Sex Life of Twenty-Two Hundred Women*, chap. 10; Blanchard and Manasses, *New Girls for Old*, 99.

51. John Chynoweth Burnham, "The New Psychology: From Narcissism to Social Control," in *Change and Continuity in Twentieth-Century America: The 1920s*, ed. John Braeman, Robert H. Bremner, and David Brody (Columbus: Ohio State University Press, 1968), 381. Even Margaret Mead noted the profound influence of magazines and films that "paraded" multiple freedoms before youth. Unlike Samoan girls, American girls had too many choices, including different standards of morality. Yet Mead's book *Coming of Age in Samoa* succumbed to the publisher's pressures to make the Samoan girls' sexuality instructive to American readers. Margaret Mead, *Coming of Age in Samoa* (New York: Morrow Quill Paperbacks, 1928), 196.

Chapter 3

1. State of Illinois, *Laws of the State of Illinois Enacted by the Forty-First Assembly* (Springfield: Phillips Brothers, 1988), 137; Timothy Hurley, "Origins of the Illinois Juvenile Court Law," in *The Child, the Clinic, and the Court* (New York: New Republic, 1925), 62. There is little scholarship about the work of probation officers; see Lorna F. Hurl and David Tucker, "The Michigan County Agents and the Development of Juvenile Probation, 1873–1900," *Journal of Social History* 30 (Summer 1997): 907–35.

2. CWCMR, Dec. 28, 1898, box 21, file 1, CHS. See also Julia C. Lathrop, "The Background of the Juvenile Court in Illinois," in *The Child, the Clinic, and the Court* (New York: New Republic, 1925), 290–297.

3. This term, again, is from Robyn Muncy, *Creating a Female Dominion in American Reform, 1890–1935* (Oxford: Oxford University Press, 1991).

4. Henriette Greenebaum Frank and Amalie Hofer Jerome, *Annals of the Chicago Woman's Club* (Chicago: Chicago Woman's Club, 1916), 181, 190.

5. Ibid., 228; Elisabeth Parker, "Personnel and Organization in the Probation Department of the Juvenile Court of Cook County (1899–1933)," (Master's thesis, University of Chicago, 1934), 7–8; Louise de Koven Bowen, *Growing Up with A City* (New York: Macmillan, 1926), 104–6; Mrs. Joseph T. [Louise de Koven] Bowen, "The Early Days of the Juvenile Court," in *The Child, the Clinic, and the Court* (New York: New Republic, 1925), 298–309. Kawin reports that the first probation officer, most likely Alzina Stevens, when asked about her district, exclaimed, "Oh, it begins at the lake and extends to the horizon." Ethel Kawin, "Anniversary of the Founding of the First Juvenile Court and the Establishment of the First Institute for Juvenile Research," *Institution Quarterly* 16 (March 1925): 95.

6. Parker, "Personnel and Organization in the Probation Department," 13, 88. By 1906, Emma Quinlan supervised nearly 240 volunteers.

7. Cited in Roy Lubove, *The Professional Altruist* (Cambridge, MA: Harvard University Press, 1965), 140.

8. Anne Meis Knupfer, *Toward a Tenderer Humanity and a Nobler Womanhood: African American Women's Clubs in Turn-of-the-Century Chicago* (New York: New York University Press, 1996), 71–72; Parker, "Personnel and Organization in the Probation Department," 18, 35.

9. 1906 CCJCAR, HWL, 4.

10. Parker, "Personnel and Organization in the Probation Department," 11, 14, 15; Knupfer, *Toward a Tenderer Humanity and a Nobler Womanhood*, 72–76; see also box 2, folder 15, JPAP, UICSC; 1915–1931 JPAAR, NU; Louise de Koven Bowen, *Five and Ten Cent Theatres: Two Investigations* (Chicago: Juvenile Protective Association, 1909 and 1911); *The Department Store Girl: Based Upon Interviews with 200 Girls* (Chicago: Juvenile Protective Association, 1911); *The Girl Employed in Hotels and Restaurants* (Chicago: Juvenile Protective Association, 1912); *Our Most Popular Recreation Controlled by the Liquor Interests: A Study of Public Dance Halls* (Chicago: Juvenile Protective Association, 1912).

11. Parker, "Personnel and Organization in the Probation Department," 121; Sophonisba P. Breckinridge, "Social Workers in Cook County Courts," *Social Service Review* 12 (June 1938): 237. See also Belle Boone Beard, *Juvenile Probation* (New York: American Book Company); and Don S. Kirschner, *The Paradox of Professionalism: Reform and Public Service in Urban America, 1900–1940* (Westport, CT: Greenwood Press, 1986).

12. Charles L. Chute, "The Needs and Future of the Probation Service," in *The Social Service of the Courts: Proceedings of the Sixteenth Annual Conference of the National Probation Association* (New York: National Probation Association, 1923), 27; Parker, "Personnel and Organization in the Probation Department," 60.

13. George B. Mangold, *Problems of Child Welfare* (New York: Macmillan, 1928), 442. Hannah Kent Schoff, president of the National Congress of Mothers (and later the Parent-Teacher Association), as well as president of the Philadelphia Juvenile Court and Probation Association, thought that probation officers should be selected from those who had "devoted" their lives to child nurture. Hannah Kent Schoff, *The Wayward Child: A Study of the Causes of Crime* (Indianapolis: Bobbs-Merrill, 1915), 234.

14. Mangold, *Problems of Child Welfare*, 234, 236; David John Hogan, *Class and Reform: School and Society in Chicago, 1880–1930* (Philadelphia: University of Pennsylvania Press, 1985), 64; Steven Schlossman, *Love and the American Delinquent: The Theory and Practice of "Progressive" Juvenile Justice, 1825–1920* (Chicago: University of Chicago Press, 1977), 61.

15. Clara E. Laughlin, *The Work-a-Day Girl* (New York: F. H. Revell, 1913; reprt., New York: Arno Press, 1974), 26.

16. Bowen, "Early Days of the Juvenile Court," 300.

17. Eleonore L. Hutzel, *The Policewoman's Handbook* (New York: Columbia University Press, 1933). The same attire was recommended for probation officers; see John J. Gasgoyne, "Standards of Probation Work," in *The Social Service of the Courts: Proceedings of the Sixteenth Annual Conference of the National Probation Association* (New York: National Probation Association, 1923), 20.

18. Herbert Lou, *Juvenile Courts in the United States* (Chapel Hill: University of North Carolina Press, 1927), 162; Mary E. Hamilton, *The Policewoman: Her Services and Ideals* (New York: Frederick H. Stokes, 1924), 31; 14th JPAAR, NU, 12; Maude E. Miner, "The Policewoman and the Girl Problem," *Proceedings of the National Probation Association* (New York: National Probation Association, 1920), 136.

19. Henrietta T. Additon, "The Policewoman," in *Community Treatment of Delinquency: Proceedings of the National Probation Association* (New York: National Probation Association, 1924), 239. See also Henrietta A. Additon, "The Functions of Policewomen," *Journal of Social Hygiene* 10 (June 1924): 321–28.

20. Additon, "The Policewoman," 238–39; Hamilton, *The Policewoman*, 4. The JPA expressed concern about the minimal qualifications for policewomen. In noting that policewomen did not perform "the work which should properly be done by police women" the association recommended a more stringent examination to attract a "higher type of woman," referring to those with some social work training. See 15th JPAAR, NU, 47. The criteria for male police officers indicated that they, too, were to exhibit sympathy and develop friendships with troubled children and youth. However, in an almost apologetic tone, Joseph Pois's study of policemen recruitment acknowledged that police work might appear "puerile," although such protective measures would prevent future criminality. The traits most desirable for policemen, he believed, were not affective ones but abstract and social intelligence. Joseph Pois, "The Recruitment of Police" (Ph.D. diss., University of Chicago, 1929), 44, 45. Nonetheless, the JPA thought probation officers more effective than male police officers, evident in their statement "a probation officer in time saves nine policemen." See "Juvenile Court Committee—Organization and Purpose, March, 1904–June 1909: Juvenile Court Committee," box 10, JPAP, UICSC. In 1910, the Chicago Police Department established a course for policemen, not policewomen. This thirty-day course, taught by the staff, covered rules and regulations, city ordinances, criminal law, attendance in court, and other related topics. 1910 PRCC, HWL, 39.

21. Ethel S. Dummer, *Why I Think So: The Autobiography of an Hypothesis* (Chicago: Clarke-McElroy, n.d.), 80–81.

22. 1927 CCJCAR, HWL, 41.

23. Steven J. Diner, *A City and Its Universities: Public Policy in Chicago, 1892–1919* (Chapel Hill: University of North Carolina Press, 1980), 112; Mary E. Odem, *Delinquent Daughters: Protecting and Policing Adolescent Female Sexuality in the United States, 1885–1920* (Chapel Hill: University of North Carolina Press, 1995), 96; Ann Sadler, "The Ideal Policewoman," *Welfare Magazine* 19 (May 1928): 638–44. Hamilton's criteria included experience as a probation officer, or relief or reformation work, plus a bachelor's degree in nursing or normal school; see Hamilton, *The Policewoman*, 20. Hutzel's descriptions of preparations of case studies necessitated psychiatric and social work backgrounds; see Hutzel, *The Policewoman's Handbook*, "Cases Relating to Preparation of Evidence," 225–54.

24. Such information was similar to the schedules of information that probation officers gathered from their clients, detailing familial and personal information, school records, and home and neighborhood conditions. Further discussions with neighbors, family doctors, teachers and principals supplemented, and in some cases, contradicted the girls' or their families' stories. Bernard Flexner and Roger N. Baldwin, *Juvenile Courts and Probation* (New York: The Century Company, 1916), 35–36.

25. Essie Mae Davidson, "Organized Boarding Homes for Self-Supporting Women in the City of Chicago" (Master's thesis, University of Chicago, 1914), 14; Hutzel, *The Policewoman's Handbook*, 21–24, 34–39, 44, 47–52. Miriam Van Waters, too, recommended trained policewomen to patrol the streets, playgrounds, and saloons for young girls' safeguard. Miriam Van Waters, *Youth in Conflict* (New York: Republic, 1925), 259.

26. Henrietta A. Additon, "Work among Delinquent Women and Girls," *Annals of the American Academy of Political and Social Sciences* 79 (September 1918): 152; "Three Pass Rigid Examination for Policewomen," *Chicago Defender*, January 15, 1916, 1; "Mrs. Grace Wilson Sworn on Thursday; Assigned to Cottage Grove Avenue Station," *Chicago Defender*, January 6, 1918, 12. African-American alderman Louis Anderson helped Grace Wilson to secure her position, as well as assisting in increasing her salary.

27. Frank T. Flyn, "Judge Merritt W. Pinckney and the Early Days of the Juvenile Court in Chicago," *Social Service Review* 28 (March 1954): 22–23; 1909 CCJCAR, HWL, 11, 14; 1913 CCJCAR, HWL, 9.

28. Despite this anecdote of Abbott's, her estimation of the civil service examinations, at least for the first twenty-five years, was that it was fairly free of partisan politics. Edith Abbott, *Social Welfare and Professional Education* (Chicago: University of Chicago Press, 1931), 90, 92. Box 4, folder 80, ICHAS, UICSC contains copies of the 1925 probation officer and assistant probation officer examinations.

29. 1906 CCJCAR, HWL, 7; Illinois Association for Criminal Justice, *Illinois Crime Survey* (Chicago: Illinois Association for Criminal Justice and the Chicago Crime Commission, 1929; reprt., Montclair, NJ: Patterson Smith, 1968, 682).

30. Flyn, "Judge Merritt W. Pinckney," 23–26; Helen Rankin Jeter, *The Chicago Juvenile Court* (Chicago: University of Chicago Press, 1922), 29; Parker, "Personnel and Organization in the Probation Department," 134.

31. The JPA cooperated with the juvenile court by establishing a corps of volunteers who were assigned city blocks near their homes. They reported to the JPA, not the court, on children's and youth's misbehavior. Although these activities were detailed in the JPA's annual reports, it was not clear whether or how many of these children were brought to the court's attention. See Juvenile Protective Association, *The "Block System" of the Juvenile Protective Association* (Chicago: Juvenile Protective Association, 1916), 1–2, 13. Herbert Lou, among others, spoke of the inadequacy of volunteers in the court system; Lou, *Juvenile Courts in the United States*, 80. For information on the expansion of the CCJC, see Jeter, *The Chicago Juvenile Court*, 31. For copies of the volunteer application for various years, see Parker, "Personnel and Organization in the Probation Department," 145–46.

32. CSCP, *Announcements*, 1, no. 1 (July 1909): 21–24, 34–35, CHS; CSCP Training for Social Work, 1910–1911, 135–41, CHS; Graham Taylor, *Pioneering on Social Frontiers* (Chicago: University of Chicago Press, 1930), 308–11; Edith Abbott, "Training in Case Work and Special Administrative Problems in a University," in *Annual Report and Proceedings of the Tenth Annual Conference of the National Probation Association* (Albany, NY: National Probation Association, 1919), 63. See also Lela B. Costin, "Edith Abbott and the Chicago Influence on Social Work Education," *Social Service Review* 51 (March 1983): 94–111.

33. Bernard Flexner, cited in William I. Trattner, *From Poor Law to Welfare State: A History of Social Welfare in America*, 2nd ed. (New York: The Free Press, 1979), 211. Mary Richmond, director of the Charity Organization Department of the Russell Sage Foundation and author of perhaps the most influential social work textbook, was very much swayed by the medical model. Mary Richmond, *Social Diagnosis* (New York: Russell Sage Foundation, 1917). For a comparison of Richmond and Jane Addams's ideologies about social work, see Donna L. Franklin, "Mary Richmond and Jane Addams: From Moral Certainty to Rational Inquiry in Social Work Practice," *Social Service Review* 60 (December 1986): 504–25.

34. Flexner and Baldwin, *Juvenile Courts and Probation*, 139; Van Waters, *Youth in Conflict*, 243–44; Henry W. Thurston, "The Training of Probation Officers in Schools of Social Work," in *The Social Service of the Courts: Proceedings of the Sixteenth Annual Conference of the National Probation Association* (New York: National Probation Association, 1923), 49–50; James E. Haggerty, "Training for Probation Workers in Colleges and Universities," in *The Social Service of the Courts: Proceedings of the Sixteenth Annual Conference of the National Probation Association* (New York: National Probation Association, 1923), 54; Leon Stern, "Report of the Committee on Training for Probation Work," in *The Social Service of the Courts: Proceedings of the Sixteenth Annual Conference of the National Probation Association* (New York: National Probation Association, 1923), 173.

35. Flexner and Baldwin, *Juvenile Courts and Probation*, 102. A. L. Jacoby, a psychiatrist with the Detroit juvenile court, actually applied the field of engineering to social work, arguing that working with delinquents required "transforming" their energy. See A. L. Jacoby, "Some Individual Causes of Delinquency," in *Community Treatment of Delinquency: Proceedings of the National Probation Association* (New York: National Probation Association, 1924), 85, 89.

36. Van Waters, *Youth in Conflict*, 246, 248; Miriam Van Waters, "Who Are Successful Workers with Delinquents?," in *Community Treatment of Delinquency: Proceedings of the National Probation Association* (New York: National Probation Association, 1924), 34.

37. Van Waters, *Youth in Conflict*, 177–78, 244.

38. Ellen Fitzpatrick, *Endless Crusade: Women Social Scientists and Progressive Reform* (New York: Oxford University Press, 1990), 176, 198.

39. Thomas D. Eliot, *The Juvenile Court and the Community* (New York: Macmillan, 1914), 12; Homer Folks, "The Probation System, Its Value and Limitations," in *Proceedings of the Child Conference for Research and Welfare, 1910* (New York: G. E. Stechert, 1910), 225.

40. Flexner and Baldwin, *Juvenile Courts and Probation*, 152; Franklin Chase Hoyt, *Quicksands of Youth* (New York: Charles Scribner's Sons, 1921), 20–25.

41. Memorandum, Aug. 1, 1922, box 92, folder 15, MB, UICSC.

42. Flexner and Baldwin, *Juvenile Courts and Probation*, 15–16.

43. Albert Sidney Beckham, "Juvenile Delinquency and the Negro," *Opportunity* 9 (October 1931): 300.

44. Jeter, *The Chicago Juvenile Court*, 32; Lou, *Juvenile Courts in the United States*, 89.

45. Clarence E. Davis, "Probation with Colored Cases," in *Community Treatment of Delinquency: Proceedings of the National Probation Association* (New York: National Probation Association, 1924), 243–45; George Haynes, "The Basis of Race Adjustment," *The Survey*, February 1, 1913, 569–70; George E. Haynes, "Negro Migration—Its Effect on Family and Community Life in the North," in *The Proceedings of the National Conference of Social Work* (Chicago: University of Chicago Press, 1924), 62–75.

46. Robert C. Dexter, "The Negro in Social Work," *The Survey* 46 (June 25, 1921): 439.

47. Forrester B. Washington, "What Professional Training Means to the Social Workers," *Annals of the American Academy of Political and Social Science* 87 (September 1926): 165.

48. Jeter, *The Juvenile Court*, 32; Lou, *Juvenile Courts in the United States*, 89; Sophonisba Breckinridge and Edith Abbott, *The Delinquent Child and the Home* (New York: Charities Publication Committee, 1912), 37.

49. Lou, *Juvenile Courts in the United States*, 160, 161.

50. Floyd Dell, *Love in the Machine Age: A Psychological Study of the Transition from Patriarchal Society* (New York: Farrar and Rinehart, 1930), 227; Lou, *Juvenile Courts in the United States*, 162.

51. Cited in Flexner and Baldwin, *Juvenile Courts and Probation*, 150.

52. Information derived from 1915–1917 CCJAR, HWL.

53. Nell L. Perkins, "Mental and Moral Problems of the Woman Probationer," in *Probation and the Prevention of Delinquency: Proceedings of the Seventeenth Annual Conference of the National Probation Association* (New York: National Probation Association, 1924), 92.

54. Jeter, *The Chicago Juvenile Court*, 29; Letter to Judge Mary Bartelme, April 24, 1924, folder 15, box 92, MB, UICSC.

55. 1913 CCJCAR, HWL, 61, 63; 1906 to 1927 CCJCAR, HWL. The U.S. Children's Bureau, in its examination of children's placements in 1929, estimated that 58 percent of delinquent boys and 50 percent of delinquent girls were cared for in their own homes pending court hearings. U.S. Children's Bureau study cited in Florence Mary Warner, *Juvenile Detention in the United States* (Chicago: University of Chicago Libraries, 1933), 9.

56. 1906 to 1912 CCJCAR, HWL.

57. Margueritte Anita Elowson, "Some Aspects of the Cook County Juvenile Court in Relation to Readjustment of the Delinquent Girl" (Master's thesis, University of Chicago, 1930), 62, 64. Ellwood's study estimated that of delinquent children in state schools, nearly 25 to 35 percent were from broken homes; Ellwood, cited in Mangold, *Problems of Child Welfare*, 408. The length of most delinquent girls' probation in 1913 was from one to three years; by 1915, the average length was one year. 1913 CCJCAR, HWL, 90; 1915 CCJCAR, HWL, 35.

58. Elowson, "Some Aspects of the Cook County Juvenile Court," 66, 69; Earl R. Moses, *The Negro Delinquent in Chicago* (Washington, DC: Washington Public Schools, 1936), 118.

59. Illinois Association for Criminal Justice, *Illinois Crime Survey*, 683, 684. Rules for probation officers in 1918 stipulated that officers visit their clients within one week and that they report on the child's progress in school monthly; 1919 CCJCAR, HWL, 10. Worthington and Topping noted how many girls eluded their probation officers, often hiding, or giving them false addresses and names. George E. Worthington and Ruth Topping, "The Morals Court of Chicago," *Social Hygiene* 7 (October 1921): 381, 388.

60. 1906 CCJCAR, HWL, 7; William Lester Bodine, *Bodine's Reference Book on Juvenile Welfare* (Chicago: William L. Bodine, 1913), 55, 119; Warner, *Juvenile Detention in the United States*, 3, 40; Parker, "Personnel and Organization in the Probation Department," 114; Caroline Meis, "Personnel Standards and Salaries of Social Workers in the Children's Agencies in Chicago" (Master's thesis, University of Chicago, 1934), 17–18, 30–33; Jeter, *The Chicago Juvenile Court*, 29–30.

61. Marguerite G. Rosenthal, "The Children's Bureau and the Juvenile Court: Delinquency Policy, 1912–1940," *Social Service Review* 70 (June 1996): 307–12.

62. Annual Report, Demonstration Probation Project, July, 1933, folder 7, box 33, EGA, UCSC; Rosenthal, "The Children's Bureau and the Juvenile Court": 312; Edith Abbott, "The Juvenile Court and a Community Program for Treating and Preventing Delinquency," *Social Service Review* 10 (June 1936): 227–42.

63. Abbott, *Social Welfare and Professional Education*, 115.

64. Letter from Edith Abbott to Isabel Dolton, February 2, 1929, EGA, UCSC; Narrative Report, Letter from Jane Culbert to Edith Abbott, November 13, 1928, box 20, folder 20, EGA, UCSC; Letter from Sophonisba Breckinridge to Edith Abbott, November 10, 1928, box 20, folder 9, EGA, UCSC; William J. Bogan, *First Annual Report of Montefiore School, 1929–1930* (Chicago: n.p., 1930), 3. For a history of the visiting teacher movement, see Anne Meis Knupfer, "'The Arm of the School Which Extends into the Home': The Visiting Teacher Movement, 1906 to 1940," *Teachers College Record* 100 (Spring 1999): 627–55.

65. Merrill F. Krughoff, *Salaries and Professional Qualifications of Social Workers in Chicago, 1935* (Chicago: University of Chicago Press, 1937), 19–20.

66. National Urban League Report, "1912–1913 Report" in *Black Heritage in Social Welfare 1860–1930,* comp. and ed. Edyth L. Ross (Metuchen, NJ: Scarecrow Press, 1978), 240–42.

67. Iris Carlton-LaNey, "Training African-American Social Workers Through the NUL Fellowship Program," *Journal of Sociology and Social Welfare* 21 (June 1994): 46, 49, 51. See also Knupfer, *Toward a Tenderer Humanity and a Nobler Womanhood*; Intercollegiate Club of Chicago, *Intercollegiate Wonder Book*, vols. 1 and 2 (Washington, DC: Intercollegiate Club of Chicago, 1917).

68. Carlton-LaNey, "Training African-American Social Workers": 44–45; George E. Haynes, "Cooperation with Colleges in Securing and Training Negro Social Workers for Urban Centers," in *Proceedings of the National Conference of Charities and Correction* (Fort Wayne, IN: Fort Wayne Printing, 1911), 385; National Urban League, "Result of the 1912–1913 Program," *Bulletin of the National League on Urban Conditions among Negroes* 3 (November 1913): 10–11: Stephanie Shaw, *What a Woman Ought to Be and to Do: Black Professional Women Workers during the Jim Crow Era* (Chicago: University of Chicago Press, 1996), 96; Nancy J. Weiss, *The National Urban League, 1910–1940* (New York: Oxford University Press, 1974), 75; Parris Guichard and Lester Brooks, *Blacks in the City: A History of the National Urban League* (Boston: Little, Brown, 1971), 26; Arvarh E. Strickland, *History of the Chicago Urban League* (Urbana: University of Illinois Press, 1966), 19.

69. Haynes, "Cooperation with Colleges in Securing and Training Negro Social Workers for Urban Centers," 384–85; n.a., "Our Negro Colleges," *Opportunity* 1 (April 1923): 12.

70. Robenia Baker Gary and Lawrence E. Gary, "The History of Social Work Education for Black People, 1900–1930," *Journal of Sociology and Social Welfare* 21 (March 1994): 73; *Chicago Defender*, November 19, 1921.

71. Atlanta School of Social Work, "1920 Announcement," in Ross, ed., *Black Heritage in Social Welfare*, 433, 434–36; E. Franklin Frazier, "Round Table No. 2: " 'Professional Education for Negro Social Workers,' " in *Proceedings of the National Conference of Social Work* (Chicago: University of Chicago Press, 1927), 640; Gary and Gary, "The History of Social Work Education": 74–75.

72. Atlanta School of Social Service, "1920 Announcement," in Ross, ed., *Black Heritage in Social Welfare*, 434; Atlanta School of Social Work, "1929–30 Bulletin," in Ross, ed., *Black Heritage in Social Welfare*, 451.

73. David King Cherry, "Vocational Activities of Educated Negroes" (Master's thesis, University of Chicago, 1931), 22.

74. Jesse O. Thomas, "A Social Program to Help the Migrant," *Opportunity* 2 (March 1924): 72.

75. George Haynes, "The Basis of Race Adjustment," *The Survey* (February 1, 1913): 569; George E. Haynes, "Race Riots in Relation to Democracy," *The Survey* (August 9, 1919): 697–99.

76. Thomas, "A Social Program to Help the Migrant": 71; George E. Haynes, "Negro Migration—Its Effect on Family and Community Life in the North," in *Proceedings of the National Conference of Social Work* (Chicago: University of Chicago Press, 1924), 69–70.

77. Ethel Ramsey Harris, "A Study of Voluntary Activity among the Professional Negroes in Chicago" (Master's thesis, University of Chicago, 1937), 10, 31.

78. Monroe N. Work, "Problems of Negro Urban Welfare," *Southern Workman* (January 1924): 11; Irene Graham, "The Negro Family in a Northern City," *Opportunity* 8 (February 1930): 49.

79. Graham, "The Negro Family in a Northern City": 49. According to Graham, as of 1929 almost 32 percent of all African-American children under 16 lived at home with lodgers in Chicago. Child-placing agencies refused to place children in these homes. Even when children lived with both parents, the presence of a lodger (especially if male) signaled moral danger. See Irene Graham, "Family Support and Dependency among Chicago Negroes: A Study of Unpublished Census Data," *Social Service Review* 3 (December 1929): 561.

80. Forrester B. Washington, "Negroes," in *Social Work Year Book: A Description of Organized Activities in Social Work and in Related Fields*, ed. Fred Hall (New York: Russell Sage Foundation, 1933), 314–15.

81. Eugene Kinckle Jones, "Social Work among Negroes," *Annals of the American Academy of Political and Social Science* 89 (November 1928): 287; Dorothy West, "Mammy," in *The Richer, The Poorer: Stories, Sketches, and Reminiscences* (New York: Doubleday, 1995), 43, 51.

82. 3rd CUL, box 1, folder 2, UICSC; 10th CUL, box 1, folder 9, UICSC; 7th CUL, box 1, folder 6, UICSC; 11th CUL, box 1, folder 10, UICSC; Strickland, *History of the Chicago Urban League*, 49–50; *Broad Ax*, September 9, 1925, April 21, 1925, and January 16, 1926; *Chicago Defender*, July 9, 1921, and February 28, 1929; Harris, "A Study of Voluntary Social Activity among the Professional Negroes in Chicago," 68. An African-American caseworker was very much needed in the Cook County Hospital, where most African-American unmarried mothers received prenatal and postpartum care. Nearly 77 percent of African-American unmarried mothers were sent to this hospital, compared to 30 percent native-born white and nearly 36 percent foreign-born white unmarried mothers. Dorothy Frances Puttee and Mary Ruth Colby, *The Illegitimate Child in Illinois* (Chicago: University of Chicago Press, 1937), 104. This pattern reflected national trends, as less than 5 percent of African-American unmarried mothers had access to social service programs, compared to 50

percent of white unmarried women in the 1920s. See Michael W. Sedlak, "Young Women and the City: Adolescent Deviance and the Transformation of Educational Policy, 1870–1960," *History of Education Quarterly* 23 (Spring 1983): 21. For a listing of Chicago's maternity hospitals, see Harvey C. Carbaugh, *Human Welfare Work in Chicago* (Chicago: A. C. McClurg, 1917), 246.

83. Memorandum dated April 24, 1924, box 4, folder 77, MB, UICSC; Jeter, *The Chicago Juvenile Court*, 32; Joanne L. Goodwin, *Gender and the Politics of Welfare Reform: Mothers' Pensions in Chicago, 1911–1929* (Chicago: University of Chicago Press, 1997), 122–23; 18th CUL, box 1, folder 10, UICSC. Iris Carlton-LaNey, "The Career of Birdye Henrietta Haynes, A Pioneer Settlement House Worker," *Social Service Review* 68 (June 1994): 259–63; Knupfer, *Toward a Tenderer Humanity and a Nobler Womanhood*, 95; Steven J. Diner, "Chicago Social Workers and Blacks in the Progressive Era," *Social Service Review* 44 (December 1970): 406.

84. "Life Story of Irene McCoy Gaines," box 1, Scrapbook, IMGP, CHS.

85. James Dorsey, *Up South: Blacks in Chicago's Suburbs, 1719–1983* (Bristol, IN: Wyndham Hall Press, 1986), 64.

86. Harris, "A Study of Voluntary Social Activity among the Professional Negroes in Chicago," 67, 69–71. See also Allan H. Spear, *Black Chicago: The Making of a Negro Ghetto, 1890–1920* (Chicago: University of Chicago Press, 1967).

87. Harris, "A Study of Voluntary Social Activity among the Professional Negroes in Chicago," 69–71.

88. Puttee and Colby, *The Illegitimate Child in Illinois*, 154; Sedlak, "Young Women and the City": 21–22. For further information about Amanda Smith's home for dependent girls, see Knupfer, *Toward a Tenderer Humanity and a Nobler Womanhood*, 76–81.

89. 1st CUL, box 1, folder 2, UICSC; "Brief Summary of the Work of the Chicago Urban League," box 1, folder 1, CUL, UICSC; Frazier, "Round Table No. 2": 641.

90. Jones, "Social Work among Negroes": 292.

91. Ibid., 287–93; Eugene Kinckle Jones, "The Negro's Struggle or Health," in *Proceedings of the National Conference of Social Work, Fiftieth Annual Session* (Washington, DC: National Conference of Social Work, 1923), 72; Washington, "Negroes," 315.

92. Regina G. Kunzel, *Fallen Women, Problem Girls: Unmarried Mothers and the Professionalization of Social Work, 1890–1945* (New Haven: Yale University Press, 1993), 45–46; Daniel J. Walkowitz, "The Making of a Feminine Professional Identity: Social Workers in the 1920s," *American Historical Review* 95 (October 1990): 1051–75.

93. Ralph G. Huslin, *Salaries and Qualifications of Child Welfare Workers in 1941* (New York: Russell Sage Foundation, 1943), 16; Margaret Elizabeth Warren, "Salaries, Education, Training and Experience of Social Workers in Six Family Welfare and Relief Agencies in Chicago" (Ph.D. diss., University of Chicago, 1933), 17–21. The average 1933 monthly salary of Chicago social workers in private agencies was only $125 whereas juvenile court employees were paid between $80 and $100. Most women employed in Chicago's public agencies were single, ages twenty-five to forty-five. The same characteristics of social workers were reported in New York City. Meis, "Personnel Standards and Salaries of Social Workers," 17, 30, 32; Edward T. Devine and Mary Van Kleeck, *Positions in Social Work* (New York: New York School of Philanthropy, 1916).

Chapter 4

1. Cited in Janet Staiger, *Bad Women: Regulating Sexuality in Early American Cinema* (Minneapolis: University of Minnesota Press, 1995), 17. This prompted one social hygienist to deplore that art and literature were imbued with sex, "more powerfully vex[ing] than nature

needs to accomplish her purpose of reproduction." Franklin O. Nichols, "The Aim and Scope of Social Hygiene," *Opportunity* 1 (April 1923): 9. For another history of changing sexual relationships, see Beth L. Bailey, *From Front Porch to Back Seat: Courtship in Twentieth-Century America* (Baltimore: Johns Hopkins University Press, 1988).

2. This is not a new argument, but one that has been amply discussed by other historians. See, for example, Kathy Peiss, *Cheap Amusements: Working Women and Leisure in Turn-of-the-Century New York* (Philadelphia: Temple University Press, 1986); and Leslie Woodcock Tentler, *Wage-Earning Women: Industrial Work and Family Life in the United States, 1900–1930* (New York: Oxford University Press, 1979).

3. John F. Kasson, *Amusing the Million: Coney Island at the Turn of the Century* (New York: Hill and Wang, 1987), 25–26.

4. William Leach, "Strategists of Display and the Production of Desire," in *Consuming Visions: Accumulation and Display of Goods in America, 1880–1920*, ed. Simon J. Bronner (New York: W. W. Norton, 1989), 131–32. See also William Leach, *Land of Desire: Merchants, Power, and the Rise of a New American Culture* (New York: Vintage, 1993).

5. Simon J. Bronner, "Object Lesson. The Work of Ethnological Museums and Collections," in *Consuming Visions: Accumulation and Display of Goods in America, 1880–1920*, ed. Simon J. Bronner (New York: W. W. Norton, 1989), 219.

6. Stuart Ewen and Elizabeth Ewen, *Channels of Desire: Mass Images and the Shaping of American Consciousness* (New York: McGraw-Hill, 1982), 68, 69. Dreiser's Sister Carrie, wandering endlessly in a Chicago department store, exemplified the woman whose identity was consumed by material goods.

7. Leach, "Strategists of Display and the Production of Desire," 117.

8. Simon J. Bronner, "Reading Consumer Culture," in *Consuming Visions: Accumulation and Display of Goods in America, 1880–1920*, ed. Simon J. Bronner (New York: W. W. Norton, 1989), 52; John H. Ehrenreich, *The Altruistic Imagination: A History of Social Work and Social Policy in the United States* (Ithaca: Cornell University Press, 1985), 40. As Thorstein Veblen properly notes, the working class, unlike the leisure class, lived "in" not "by" industry; Thorstein Veblen, *The Theory of the Leisure Class* (New York: Penguin Books, 1994), 167. Maxim Gorky's criticism of Coney Island, that it was simply a mechanized version of the working-class's work, reflected, like Veblen, the difference between leisure and amusement; cited in Kasson, *Amusing the Million*, 108.

9. Carl A. Naether, *Advertising to Women* (New York: Prentice-Hall, 1929), 27. See also Elaine Tyler May, "The Pressure to Provide: Class, Consumerism, and Divorce in Urban America, 1880–1920," in *The American Family in Social-Historical Perspective*, 3rd ed., ed. Michael Gordon (New York: St. Martin's Press, 1983), 154–68.

10. Naether, *Advertising to Women*, 77–91, 99, 252.

11. Ibid., 4, 105; Dorothy M. Brown, *American Women in the 1920s: Setting a Course* (Boston: Twayne, 1987), 7; Ehrenreich, *The Altruistic Imagination*, 50; Virginia Scharff, *Taking the Wheel: Women and the Coming of the Motor Age* (New York: The Free Press, 1991), 116. The famous sociological study of Middletown (a ficticious name for a small city in Indiana) likewise discussed the influence of the automobile on youth; Robert S. Lynd and Helen Merrell Lynd, *Middletown in Transition: A Study in Cultural Conflict* (New York: Harcourt Brace Jovanovich, 1937), 242–94. See also John Henry Mueller, "The Automobile: A Sociological Study" (Ph.D. diss., University of Chicago, 1929) for a discussion of how the automobile influenced social behavior.

12. T. V. Smith and Leonard D. White, eds., *Chicago: An Experiment in Social Science Research* (Chicago: University of Chicago Press, 1929), 127, 166. See also the 1932 White House Conference on Health and Protection, *The Delinquent Child* (New York: The Century Company, 1932), 215. Despite the promotion of parks as places of respectability and of wholesome

recreation, their placement near tenements did not encourage young women to use them as such. See Galen Cranz, "Women in Urban Parks," *Signs* 5 (Spring 1980): S80–S95. For descriptions of the red districts and dance halls of Chicago, see Mark H. Haller, "Policy Gambling, Entertainment, and the Emergence of Black Politics: Chicago from 1900 to 1940," *Journal of Social History* 24 (Summer 1991): 719–40.

13. Young women, because of their busy schedules, were thought to be predisposed toward neurasthenia and neurosis. This was another form of recapitulation of earlier-nineteenth-century thought. Young women's stress could best be alleviated through relaxation, outdoor activities, and light exercises. Paul Hanley Furfey, *Social Problems of Childhood* (New York: Macmillan, 1929), 95; William A. McKeever, *Industrial Training of the Girl* (New York: Macmillan, 1914), 50–51, 53. A number of surveys were conducted about adolescent girls' leisurely activities. See, for example, Lorraine Solomon's survey based on a questionnaire developed by Burgess in 1932: "Things I Like to Do," box 134, folder 4, EB, UCSC; John M. Eddy, "Unsupervised Club Life among Girls Attending Secondary School," *Journal of Educational Sociology* 2 (1928): 210–20; Ralph W. Pringle, *Adolescence and High-School Problems* (Boston: D. C. Heath, 1922); and Inez M. Cook and T. V. Goodrich, "How High School Pupils Spend Their Time," *School Review* 36 (1929): 721–28. Many of their conclusions were influenced by G. Stanley Hall and William Thomas. Pringle insisted that mental growth was charted into emotional channels, including charms, fetishes, migratory instinct, and reverie. Youth craved emotional experiences almost as much as food and drink. One cannot help but wonder how self-fulfilling many of these prophecies were. A study of New York City's delinquent girls' favorite pastimes noted that 90 percent of them listed reading, again mostly love stories. Dorothy Reed, *Leisure Time of Girls in a "Little Italy"* (Portland, OR: n.p., 1932), 47.

14. Ruth Shonle Cavan, *Business Girls: A Study of Their Interests and Problems* (Chicago: Religious Education Association, 1929), 36. One survey that questioned college girls' fiction preferences found romantic literature to be their favorite as well. Phyllis Blanchard and Carlyn Manasses, *New Girls for Old* (New York: Macaulay, 1930), 172.

15. Henriette R. Walter, *Girl Life in America: A Study of Backgrounds* (New York: National Committee for the Study of Juvenile Reading, 1927), 120, 123.

16. George B. Mangold, *Problems of Child Welfare* (New York: Macmillan, 1928), 212; Louise de Koven Bowen, *Five and Ten Cent Theatres: Two Investigations* (Chicago: Juvenile Protective Association, 1909 and 1911), n.p. Lloyd Allen Cook found that movie pictures portrayed love, crime, and sex, in that order; Lloyd Allen Cook, *Community Backgrounds of Education: A Textbook in Educational Sociology*, 1st ed. (New York: McGraw-Hill, 1938), 219. By 1913, there were six hundred movie theaters in New York City, with an approximate attendance of 400,000 daily. As admission was only a nickel, many poor and working-class flocked there. See Harriet McDoual Daniels, *The Girl and Her Chance: A Study of Conditions surrounding the Young Girl between Fourteen and Eighteen Years of Age in New York City* (New York: Fleming H. Revell, 1914), 71.

17. Lois Kate Halley, "A Study of Motion Pictures in Chicago as a Medium of Communication" (Master's thesis, University of Chicago, 1924), 44–45. As of 1909, there were forty-one such "first-class" theaters in Chicago.

18. Cited in Ewen and Ewen, *Channels of Desire*, 88. Charles Cooper conjectured that after the public schools, the two agencies which most educated the immigrants were the movies and the press. He thought that immigrants accepted the lurid plots of early films as typically American. Charles C. Cooper, "The Necessity for Changes in Americanization Methods," in *The 1918 National Conference of Social Work* (Chicago: Rogers and Hall, 1919), 440.

19. Halley, "A Study of Motion Pictures in Chicago as a Medium of Communication," 33–34; Lizabeth Cohen, *Making a New Deal: Industrial Workers in Chicago, 1919–1930* (New York: Cambridge University Press, 1990), 121, 127; Bowen, *Five and Ten Cent Theatres*, n.p.

20. Ewen and Ewen, *Channels of Desire*, 97; see also Elizabeth Ewen, "City Lights: Immigrant Women and the Rise of the Movies," *Signs* 5 (Spring 1980): S45–S65; Staiger, *Bad Women*. For further information about the characterization of white slaves, see Mark Thomas Connelly, *The Response to Prostitution in the Progressive Era* (Chapel Hill: University of North Carolina Press, 1980), chap. 6.

21. Halley, "A Study of Motion Pictures in Chicago as a Medium of Communication," 46, 48.

22. Bowen, *Five and Ten Cent Theatres*, n.p.

23. Halley, "A Study of Motion Pictures in Chicago as a Medium of Communication," 22–23, 27, 29–30. For a history of the JPA, see Paul Gerard Anderson, "The Good to Be Done: A History of the Juvenile Protective Association of Chicago, 1898–1976" (Ph.D. diss., University of Chicago, 1988).

24. Halley, "A Study of Motion Pictures in Chicago as a Medium of Communication," 7, 56; William Healy and Augusta F. Bronner, *Delinquents and Criminals: Their Making and Unmaking. Studies in Two American Cities* (New York: AMS Press, 1926), 174.

25. Ernest Burgess cited in Halley, "A Study of Motion Pictures in Chicago as a Medium of Communication," 56–58. Fatigue from movie watching could be misconstrued as laziness or lack of intelligence. Ella Ruth Boyce argued that there were scientific ways for teachers to differentiate between the two; Ella Ruth Boyce, "Magazine Articles on Parent Education," in *Parent Education: The First Yearbook*, ed. National Congress of Parents and Teachers (Washington, DC: National Congress of Parents and Teachers, 1930), 140. The maternalist organizations undoubtedly worked in conjunction with the Bureau of Moving Pictures, which was part of the Chicago Police Department. Established in 1912, the bureau reviewed movie picture films, burlesque, and vaudeville theaters for objectionable materials. In 1912 alone, the bureau visited over 8,000 theaters and eliminated over three hundred objectionable episodes from burlesque and vaudeville plays and rejected almost 316,000 feet of film. See 1913 PRCC, HWL, 101.

26. Herbert Blumer and Philip M. Hauser, *Movies, Delinquency, and Crime* (New York: Macmillan, 1933), 88, 97. The stars most admired by the delinquent girls were Greta Garbo, Mary Pickford, Clara Bow, and Nita Naldi. Many of these girls claimed to have dreamed of Rudolph Valentino and John Gilbert, their favorite male stars. Herbert Blumer, *Movies and Conduct* (New York: Macmillan, 1933), 31.

27. Blumer and Hauser, *Movies, Delinquency, and Crime*, 85.

28. Louise de Koven Bowen, *Speeches, Addresses, and Letters of Louise de Koven Bowen*, vol. 2. (Ann Arbor: Edwards Brother, 1937), 299. By 1924, at least 240 cities had regulatory ordinances for dance halls, which entailed licenses, permits, and inspections. In twelve of fifteen cities studied by the Children's Bureau in 1925 and 1927, women were hired as inspectors. Some dance halls specifically hired women managers and hostesses to keep young children out and maintain order. See *The 1929 Social Work Yearbook* (Chicago: University of Chicago Press, 1929), 347.

29. William Lester Bodine, *Bodine's Reference Book on Juvenile Welfare. A Review of the Chicago Social Service System* (Chicago: W. L. Bodine, 1913), 35. Greenwich Village writer Hutchin Hapgood differentiated between the "spieler" girl, who was "too simple to be practical" and the "swell" girl described as "hard" and "tough." Hutchin Hapgood, *Types from City Streets* (New York: Funk and Wagnalls, 1910), 135.

30. Peiss, *Cheap Amusements*, 102.

31. Staiger, *Bad Women*, 8–9; William Burgess, "The Moral Decay of the Modern Stage," in *The 1919 National Conference of Social Work* (Chicago: Rogers and Hall, 1920), 503–4.

32. James T. Farrell, "The Dance Marathon," box 141, folder 8 and 10, EB, UCSC. At the Chicago Dancing Academy, most of the patrons were Greek, Italian, Polish, and American-born men, who spent up to six dollars an evening on dances. See also Walter C. Reckless, *Vice in Chicago* (Chicago: University of Chicago Press, 1933), 160–163.

33. Bert Perkins, "The Taxi-Dance Hall," box 143, folder 5, EB, UCSC. See also Paul Goalby Cressey, *The Taxi-Dance Hall: A Sociological Study in Commercilized Recreation and City Life* (Montclair, NJ: Pattterson Smith, 1969; University of Chicago, 1932, reprt.).

34. Ibid.

35. Addams, cited in Ewen and Ewen, *Channels of Desire*, 214.

36. See box 2, folder 26, MB, UICSC; "The Girl Prisoners," *Oak Leaves*, January 17, 1920, box 5, folder 107, MB, UICSC. As Clara E. Laughlin observed, "The effect [of high fashion] was far from inconspicuous in Halsted Street—where a willow plume would have passed unnoticed." Clara E. Laughlin, *The Penny Philanthropist: A Story That Could Be True* (New York: Fleming H. Revell, 1912), 86. One argument used by Bartelme for female probation officers was that they could best ferret out the girls' stories because they understood the girls' desires for finery and makeup. 1913 CCJCAR, HWL, 38.

37. "The Gun Girl," box 138, folder 9, EB, UCSC. See also "Gangs—Girls Report: 1934," box 1, folder 75, SB, UICSC. Peiss, too, noted how girls bragged about their conquests; see Peiss, *Cheap Amusements*, 65.

38. "The Gun Girl," box 138, folder 9, EB, UCSC.

39. Many of these were prostitution roadhouses, such as the Old Blue Goose, which routinely inspected its male customers for venereal disease. Daniel Russell, "The Road House: A Study of Commercialized Amusements in the Environs of Chicago (Master's thesis, University of Chicago, 1931), 10, 17, 53, 136–38; Reckless, 120–36; Jessie F. Binford, "Cook County (Illinois) Roadhouse," *Journal of Social Hygiene* 6 (May 1930): 259, 262. Binford was affiliated with the JPA for many years.

40. Floyd Dell, *Love without Money* (New York: Farrar and Rinehart, 1931), 93.

41. David John Hogan, *Class and Reform: School and Society in Chicago, 1880–1930* (Philadelphia: University of Pennsylvania Press, 1985); Perry R. Duis, *The Saloons: Public Drinking in Chicago and Boston 1880–1920* (Urbana: University of Illinois Press, 1983), 69, 145; Albert Ellis Webster, "The Relation of the Saloon to Juvenile Delinquency" (Ph.D. diss., University of Chicago, 1912), 16; Webster was a member of the Illinois Vigilance Association. See also Dominic A. Pacyga, *Polish Immigrants and Industrial Chicago: Workers on the South Side, 1880–1922* (Columbus: Ohio State University Press, 1991); Hannah Kent Schoff, *The Wayward Child: A Study of the Causes of Crime* (Indianapolis: Bobbs-Merrill, 1915), 137–57.

42. Peiss, *Cheap Amusements*, 28–30; Webster, "The Relation of the Saloon to Juvenile Delinquency," 4–6; Samuel Paynter Wilson, *Chicago and Its Cess-Pools of Infamy* (Chicago: Samuel Paynter Wilson, 1910), 51–53; Royal L. Melendy, "The Saloon in Chicago," *American Journal of Sociology* 6 (November 1900): 289–306. Christina Simmons, too, has discussed the masculine ethos in recreational activities; Christina Simmons, "Modern Sexuality and the Myth of Victorian Repression," in *Passion and Power: Sexuality in History*, ed. Kathy Peiss and Christina Simmons with Robert A. Padgug (Philadelphia: Temple University Press, 1989), 160.

43. Vice Commission of Chicago, *The Social Evil in Chicago* (Chicago: Gunthorp, 1911), 42; Tentler, *Wage-Earning Women*, 190; Cavan, *Business Girls*, 56–57. Cavan also noted how fewer than 10 percent of business girls in Chicago were immigrants and slightly over 1 percent African American; Cavan, *Business Girls*, 8–10. Cavan's discussion of business girls as a "cultural group" who exhibited a body of customs, traditions, and opinions reflected the influence of Margaret Mead's *Coming of Age in Samoa* (New York: Morrow Quill Paperbacks, 1928), published a year earlier.

44. Annie Marion MacLean, "Two Weeks in Department Stories," *American Journal of Sociology* 4 (May 1989): 723. Ann Elizabeth Trotter, *Housing of Non-Family Women in Chicago* (Chicago: Chicago Community Trust, 1921), 1.

45. Essie Mae Davidson, "Organized Boarding Homes for Self-Supporting Women in the City of Chicago" (Master's thesis, University of Chicago, 1914), 10, 25.

46. Davidson, "Organized Boarding Homes," 18, 24, 29. See also Joanne J. Meyerowitz, *Women Adrift: Independent Wage Earners in Chicago, 1880–1930* (Chicago: University of Chicago Press, 1988).

47. Davidson, "Organized Boarding Homes," 32; Josephine Taylor, YWCA of Chicago, Room Registry Bureau, "Room Registry and Housing Study—1928," box 138, folder 9, EB, UCSC; Smith and White, *An Experiment in Social Science Research*, 129; Edith Abbott and Evelyn Heacox Wilson, "The Problem of the Furnished Rooms," in *The Tenements of Chicago, 1908–1935*, ed. Edith Abbott (Chicago: University of Chicago Press, 1936), 327.

48. "Tables on Room Registry—1928," box 138, folder 9, EB, UCSC.

49. Clara E. Laughlin, *The Work-a-Day Girl* (New York: F. H. Revell, 1913; Reprt., New York: Arno Press, 1974), 96, 97.

50. Miriam Van Waters, *Youth in Conflict* (New York: Republic, 1925), 116; Cavan, *Business Girls*, 48; William LeRoy Zabel, "Street Trades and Juvenile Delinquency" (Master's thesis, University of Chicago, 1918), 50.

51. John D'Emilio and Estelle Freedman, *Intimate Matters: A History of Sexuality in America* (New York: Harper and Row, 1988), 189; "Editorial," *Opportunity* 3 (August 1925): 1.

52. Louise de Koven Bowen, *The Colored People of Chicago* (Chicago: Juvenile Protective Association, 1913), 173–74, 176; see also Anne Meis Knupfer, *Toward a Tenderer Humanity and a Nobler Womanhood: African American Women's Clubs in Turn-of-the Century Chicago* (New York: New York University Press, 1996), chap. 5.

53. Joy K. Lintelman, "'On My Own': Single, Swedish, and Female in Turn-of-the-Century Chicago," in *Swedish-American Life in Chicago: Cultural and Urban Aspects of an Immigrant People, 1850–1930*, ed. Philip J. Anderson and Dag Lanck (Urbana: University of Illinois Press, 1992), 89, 96.

54. Louise de Koven Bowen, *The Girl Employed in Hotels and Restaurants* (Chicago: Juvenile Protective Association, 1912), n.p.

55. Frances R. Donovan, *The Saleslady* (Chicago: University of Chicago Press, 1929), 131.

56. Ibid., 126–27, 195.

57. Ibid., 208–9. See also William A. McKeever's fascinating discussion of the psychology of girls' clothes, which examined the connection between clothes and democracy, as well as clothes as an "instinct." William A. McKeever, *Training the Girl* (New York: Macmillan, 1916), chap. 9.

58. Donovan, *The Saleslady*, 55. These clothes conjured up the idea of respectability for the young women. Donovan noted that when a waitress was released from a hospital, she insisted that she not leave wearing her waitress uniform. Instead, she asked one of her friends to go home and get a more suitable outfit for her. She left the hospital "decked out in silk stockings, slippers, a hat with roses around the crown and a brown crepe de chine dress." Donovan, *The Saleslady*, 158.

59. Ibid., 213.

60. Ibid., 138.

61. See also Harriet McDoual Daniels, *The Girl and Her Chance: A Study of Conditions surrounding the Young Girl between Fourteen and Eighteen Years of Age in New York City* (New York: Fleming H. Revell, 1914), 58–59.

62. MacLean, "Two Weeks in Department Stories," 729. The Vice Commission of Chicago stressed that economic conditions often led to prostitution. In their study of 119 prostitutes, they found that eighteen had worked in department stores. Vice Commission of Chicago, cited in Louise de Koven Bowen, *The Department Store Girl: Based upon Interviews with 200 Girls* (Chicago: Juvenile Protective Association, 1911), n.p.

63. MacLean, "Two Weeks in Department Stories": 737.

64. Edith Livingston Smith and Hugh Cabot, M.D., "A Study in Sexual Morality," *Journal of Social Hygiene* 2 (October 1916): 541.

65. Bowen, *The Department Store Girl*, n.p.

66. MacLean, "Two Weeks in Department Stories": 731. Hutchin Hapgood discussed different types of shop girls: again, the "swell" types, who imitated the better elements of society; and the "speilers," who remained true to themselves. Characterizing the first type, he commented, "Shop-girl refinement is like stage scenery—unreal, but prominent and obvious." Hapgood, *Types from City Streets*, 127.

67. True, *The Neglected Girl*, 43; see also Meyerowitz, *Women Adrift*.

68. Dorothy Richardson, *The Long Day: The Story of a New York Working Girl*, ed. William L. O'Neill (Chicago: Quadrangle Books, 1972), 97; Tentler, Wage-Earning Women; Ernest L. Talbert, *Opportunities in School and Industry for Children of the Stockyard District* (Chicago: University of Chicago Press, 1912), 9, 13, 26, 47.

69. Tentler, *Wage-Earning Women*, 85. One study of New York City workers noted that of 344 department store girls, about 84 percent turned over all of their wages to their mothers; 88 percent of factory girls gave their wages to their families. Daniels, *The Girl and Her Chance*, 21.

Chapter 5

1. Selected members of the CWC frequently traveled to Springfield to attend legislative sessions, then reported back to the club until the juvenile court officially opened its doors in July of 1899. Oct. 26, 1898 Minutes, CWCMR, CHS; Dec. 28, 1898 Minutes, CWCMR, CHS; Jan. 25, 1899 Minutes, CWCMR, CHS. See also Julia C. Lathrop, "The Background of the Juvenile Court in Illinois," in *The Child, the Clinic, and the Court* (New York: New Republic, 1925), 291; 1913 CCJCAR, HWL, 5–6. For other histories of the establishment of the Chicago juvenile court, see Timothy D. Hurley, comp., *Origin of the Illinois Juvenile Court Law: Juvenile Courts and What They Have Accomplished* (Chicago: Visitation and Aid Society, 1907); Ellen Ryerson, *The Best-Laid Plans: America's Juvenile Court Experiment* (New York: Hill and Wang, 1978); and Susan Tiffin, *In Whose Best Interest? Child Welfare Reform in the Progressive Era* (Westport, CT: Greenwood Press, 1982).

2. Feb. 22, 1899 Minutes, CWCMR, CHS; Mar. 1, 1899 Minutes, CWCMR, CHS; Mar. 22, 1899 Minutes, CWCMR, CHS; April 29, 1899 Minutes, CWCMR, CHS; Grace Abbott, *The Child and the State*, vol 2. *The Dependent and the Delinquent Child: The Child of Unmarried Parents. Selected Documents, with Introductory Notes* (Chicago: University of Chicago Press, 1938), 330–31; Timothy D. Hurley, "Origins of the Illinois Juvenile Court Law," in *The Child, the Clinic, and the Court* (New York: New Republic, 1925), 323–24. As a member of the State Board of Charities, Lathrop was familiar with conditions in the Illinois industrial and reformatory schools. To be expected, most of the opposition to the Juvenile Court Act came from these institutions' administrators. Victoria Lynn Getis, "A Disciplined Society: The Juvenile Court, Reform, and the Social Sciences in Chicago, 1890–1930" (Ph.D. diss., University of Michigan, 1994), 121.

3. Hurley, comp., *Origin of the Illinois Juvenile Court Law*, 18. Flower and Lathrop even arranged luncheons to garner additional support for the bill; Getis, *A Disciplined Society*, 114–15.

4. Getis, "A Disciplined Society," 92; Hurley, comp., *Origin of the Illinois Juvenile Court Law*, 17–18; Louise de Koven Bowen, *Speeches, Addresses, and Letters of Louise de Koven Bowen*, vol. 1 (Ann Arbor: Edwards Brother, 1937), 63; Kathryn Kish Sklar, "The Historical Foundation of Women's Power in the Creation of the American Welfare State, 1830–1930," in *Mothers of a New World: Maternalist Politics and the Origins of Welfare States*, ed. Seth Koven and Sonya Michel (New York: Routledge, 1993), 67, 69. Such studies have elaborated on the portraits of Chicago reformers as presented earlier by Steven J. Diner in *A City and Its Universi-*

ties: Public Policy in Chicago, 1892–1919 (Chapel Hill: University of North Carolina Press, 1980).

5. State of Illinois, *Laws of the State of Illinois Enacted by the Forty-First Assembly* (Springfield: Phillips Brothers, 1899), 137; Illinois Association for Criminal Justice, *Illinois Crime Survey* (Chicago: Illinois Association for Criminal Justice and The Chicago Crime Commission, 1929, reprt., Montclair, NJ: Patterson Smith, 1968), 681; David John Hogan, *Class and Reform: School and Society in Chicago, 1880–1930* (Philadelphia: University of Pennsylvania Press, 1985), 63–64; Abbott, *The Child and the State*, 393–401; Hurley, comp., *Origin of the Illinois Juvenile Court Law*, 62. The Cook County Juvenile Court was a civil, not a criminal, court; as such, parents were codefendants with their daughters.

6. "Juvenile Court Committee—Organization and Purpose, March, 1904–June, 1909," box 15, folder 9, JPAP, UICSC; Juvenile Protective Leagues, "Suggestions for Organization and Plan of Work," Organization and Purpose, 1910," box 15, folder 15, JPAP, UICSC.

7. Emma Lundberg, *Unto the Least of These* (New York: D. Appleton-Century, 1947), 115. For a legal history of the CCJC, see David S. Tanenhaus, "Policing the Child: Juvenile Justice in Chicago, 1870–1925" (Ph.D. diss., University of Chicago, 1997).

8. Mary E. Odem, *Delinquent Daughters: Protecting and Policing Adolescent Female Sexuality in the United States, 1885–1920* (Chapel Hill: University of North Carolina Press, 1995), 109. See also Christopher Lasch, *Haven in a Heartless World: The Family Besieged* (New York: Basic Books, 1977).

9. Jane Addams, *My Friend, Julia Lathrop* (New York: Macmillan Company, 1935), 143–44. Greatly concerned about mental hygiene, Lathrop was a member of related national organizations, along with Clifford Beers. See Clifford Whittingham Beers, *A Mind That Found Itself: An Autobiography*, 7th ed. (Garden City, NY: Doubleday, Doran, 1948).

10. Molly Ladd-Taylor, *Mother-Work: Women, Child Welfare, and the State, 1890–1930* (Urbana: University of Illinois Press, 1994), 149–50; Louise de Koven Bowen, *Speeches, Letters and Addresses*, 302; William Lester Bodine, *Bodine's Reference Book on Juvenile Welfare: A Review of the Chicago Social Service System* (Chicago: W. L. Bodine, 1913), 131; Lundberg, *Unto the Least of These*, 199.

11. Louise de Koven Bowen, *Safeguards for City Youth at Work and at Play* (New York: Macmillan, 1914), 22; Susan Tiffin, *In Whose Best Interest?*, 219, 228; Getis, "A Disciplined Society," 127. This was especially true for African-American dependent and delinquent girls in Chicago. See Anne Meis Knupfer, *Toward a Tenderer Humanity and a Nobler Womanhood: African American Women's Clubs in Turn-of-the-Century Chicago* (New York: New York University Press, 1996), 66–70, 79–80. States varied in their legal definitions of dependency and delinquency. See Sophonisba P. Breckinridge and Helen R. Jeter, *A Summary of Juvenile-Court Legislation in the United States* (Washington, DC: Government Printing Office, 1920), 15–19.

12. Cited in Joan Gittens, *Poor Relations: The Children of the State of Illinois, 1818–1990* (Urbana: University of Illinois Press, 1994), 116; Ralph J. Riley, *A Working Manual for Juvenile Court Officers* (Chicago: University of Chicago Press, 1932), 37. The Illinois definitions of delinquency were similar to those of other states, such as New York; see Arthur B. Spingarn, *Laws Relating to Sex Morality in New York City* (New York: The Century Company, 1926), 87. That parents used the juvenile courts to discipline their children was noted early by Thomas Eliot and Grace Abbott. See Thomas D. Eliot, *The Juvenile Court and the Community* (New York: Macmillan, 1914), 131, and Abbott, *The Child and the State*, 337. Recent scholarship, too, has emphasized how children and parents used the judicial system for their own purposes, encouraging us to revisit our views of juvenile courts as hegemonic institutions. See Mary E. Odem and Steven Schlossman, "Guardians of Virtue: The Juvenile Court and Female Delinquency in Early-Twentieth-Century Los Angeles," *Crime and Delinquency* 37 (April 1991): 186–203; and Carolyn Strange, *Toronto's Girl Problem: The Perils and Pleasures of the City, 1880–1930* (Toronto: University of Toronto Press, 1995).

13. Probation officers were encouraged when investigating homes to be friendly yet look surreptitiously around the houses to assess conditions. Margueritte Anita Elowson, "Some Aspects of the Cook County Juvenile Court in Relation to Readjustment of the Delinquent Girl" (Master's thesis, University of Chicago, 1930), 9; 1917 CCJCAR, HWL, 8. Elowson examined seven hundred delinquent girls from 1928 to 1929 but accessed CCJC files from as far back as 1921 for complete records on each girl. In the early years of the juvenile court, two members of the Juvenile Court Committee sat next to the judge to advise him; Bowen, *Speeches, Letters, and Addresses*, 825. Superintendents and staff from the Chicago Home for Girls and the State Industrial School for Delinquent Girls (at Geneva) also attended the sessions and assisted in the commitments.

14. Elowson, "Some Aspects of the Cook County Juvenile Court," 12–13; Abbott, *The Child and the State*, 415; Hurley, comp., "Origins of the Illinois Juvenile Court Law," 328.

15. Clara E. Laughlin, "A Court of Kindly Eyes," box 5, folder 107, MB, UICSC. Judge Pinckney, too, talked about how he could differentiate "crocodile tears" from "genuine sorrow"; "A Day in the Juvenile Court-Delinquent, Monday, June 10, 1901," in Hurley, comp., *Origin of the Illinois Juvenile Court Law*, 88.

16. 1909 CCJCAR, HWL, 27; 1915 CCJCAR, HWL, 57; Elowson, "Some Aspects of the Cook County Juvenile Court," 14; Gittens, *Poor Relations*, 117; 1909 CCJCAR, HWL, 28. The only staff members permitted in Bartelme's room were a female stenographer and probation officer, further ensuring the girls' privacy as well as reinforcing women's moral domain.

17. Elowson, "Some Aspects of the Cook County Juvenile Court," 17–18, 34; David Henry Hoover, "A Study of Juvenile Probation in Cook County" (B.A. thesis, University of Chicago, 1918), 31, 34, 61; 1914 CCJCAR, HWL, 5; "The Girl Prisoners," *Oak Leaves*, January 17, 1920, box 5, folder 107, MB, UICSC. Percy Kammerer also noted many victims of rape and incest; Percy Gamble Kammerer, "The Social Consequences of Illegitimacy," *Social Hygiene* 6 (April 1920): 169. Mary Odem, too, noted many girls were sexually assaulted by a male relative, although self-reporting should be questioned; Odem, *Delinquent Daughters*, 58. For another assessment on foster care, see William Healy, Augusta F. Bronner, Edith M. H. Baylor, and J. Prentice Murphy, *Reconstructing Behavior in Youth: A Study of Problem Children in Foster Families* (New York: Alfred A. Knopf, 1929).

18. 1906 CCJCAR, HWL, 6, 23; Louise de Koven Bowen, *Growing Up with a City* (New York: Macmillan, 1926), chap. 7.

19. Bowen, *Growing Up with a City*, 75. As Seth Koven and Sonya Michel have argued, maternalism operated at two levels, reinscribing traditional women's roles while at the same time promoting women's involvement in the state. Seth Koven and Sonya Michel, eds., *Mothers of a New World: Maternalist Politics and the Origins of Welfare States* (New York: Routledge, 1993), 7–10. The female club members of San Francisco that Gayle Gullett examined were as zealous as the JPA members in their investigations of dance halls; see Gullet, " 'City Mothers, City Daughters, and the Dance Hall Girls': The Limits of Female Political Power in San Francisco, 1913," in *Women and the Structure of Society: Selected Research from the Fifth Berkshire Conference on the History of Women*, ed. Barbara J. Harris and JoAnne K. McNamara (Durham, NC: Duke University Press, 1984), 149–59. On an individual level, upper-class women were encouraged to "study" a family, even their "back-door world[s]" of domestic servants, and create miniature social settlements. See Clara E. Laughlin, *The Work-a-Day Girl* (New York: F. H. Revell, 1913; reprt., New York: Arno Press, 1974), 103–4.

20. Lathrop, "The Background of the Juvenile Court in Illinois," 293; Dec. 28, 1898 Minutes, CWCMR, CHS. For further information on Mary Bartelme, see Estelle Freedman, "Bartelme, Mary Margaret," in *Notable American Women: The Modern Period*, ed. Barbara Sicherman and Carol Hurd Green with Ilene Kantrov and Harriette Walker (Cambridge, MA: Belknap Press of Harvard University Press, 1980), 60–61.

21. Helen Rankin Jeter, *The Chicago Juvenile Court* (Chicago: University of Chicago Libraries, 1922), 27–28; "First Chicago Woman Judge Will Hear Girl Cases," *Record Herald*, December 11, 1912.

22. 1915 CCJCAR, HWL, 11.

23. "Miss Mary M. Bartelme and the November Election," *Eleanor Record* 9 (1923), box 4, folder 67, MB, UICSC; see also box 5, folder 107, MB, UICSC. The Chicago Woman's Club had made recommendations for a female state attorney with the juvenile court, as well as for the staffing, training and activities of juvenile court and related agencies, such as the Institute for Psychopathic Research; Twenty-First JPAAR, NU, 77–78.

24. 1913 CCJCAR, HWL, 38–40; September 11, 1925 letter, box 5, folder 107, MB, UICSC; Case #6, "Social Work-Delinquents, Restricted," box 4, folder 75a, CFR, UICSC.

25. "'Suitcase Mary' Inspired Bartelme School's Name," *Chicago Tribune*, October 13, 1926, box 126, folder 8, CFR, UICSC.

26. "Social Work-Delinquents, Restricted," box 4, folder 75a, CFR, UICSC. Healy thought that there was "golden moment" when parents and youth could mutually resolve a problem. Murray Levine and Adeline Levine, *A Social History of Helping Services: Clinic, Court, School, and Community* (New York: Appleton-Century-Crofts, 1970), 171.

27. "Social Work-Delinquents, Restricted," box 4, folder 75a, CFR, UICSC.

28. Bartelme thought that immigrant parents', especially mothers', lack of understanding of their children's lives in America, was an enormous problem. Box 2, folder 26, MB, UICSC. Accordingly, probation officers in the Lower North Side and South Side districts formed mothers' clubs and citizen classes. See Annette Marie Garrett, "The Administration of the Aid to Mothers' Law in Illinois 1917 to 1925" (Ph.D. diss., University of Chicago, 1925), 19.

29. 1913 CCJCAR, HWL, 38.

30. Clara E. Laughlin, "A Court of Kindly Eyes," folder 107, box 5, MB, UICSC.

31. "Social Work-Delinquents," box 4, folder 75a, CFR, UICSC.

32. "The Girl Prisoners," *Oak Leaves*, January 17, 1920, box 5, folder 107, MB, UICSC.

33. Mary E. McChristie, "What Is Success and What Is Failure?" in *The 1928 Proceedings of the National Probation Association* (New York: National Probation Association, 1928), 249; George E. Worthington and Ruth Topping, "The Morals Court of Chicago," *Social Hygiene* 7 (October 1921): 379; box 2, folder 15, MB, UICSC.

34. "The Girl Prisoners," *Oak Leaves*, January 17, 1920, box 5, folder 107, MB, UICSC.

35. Ethel S. Dummer, *Why I Think So: The Autobiography of an Hypothesis* (Chicago: Clarke-McElroy, n.d.), 45–46.

36. "Social Work-Delinquents, Restricted," box 4, folder 75a, CFR, UICSC.

37. Ibid.

38. Ibid. Parents also wrongly accused their daughters of sexual misbehavior. For example, in at least four of the recorded court cases in 1913, parents had insisted their daughters had sexual relations, despite the girls' denial. Pelvic examinations revealed that the girls were truthful. Examinations, then, were not only performed to verify sexual involvement but to exonerate the girls. 1913 CCJCAR, HWL, 37.

39. "Social Work Restricted," box 4, folder 72, CFR, UICSC. As early as 1945, a merger between the Chicago Home for Girls and the Mary Bartelme Club was recommended. In 1960, the organizations were finally unified and the name changed to the Mary Bartelme Home for Girls of Metropolitan Chicago. "Mary Bartelme Home for Girls of Metropolitan Chicago, 1932–69"; January 15, 1960 letter, box 370, file 7, WCMC, CHS.

40. "Mary Clubs, November 13, 1938," box 370, folder 7, WCMC, CHS; "Mary Clubs #1 and #2," December 20, 1934, box 370, folder 3, WCMC, CHS. Hoover, "A Study of Juvenile Probation in Cook County," 61.

41. "Mary Clubs, November 13, 1938," box 370, folder 7, WCMC, CHS; 1916 CCJCAR, HWL, 61–63.

42. 1918 CCJCAR, HWL, 21; "Mary Clubs, November 13, 1938," box 370, folder 7, WCMC, CHS; 1916 CCJCAR, HWL, 64.

43. Box 5, folder 107, MB, UICSC.

44. "The Girl Prisoners," box 5, folder 107, MB, UICSC. Other homes for delinquent and dependent girls included the Melissa Evans Club, discussed in chapter 7; the Eleanor Junior League for dependent girls; and the Home Training School, supported by the Chicago Woman's Club, which gave four to five dependent girls "intensive home training." All of the clubs, established before the war years, cooperated with the juvenile court. 1916 CCJCAR, HWL, 63; Hoover, "A Study of Juvenile Probation in Cook County," 61. The Home for Working Girls, although receiving public funds, took a different turn. Because of insufficient funds and thus, limited staff, the doors were locked at 10:30 each night. Many girls were subsequently forced to stay out all night and some were accosted and became pregnant. Other girls danced seductively before their bedroom windows, causing men to knock at the door, thinking it was a house of prostitution. See Louise de Koven Bowen, *Fighting to Make Chicago Safe for Children* (Chicago: Juvenile Protective Association, n.d.), 9.

45. Maude Mary Firth, "The Use of the Foster Home for the Care of the Delinquent Girls of the Cook County Juvenile Court" (Master's thesis, University of Chicago, 1924), 115–18, 97–110, 37–42.

46. Box 5, folder 107, MB, UICSC.

47. "Speeches—Girls Court Committee," box 2, folder 33, MB, UICSC. There were many letters of thanks from the Mary Club girls for the suits and money; "Mary Bartelme Home for Girls of Metro Chicago, 1959," box 126, folder 8, CFR, UICSC.

48. Christopher Lasch, "Social Pathologists and the Socialization of Reproduction," in *The American Family in Social-Historical Perspective*, ed. Michael Gordon, 3rd ed. (New York: St. Martin's Press, 1983), 89.

49. See table 11 in Appendix 2 for the numbers and types of charges from 1904 to 1927, including the more violent and aggressive charges of robbery, burglary, forgery, assault, arson, and concealed weapons. Elowson's 1930 study noted that African-American girls, more than white girls, were held three times more often for stealing and twice as often for disorderly fighting and street disturbance. Elowson, "Some Aspects of the Cook County Juvenile Court in Relation to Readjustment of the Delinquent Girl," 51, 82–83.

50. See chapter 1 for a discussion of women's marginality in the Chicago School.

51. Information is from 1904 to 1926 CCJCAR, HWL. Peter Kasius's study of over fifteen thousand sex delinquents found that nearly 60 percent of first-time offenders were under seventeen years of age. Peter Kasius, "Venereal Disease Aspects of Delinquency," in *The Development of Juvenile Courts and Probation: Annual Report and Proceedings of the Nineteenth Annual Conference of the National Probation Association* (New York: National Probation Association, 1925), 151.

52. Steven Schlossman and Stephanie Wallach, "The Crime of Precocious Sexuality: Female Juvenile Delinquency in the Progressive Era" *Harvard Educational Review* 48 (February 1978): 69, 75.

53. Knupfer, *Toward a Tenderer Humanity and a Nobler Womanhood*, 79. According to Elowson, only 25 percent of native-born white girls (based upon both parents' nativity) from 1928 to 1929 were placed on probation, compared to almost 40 percent of African-American girls. In contrast, native-born white delinquent girls' rates for case dismissals were generally higher than most other ethnic groups for the same years. Elowson, "Some Aspects of the Cook County Juvenile Court," 66, 69.

54. See Earl R. Moses, *The Negro Delinquent in Chicago* (Washington, DC: Washington Public Schools, 1936). In other cities, such as Boston, African-American children and youth

experienced similar discrimination in institutional placement. See Eric C. Schneider, *In the Web of Class: Delinquents and Reformers in Boston, 1810s–1930s* (New York: New York University Press, 1992), 63.

55. These issues are fully discussed in David Tyack and Elisabeth Hansot, *Learning Together: A History of Co-Education in American Schools* (New York: Russell Sage Foundation, 1990).

56. Elowson, "Some Aspects of the Cook County Juvenile Court in Relation to Readjustment of the Delinquent Girl," 43–47.

57. Sophonisba Breckinridge and Edith Abbott, *The Delinquent Child and the Home* (New York: Russell Sage Foundation, 1912), 37; Laughlin, *The Work-a-Day Girl*, 95; Gittens, *Poor Relations*, 117; 1917 CCJCAR, HWL, 70.

58. Thomas Minehan, *Boy and Girl Tramps of America* (New York: Farrar and Rinehart, 1934), 170; Moses, *The Negro Delinquent in Chicago*, 128, 132. The category of mothers' "moral unfitness" was often designated as a cause for female delinquency, but rarely so for its male counterpart. By 1917, fathers, not only mothers, could be termed "immoral," although few were categorized as such. Further, early court records do not list immorality as a charge for boys; 1910 CCJCAR, HWL, 7.

59. 1906 to 1912 CCJCAR, HWL.

60. Moses, *The Negro Delinquent in Chicago*, 77; 1923 CCJCAR, HWL, 25. The percentage of Polish delinquent girls likewise exceeded the Polish population in Chicago in 1923 by almost 9 percent. 1923 CCJCAR, HWL, 25; see also table 10 in Appendix 2.

61. 1913 CCJCAR, HWL, 43, 50.

62. Ibid., 48–49.

63. 1909 CCJCAR, HWL, 76.

64. As of 1913, six divisions of the CCJC served dependent children, male and female delinquents, and mother pensioners. There appeared to be little communication among the divisions about cases. Just as the juvenile court lagged in its payments for delinquent children so, too, did it fall behind in the mothers' pensions. It should come as no surprise that maternalist clubs and individuals stepped in and assisted, perhaps aware that a lack of funds would have a deleterious effect on all of the juvenile court's programs. Louise de Koven Bowen, for one, donated $1,000 to the pension fund; the Chicago Woman's Club also paid the salaries of staff in that division. Box 2, folder 26, MB, UICSC. See also Edith Abbott and Sophonisba P. Breckinridge, "The Administration of the Aid-to-Mothers Law in Illinois," in *The Family in America*, ed. David J. Rothman and Sheila Rothman (Washington, DC: Government Printing Office, 1921, Reprt., New York: Arno Press and The New York Times, 1972), 7, 116; Joanne L. Goodwin, *Gender and the Politics of Welfare Reform: Mothers' Pensions in Chicago, 1911–1929* (Chicago: University of Chicago Press, 1997).

65. *Proceedings of the Conference on the Care of Dependent Children* (Washington, DC: Government Printing Office, 1909).

66. 1916 CCJCAR, HWL, 10. See also E. C. Lindeman, "Parent Education as a Social Movement," in *Parent Education: The First Yearbook*, ed. National Congress of Parents and Teachers (Washington, DC: National Congress of Parents and Teachers, 1930), 13; F. Emory Lyon, "Home Neglect, A Factor in Delinquency: How It May Be Met?" in *Community Treatment of Delinquency: Proceedings of the National Probation Association* (New York: National Probation Association, 1924), 313–14; White House Conference on Child Health and Protection, *White House Conference, Addresses and Abstracts of Committee Reports* (New York: The Century Company, 1930), 147–51.

67. Merritt W. Pinckney, "The Delinquent Girl and the Juvenile Court," in *The Child in the City; A Series of Papers Presented at the Conferences Held During the Chicago Child Welfare Exhibit,* ed. Sophonisba Breckinridge (Chicago: Department of Social Investigation, Chicago School of Civics and Philanthropy, 1912), 350–51.

68. Strange, *Toronto's Girl Problem*, 139.

69. 1913 CCJCAR, HWL, 61. Hoover, "A Study of Juvenile Probation in Cook County," 9; Firth, "The Use of the Foster Home," 64.

70. Firth, "The Use of the Foster Home," 63.

71. Ibid. Girls who did not return to their homes were sent to private homes where employment compensation and bank accounts were established. Families were to comply with the probation officers' recommendations that the girls be paid a regular wage, and that they not engage in heavy work, such as washing or scrubbing. 1913 CCJC records indicated that most girls were paid an average of six to eight dollars per week. But it was not clear whether they were required to do more strenuous housework or if they were allowed to spend part of their earnings.

72. Elowson, "Some Aspects of the Cook County Juvenile Court," 62, 64. In 1915, Grace M. Fernald found that only 13 percent of delinquent girls she studied were from two-parent families; thus, broken homes were considered one of the primary reasons for delinquency, as well as little parental discipline, truancy from school, and child employment; Grace Fernald, cited in Kelley, *Mental Aspects of Delinquency*, 55. Ellwood's study estimated that of delinquent children in state schools, nearly 25 to 35 percent were from broken homes; Ellwood cited in George B. Mangold, *Problems of Child Welfare* (New York: Macmillan, 1928), 408. The length of most delinquent girls' probation in 1913 was from one to three years; by 1915, the average length was one year. 1913 CCJCAR, HWL, 90; 1915 CCJCAR, HWL, 35.

73. Warner, *Juvenile Detention in the United States*, 115.

74. Elowson, "Some Aspects of the Cook County Juvenile Court," 47, 53. The multiple accounts of incest in Chicago were consistent with accounts noted by Odem and Gordon. See Odem, *Delinquent Daughters*; and Gordon, *Heroes of Their Own Lives*. Breckinridge and Abbott's study of delinquent girls' homes found that of 254 girls, 101 said they were initially victims of force or fraud; in 46 cases, many reported to be victims of their own family members; Sophonisba P. Breckinridge and Edith Abbott, *The Delinquent Child and the Home* (New York: Charities Publication Committee, 1912), 315. Again, the problems of self-reporting should be taken into account.

75. See 1918 to 1920 CCJCAR, HWL, as well as chapter 7 of this book.

76. See table 14 in appendix 2.

77. Ibid. According to one study of delinquent girls' institutional commitments from 1928 to 1931, Polish girls were usually sent to the House of the Good Shepherd. Edna Ruth Davis, "A Comparison of Four National and Racial Groups," *Smith College Studies in Social Work* 13 (March 1933): 256–58.

78. The Chicago Home for Girls and the Geneva School's failure rates were respectively 51 percent and 52 percent; see William Healy and Augusta F. Bronner, *Delinquents and Criminals: Their Making and Unmaking. Studies in Two American Cities* (New York: AMS Press, 1926), 80. Other facilities for delinquent and dependent girls included the Home for the Friendless, the Salvation Army, and the Beulah Home and Maternity Hospital. The juvenile court sent very few girls to the Beulah Home, and for good reason. The deaths of over twenty-five infants at its other maternity home in Michigan prompted a grand jury investigation. "Annual Service Report of the Beulah Home and Maternity Hospital of Chicago, 10/1/1929 to 10/30/1930," box 253, folder 5, WCMC, CHS; "Launch Michigan Maternity Home Deaths Inquiry," box 253, folder 5, WCMC, CHS.

79. See chapter 9 for further discussion of the Catholic archdiocese.

80. 1910 CCJCAR, HWL, 11. Worthington and Topping noted how many girls eluded their probation officers, often hiding or giving them false addresses and names; Worthington and Topping, "The Morals Court of Chicago," 381, 388.

81. Healy and Bronner, *Delinquents and Criminals*, 252, 263.

Chapter 6

1. Elizabeth Frances Hirsch, "A Study of the Chicago and Cook County School for Boys" (Master's thesis, University of Chicago, 1926), 6.

2. Henriette Greenebaum Frank and Amalie Hofer Jerome, comps., *Annals of the Chicago Woman's Club for the First Forty Years of Its Organization, 1876–1916* (Chicago: Chicago Woman's Club, 1916), 125, 126–27; William Irvin, "Miss Florence Scully, Friend, Guide of Friendless, Retires," *Chicago Tribune*, February 11, 1934, sec. 3, 1–2.

3. Phyllis Rae Osborn, "A Study of the Detention of Two Hundred Six Children" (Master's thesis, University of Chicago, 1931), 6. The quotation is from the author, not the statute. Savilla Millis, *The Juvenile Detention Home in Relation to Juvenile Court Policy: A Study of Intake in the Cook County Chicago Juvenile Detention Home* (Chicago: University of Chicago Press, 1927), 17; Frank and Jerome, *Annals of the Chicago Woman's Club*, 163.

4. David J. Rothman, *The Discovery of the Asylum: Social Order and Disorder in the New Republic* (Boston: Little, Brown, 1971).

5. Louise de Koven Bowen, *Growing Up with a City* (New York: Macmillan, 1926), 300–305. See also Mrs. Joseph T. [Louise de Koven] Bowen, *Open Windows: Stories of People and Places* (Chicago: Ralph Fletcher Seymour, 1946), 187–88. Donations were also received from the Hull House, and individual philanthropists Mrs. Julius Rosenwald, Louise de Koven Bowen, and several judges; 1908 CCJCAR, HWL, 69–70.

6. Bowen, *Growing Up with A City*, 302.

7. 1906 CCJCAR, HWL, 8, 10–11. Osborn, "A Study of the Detention of Two Hundred Six Children," 5–6. It was not until 1919, however, that a law was passed which authorized the county to levy a property tax to meet the expenses; Hirsch, "A Study of the Chicago and Cook County School for Boys," 8.

8. 1909 CCJCAR, HWL, 34, 82.

9. Florence Mary Warner, *Juvenile Detention in the United States* (Chicago: University of Chicago Press, 1933), 38; Mary Bartelme, "The Girl Prisoners," *Oak Leaves*, January 7, 1920, folder 107, box 5, MB, UICSC. The Illinois Association for Criminal Justice was concerned that young children not be placed in the Chicago Detention Home because of association with bad companions; Illinois Association for Criminal Justice, *Illinois Crime Survey* (Illinois Association for Criminal Justice and The Chicago Crime Commission, 1929; reprt., Montclair, NJ: Patterson Smith, 1968), 730.

10. 1926 CCJCAR, HWL, 187; 1909 CCJCAR, HWL, 81.

11. Warner, *Juvenile Detention in the United States*, 17–18; Millis, *The Juvenile Detention Home in Relation to Juvenile Court Policy*, 18.

12. 1913 CCJCAR, HWL, 120, 121; 1911 CCJCAR, HWL, 80; 1917 CCJCAR, HWL, 66. The Illinois Association for Criminal Justice also recommended that children not be transported in patrol wagons but instead on a trolley, the el, or in a police motor car, and also accompanied by plain clothes officers; Illinois Association for Criminal Justice, *Illinois Crime Survey*, 730.

13. 1915 CCJCAR, HWL, 54; Millis, *The Juvenile Detention Home in Relation to Juvenile Court Policy*, 20; 1915 CCJCAR, HWL, 53, 54. Regardless of the girls' duties, the proximity of their dormitories to the hospital, kitchen, and pantry indicated the intended course of reform proposed by the Home; 1906 CCJCAR, HWL, 10, 23.

14. 1917 CCJCAR, HWL, 76; 1918 CCJCAR, HWL, 60.

15. 1908 CCJCAR, HWL, 66; 1917 CCJCAR, HWL, 66; 1923 CCJCAR, HWL, 5; Warner, *Juvenile Detention in the United States*, 5. The Home was described as a prison with its high stone wall and barred windows by the Illinois Association for Criminal Justice, *Illinois Crime Survey*, 681. Unfortunately, the Home did not record the number of children detained there each year so I am unable to determine what percentage of them escaped.

16. 1925 CCJCAR, HWL, 67.

17. 1926 CCJCAR, HWL, 66. In cooperation with the Chicago Public Library, the Home provided books for boys awaiting trial. Carefully selected to appeal to boys ages 17 to 21, the list included adventures, mysteries, and westerns. Unfortunately, there was no book list for girls. Other forms of entertainment included movies, although again no listing was provided. 1916 CCJCAR, HWL, 10–11; 1920 CCJCAR, HWL, 57.

18. 1908 CCJCAR, HWL, 68–69.

19. 1926 CCJCAR, HWL, 69; Osborn, "A Study of the Detention of Two Hundred Six Children," 5. Sociologist Thomas Eliot of Northwestern University had declared that the very best of detention homes were like "special schools," although the worst were like jails. He also argued that detention homes should be administered by public school systems. Thomas D. Eliot, *The Juvenile Court and the Community* (New York: Macmillan, 1914), 19. Noticeable changes were made in 1923 so that the facility would "carry no suggestions of bleak and chilling austerities." See 1924 CCJCAR, HWL, 67. The Home, like other physical plants, was subject to standards. The Children's Bureau had recommended that there be sufficient space to avoid overcrowding, even though rooms were to be arranged to allow segregation by gender, character, and medical conditions. Proper lighting and ventilation were also thought essential, as well as security against escape and fire protection. See Millis, *The Juvenile Detention Home in Relation to Juvenile Court Policy*, 19; Warner, *Juvenile Detention in the United States*, 41.

20. 1917 CCJCAR, HWL, 75. Costs in 1930 were $2.61 per child, not including overhead or education. Nearly 73 percent of the Home's monies, though, was allocated for salaries. By 1930, there was a greater tendency for girls to be committed to institutions than boys; more precisely, there was a ratio of forty-one boys to fifty girls; Warner, *Juvenile Detention in the United States*, 8–9, 44.

21. Osborn, "A Study of the Detention of Two Hundred Six Children," 41–42. Girls were thought to be so suggestible that Healy recommended they be examined by a female, not male, doctor; Healy, *The Individual Delinquent*, 65. Further, he discouraged the practice of examining girls for evidence of virginity, pointing out that some may be virgins physically but their minds were so charged with sexuality that their outcomes were not promising. Thus, physical evidence never presented the complete portrait; Healy, *The Individual Delinquent: A Text-Book of Diagnosis and Prognosis for All Concerned in Understanding Offenders* (Boston: Little, Brown, 1929), 66. In the case of African-American girls, Healy was not so concerned with individual suggestibility. Following a retrogressionist model, he and Bronner referred instead to their extreme suggestibility as a group, especially their love of excitement, gambling, and obsessive mental imagery; William Healy and Augusta F. Bronner, "Youthful Offenders. A Comparative Study of Two Groups, Each of 1,000 Young Recidivists," *American Journal of Sociology* 22 (July 1916): 49–50.

22. Osborn, "A Study of the Detention of Two Hundred Six Children," 89–90.

23. William Healy, *The Individual Delinquent*, 449, 491.

24. 1913 CCJCAR, HWL, 111; Millis, *The Juvenile Detention Home in Relation to Juvenile Court Policy*, 38, 49; 1912 CCJCAR, HWL, 89, 90; 1911 CCJCAR, HWL, 81. Eighty percent of the children sent to the Chicago Detention Home were brought in by the police; 1918 CCJCAR, HWL, 10. This prompted the Illinois Association for Criminal Justice to recommend that social workers, not police officers, make the initial investigation; Illinois Association for Criminal Justice, *Illinois Crime Survey*, 680. In 1913, a CWC committee cooperated with the JPA in hiring a social worker to interview boys and girls detained in the county jail, as well as to assist in their dispositions. Frank and Jerome, *Annals of the Chicago Woman's Club*, 317.

25. Warner, *Juvenile Detention in the United States*, 44; 1918 CCJCAR, HWL, 11.

26. 1924 CCJCAR, HWL; Warner, *Juvenile Detention in the United States*, 30, 101, 103. According to the JPA, at least one-third of the girls and young women in Chicago jails in 1913

were African American; Joan Gittens, *Poor Relations: The Children of the State of Illinois, 1818–1990* (Urbana: University of Illinois Press, 1994), 43. See also Earl R. Moses, *The Negro Delinquent in Chicago* (Washington, DC: Washington Public Schools, 1936),109; White House Conference on Child Health and Protection, *The Delinquent Child* (New York: The Century Company, 1932), 323. In one newspaper article, African-American club woman Ida B. Wells Barnett described police brutality against fifteen-year-old Frances Jordan. As Barnett recounted, "three big burly policemen put her in the wagon, threatened to shoot her legs off if she attempted to run." See "Club Woman Tells of Rotten Conditions in Chicago's Public Schools," *Chicago Defender*, March 1, 1930.

27. 1909 CCJCAR, HWL, 7; Millis, *The Juvenile Detention Home in Relation to Juvenile Court Policy*, 23; Osborn, "A Study of the Detention of Two Hundred Six Children," 45.

28. 1915 CCJCAR, HWL, 50–51; 1912 CCJCAR, HWL, 89.

29. 1912 CCJCAR, HWL, 88, 89; 1909 CCJCAR, HWL, 81; 1913 CCJCAR, HWL, 114.

30. 1913 CCJCAR, HWL, 118; Mary E. Odem, *Delinquent Daughters: Protecting and Policing Adolescent Female Sexuality in the United States, 1885–1920* (Chapel Hill: University of North Carolina Press, 1995), 65, 72; 1917 CCJCAR, HWL, 83; 1912 CCJCAR, HWL, 91. See also Joel D. Hunter, "The History and Development of Institute for the Study of Children," in *The Child, the Clinic and the Court* (New York: New Republic, 1925), 204–14; and *Proceedings of the Twelfth Annual Conference on the Education of Dependent, Truant, Backward and Delinquent Children* (Baltimore: n.p., 1915). In 1908, 18 percent of the delinquent girls in the Chicago Detention Home had a venereal disease, compared to 1 percent of the delinquent boys. One year later, the percentage for girls increased to 33 percent; 1908 CCJCAR, HWL, 74; 1909 CCJCAR, HWL, 88. A survey of the U.S. Public Health Service of 236 white female delinquents substantiated that over half were infected with gonorrhea; cited in Peter Kasius, "Venereal Disease Aspects of Delinquency," in *The Development of Juvenile Courts and Probation: Annual Report and Proceedings of the Nineteenth Annual Conference of the National Probation Association* (New York: National Probation Association, 1925), 148. Mary Odem and Linda Gordon have written about the abiding concerns of the girls' loss of virginity, verified through pelvic examinations; Odem, *Delinquent Daughters*, 65; Linda Gordon, *Heroes of Their Own Lives: The Politics and History of Family Violence* (New York: Penquin Books, 1988), 216–17. The hospital also performed abortions; see 1909 CCJCAR, HWL, 92.

31. 1910 CCJCAR, HWL, 74; 1916 CCJCAR, HWL, 65; 1918 CCJCAR, HWL, 69; 1924 CCJCAR, HWL, 81.

32. 1917 CCJCAR, HWL, 84–85, 90, 91; 1910 CCJCAR, HWL, 75. One dentist discussed how the multitude of germs in the mouth, from 60 to 70 different strains, traveled to "remote" parts of the body; 1919 CCJCAR, HWL, 83.

33. Osborn, "A Study of Detention of Two Hundred Six Children," 53–54. Lizabeth Cohen has argued that ethnic communities generally took care of their own but this did not seem to be quite true with delinquent children. I believe this was because of the penetration of the state and county and because of the steadfastness of maternalist organizations. As noted, it is probable that in seeking outside medical help, immigrant parents often relied upon the juvenile court services. Lizabeth Cohen, *Making a New Deal: Industrial Workers in Chicago, 1919–1930* (New York: Cambridge University Press, 1990), 57, 62.

34. The Illinois Association for Criminal Justice, *Illinois Crime Survey*, 783.

35. 1910 CCJCAR, HWL, 74.

36. Warner, *Juvenile Detention in the United States*, 51; William Healy and Augusta Bronner, "Juvenile Detention Homes," *Annals of the American Academy of Political and Social Sciences* 151 (September 1930): 186–87. The Illinois Association for Criminal Justice estimated that nearly two-thirds to three-fourths alleged delinquents in the Home were released without a hearing; Illinois Association for Criminal Justice, *Illinois Crime Survey*, 681, 782.

37. Moses, *The Negro Delinquent in Chicago*, 18.

38. Osborn, "A Study of Detention of Two Hundred Six Children," 54–55, 57.

39. Ibid., 54–55.

40. Ibid., 7; Warner, *Juvenile Detention in the United States*, 11.

41. Percentages were figured from CCJCAR, from 1901 to 1913, HWL. These percentages reflected a national trend. By 1930, nearly 84 percent of most detention homes' populations were delinquent children; Warner, *Juvenile Detention in the United States*, 38.

42. 1912 CCJCAR, HWL, 88–89. As of 1915, the Home's staff included a superintendent, doctor, dentist, dispensary nurse, dental nurse, graduate nurse, head nurse, typist, three clerks, a head janitor, four assistants, three janitresses, one laborer, and forty-four attendants. By 1926, the staff consisted of twenty-one employees with eight-hour shifts to supervise the children and maintain the building. Well-trained staff were difficult to procure, as noted: "A calm dignity, an endless tact, a trained approach, an untiring interest and a high idealism, as protecting influences of the child in detention, ought to characterize each employee. Regretfully it is stated that some staff still have far to go toward the realization of these standards." 1915 CCJCAR, HWL, 51; 1926 CCJCAR, HWL, 71.

43. 1913 CCJCAR, HWL, 130. Zuerner thought that most girls did not know how to sew, mend or darn, considered essential skills for their future as wives and mothers; William F. Zuerner, "Detention Homes Report of the Committees," in *The Social Service of the Courts: Proceedings of the Sixteenth Annual Conference of the National Probation Association* (New York: National Probation Association, 1923), 115.

44. 1913 CCJCAR, HWL, 132.

45. 1921 CCJCAR, HWL, 51; Zuerner, "Detention Homes Report of the Committees," 112–13; 1908 CCJCAR, HWL, 67.

46. 1925 CCJCAR, HWL, 77.

47. 1926 CCJCAR, HWL, 71, 73. Recreation periods were also intended "to correct posture, inattention, and above all to create a spirit of good sportsmanship—a trait generally found lacking in our girls." See 1926 CCJCAR, HWL, 71; 1921 CCJCAR, HWL, 50.

48. 1912 CCJCAR, HWL, 91.

49. 1909 CCJCAR, HWL, 93, 94; 1912 CCJCAR, HWL, 90; 1913 CCJCAR, HWL, 130. The Juvenile Court School, part of Dore Public School, was staffed by five teachers, two for delinquent girls only; 1913 CCJCAR, HWL, 13. Other teachers were hired to teach gym and sewing. By 1922, there were six teachers for the school, which followed the public school's curricula, although the school was in session year-round, as well as six days a week; 1922 CCJCAR, HWL, 48.

50. 1912 CCJCAR, HWL, 90; 1921 CCJCAR, HWL, 48; George B. Mangold, *Problems of Child Welfare* (New York: Macmillan, 1928), 452.

51. 1912 CCJCAR, HWL, 89; 1918 CCJCAR, HWL, 60; Millis, *The Juvenile Detention Home in Relation to Juvenile Court Policy*, 22.

52. 1913 CCJCAR, HWL, 115.

53. Osborn, "A Study of Detention of Six Hundred Children," 59–60; 1925 CCJCAR, HWL, 77.

54. Jane Addams, *My Friend, Julia Lathrop* (New York: Macmillan, 1935), 163; Murray Levine and Adeline Levine, *A Social History of Helping Services: Clinic, Court, School, and Community* (New York: Appleton-Century-Crofts, 1970), 147; Emma Lundberg, *Unto the Least of These: Social Services for Children* (New York: D. Appleton-Century, 1947), 121. Joining Ethyl Sturges Dummer on the executive committee were Jane Addams and Julia Lathrop.

55. Addams, *My Friend, Julia Lathrop*, 165; Illinois Association for Criminal Justice, *Illinois Crime Survey*, 778; Jon Snodgrass, "William Healy (1869–1963): Pioneer Child Psychiatrist and Criminologist," *Journal of the History of the Behavioral Sciences* 20 (October 1984): 335; see

also Ellen Ryerson, *The Best-Laid Plans: Americans Juvenile Court Experiment* (New York: Hill and Wang, 1978). Healy's *The Individual Delinquent* was dedicated to Dummer. Healy and Bronner, in their *Delinquents and Criminals: Their Making and Unmaking: Studies in Two American Cities* (New York: AMS Press, 1926), acknowledged Dummer's "inspiration" and financial support. Along with Dummer, members of the JPI's executive committee included Addams, Lathrop, and Graham Taylor; Lathrop was the JPI's first president and Dummer its first secretary. Court clinics became increasingly important as judges and court officials sought psychological and psychiatric assessments to inform their deliberations on delinquents' commitments and treatment plans; Paul Hanly Furfey, *Social Problems of Childhood* (New York: Macmillan, 1929), 117.

56. 1913 CCJCAR, HWL, 118; Zuerner, "Detention Homes Report of the Committees," 111; Katharine F. Lenroot, "Juvenile Detention Homes," in *Social Treatment of the Delinquent: Annual Report and Proceedings of the Fifteenth Annual Conference of the National Probation Association* (New York: National Probation Association, 1922), 93; Leon Stern, "Detention Homes for Children," in *Social Work Year Book, 1933: A Description of Organized Activities in Social Work and in Related Fields*, ed. Fred S. Hall (New York: Russell Sage Foundation, 1933), 131.

57. Bernard Flexner and Roger N. Baldwin, *Juvenile Courts and Probation* (New York: The Century Company, 1916), 41; 1910 CCJCAR, HWL, 10. Healy thought the original name of the institute was "silly" as most youth were not psychopathic; Snodgrass, "William Healy (1869–1963)": 335.

58. Snodgrass, "William Healy (1869–1963)": 332–34; Victoria Lynn Getis, "A Disciplined Society: The Juvenile Court, Reform, and the Social Sciences in Chicago, 1890–1930" (Ph.D. diss., University of Michigan, 1994), 179–80. The social construction of female psychiatric aberrations, guided by moral prescriptions, was particularly apparent in the preponderance of girls diagnosed as psychopathological liars and as overly influenced by suggestibility. Boys' deviance, on the other hand, often resulted from their love of adventure; Healy and Bronner, *Delinquents and Criminals*, 181.

59. Lundberg, *Unto the Least of These*, 267; Healy, *The Individual Delinquent*, 134; Snodgrass, "William Healy (1869–1963)": 337. Based upon his study of the probation officers' case records, as well as children's physical, psychological, and psychiatric examinations, Healy concluded, at least by 1915, that approximately 72 percent of the girls became delinquent through demoralized home conditions, especially alcoholism, immorality, criminality, and poverty; 1915 CCJCAR, HWL, 22.

60. Healy, *The Individual Delinquent*, 53, 57–58.

61. Ibid., 75–103; for the schedule of data on delinquents, see 53–67. In her early work, Bronner did most of the psychological testing; Healy supervised most of the medical work.

62. Ibid., 58, 77, 89, 98.

63. 1909 CCJCAR, HWL, 29; 1920 CCJCAR, HWL, 22.

64. William Healy and Mary Tenney Healy, *Pathological Lying, Accusation, and Swindling* (Boston: Little, Brown, 1926), 15; 1920 CCJCAR, HWL, 22. Case records of immigrant girls classified as feebleminded can be found in Sophonisba P. Breckinridge, *Family Welfare Work in a Metropolitan Community: Selected Case Records* (Chicago: University of Chicago Press, 1924). Unfortunately, the JPI's annual reports were not available and so I am unable to determine the percentages of children classified as feebleminded annually.

65. Healy, *The Individual Delinquent*, 408–9.

66. Ibid., 563–64.

67. Ibid., 245, 410. See also William Healy and Augusta F. Bronner, *Delinquents and Criminals*, 138.

68. Ibid., 403. This was not an isolated incident. Healy often referred to the beauty of his female patients, evident in such phrases as "magnificently endowed physically," "considerable

measure of good looks," "very well developed and nourished," and "pleasant features and expression." Ibid., 14, 124.

69. Ibid., 374–75.

70. Ibid., 714–17.

71. Ibid., 627.

72. Ibid., 627–31.

73. Warner, *Juvenile Detention in the United States*, 133.

74. Healy and Healy, *Pathological Lying*, 186. Another girl, found to be an extreme fabricator, produced brilliant scores on all the abilities tests. She was so skilled at stealing that she returned the items to the very stores from which she had stolen and then requested refunds. Healy found no evidence of any mental aberration other than her persistent lying. Instead of considering her family's extreme poverty as one causative factor, he chose to focus on her pathological lying; Healy, *The Individual Delinquent*, 612–13.

75. Healy, *The Individual Delinquent*, 70; Robert M. Mennel, *Thorns and Thistles: Juvenile Delinquents in the United States 1825–1940* (Hanover, NH: University Press of New England, 1973), 164; 44. The delinquents' "own story," then, assumed multiple purposes: as instructional material; a diagnostic tool; a form of "confession" to the judge; an experimental methodology; and data for Healy's longitudinal studies on delinquents. For research purposes, as well as to make this prodigious amount of material available to professional audiences, Healy condensed this vital information onto note cards and so created another genre of medical literature: psychograms. Healy, *The Individual Delinquent*, 53. Ironically, the girls undermined Healy's contention that every situation comprised part of a process "continually in the making." Although Healy was referring specifically to the ways in which the court and clinic affected the offender, he did not consider how the girls took an active role in these processes. Ethel Kawin, "Anniversary of the Founding of the First Juvenile Court and the Establishment of the First Institute for Juvenile Research," *Institution Quarterly* 16 (March 1925): 98.

76. William Healy, "Knowing Your Individual," in *The Social Service of the Courts: Proceedings of the Sixteenth Annual Conference of the National Probation Association* (New York: National Probation Association, 1923), 231. See also William Healy, "The Psychology of the Situation: A Fundamental for Understanding and Treatment of Delinquency and Crime," in *The Child, the Clinic, and the Court* (New York: New Republic, 1927), 44–45, for his retrospective view on the method of the child's "own story."

77. William Healy, *Case Studies of Mentally and Morally Abnormal Types* (Cambridge: Harvard University Summer School, 1912), 50–51.

78. Ibid.

79. Healy, *The Individual Delinquent*, 475–81.

80. Ibid., 477. Perhaps the most baffling cases were young, intelligent, and attractive women who chose to lead undesirable lives. One nineteen-year-old girl had deliberately become a prostitute because it was the quickest way to make money. In her own words, she preferred this line of work to more strenuous employment. Despite her logic and fine mental abilities, Healy and Bronner found her to be a "frankly lazy and sensuous type," following in her father's path, a "notoriously lazy and shiftless" man, despite his mentally acuity. Ibid., 336–37.

81. Ibid., 609–12.

82. Mennel, *Thorns and Thistles*, 167; Healy and Bronner, "Juvenile Detention Homes," 180–81, 182.

83. Kathleen W. Jones, *Taming the Troublesome Child: American Families, Child Guidance, and the Limits of Psychiatric Authority* (Cambridge, MA: Harvard University Press, 1999). Unlike Edith Abbott's model of social work, child guidance clinics reinstated the critical importance of the probation officer's personality. See Levine and Levine, *A Social History of Helping Services*, 168. Some reformers felt clinics should be taken from juvenile courts and placed in the

schools. As Jessie Binford recommended, "The successful program [to prevent juvenile delinquency] must begin, not with the criminal and the law, but with the child, the home, the school, the community, and the body politic." Jessie F. Binford, "Community Responsibility," *Welfare Magazine* 19 (February 1928): 148. Healy increasingly faulted schools for their lack of concern with students' personalities. See William Healy, "The Constructive Values of Conflicts, Successes and Failures" in *Building Character: Proceedings of the Midwest Conference on Parent Education, February, 1928* (Chicago: University of Chicago Press, 1928), 132–60; William Healy, "How Does the School Produce or Prevent Delinquency?," *Journal of Educational Sociology* 6 (April 1933): 450–70.

84. Albert Sidney Beckham, "The Behavior Problem Clinic and the Negro Child," *Journal of Negro Life* 9 (April 1931): 111, 112; Getis, "A Disciplined Society," 264. Beckham found 12 percent of the African-American children he studied to be feebleminded; Beckham, "The Behavior Problem Clinic and the Negro Child": 112. Other works by Beckham include "A Study of Race Attitudes in Negro Children of Adolescent Age," *Journal of Abnormal and Social Psychology* 29 (April–June 1934): 18–29; "Juvenile Crime," *Journal of Juvenile Research* 16 (January 1932): 66–76; and "Juvenile Delinquency and the Negro," *Opportunity* 9 (October 1931): 300–2. Beginning in 1920, Burgess and Park sent sociology students to the IJR for field studies, where they learned to conduct social histories, mental tests, and interviews; Getis, "A Disciplined Society," 250. The sociological and psychological worlds of professionals would became even more conjoined in 1930, when Ernest Burgess became director of the Behavior Research Fund, affiliated with the IJR.

85. Kawin, "Anniversary of the Founding of the First Juvenile Court": 97; 1917 CCJ-CAR, HWL, 6; Herman M. Adler, M.D., "The Juvenile Psychopathic Institute and the Work of the Division of the Criminologist," *Institution Quarterly* 9 (March 31, 1918): 5; Joel D. Hunter, "The History and Development of the Institute for the Study of Children," in *The Child, the Clinic, and the Court* (New York: New Republic, 1925), 206; Getis, "A Disciplined Society," 244. A committee, the Friends of the Institute for Juvenile Research, helped raise monies to support scientific research. The committee was comprised of attorneys, businessmen, doctors, and social welfare leaders of Chicago. Adler's board membership with the JPA undoubtedly helped to garner their financial support; Getis, "A Disciplined Society," 249.

86. 7th DPWAR, NU, 94, 95; Adler, "The Juvenile Psychopathic Institute": 11. Similar to child guidance clinics, a hierarchy developed where the psychiatrist diagnosed and the psychiatric social worker—variously titled the "steerer[s]" and "active therapeutic assistant[s]"—carried out the treatment plans. David M. Levy, M.D., "Notes on Psychotherapy," *Social Service Review* 1 (March 1927): 78.

Chapter 7

1. Michael W. Sedlak, "Young Women and the City: Adolescent Deviance and the Transformation of Educational Policy, 1870–1960," *History of Education Quarterly* 23 (Spring 1983): 12. For purposes of continuity, the institution is herein referred to as the Chicago Home for Girls throughout, despite the earlier names of the Erring Women's Refuge of Chicago and Chicago Refuge for Girls.

2. Dr. Kate Waller Barrett, *Some Practical Suggestions on the Conduct of a Rescue Home* (Washington, DC: 1903; reprt., New York: Arno Press, 1974). For other works on rescue homes, see Regina G. Kunzel, *Fall Women, Problem Girls: Unmarried Mothers and the Professionalization of Social Work, 1890–1945* (New Haven: Yale University Press, 1993); and Peggy Pascoe, *Relations of Rescue: The Search for Female Moral Authority in the American West, 1874–1939* (New York: Oxford University Press, 1990); Barbara Brenzel, *Daughters of the State: A Social*

Portrait of the First Reform School for Girls in North America, 1856–1905 (Cambridge, MA: MIT Press, 1983); Joan Jacobs Brumberg, " 'Ruined' Girls: Changing Community Responses to Illegitimacy in Upstate New York, 1890–1920," *Journal of Social History* 15 (Winter 1984); 247–87.

3. 65th CHGAR, UCRL, 18; 42nd CRGAR, UCRL, 1.

4. Helen D. Haseltine, "A History of the Chicago Home for Girls Founded in 1863 as the Chicago Erring Woman's Refuge for Reform" (Master's thesis, University of Chicago, 1934), 87.

5. 33rd CHGAR, UCRL, 10; 41st EWRCAR, UCRL, 20; 65th CHGAR, UCRL, 19.

6. Most of the female board and committee members' addresses indicated that they resided in the wealthy neighborhoods of Evanston and Lake Forest on the North Shore, as well as in Hyde Park. Such women's volunteer work extended to other child welfare institutions; see Kenneth Cmiel, *A Home of Another Kind: One Chicago Orphanage and the Tangle of Child Welfare* (Chicago: University of Chicago Press, 1995), 199. But only 30 percent of other Chicago social agencies' board members lived in the northern suburbs; see Howard Moore, *The Care of Illegitimate Children in Chicago* (Chicago: Juvenile Protective Association, 1912), 99. That the Chicago Home for Girls' board was comprised of only women through the 1930s was unusual; by 1928, the Home was only one of seven facilities for delinquent girls nationwide that still had an all-female board. Margaret Reeves, *Training Schools for Delinquent Girls* (New York: Russell Sage Foundation, 1929), 57. For further discussion of such institutions' ideologies, see Pascoe, *Relations of Rescue*; and Marian J. Morton, "Fallen Women, Federated Charities, and Maternity Homes, 1913–1973," *Social Service Review* 62 (March 1988): 61–82.

7. 34th EWRCAR, UCRL, 15; 72nd CHGAR, UCRL, 1. Ophelia Amigh, an administrator at the Home for many years, accepted a position at the Illinois Industrial School for Delinquent Girls in Geneva, Illinois, in 1904; *Refuge Journal* (March 1, 1904), 2. Her difficulties with the state institution are detailed in chapter 8. Cynthia Embree remained with the Home until 1940.

8. 45th CRGAR, UCRL, 9; 52nd CHGAR, UCRL, 8; 60th CHGAR, UCRL, 14; 42nd CRGAR, UCRL, 8. Percentages are averaged from 1896–1935 annual reports' financial statements. Donations were a steady source of income, except during the war years. The Florence Crittenton Anchorage in Chicago likewise expressed financial difficulty in caring for its population of twenty-five girls and their babies. There, one female volunteer solicited $4,000 alone in 1905; and in 1910 and 1923, the institution received two financial windfalls from wealthy donors. See Otto Wilson, *Fifty Years' Work with Girls, 1883–1933: A Story of the Florence Crittenton Homes* (Alexandria, VA: National Florence Crittenton Mission, 1933), 252.

9. These figures pointed to the financial savvy of the trustees, as well as the "masculinized" rhetoric that Kunzel has so aptly described; Kunzel, *Fallen Women, Problem Girls*, 50. Through legislation from 1869, these monies from fines had been equally divided between the Chicago Home for Girls and the House of the Good Shepherd.

10. Haseltine, "A History of the Chicago Home," 62, 90. Another house of correction, Bridewell, was located near the Stockyard. Its interior was equally dismal: each cell was furnished with only a bed, running cold water, and a toilet. Most inmates were women over the age of eighteen committed for adultery, prostitution, or pandering. But young girls were sometimes admitted and not segregated from the older inmates. See George E. Worthington and Ruth Topping, "The Morals Court of Chicago," *Social Hygiene* 7 (October 1921): 396–98.

11. Haseltine, "A History of the Chicago Home," 91, 94. By 1900, the per diem cost of each girl's care was calculated at thirty-nine cents; 36th EWRCAR, UCRL, 10; 39th EWRCAR, UCRL, 13.

12. 59th CHGAR, UCRL, 9.

13. The Home did acknowledge that sewing brought in a "considerable income"; 35th EWRCAR, UCRL, 8. Unfortunately, the number of girls committed by parents or guardians was not recorded.

14. Haseltine, "A History of the Chicago Home," 122–23. These events occurred despite and perhaps because of the barred windows; 63rd CHGAR, UCRL, 18. The Home was in the center of one of the busiest African-American business communities in Chicago.

15. 59th CHGAR, UCRL, 11–12; 60th CHGAR, UCRL, 10; 38th EWRCAR, UCRL, 18.

16. 36th EWRCAR, UCRL, 17; 60th CHGAR, UCRL, 17; 68th CHGAR, UCRL, 14.

17. 40th EWRCAR, UCRL, 7; 52nd CHGAR, UCRL, 17; 49th CRGAR, UCRL, 20. Some reformers recommended legislation requiring that a mother care for her illegitimate child for at least one year and nurse it for no less than six months. Moore, *The Care of Illegitimate Children in Chicago*, 21. The Florence Crittenton Mission and the Children's Bureau would also promote breastfeeding, at least for the first six months. Katherine G. Aiken, *Harnessing the Power of Motherhood: The National Florence Crittenton Mission, 1883–1925* (Knoxville: University of Tennessee Press, 1999), 78.

18. 58th CHGAR, UCRL, 15; 66th CHGAR, UCRL, 13.

19. 58th CHGAR, UCRL, 15–16; 59th CHGAR, UCRL, 14.

20. 58th CHGAR, UCRL, 15; 59th CHGAR, UCRL, 12; 60th CHGAR, UCRL, 12; 64th CHGAR, UCRL, 14. By 1928, 77 percent of unmarried African-American mothers in Chicago were generally sent to Cook County Hospital for deliveries, as opposed to 30 percent native-born white mothers. Slightly less than 5 percent of unmarried African-American mothers delivered their babies at maternity homes. Some hospitals, such as the Presbyterian Hospital, provided services to African-American mothers in their own homes but did not admit them into the hospital. Dorothy Frances Puttee and Mary Ruth Colby, *The Illegitimate Child in Illinois* (Chicago: University of Chicago Press, 1937), 103–4.

21. 57th CHGAR, UCRL, 2; 65th CHGAR, UCRL, 14; Josephine Gordon Taylor, "The Development of Social Service at Cook County Hospital, 1911–1933" (Master's thesis, University of Chicago, 1935), 19. The Chicago Home for Girls was only one of four maternity homes in Chicago that admitted unmarried African-American mothers; Puttee and Colby, *The Illegitimate Child in Illinois*, 129. The Salvation Army Rescue and Maternity Home in Chicago also reserved a limited number of beds for unmarried African-American mothers; *Refuge Journal* (April 1, 1906), 4. In New York City, of 435 unmarried African-American mothers, only 83 were sent to maternity homes; Reed cited in R. Insley-Casper, "The Negro Unmarried Mother of New York," *Opportunity* 12 (June 1934): 172.

22. 72nd CHGAR, UCRL, 13; Reeves, *Training Schools for Delinquent Girls*, 222–23. By 1928, only six of seventy-eight surveyed facilities had provisions for baby care.

23. 71st CHGAR, UCRL, 15; see also Children's Bureau, *A Study of Maternity Homes in Minnesota and Pennsylvania* (Washington, DC: Government Printing Office, 1926), 10; and Kunzel, *Fallen Women, Problem Girls*.

24. 44th CRGAR, UCRL, 25; 63rd CHGAR, UCRL, 12; Haseltine, "A History of the Chicago Home," 42. Babies were often adopted by families, and one by "a wealthy woman." *Refuge Journal* (April 1, 1908), 3, 8. Although there has been recent criticism of the rescue homes' treatment of pregnant unmarried women, my estimation is that their moral indictments were less harsh than the later scientific classifications and treatments. Benevolence and the women's Christian duty tempered their criticism of the girls. Emma Lundberg, for one, in assessing such girls' personalities, believed that "inferior mentality and psychopathic traits [were] without doubt of important as predisposing factors." Emma Lundberg, *Children of Illegitimate Birth and Measures for Their Protection* (Washington, DC: Government Printing Office, 1926), 13–14.

25. 53rd CHGAR, UCRL, 22; 34th CRGAR, UCRL, 19; 55th CHGAR, UCRL, 22; Haseltine, "A History of the Chicago Home," 82–83; 54th CHGAR, UCRL, 19. Most employed girls' salaries ranged from $2.50 to $7 per week. Such wages would not have been sufficient to pay for room and board in other Chicago boarding houses. See Joanne J. Meyerowitz, *Women Adrift: Independent Wages Earners in Chicago, 1880–1930* (Chicago: University of Chicago Press, 1988).

26. 52nd CHGAR, UCRL, 6, 19.

27. 58th CHGAR, UCRL, 22.

28. Haseltine, "A History of the Chicago Home," 84.

29. 34th EWRCAR, UCRUL, 19. Although the Home initially welcomed young girls from the juvenile court, in the later years, staff members spoke increasingly of the girls' "defiance" and "anarchy"; see 34th EWRCAR, UCRL, 7–8; 46th CRGAR, UCRL, 14.

30. To some extent, the ethnic populations of the Chicago Home for Girls reflected those of Chicago's juvenile court. That is, the percentages of native-born white, German-American, and African-American girls were high at the Home, as well as in the CCJC. However, I suspect that more Swedish-American girls were accepted at the Home because it was a Protestant home, whereas fewer Polish-American girls were there because they resided at the House of the Good Shepherd, the Catholic institution for delinquent girls. See table 10 in appendix 2 for percentages of delinquent girls appearing before the CCJC from 1906 to 1927 based upon ethnicity. Unfortunately, the Home's records do not distinguish between first- and second-generation immigrants. 43rd CRGAR, UCRL, 16; 54th CHGAR, UCRL, 11; 53rd CHGAR, UCRL, 19.

31. The 1915 CCJCAR, for example, declared that three quarters of delinquent girls' cases resulted from environmental problems of poverty, bad companions, alcoholism, and immorality. The remaining cases were due to either physiological or mental problems, the latter including feeblemindedness, psychoses, or subnormal intelligence.

32. 44th CRGAR, UCRL, 17; 45th CRGAR, UCRL, 10; 39th EWRCAR, UCRL, 22; 55th CHGAR, UCRL, 15. Odem, too, noted the ways in which the parents of rebellious girls used the courts to discipline them. Mary E. Odem, *Delinquent Daughters: Protecting and Policing Female Sexuality in the United States, 1885–1920* (Chapel Hill: University of North Carolina Press, 1995).

33. Margueritte Anita Elowson, "Some Aspects of the Cook County Juvenile Court in Relation to Readjustment of the Delinquent Girl" (Master's thesis, University of Chicago, 1930), 21–22.

34. 35th EWRCAR, UCRL, 12; 64th CHGAR, UCRL, 12. Often the girls lifted their scripts directly from movies. See Judith Staiger, *Bad Women: Regulating Sexuality in Early American Cinema* (Minneapolis: University of Minnesota Press, 1995); and Herbert Blumer, *Movies and Conduct* (New York: Macmillan, 1933).

35. 37th EWRCAR, UCRL, 12; 39th EWRCAR, UCRL, 20–21.

36. 43rd CRGAR, UCRL, 17. The morals court, a branch of the municipal court, was established through the recommendation of the Chicago Vice Commission in 1913. See Worthington and Topping, "The Morals Court of Chicago": 353–57.

37. For further information on the morals and municipal courts of Chicago, see George E. Worthington and Ruth Topping, *Specialized Courts Dealing with Sex Delinquency* (New York: F. H. Hitchcock, 1925), chap. 1. In 1942, Ruth Topping became the superintendent of the Chicago Home for Girls.

38. 43rd CRGAR, UCRL, 17; 40th EWRCAR, UCRL, 19; 53rd CHGAR, UCRL, 9.

39. 40th EWRCAR, UCRL, 19; 41st EWRCAR, UCRL, 18.

40. The percentages of young women received by the Chicago Home for Girls from the municipal court for the years 1906, 1907, and 1908 were respectively 22, 17, and 15. 46th CRGAR, UCRL, 17; 47th CRGAR, UCRL, 18; 48th CRGAR, UCRL, 11. Police reports from 1905 to 1912 indicated that nearly half of the female cases brought before the municipal court were fined; the rest were discharged. 1906–1913 RGSP, UCRL.

41. The percentages of young women accepted by the Chicago Home for Girls from the morals court for the years 1913, 1914, and 1917 were respectively 17, 23, and 38. 52nd CHGAR, UCRL, 14; 53rd CHGAR, UCRL, 15; 56th CHGAR, UCRL, 11. The percentage

of 38 in 1917 is quite large. But of all female reform institutions serving Chicago girls from the juvenile court, the Chicago Home for Girls received the lowest number that year. For further information on the morals court, see Worthington and Topping, *Specialized Courts Dealing with Sex Delinquency*, and Judge Joseph W. Schulman, "The Moral Court," in the 1928–1929 CMCAR, HWL, 36–39.

42. Elisabeth Parker, "Personnel and Organization in the Probation Department of the Juvenile Court of Cook County (1899–1933)" (Master's thesis, University of Chicago, 1934), 7–8; Henriette Greenebaum Frank and Amalie Hofer Jerome, comps., *Annals of the Chicago Woman's Club for the First Forty Years of Its Organization, 1876–1916* (Chicago: Chicago Woman's Club, 1916), 228; Louise de Koven Bowen, *Growing Up with a City* (New York: Macmillan, 1926), 104–6; Mrs. Joseph T. [Louise de Koven] Bowen, "The Early Days of the Juvenile Court," in *The Child, the Clinic, and the Court* (New York: New Republic, 1925), 298–309.

43. Haseltine, "A History of the Chicago Home for Girls," 133–34. Part of this criticism may have been well-founded, as the Home staff noted that more attention was given to dependent and delinquent boys than girls. As they questioned, "[W]hat of the girls? Are they not entitled to the same consideration and sympathy? Ought we not to put forth the same effort to reclaim them?" 43rd CRGAR, UCRL, 12. What the Home staff did not consider was that generally three to four times more boys than girls were brought before the juvenile court judge. Additional tensions between the superintendent and the juvenile court in the early 1900s arose because the superintendent wanted to use her own parole system, but the court required that all juvenile court girls be released to them for supervision. Even the later superintendent Cynthia H. Embree would argue that the juvenile court girls, upon their release, would resort to their previous delinquent behaviors because they were under the juvenile court's jurisdiction. And so, as late as 1930 the Home staff disregarded the court's records, acknowledging that they rarely looked at the girls' papers before embarking on their own plan of reform. 40th EWRCAR, UCRL, 17; 53rd CHGAR, UCRL, 19–20; Haseltine, "A History of the Chicago Home," 135; 67th CHGAR, UCRL, 10–11, 14.

44. See chapter 9 for a fuller discussion of Tuthill's deliberation.

45. 39th EWRCAR, UCRL, 21.

46. Percentages are averaged from the superintendent's reports from 1898 to 1909 and the probation officer's reports from 1910–1921 in the Chicago Home for Girls' annual reports.

47. 59th CHGAR, UCRL, 21–22; 60th CHGAR, UCRL, 19; 63rd CHGAR, UCRL, 18; 66th CHGAR, UCRL, 16; 72nd CHGAR, UCRL, 16; 60th CHGAR, UCRL, 19; Haseltine, "A History of the Chicago Home," 126.

48. Enumerations tallied from the Home's 33rd through 72nd annual reports. In the early 1900s, the Home's average daily number of girls only exceeded the facility's capacity by ten. But by 1905, the daily average was generally 100 more girls than the Home could comfortably accommodate, although the girls' duration of stay varied. The large number of girls undoubtedly came from the juvenile court.

49. Kunzel, *Fallen Women, Problem Girls*.

50. 37th EWRCAR, UCRL, 9. The girls were not allowed to talk about their past, except with the superintendent. The matrons were not informed of the girls' charges nor could they read the court records. This kept the locus of control even more so with the superintendent. Illinois Association of Criminal Justice, *Illinois Crime Survey* (Chicago: Illinois Association of Criminal Justice and The Chicago Crime Commission, 1929, reprt., Montclair, NJ: Patterson Smith, 1968), 702. For other letters of gratitude see "Mary Bartelme Home for Girls of Metro Chicago, 1959," box 126, folder 8, CFR, UICSC; and in the Home's publication *Refuge Journal*, published from 1902 to 1912. Some letters of gratitude were similar to those of the State Industrial School for Delinquent Girls at Geneva, where the girls highlighted their reformed character and gratitude, then requested favors from the superintendent. For

example, one girl's letter to Miss Stone in 1905 graciously thanked her, then asked that the girl's "little trunk" be sent. Chicago Home for Girls, *Refuge Journal* (July 1, 1905): 6.

51. 42nd CRGAR, UCRL, 19.

52. 33rd EWRCAR, UCRL, 9.

53. 40th EWRCAR, UCRL, 18; 58th CHGAR, UCRL, 13–14.

54. 58th CHGAR, UCRL, 25.

55. From probation reports published in the Home's 1910–1922 annual reports and superintendent's reports 1926–1934.

56. Betty Marwood Hill, "A Comparative Study of Delinquency in Four National Groups in Cook County Juvenile Court of 1930" (Master's thesis, University of Chicago, 1932), 38–39.

57. 61st CHGAR, UCRL, 17; 71st CHGAR, UCRL, 18; Haseltine, "A History of the Chicago Home," 125. See also "Annual Report of the South Side Child Guidance Center, Chicago 1930," box 21, folder 9, EB, UCSC.

58. 61st CHGAR, UCRL, 18; 52nd CHGAR, UCRL, 6. The Home wanted it both ways: to maintain its own vision of spiritual reform, as well as to present to the public a "scientized" version. To illustrate, even "after rectifying as far as possible the hampering cause of delinquency through our medical department through a study of each girl's mentality," the Home still persisted in giving the girls "insight" into a "simple, dignified home life." 60th CHGAR, UCRL, 20.

59. 60th CHGAR, UCRL, 18. The superintendent, in her own desexualized manner, vivified the medical description of psychopathic girls as "egocentric, temperamental, and extremely selfish . . . intent on pleasure, clothes, and friends . . . a whirlpool of emotions"; 68th CHGAR, UCRL, 14.

60. Haseltine, "A History of the Chicago Home," 125.

61. Reeves, cited in Haseltine, "A History of the Chicago Home," 125.

62. 71st CHGAR, UCRL, 11–14; 73rd CHGAR, UCRL, 11. In 1937, a caseworker was officially hired by the Home; 73rd CHGAR, UCRL, 11–18. See also "Monthly Report, Chicago Probation Project, April, 1935," box 33, folder 6, EGA, UCSC. In October of 1935, Haseltine and the Chicago Home for Girls' fieldwork unit had thirty-four active cases. Increasingly, they were referred to the IJR, although Haseltine also increased expenses for recreation, favoring the community services approach. This paralleled Abbott's Chicago Probation Project, which emphasized more community involvement in the prevention of delinquency and prefigured the Chicago School's Chicago Area Project initiative. See "Letter from Helen Haseltine to Grace Abbott, 6 June, 1936," box 33, folder 7, EGA, UCSC.

63. 33rd EWRCAR, UCRL, 9.

64. 33rd EWRCAR, UCRL, 9; 36th EWRCAR, UCRL, 16.

65. 61st CHGAR, UCRL, 15; 41st EWRCAR, UCRL, 28; 46th CRGAR, UCRL, 21; 61st CHGAR, UCRL, 16.

66. 34th EWRCAR, UCRL, 16, 26, 27; 37th EWRCAR, UCRL, 18; 36th EWRCAR, UCRL, 15; 41st EWRCAR, UCRL, 26; 43rd CRGAR, UCRL, 21; 57th CHGAR, UCRL, 18. Clifford Roe was a popular author of white-slave-traffic novels.

67. 35th EWRCAR, UCRL, 16; 59th CHGAR, UCRL, 18–19; 64th CHGAR, UCRL, 19.

68. 39th EWRCAR, UCRL, 8.

69. 33rd EWRCAR, UCRL, 9; 38th EWRCAR, UCRL, 17.

70. 55th CHGAR, UCRL, 20.

71. 34th EWRCAR, UCRL, 16, 19; 35th EWRCAR, UCRL, 8; 41st EWRCAR, UCRL, 10, 16.

72. 33rd EWRCAR, UCRL, 9; 52nd CHGAR, UCRL, 7.

73. 55th CHGAR, UCRL, 13; 56th CHGAR, UCRL, 17; 35th EWRCAR, UCRL, 15; 38th EWRCAR, UCRL, 14.

74. 33rd EWRCAR, UCRL, 17.

75. 34th EWRCAR, UCRL, 24; 40th EWRCAR, UCRL, 20.

76. 34th EWRCAR, UCRL, 25.

77. 34th EWRCAR, UCRL, 16; 35th EWRCAR, UCRL, 17; 37th EWRCAR, UCRL, 17. One African-American girl earned as much as eight dollars a week, but she seemed to be an exception; 51st CHGAR, UCRL, 13.

78. 33rd EWRCAR, UCRL, 9; 35th EWRCAR, UCRL, 8.

79. Edith N. Burleigh, "Principles of Parole," in *The Social Work of the Courts: Annual Report and Proceedings of the Tenth Annual Conference of the National Probation Association* (Albany, NY: National Probation Association, 1919), 162; 44th CRGAR, UCRL, 23; 64th CHGAR, UCRL, 19.

80. 46th CRGAR, UCRL, 24–25; 52nd CHGAR, UCRL, 14; 53rd CHGAR, UCRL, 12; 58th CHGAR, UCRL, 18. In order to teach thrift, they made babies' clothes from left-over cloth.

81. 43rd CRGAR, UCRL, 7; 45th CRGAR, UCRL, 26; 58th CHGAR, UCRL, 18.

82. 44th CRGAR, UCRL, 6; 45th CRGAR, UCRL, 27; 55th CHGAR, UCRL, 14; 56th CHGAR, UCRL, 19; 57th CHGAR, UCRL, 18; 41st CRGAR, UCRL, 17.

83. 57th CHGAR, UCRL, 21; 59th CHGAR, UCRL, 14; 60th CHGAR, UCRL, 13; 63rd CHGAR, UCRL, 19; 69th CHGAR, UCRL, 15.

84. 35th EWRCAR, UCRL, 7.

85. Deaconess Weaver of the Chase House came to give "helpful" talks to the Protestant girls; a rabbi and the Jewish Woman's Aid Society visited the Jewish girls. 36th EWRCAR, UCRL, 8; 35th EWRCAR, 7, 10; 46th CRGAR, UCRL, 17; 59th CHGAR, UCRL, 15.

86. 33rd EWRCAR, UCRL, 7.

87. Ibid., 9.

88. Ibid., 10; 34th EWRCAR, UCRL, 14; 35th EWRCAR, UCRL, 9, 10; 39th EWRCAR, UCRL, 10; 58th CHGAR, UCRL, 24. Like other girls, the inmates celebrated the seasons by swinging in hammocks, playing croquet, and going for summer drives in the park or winter sleigh rides.

89. 52d CHGAR, UCRL, 8; 57th CHGAR, UCRL, 22; 58th CHGAR, UCRL, 23; 59th CHGAR, UCRL, 16; 60th CHGAR, UCRL, 15. See also Sedlak, "Young Women and the City": 10.

90. 64th CHGAR, UCRL, 13; 59th CHGAR, UCRL, 17.

91. 59th CHGAR, UCRL, 21–22; 60th CHGAR, UCRL, 19; 63rd CHGAR, UCRL, 18. For further information on beauty culture in the early twentieth century, see Kathy Peiss, *Hope in a Jar: The Making of American's Beauty Culture* (New York: Henry Holt, 1998).

92. 66th CHGAR, UCRL, 16; 72nd CHGAR, UCRL, 16; 60th CHGAR, UCRL, 19; Haseltine, "A History of the Chicago Home," 126.

93. 59th CHGAR, UCRL, 15.

Chapter 8

1. Ophelia Amigh, "More about the Traffic in Shame," in *Fighting the Traffic in Young Girls or War on the White Slave Trade*, ed. Ernest A. Bell (N.p.: G. S. Ball, 1910), 120–23.

2. See table 10 in appendix 2 for the percentages of delinquent girls appearing before the CCJC from 1906 to 1927, based on ethnicity. The Geneva School's portrait is drawn from multiple texts within the biennial reports from 1896 to 1935, as well as medical and psychiatric studies of the Geneva girls. Within the biennial reports were medical, parole, and school reports, as well as psychiatric, psychological, and intelligence correlations from the IJR. Ad-

ditionally, nearly one hundred letters from parolees, their relatives, and men requesting permission for marriage or visits were not examined. Case records were not available as they were destroyed in the 1960s.

3. 3rd GBR, UCRL, 9; 8th GBR, UCRL, 13; 15th DPWAR, NU, 200; 25th DPWAR, NU, 303. By the 1930s, over half of the African-American girls at Geneva were from Cook County. Charlotte Ruth Klein, "Success and Failure on Parole: A Study of 160 Girls Paroled from the State Training School at Geneva, Illinois" (Master's thesis, University of Chicago, 1935), 5; Illinois Association for Criminal Justice, *Illinois Crime Survey* (Chicago: Illinois Association for Criminal Justice and The Chicago Crime Commission, 1929; Reprt., Montclair, NJ: Patterson Smith, 1968), 675.

4. See tables 13 and 14 in appendix 2 for the number and percentages of dispositions of delinquent girls brought before the CCJC from 1906 to 1927. Anne Meis Knupfer, *Toward a Tenderer Humanity and a Nobler Womanhood: African American Women's Clubs in Turn-of-the-Century Chicago* (New York: New York University Press, 1996), chap. 4; Illinois Association for Criminal Justice, *Illinois Crime Survey*, 719.

5. Elisabeth Parker, "Personnel and Organization in the Probation Department of the Juvenile Court of Cook County (1899–1933)" (Master's thesis, University of Chicago, 1934), 81–82; 1911 CCJCAR, HWL, 81. Correspondence from the CSCP, too, expressed concern about the number of African-American dependent girls sent to the Geneva School. See "The Colored Children's Aid Society," box 30, folder 10, ICHAS, UICSC.

6. 7th GBR, UCRL, 7–8; T. H. MacQueary, "Schools for Dependent, Delinquent, and Truant Children in Illinois," *American Journal of Sociology* 9 (July 1903): 1–23; Arlien Johnson, "Subsidies from Public Funds to Private Children's Institutions and Agencies in Chicago," *Social Service Review* 3 (June 1929): 169–206; 10 April, 1918 letter to Breckinridge, box 30, file 57, ICHAS, UICSC.

7. Florence Monahan, *Women in Crime* (New York: Ives Washburn, 1941), 112.

8. Carolyn Strange, *Toronto's Girl Problem: The Perils and Pleasure of the City, 1880–1930* (Toronto: University of Toronto Press, 1995), 135; Mary E. Odem, *Delinquent Daughters: Protecting and Policing Adolescent Female Sexuality in the United States, 1885–1920* (Chapel Hill: University of North Carolina Press, 1995), 58; 1913 CCJCAR, HWL, 37. See also Sophonisba Breckinridge and Edith Abbott, *The Delinquent Child and the Home* (New York: Charities Publication Committee, 1912), appendix 5, "Family Paragraphs Relating to the Delinquency of 50 Girls."

9. 1913 CCJCAR, HWL, 37.

10. Monahan, *Women in Crime*, 110. James Beane, too, reported that most delinquent girls at the Indiana State School for Delinquent Girls came from poor households and had committed sex-related offenses; James C. Beane, "A Survey of Three Hundred Delinquent Girls," *Journal of Juvenile Research* 15 (July 1931): 198–208.

11. Edith Livingston Smith and Hugh Cabot, M.D., "A Study in Sexual Morality," *Journal of Social Hygiene* 2 (October 1916): 527.

12. Ibid., 529; Hutchin Hapgood, *Types from City Streets* (New York: Funk and Wagnalls, 1910), 135–36; Kathy Peiss, *Cheap Amusements: Working Women and Leisure in Turn-of-the-Century New York* (Philadelphia: Temple University Press, 1986); Joanne J. Meyerowitz, *Women Adrift: Independent Wage Earners in Chicago, 1880–1930* (Chicago: University of Chicago Press, 1988).

13. Elizabeth Lunbeck, *The Psychiatric Persuasion: Knowledge, Gender, and Power in Modern America* (Princeton: Princeton University Press, 1994).

14. George Chauncey Jr., "From Sexual Inversion to Homosexuality: The Changing Medical Conceptualization of Female 'Deviance,'" in *Passion and Power: Sexuality in History*, eds. Kathy Peiss and Christina Simmons with Robert A. Padgug (Philadelphia: Temple University Press, 1989), 87–117. See also Walter M. Gallichan, *Sexual Apathy and Coldness in*

Women (Boston: Stratford, 1930) and Robert Latou Dickinson and Lura Beam, *The Single Woman: A Medical Study in Sex Education* (Baltimore: Williams and Wilkins, 1934).

15. George Chauncey Jr., "From Sexual Inversion to Homosexuality," 114–46; Havelock Ellis, *Studies in the Psychology of Sex*, 3rd ed. (Philadelphia: F. A. Davis, 1929), 261; Phyllis Blanchard and Carlyn Manasses, *New Girls for Old* (New York: Macaulay, 1930), 60; Maurice Chideckel, M.D., *Female Sex Perversion: The Sexually Aberrated Woman as She Is* (New York: Eugenics Publishing, 1935); Floyd Dell, *Love in the Machine Age: A Psychological Study of the Transition from Patriarchal Society* (New York: Farrar and Rinehart, 1930).

16. Louise E. Ordahl and George Ordahl, "A Study of Delinquent and Dependent Girls at Geneva," *Institution Quarterly* 9 (September 30, 1918): 57; 24th GBR, UCRL; 28th GBR, UCRL, 305; 26th GBR, UCRL, 53; Klein, "Success and Failure on Parole," 28; Regina Kunzel, *Fallen Women, Problem Girls: Married Mothers and the Professionalization of Social Work, 1890–1945* (New Haven: Yale University Press, 1993), 52–53; Stuart Alfred Queen, Walter Blaine Bodenhafer, and Ernest Bouldin Harper, *Social Organization and Disorganization* (New York: Thomas Y. Crowell, 1930), 510.

17. Paul Hanly Furfey, *Social Problems of Childhood* (New York: Macmillan, 1929), 95–96; Knight Dunlap, *Personal Beauty and Racial Betterment* (St. Louis: C. V. Mosby, 1920), 66. Numerous texts linked feeblemindedness to promiscuity; see, for example, Charles Richmond Henderson, *Introduction to the Study of the Dependent, Defective, and Delinquent Classes and of Their Social Treatment*, 2nd ed. (Boston: D. C. Heath, 1908); Edith Houghton Hooker, *Life's Clinic: A Series of Sketches Written from between the Lines of Some Medical Case Histories* (New York: Association Press, 1918); Truman Lee Kelley, *Mental Aspects of Delinquency* (Austin: University of Texas Press, 1917); and Mary Vanuxem, *Education of Feeble-Minded Women* (New York: Teachers College Press, 1925).

18. 4th GBR, UCRL, 7–8.

19. 5th GBR, UCRL, 7; 9th GBR, UCRL, 9.

20. Queen, Bodenhafer, and Harper, *Social Organization and Disorganization*, 514–15; Lunbeck, *The Psychiatric Persuasion*, 65–67, 122–23, 527; Estelle B. Freedman, *Their Sisters' Keepers: Women's Prison Reform in America, 1830–1930* (Ann Arbor: University of Michigan Press, 1984), 119; Anne T. Bingham, "Determinants of Sex Delinquency in Adolescent Girls Based on Intensive Studies of 500 Cases," *Journal of the American Institute of Criminal Law and Criminology* 13 (February 1923): 553, 555–56. The Juvenile Psychopathic Institute, affiliated with the Cook County Juvenile Court, also documented a higher number of female than male psychoses and feeblemindedness; see, for example, 1915 CCJCAR, HWL, 21.

21. 23rd DPWAR, NU, 291.

22. 3rd GBR, UCRL, 10; 21st DPWAR, NU, 266; 12th GBR, UCRL, 12; 26th DPWAR, NU, 323; 9th GBR, UCRL, 7.

23. 8th GBR, UCRL, 30.

24. 4th GBR, UCRL, 13; 9th GBR, UCRL, 13; 20th DPWAR, NU, 239; Lucy D. Ball, "State Training School for Girls," *Institution Quarterly* 14 (December 1923): 340; 30th DPWAR, NU, 175–76. As of 1929, most girls' reformatory schools had no obstetrical services; only six institutions had provisions for infant care, including the Chicago Home for Girls. See Margaret Reeves, *Training Schools for Delinquent Girls* (New York: Russell Sage Foundation, 1929), 222–23. The Chicago Woman's Club's State Training School for Girls' Committee advocated for a psychiatric staff at Geneva, as well as setting up maternity facilities. Jan. 3, 1925 letter, State Training School for Girls Committee, Chicago Woman's Club, box 3, folder 50, MB, UICSC; "Plan for the Development of the Juvenile Court of Cook County" (n.d.), box 4, folder 77, MB, UICSC.

25. Kunzel, *Fallen Women, Problem Girls*, 32–33; Alice D. Menken, "A Social Aspect of the Unmarried Mother," *Journal of Delinquency* 7 (March 1922): 99–103. Marian Morton has

documented that some African-American maternity homes held similar beliefs; see Marian J. Morton, "Fallen Women, Federated Charities, and Maternity Homes, 1913–1973," *Social Service Review* 62 (March 1988): 61–82. Mary Dewson, however, had forewarned that some girls used marriage as a means of escape. In such cases, parole officers could assist the girls through their advice. Mary W. Dewson, "Probation and Institutional Care of Girls," in *The Child in the City: A Series of Papers Presented at the Conferences Held during the Chicago Child Welfare Exhibit*, ed. Sophonisba P. Breckinridge (Chicago: Department of Social Investigation, Chicago School of Civics and Philanthropy, 1912), 366.

26. 4th GBR, UCRL 8.

27. Klein, "Success and Failure on Parole," 63. It is not clear whether the girls had only one or several sexual partners. In Bingham's study of five hundred delinquent girls, she noted that two-fifths of the girls self-reported to have had only one sexual experience or one partner only. Bingham, "Determinants of Sex Delinquency": 528. Referencing works by William I. Thomas and Havelock Ellis, Evelyn Buchan devoted one of her thesis chapters to the "breakdown" of modesty. In her interviews of Geneva girls, in which she directly asked them whether they had been immoral or diseased, all flatly denied it, instead claiming they had been unwillingly molested. She attributed their responses in part to modesty, although she also argued that many delinquent girls had no concept of appropriate codes of behavior. Evelyn Buchan, "The Delinquency of Girls" (Master's thesis, University of Chicago, 1922), 33, 44.

28. Dickinson and Beam, *The Single Woman*, 79, 238; Freud, cited in Ellis, *Studies in the Psychology of Sex*, 261.

29. Wile, "The Sex Problem of Youth": 422; Ellis, cited in Chauncey, "From Sexual Inversion to Homosexuality," 104.

30. 13th DPWAR, NU, 7. For information on other reform schools, see Mary W. Dewson, "Probation and Institutional Care of Girls," 355–70; Mabel Ruth Fernald, Mary Holmes Stevens Hayes, and Almena Dawley, *A Study of Women Delinquents in New York State* (New York: The Century Company, 1920).

31. 13th DPWAR, NU, 5. Per capita costs of Geneva reached their highest in 1935 at $620; 15th DPWAR, NU, 23.

32. 15th DPWAR, NU, 222.

33. Ibid., 224.

34. William LeRoy Zabel, "Street Trades and Juvenile Delinquency" (Master's thesis, University of Chicago, 1918), 50; see also 1913 CCJCAR, HWL, 63.

35. Miriam Van Waters, *Youth in Conflict* (New York: Republic, 1925), 115–16.

36. 3rd GBR, UCRL, 4; 11th GBR, UCRL, 20–23; 12th GBR, UCRL, 7; 1935 GBR, UCRL, 175.

37. 20th DPWAR, NU, 229; Lucy D. Ball, "The Delinquent Girl—and Music," *Institution Quarterly* 8 (January 1927): 95–96.

38. CWCMR, Apr. 26, 1901, CHS.

39. 20th DPWAR, NU, 233; 21st DPWAR, NU, 266; *Broad Ax*, September 19, 1925. Cottages for the white girls averaged twenty-two to twenty-four inmates, compared to fifty African-American inmates per cottage; Illinois Association for Criminal Justice, *Illinois Crime Survey*, 719.

40. 20th DPWAR, NU, 230–32.

41. 8th GBR, UCRL, 34–35.

42. Bertha Corman, "Study of 446 Delinquent Girls with Institutional Experience" (Master's thesis, University of Chicago, 1923), 43, 52.

43. Ordahl and Ordahl, "A Study of Delinquent and Dependent Girls at Geneva": 58.

44. Miriam Van Waters, "What Is the Test of Success?" in *Proceedings of the National Conference of Social Work* (Chicago: University of Chicago Press, 1925), 119; Illinois Association for Criminal Justice, *Illinois Crime Survey*, 719.

45. Illinois Association for Criminal Justice, *Illinois Crime Survey*, 723; Personal communication with Dolores Guinnee, Geneva, Illinois, October, 1996. Before 1924, there were four resident social workers, called "home visitors," who inspected homes, located escapees, and consulted with community agencies. But Klein assessed their work with the girls as marginal; Klein, "Success and Failure on Parole," 102-3. See also Jessie F. Binford, "Delinquent Geneva Girls and Co-Operation," *Institution Quarterly* 14 (December 1923): 141–44.

46. Information on first-, second-, and third-time female offenders from Chicago is contained in the 1906 to 1927 CCJCAR, HWL; Illinois Association for Criminal Justice, *Illinois Crime Survey*, 723, 788; A. L. Bowen, "State Training School for Girls," *Institution Quarterly* 5 (1914): 43; Corman, "Study of 446 Delinquent Girls with Institutional Experience," 43. Healy and Bronner also noted that many delinquent girls were reparoled; see William Healy and Augusta F. Bronner, *Delinquents and Criminals: Their Making and Unmaking: Studies in Ten American Cities* (New York: AMS Press, 1926); Edith N. Burleigh and Frances R. Harris, *The Delinquent Girl: A Study of the Girl on Parole in Massachusetts* (New York: New York School of Social Work, 1923).

47. Corman, "Study of 446 Delinquent Girls with Institutional Experience," 46, 48, 50, 54; Monahan, *Women in Crime*, 128–30.

48. Corman, "Study of 446 Delinquent Girls with Institutional Experience," 54.

49. 10th GBR, UCRL, 12; 12th GBR, UCRL, 16; Meyerowitz, *Women Adrift*, 34. The Geneva School was situated idyllically on a hill overlooking Fox River, just south of the village of Geneva, nearly thirty miles from Chicago. It was a self-sufficient facility, with its own meat locker, ice-making plant, barns, silo, hog house, and boarding house for male farmhands. Illinois Association for Criminal Justice, *Illinois Crime Survey*, 718.

50. 25th DPWAR, NU, 302. Other recommendations for delinquent girls' rehabilitation included the reestablishment of a girls' parental school, a better parole system, and hiring more probation officers. "Plan for the Development of the Juvenile Court of Cook County," box 92, folder 15, MB, UICSC.

51. 7th GBR, UCRL, 15–16; 5th GBR, UCRL, 11; 4th GBR, UCRL, 10; 9th GBR, UCRL, 22; 7th GBR, UCRL, 20.

52. 7th GBR, UCRL, 18; 8th GBR, UCRL, 24.

53. 7th GBR, UCRL, 19, 22, 24.

54. 8th GBR, UCRL, 18, 20.

55. Ibid., 19.

56. Ibid., 21, 22, 24.

57. Kunzel, *Fallen Women, Problem Girls*, 96, 103–5. See also Odem, *Delinquent Daughters*, 24.

58. Reeves, *Training Schools for Delinquent Girls*, 120; "Illinois State Training School for Girls," *Institution Quarterly* 3 (December 31, 1912): 52; Ball, "State Training School for Girls": 339; Klein, "Success and Failure on Parole," 77. Although escapes were clearly an embarrassment to the school, some progressive reformatory educators thought otherwise. Carrie Weaver Smith of Texas, referring to the girls' escape attempts, responded, "Thank Heavens! they still live." See Carrie Weaver Smith, "Can the Institution Equip the Girl for Normal Social Relationships?" in *Proceedings of the National Conference of Social Work* (Chicago: University of Chicago Press, 1925), 115.

59. "The Story of Four Girls," *Institution Quarterly* 3 (December 31, 1912): 28.

60. "State Training School for Girls Notes," *Institution Quarterly* 9 (June 30, 1918): 69; Klein, "Success and Failure on Parole," 78.

61. Illinois Association for Criminal Justice, *Illinois Crime Survey*, 721; Monahan, *Women in Crime*, 128.

62. Klein, "Success and Failure on Parole," 5.

63. Corman, "Study of 446 Delinquent Girls with Institutional Experience," 39–40; Bingham, "Determinants of Sex Delinquency," 546, 548.

64. Corman, "Study of 446 Delinquent Girls with Institutional Experience," 39–40.

65. Ibid., 23–25.

66. Anne Burnet, M.D., "A Study of Delinquent Girls," *Institution Quarterly* 3 (June 30, 1912): 51. Lunbeck, too, suggests evidence of resistance in the "brief, telegraphic comments" of case records; Lunbeck, *The Psychiatric Persuasion*, 96.

67. Monahan, *Women in Crime*, 133–34. Susan Cahn, too, discusses girls' defiance and boredom in similar incidents; see Susan Cahn, "Spirited Youth or Fiends Incarnate: The Samarcand Arson Case and Female Adolescence in the American South," *Journal of Women's History* 9 (Winter 1988): 152–80.

68. Esther H. Stone, M. D., "A Plea for Early Commitment to Correctional Institutions of Delinquent Children, and an Endorsement of Industrial and Vocational Training in These Institutions," *Institution Quarterly* 9 (March 31, 1918): 62. Kahn also discusses how child experts were concerned about being tricked by clever girls. She referred to this strategy of the girls as "the masquerading mental defective." See Kahn, "Spirited Youth or Fiends Incarnate": 186.

69. Lunbeck, *The Psychiatric Persuasion*, 240.

70. Stone, "A Plea for Early Commitment to Correctional Institutions": 63.

71. Ibid., 63–64.

72. Ibid., 63.

73. Ibid., 65.

74. Ibid., 64, 66.

75. Klein, "Success and Failure on Parole," 28–29.

76. Ibid., 29.

77. Ibid., 77, 75.

78. Illinois Association for Criminal Justice, *Illinois Crime Survey*, 721; Monahan, *Women in Crime*, 114.

79. Although no reasons were given for Amigh's resignation from the Chicago Refuge for Girls (later the Chicago Home for Girls) in 1904, it is noteworthy that that year marked a significant change in the Home's relationship with the juvenile court. Beginning then, court monies became the mainstay of the Home's financial resources. Amigh may well have feared that her autonomy and control would be compromised by the CCJC.

80. Joan Gittens, *Poor Relations: The Children of the State of Illinois, 1818–1990* (Urbana: University of Illinois Press, 1994), 119; "Miss Bartelme Urges Reforms for Geneva Girls," *Chicago Tribune*, October 15, 1915.

81. "State Training School for Girls," *Institution Quarterly* 4 (June 30, 1913): 188–219. The two African-American cottages were adjacent to one another, prompting some to recommend that they be placed on opposite ends of the school grounds. See "Illinois State Training for Girls," *Institution Quarterly* 3 (December 31, 1912): 49.

82. Buchan, "The Delinquency of Girls," 57.

83. Klein, "Success and Failure on Parole," 67.

84. Illinois Association for Criminal Justice, *Illinois Crime Survey*, 720; Monahan, *Women in Crime*, 111, 114, 117.

85. Monahan, *Women in Crime*, 131, 142, 149. Mary Dewson advised that reform schools not hire male farmhands and that girls not be paroled to families with adolescent sons. Mary W. Dewson, "Probation and Institutional Care of Girls," 362. Miriam Van Waters, too, has discussed riots, violence, and obscene language used in the girls' reformatories. See Miriam Van Waters, "The Delinquent Attitude," in *Community Treatment of Delinquency: Proceedings of the National Probation Association* (New York: National Probation Association, 1924), 72–79.

86. Klein, "Success and Failure on Parole," 65; see also Ordahl and Ordahl, "A Study of Delinquent and Dependent Girls at Geneva": 58.

87. Klein, "Success and Failure on Parole," 66.

88. Ibid., 73.

89. Ibid., 67; Illinois Association for Criminal Justice, *Illinois Crime Survey*, 721.

90. Klein, "Success and Failure on Parole," 66, 67. Lesbian relationships were not singular to Geneva but occurred at other reformatories and prisons. See Freedman, *Their Sisters' Keepers*, 131; Mara Dodge, "One Female Prisoner Is of More Trouble than Twenty Males: Women Convicts in Illinois Prisons, 1835–1896," *Journal of Social History* 32 (Summer 1999): 907–30; Ruth Alexander, *The "Girl Problem": Female Sexual Delinquency in New York, 1900–1930* (Ithaca: Cornell University Press, 1995), 91–92; Robert M. Mennel, *Thorns and Thistles: Juvenile Delinquents in the United States 1825–1940* (Hanover, NH: University Press of New England, 1973), 94, 108, 175. Floyd Dell has argued that single-sex schools, in their patriarchal structure, encouraged lesbian relations; Floyd Dell, *Love in the Machine Age*, 28.

91. Edith R. Spaulding, *An Experimental Study of Psychopathic Delinquent Women* (New York: Rand McNally, 1923), 273.

92. Margaret Otis, "A Perversion Not Commonly Noted," *Journal of Abnormal and Social Psychology* 8 (April–May, 1913): 114, 116; Klein, "Success and Failure on Parole," 66; Stone, "A Plea for Early Commitment to Correctional Institutions": 64, 65; Illinois Association for Criminal Justice, *Illinois Crime Survey*, 720.

93. Klein, "Success and Failure on Parole," 66. In such situations, white girls were not redeemed of their lesbian activities through interracial heterosexual relationships. However, heterosexuality—reconciliation with her white husband—was the solution for another white girl, described as lesbian because she wore overalls and preferred women's company; 1925–26 GBR, UCRL, 30. Psychologist Winifred Richmond termed lesbians who were active as "masculine" and those who were passive as "female"; Winifred Richmond, *The Adolescent Girl: A Book for Parents and Teachers* (New York: Macmillan, 1925), 125–126.

94. Klein, "Success and Failure on Parole," 66–67; Otis, "A Perversion Not Commonly Noted": 113.

95. Philip Morris Hauser, "Motion Pictures in Penal and Correctional Institutions. A Study of the Reactions of Prisoners to Movies" (Master's thesis, University of Chicago, 1933), 31, 51.

96. Ibid., 40.

97. Ibid.

98. Ibid., 39.

99. Ibid.

100. Ibid., 73–74, 76.

101. One neurologist in 1894 chided asylum physicians for their "odd little statements, reports of a case or two, a few useless pages of isolated post-mortem records, and these are sandwiched among incomprehensible statistics and farm balance-sheets." Quoted in Edward Shorter, *A History of Psychiatry: From the Era of the Asylum to the Age of Prozac* (New York: John Wiley, 1997), 68.

Chapter 9

1. Rev. Msgr. Harry C. Koenig, S.T.D., ed., *Caritas Christi, Urget Nos: A History of the Offices, Agencies, and Institutions of the Archdiocese of Chicago*, vol. 2 (Chicago: The Archdiocese of Chicago, 1981), 895; Sister Mary Patrice, "Psycho-Social Factors in the Case Histories of Seventy Girls Admitted to the House of the Good Shepherd" (Master's thesis, Loyola University, 1955), 3; Illinois Association for Criminal Justice, *Illinois Crime Survey* (Chicago: Illinois Association for Criminal Justice and The Chicago Crime Commission, 1929, reprt., Montclair, NJ: Patterson Smith, 1968), 699; Margaret Anne Gould, "An Historical Study of

the House of the Good Shepherd, A Specialized Child-Caring Institution" (Master's thesis, Loyola University, 1946), 37, 39; Suellen Hoy, "Caring for Chicago's Women and Girls: The Sisters of the Good Shepherd, 1859–1911," *Journal of Urban History* 23 (March 1997): 270. For further information on the order, see "Sisters of the Good Shepherd," in *Religious Orders of Women in the United States: Accounts of Their Origin and of Their Most Important Institutions*, 1st ed., comp. Elinor Tong Dehey (Hammond, IN: W. B. Conkey, 1913), 144–50. In every fallen woman, the Sisters saw the image of Mary Magdalen. John Patrick Walsh, "The Catholic Church in Chicago and Problems of an Urban Society: 1893–1915" (Ph.D. diss., University of Chicago, 1948), 193.

2. Illinois Association for Criminal Justice, *Illinois Crime Survey*, 699; n.a., *If I Forget Thee: The History of the Saint Louis Province of the Sisters of the Good Shepherd 1849–1976* (Chicago, April 10, 1977), 139, HGSC; Roger J. Coughlin and Cathryn A. Riplinger, *The Story of Charitable Care in the Archdiocese of Chicago 1844–1959* (Chicago: The Catholic Charities of Chicago, 1981), 126; Walsh, "The Catholic Church in Chicago," 185.

3. Mary C. Tinney, "Catholic Charities, with Illustrations from Chicago" (Master's thesis, University of Chicago, 1910), 12–13; Walsh, "The Catholic Church in Chicago," 188; n.a., *History of the Illinois Technical School for Colored Girls*, n.d., HGSC; Joseph J. Thompson, *Diamond Jubilee of the Archdiocese of Chicago* (Des Plaines, IL: St. Mary's Training Schooling Press, 1920), 744–45, 755–56.

4. "The Sisters of the Good Shepherd in the Archdiocese of Chicago, Illinois," n.d., 10, HGSC; Walsh, "The Catholic Church in Chicago," 189–90; *If I Forget Thee*, 140; *New World*, September 24, 1915. See also Sandra Stehno, "Foster Care for Dependent Black Children in Chicago 1899–1934" (Ph.D. diss., University of Chicago, 1985). The Illinois Technical School for Colored Girls was located several blocks from the Chicago Home for Girls in a predominantly African-American neighborhood at 4910 South Prairie Street. Although Edward Kantowicz has argued that Chicago Catholic leaders did not adequately address the "Negro question," he did not include this school in his discussion. Edward R. Kantowicz, *Corporation Sole: Cardinal Mundelein and Chicago Catholicism* (Notre Dame, IN: University of Notre Dame Press, 1983), 212.

5. *History of the Illinois Technical School for Colored Girls*, 15–16.

6. Ibid., 12, 13, 23.

7. *Broad Ax*, August 17, 1913. In 1912, Mrs. Ida D. Lewis of the West Side Woman's Club opened a three-story home for dependent African-American girls. It remained open for only one year and did not greatly affect enrollment at the Illinois Technical School for Colored Girls. See *History of the Illinois Technical School for Colored Girls*, 26. In New York City, even African-American boys were sent to the House of the Good Shepherd because of the paucity of institutions for African-American children; Joint Committee on Negro Child Study in New York City, *A Study of Delinquent and Neglected Negro Children before the New York City Children's Court* (New York: Joint Committee on Negro Child Study in New York City, 1927), 28.

8. African-American banker Jesse Binga made a substantial financial contribution to the school. Koenig, *Caritas Christi*, 897; "The Junior Auxiliary," *New World*, December 5, 1908, 5; *History of the Illinois Technical School for Colored Girls*, 26; *If I Forget Thee*, 145; Anne Meis Knupfer, *Toward a Tenderer Humanity and a Nobler Womanhood: African American Women's Clubs in Turn-of-the-Century Chicago* (New York: New York University Press, 1996), 79–80.

9. Thompson, *Diamond Jubilee of the Archdiocese of Chicago*, 756–57.

10. "Program by Colored Girls," *New World*, June 5, 1914, 1; Rae Dickerson, "What the Catholic Church Is Doing for the Negro in This City," *New World*, September 24, 1915, 1. Although the Sisters taught domestic skills to the girls, they did not minimize academic prepa-

ration which followed public school instruction. The school remained open until 1953. Koenig, *Caritas Christi*, 895.

11. Walsh, "The Catholic Church in Chicago," 197. Cumulative House records from 1859 until 1924 enumerated that the Sisters had cared for 228 Magdalens, 7,650 Penitents, and 5,720 Juniors. They celebrated 624 baptisms, 1615 confirmations, and 26 marriages; 1924 Ledger, HGSC. Ledgers contained information on each girl's birth place and date, her religious status (whether baptized and confirmed), family members, home address, and school level.

12. Walsh, "The Catholic Church in Chicago," 196; Gould, "An Historical Study of the House of the Good Shepherd," ii–v. Clifton Wooldridge, a detective for the Chicago Police Department, also sent underaged girls from prostitution houses to the Chicago Detention Home and the House of the Good Shepherd. Clifton F. Wooldridge, *Twenty Years a Detective in the Wickedest City in the World* (Chicago: Clifton F. Wooldridge, 1908), 33.

13. Walsh, "The Catholic Church in Chicago," 103, 178; Charles Shanabruch, *Chicago's Catholics: The Evolution of an American Identity* (Notre Dame, IN: University of Notre Dame, 1981), 59–60, 68, 73.

14. Coughlin and Riplinger, *The Story of Charitable Care*, 132.

15. Walsh, "The Catholic Church in Chicago," 37; Shanabruch, *Chicago's Catholics*, 138.

16. Gould, "An Historical Study of the House of the Good Shepherd," i, 13; Mary Foote Coughlin, *A New Commandment: A Little Memoir of the Work Accomplished by the Shepherd Nuns in Chicago during a Half Century, 1859–1909* (Chicago: Sisters of the Good Shepherd, 1909), 153; Gould, "An Historical Study of the House of the Good Shepherd," 15.

17. Walsh, "The Catholic Church in Chicago," 199–200.

18. Sisters of the Good Shepherd, n.t., n.d., 69, HGSC; Hoy, "Caring for Chicago's Women and Girls": 283–84. Organized in 1889, the Illinois Woman's Alliance was comprised of various women's clubs, including the CWC, that worked on behalf of children's and women's issues. As such, they advocated for the enforcement of factory ordinances, compulsory education laws, and the creation of child labor laws. Additionally, they publicized the dismal conditions they found in children's institutions and police stations. Kathryn Kish Sklar, *Florence Kelley and the Nation's Work* (New Haven: Yale University Press, 1995), 211, 213.

19. Walsh, "The Catholic Church in Chicago," 201.

20. 1900, 1901, 1902, 1903 Ledgers, HGSC.

21. Coughlin, *A New Commandment*, 139. Richard Tuthill was juvenile court judge from 1899 to 1905.

22. Walsh, "The Catholic Church in Chicago," 202.

23. Maureen Flanagan, "Gender and Urban Political Reform: The City Club and the Woman's City Club of Chicago in the Progressive Era," *American Historical Review* 95 (October 1990): 1032–50, 1109–14.

24. Walsh, "The Catholic Church in Chicago," 104, 198, 199.

25. Coughlin, *A New Commandment*, 139, 149; *If I Forget Thee*, 80.

26. Walsh, "The Catholic Church in Chicago," 198. In 1905, for example, the Visitation and Aid Society had filed in the CCJC 48 percent of all dependent cases. Dependent as well as delinquent children who were not committed to Catholic institutions were placed under the supervision of probation officers affiliated with the society. *Juvenile Court Record* (January 1905), 5.

27. Gould, "An Historical Study of the House of the Good Shepherd," 15, 19–20, 22–24; "History of the Sisters of the Good Shepherd. The Centennial Jubilee, 1859–1959," in *The House of the Good Shepherd: A Century of Service to Chicago Land* (Chicago: HGSC, 1959), n.p.;

Untitled List of Benefactors, 1905–1942, HGSC, n.d.; Letter to Rev. Quigley from Sisters of the Good Shepherd, September 30, 1904, item 10, folder Q, box 1904, MC, JCBRC; n.a., "Little Journeys to Institutions of Interest," *Charity Watchman* (December, 1919), 14–15. See also "Fifty Years of Earnest Work," *New World*, October 3, 1905, 1.

28. Untitled and Typed Manuscript on the History of the House of the Good Shepherd, HGSC, n.d., 79; Gould, "An Historical Study of the House of the Good Shepherd," 13, 14, 18; Walsh, "The Catholic Church in Chicago," 203; Coughlin, *A New Commandment*, 153.

29. 1910–1926 CCJCAR, HWL; see table 8 in appendix 2.

30. During the prewar years, there were three to four times more delinquent girls in the Sacred Heart Class than in the industrial class. This was, in part, because most girls in the industrial class were first-time offenders, not recidivists. During the war years, roughly half or more of the delinquent girls attended the industrial class. 1909–1920 CCJCAR, HWL.

31. Letter to Rev. Quigley from Sisters of the Good Shepherd, September 30, 1904, item 10, folder Q, box 1904, MC, JCBRC.

32. Walsh, "The Catholic Church in Chicago," 202.

33. Sisters of the Good Shepherd, Untitled List of Benefactors Book, 1899–1935, HGSC; Untitled List of Benefactors, 1905–1942, HSGC. According to the Sisters, Al Capone occasionally gave a $1,000 gift as an anonymous visitor; Koenig, *Caritas Christi*, 896.

34. Untitled and typed manuscript on the History of the House of the Good Shepherd, 79; Untitled and handwritten manuscript, HGSC.

35. "To Hold Christmas Sale at House of Good Shepherd," *New World*, November 30, 1912, 5; Coughlin, *A New Commandment*, 135. The number of members is calculated from the total of membership fees at $2,000, with an individual annual membership fee of $5.

36. *If I Forget Thee*, 79; Untitled and typed manuscript on the History of the House of the Good Shepherd, 79; Walsh, "The Catholic Church in Chicago," 201; "Good Shepherd Benefit Baseball Nets $5,000," *New World*, July 25, 1908, 5; *New World*, July 11, 1908, 1.

37. 1917 Receipts, item 22 (3), pp. 1–4, folder C, box 1918, MC, JCBRC.

38. Shanabruch, *Chicago's Catholics*, 39, 49, 80, 115; Edward R. Kantowicz, "The Ethnic Church," in *Catholicism, Chicago Style*, ed. Ellen Skerrett, Edward R. Kantowicz, and Steven M. Avella (Chicago: Loyola University Press, 1993), 12; Ellen Skerrett, "The Irish in Chicago: The Catholic Dimension," in *Catholicism, Chicago Style*, 54–55. As late as 1926, nearly half of Chicago's parishes were Irish. One Gaelic Club had sponsored an "entertainment" for the House of the Good Shepherd; Koenig, *Caritas Christi*, 896. Mundelein praised the Ladies' Auxiliary of the Ancient Order of Hibernians for promoting the study of Irish history in the Chicago public schools. See "Letter to the Ladies' Auxiliary of the Ancient Order of Hibernians, Commending the Study of Irish History," in *Two Crowded Years: Being Selected Addresses, Pastorals, and Letters Issued during the First Twenty-Four Months of the Episcopate of the Most Rev. George William Mundelein, D.D.* (Chicago: Extension Press, 1918), 310–11.

39. Shanabruch, *Chicago's Catholics*, 1; Kantowicz, *Corporation Sole*, 33–34, 35; Koenig, *Caritas Christi*, 813–814.

40. Kantowicz, *Corporation Sole*, 15; Shanabruch, *Chicago's Catholics*, 178. Mundelein believed strongly in the Americanization of immigrant children, for example, teaching them in English and not in their native languages in the parochial schools. Edward R. Kantowicz, "Cardinal Mundelein of Chicago and the Shaping of Twentieth-Century American Catholicism," in *Catholicism, Chicago Style*, 74.

41. Kantowicz, *Corporation Sole*, 22–23. For examples of patriotic activity advocated by Mundelein, see "Letter in Favor of the Work of the Red Cross," "Second Letter in Favor of

the Work of the Red Cross," "Letter in Favor of the Liberty Loan," in *Two Crowded Years*, 284–85, 286–87, 288–89. One of Mundelein's letters to Timothy Hurley revealed his strategies regarding the *Dunn* case. Apparently a committee of social welfare workers was to meet to consider proposed changes in juvenile court law. One amendment of the law was that the child's guardian need not be of the same religion. But the two persons appointed by the cardinal had not been notified of the meetings. The cardinal was opposed to the amendment and recommended that the committee be allowed to do "a whole lot of talking" and then "we simply put down our foot on any kind of a suggestion." Letter to Timothy Hurley from Archbishop Mundelein, November 16, 1916, item 41, folder H, box 1916, MC, JCBRC. For further information on the *Dunn* case, see David S. Tanenhaus, " 'Rotten to the Core': The Juvenile Court and the Problem of Legitimacy in the Progressive Era," in *A Noble Social Experiment? The First 100 Years of the Cook County Juvenile Court 1899–1999*, ed. Gwen Hoerr McNamee (Chicago: Chicago Bar Association and the Children's Court Centennial Committee, 1999), 24–29.

42. Kantowicz, *Corporation Sole*, 24; "State Aid Sustained in Illinois," *The Catholic Charities Review* 1 (December 1917): 309–10.

43. Shanabruch, *Chicago's Catholics*, 160–61; Kantowicz, *Corporation Sole*, 45–46, 132–33, 135. Sister Mary referred to Mundelein "working through" the Catholic senators. Letter to Archbishop Mundelein from Sister Mary, November 1, 1918, item 120 (3), folder M, box 1918, MC, JCBRC; "Address on the Occasion When the Associated Catholic Charities of Chicago Was Formed, April 10th, 1917," in *Two Crowded Years*, 145. See also Paul R. Martin, *The First Cardinal of the West: The Story of the Church in the Archdiocese of Chicago* (Chicago: New World, 1934), chap. 26.

44. Kantowicz, *Corporation Sole*, 133–34; Kantowicz, "Cardinal Mundelein of Chicago," 73.

45. Koenig, *Caritas Christi*, 812; Coughlin and Riplinger, *The Story of Charitable Care*, 210.

46. Kantowicz, *Corporation Sole*, 132, 190; Thompson, *Diamond Jubilee of the Archdiocese of Chicago*, 794–95; "New Boarding Homes for Chicago," *Catholic Charities Review* 5 (October 1921): 274. Mundelein charged the Women's Catholic Order of Foresters with caring for working girls in downtown Chicago, pointing out that this would be their particular accomplishment. See "Address of the Silver Jubilee of the Women's Catholic Order of Foresters, Auditorium, Chicago, April 28th, 1916," in *Two Crowded Years*, 195–204. Similarly he charged the Knights of Columbus with care of delinquent boys. See "Address to the Knights of Columbus—The Care of Delinquent Boys, February 22nd, 1916," in *Two Crowded Years*, 180–87.

47. Shanabruch, *Chicago's Catholics*, 186; Kantowicz, *Corporation Sole*, 20.

48. Kantowicz, *Corporation Sole*, 134, 146. In January of 1918, expenditures for the House exceeded $20,000 and so the Sisters had not paid a number of bills. They hoped to do so when the city reimbursed them. Letter from Sister Mary Superior to Mundelein, January 19, 1918, item 221, folder M, box 1918, MC, JCBRC. Mundelein provided substantial sums of the ACC's monies to the House of the Good Shepherd and St. Mary's School, prompting Reverend George Eisenbacher of the Angel Guardian Orphanage to complain because his orphanage received so little. Letter from Rev. George Eisenbacher to Cardinal Mundelein, May 30, 1919, item 154, folder M, box 1919, MC, JCBRC.

49. Coughlin and Riplinger, *The Story of Charitable Care*, 212.

50. Walsh, "The Catholic Church in Chicago," 49–50.

51. 1934–1935 contributors listed in Untitled List of Benefactors, 1899–1935.

52. Coughlin, *A New Commandment*, 150.

53. *Practical Rules for the Use of the Religious of the Good Shepherd for Direction of the Classes* (St. Paul: Convent of the Good Shepherd, 1943), 53.

54. "The Good Shepherd's Black Sheep," *American Mercury* 26 (June 1932): 157.

55. Walsh, "The Catholic Church in Chicago," 196.

56. *Practical Rules for the Use of the Religious of the Good Shepherd*, 89, 113; Ella M. Cullen, "The House of the Good Shepherd. No Corporal Punishment Been Resorted To," *New World*, November 16, 1912, 1.

57. Emma Quinlan, "Cases Cared for by the Chicago Juvenile Court and the House of the Good Shepherd," *Catholic Charities Review* 9 (June 1925): 213.

58. Toward this end, Mother Superior asked the superintendent of the Chicago Public Schools, Ella Flagg Young, for advice in improving the House's domestic department. Responding to this request, the supervisor of the household arts program of the Chicago Public Schools visited the House and commended its existing program. Kantowicz, "Cardinal Mundelein of Chicago," 52.

59. Letter from Archbishop Mundelein to Sister Mary Superior, November 11, 1917, item 51, folder M, box 1917, MC, JCBRC; "Letter in Favor of the Work of the Sisters of the Good Shepherd, Chicago," in *Two Crowded Years*, 339.

60. Letter from Archbishop Mundelein to Sister Mary Superior, November 11, 1917, item 51, folder M, box 1917, MC, JCBRC.

61. The Sisters kept the juniors' and seniors' accounts in separate banks so the older delinquent girls wouldn't influence the younger ones once they were released. Gould, "An Historical Study of the House of the Good Shepherd," 34–35; *If I Forget Thee*, 4, 81.

62. "Little Journeys to Institutions of Interest": 15; Letter from Archbishop Mundelein to Mr. Kelly, president of the Associated Catholic Charities of Chicago, May 23, 1918, item 13, folder K, box 1918, MC, JCBRC.

63. Letter from Archbishop Mundelein to Sister Mary Superior, March 28, 1918, item 164 (2), folder M, box 1918, MC, JCBRC; Quinlan, "Cases Cared for by the Chicago Juvenile Court": 213.

64. Letter from Archbishop Mundelein to Sister Mary Superior, November 11, 1917, item 51, folder M, box 1917, MC, JCBRC.

65. Quinlan, "Cases Cared for by the Chicago Juvenile Court," 210.

66. Letter to Rev. Mundelein from House of the Good Shepherd Sister, April, 1918, item 120 (3), folder M, box 1918, MC, JCBRC.

67. Letter from Sister Superior to Mundelein, March 28, 1918, item 164 (2), folder M, box 1918, MC, JCBRC; Coughlin and Riplinger, *The Story of Charitable Care*, 19.

68. As of 1927, there was a staff of forty-five nuns at the House; Illinois Association for Criminal Justice, *Illinois Crime Survey*, 700.

69. Walsh, "The Catholic Church in Chicago," 104–7; Coughlin and Riplinger, *The Story of Charitable Care*, 129, 130, 190.

70. The league also hung notices of their social services at the railway stations and cooperated with Jewish and Protestant travelers' aid groups and the YWCA to ensure the protection of Catholic girls. Shanabruch, *Chicago's Catholics*, 131; Mary Jane Burns, "The Catholic Woman's League of Chicago," *Catholic Charities Review* 2 (February 1918): 54; Thompson, *Diamond Jubilee of the Archdiocese of Chicago*, 801–3; Walsh, "The Catholic Church in Chicago," 151; YWCA 1912 Annual Report, box 43, folder 1, UICSC. See also Mary Jane Burns, "Twenty-Five Years of the Catholic Women's League of Chicago," *Catholic Charities Review* 2 (December 1918): 308–10; Harvey C. Carbaugh, *Human Welfare Work in Chicago* (Chicago: A. C. McClurg, 1917), 188–190.

71. Additionally, the women sewed clothing for the girls, including first communion outfits. Thompson, *Diamond Jubilee of the Archdiocese of Chicago*, 795–96; Burns, "The Catholic Women's League of Chicago": 53–54.

72. Kantowicz, *Corporation Sole*, 132; Letter from Edward Garesche to Archbishop Mundelein, April 16, 1918, item 218, folder M, box 1918, MC, JCBRC. Garesche was the editor of *The Queen's Work*, a magazine that covered Catholic activities in St. Louis. For information about the Protestant Big Sister organizations, whose volunteerism Bartelme encouraged, see "Service Council for Girls," folder 4, box 427, WCMC, CHS.

73. "The Chicago Big Sisters," *Catholic Charities Review* 5 (February 1921): 91.

74. Ibid.

75. Ibid. See also Rosemary Tuttle, "The Big Sister," *Catholic Charities Review* 9 (February 1925): 68–69.

76. Form letter of Catholic Big Sisters, January 1917, item 4, folder S, box 1917, MC, JCBRC.

77. Untitled List of Benefactors Book, 1889 to 1935, n.p.; Untitled List of Benefactors, 1905 to 1942, n.p.; Gould, "An Historical Study of the House of the Good Shepherd," 13; Thompson, *Diamond Jubilee of the Archdiocese of Chicago*, 110.

78. 1900, 1905 Ledgers, HGSC. For comparative information on the House of the Good Shepherd's delinquent court girls in Cleveland, see *Catholic Charities Review* 9 (April 1925): 144–47; 9 (May 1925): 181–84; and 9 (June 1925): 221–24.

79. Shanabruch, *Chicago's Catholics*, 132–33, 153; Marie Sheahan, "A Catholic School of Sociology," *Catholic Charities Review* 5 (June 1921): 197–98.

80. 1905 Ledger, HGSC; William I. Thomas and Dorothy Swaine Thomas, *The Child in America: Behavior Problems and Programs* (New York: Alfred A. Knopf, 1928), 104–5.

81. "Social Work-Delinquents, Restricted," box 4, folder 75a, CFR, UICSC.

82. Ibid.

83. "Charity Workers in Conference," *New World*, November 25, 1914, 1, 4.

84. Maude Mary Firth, "The Use of the Foster Home for the Care of Delinquent Girls of the Cook County Juvenile Court" (Master's thesis, University of Chicago), 34–37.

85. 1906–1912 CCJCAR, HWL.

86. Firth, "The Use of the Foster Home for the Care of Delinquent Girls," 106–11.

87. Ibid.

Conclusion

1. Steve Drizan, "Race Does Matter in Juvenile Justice System," *Chicago Tribune*, May 13, 1999, sec. 1, 23. See also Charles H. Shireman and Frederic G. Reamer, *Rehabilitating Juvenile Justice* (New York: Columbia University Press, 1986), 28–29.

2. Thomas F. Geraghty, "Justice for Children: How Do We Get There?," *Journal of Criminal Law and Criminology* 88 (Fall 1997): 195.

3. Shireman and Reamer, *Rehabilitating Juvenile Justice*, 134–36, 137.

4. Ibid., 142.

5. Meda Chesney-Lind and Randall G. Shelden, *Girls, Delinquency, and Juvenile Justice*, 2nd ed. (Belmont, CA: Wadsworth, 1997), 2, 3, 9.

6. Ibid., 33, 112–16, 204–8.

7. Shireman and Reamer, *Rehabilitating Juvenile Justice*, 125.

8. Barry C. Feld, "Abolish the Juvenile Court: Youthfulness, Criminal Responsibility, and Sentencing Policy," *Journal of Criminal Law and Criminology* 88 (Fall 1997): 68–136.

9. *Chicago Tribune*, September 17, 1999, sec. 1, 7.

10. Sudhir Alladi Venkatesh, "Gender and Outlaw Capitalism: A Historical Account of the Black Sisters United 'Girl Gang,'" *Signs* 23 (Fall 1998): 683–709.

Appendix One

1. Emil Frankel, "Statistics on Juvenile Delinquency," *Social Service Review* 4 (December 1930): 563–74.

Bibliography

Archive Collections Consulted

Chicago Historical Society
Bowen, Louise de Koven Scrapbooks
Chicago Council of Social Agencies, 1928–1935
Chicago School of Civics and Philanthropy
Chicago Woman's Club Meeting Records, 1898–1902
McCoy-Gaines, Irene Collection
Welfare Council of Metropolitan Chicago Records

Harold Washington Library, Chicago, Municipal Reference Collection
Chicago Municipal Court Annual Reports, 1906 to 1935
Cook County Juvenile Court Annual Reports, 1901 to 1926
Cook County Municipal Court Annual Reports, 1907 to 1917
Police Reports of the City of Chicago to the City Council, 1901 to 1919

House of the Good Shepherd Convent, Chicago
Private Collection

Joseph Cardinal Bernadin Archival Research Center, Chicago
Madaj Collection

Northwestern University
Department of Public Welfare Annual Reports, 1900 to 1930
Juvenile Protective Association of Chicago, Annual Reports, 1915 to 1931

University of Chicago, Special Collections
Abbott, Edith and Grace Papers
Breckinridge, Sophonisba B. Papers
Burgess, Ernest Collection
Chicago Committee of Fifteen Papers
Chicago School of Civics and Philanthropy Collection
Henderson, Charles R. Collection
Park, Robert E. Papers
Small, Albion Paper

University of Chicago, Regenstein Library
Chicago Home for Girls Annual Reports, 1916 to 1930
Chicago Refuge for Girls Annual Reports, 1907 to 1915
Erring Women's Refuge of Chicago Annual Reports, 1896 to 1906
Report of the General Superintendent of Police of the City of Chicago to the City, 1899 to 1930
State Training School for Girls at Geneva, Illinois (formerly the State Home for Juvenile Female Offenders at
    Geneva) Biennial Reports, 1896 to 1935

University of Illinois at Chicago
Bartelme, Mary Papers
Bubasz, Steven S. Papers
Chicago Urban League Annual Reports, 1917 to 1935
Community Funds Records
Illinois Children's Home and Aid Society
Juvenile Protective Association Papers

Kawin, Irene Papers
YWCA of Metropolitan Chicago

University of Iowa
National Probation Association Conference Proceedings and Annual Reports, 1916 to 1935

Newspapers and Journals Examined
American Journal of Sociology
Broad Ax
Catholic Charities Review
Chicago Defender
Crisis
Institution Quarterly
Journal of Abnormal and Social Psychology
Journal of the American Institute of Criminal Law and Criminology
Journal of Applied Sociology
Journal of Delinquency
Journal of Juvenile Research
Journal of Negro Life
Journal of Social Hygiene
New World
Opportunity
Refuge Journal
Smith College Studies in Social Work
Social Forces
Social Hygiene
Social Service Review
Survey
Welfare Magazine

Sources

Abbott, Andrew. *Department and Discipline: Chicago Sociology at One Hundred*. Chicago: University of Chicago Press, 1999.
——— . *The System of Professions: An Essay on the Division of Expert Labor*. Chicago: University of Chicago Press, 1988.
Abbott, Edith. *The Tenements of Chicago, 1908–1935*. Chicago: University of Chicago Press, 1936.
——— . "The Juvenile Court and a Community Program for Treating and Preventing Delinquency." *Social Service Review* 10 (June 1936): 227–42.
——— . *Social Welfare and Professional Education*. Chicago: University of Chicago Press, 1931.
——— . "Training in Case Work and Special Administrative Problems in a University." In *The Social Service of the Courts: Proceedings of the Sixteenth Annual Conference of the National Probation Association*. New York: National Probation Association, 1923. 59–68.
——— . *The Experimental Period of Widows' Pension Legislation*. Chicago: University of Chicago Press, 1917.
——— . *The One Hundred and One County Jails of Illinois and Why They Ought to Be Abolished*. Chicago: Juvenile Protective Association, 1916.
——— . *Statistics Relating to Crime in Chicago*. Chicago: Chicago School of Civics and Philanthropy, 1915.
Abbott, Edith and Sophonisba P. Breckinridge. "The Administration of the Aid-to-Mothers Law in Illinois." In *Family in America*, edited by David J. Rothman and Sheila M. Rothman. Washington, DC: Government Printing Office, 1921; reprt., New York: Arno Press and the New York Times, 1972.
——— . *Truancy and Non-Attendance in the Chicago Schools*. Chicago: University of Chicago Press, 1917; reprt., New York: Arno Press and the New York Times, 1970.
Abbott, Edith and Evelyn Heacox Wilson. "The Problem of the Furnished Rooms." In *The Tenements of Chicago, 1908–1935*, by Edith Abbott. Chicago: University of Chicago Press, 1936. 305–40.
Abbott, Grace. *The Child and the State*, vol. 2. *The Dependent and the Delinquent Child: The Child of Unmarried Parents. Selected Documents with Introductory Notes*. Chicago: University of Chicago Press, 1938.
Addams, Jane. *The Spirit of Youth and the City Streets*. New York: Macmillan, 1909; reprt., Urbana: University of Illinois Press, 1972.
——— . *My Friend, Julia Lathrop*. New York: Macmillan, 1935.
Additon, Henrietta A. "The Functions of Policewomen." *Journal of Social Hygiene* 10 (June 1924): 321–28.

————. "The Policewoman." In *Community Treatment of Delinquency: Proceedings of the National Probation Association*. New York: National Probation Association, 1924. 238–43.

————. "Work among Delinquent Women and Girls." *Annals of the American Academy of Political and Social Sciences* 79 (September 1918): 152–59.

Adler, Herman M., M.D. "Prevention of Delinquency and Criminality by Psychiatry." *Welfare Magazine* 17 (January 1926): 195–207.

————. "Our Responsibility for the Future." In *The Child, the Clinic and the Court*. New York: New Republic, 1925. 66–72.

————. "The Juvenile Psychopathic Institute and the Work of the Division of the Criminologist." *Institution Quarterly* 9 (March 31, 1918): 5–13.

Aiken, Katherine G. *Harnessing the Power of Motherhood: The National Florence Crittenton Mission, 1883–1925.* Knoxville: University of Tennessee Press, 1999.

Alexander, Ruth. *The "Girl Problem." Female Sexual Delinquency in New York, 1900–1930.* Ithaca: Cornell University Press, 1995.

Amigh, Ophelia. "More about the Traffic in Shame." In *Fighting the Traffic in Young Girls or War on the White Slave Trade*, edited by Ernest A. Bell. N.p.: G. S. Ball, 1910. 120–23.

Anderson, Paul Gerard. "The Good to Be Done: A History of the Juvenile Protective Association of Chicago, 1898–1976." Ph.D. diss., University of Chicago, 1988.

Anderson, Philip J. and Dag Lanck, eds. *Swedish-American Life in Chicago: Cultural and Urban Aspects of an Immigrant People, 1850–1930.* Urbana: University of Illinois Press, 1992.

Atlanta School of Social Work. "1920 Announcement." In *Black Heritage in Social Welfare 1860–1930*, compiled and edited by Edith L. Ross. Metuchen, NJ: Scarecrow Press, 1978. 433–36.

————. "1929–1930 Bulletin." In *Black Heritage in Social Welfare 1860–1930*, compiled and edited by Edith L. Ross. Metuchen, NJ: Scarecrow Press, 1978. 450–55.

Bailey, Beth L. *From Front Porch to Back Seat: Courtship in Twentieth-Century America.* Baltimore: Johns Hopkins University Press, 1988.

Bain, Reed. "The Impersonal Confessions and Social Research." *Journal of Applied Sociology* 9 (July 1925): 356–61.

Baker, Lee. *From Savage to Negro: Anthropology and the Construction of Race, 1896–1954.* Berkeley and Los Angeles: University of California Press, 1998.

Ball, Lucy D. "The Delinquent Girl—and Music." *Institution Quarterly* 8 (January 1927): 93–96.

————. "State Training School for Girls." *Institution Quarterly* 14 (December 1923): 336–45.

Barrett, Dr. Kate Waller. *Some Practical Suggestions on the Conduct of a Rescue Home.* Washington, DC: n.p., 1903; reprt., New York: Arno Press, 1974.

Beane, James C. "A Survey of Three Hundred Delinquent Girls." *Journal of Juvenile Research* 15 (July 1931): 198–208.

Beard, Belle Boone. *Juvenile Probation.* New York: American Book Company, 1934.

Becker, Howard. "Mental Subnormality and the Local Community: An Outline of a Practical Program." *Social Service Review* 6 (June 1932): 256–69.

Beckham, Albert Sidney. "A Study of Race Attitudes in Negro Children of Adolescent Age." *Journal of Abnormal and Social Psychology* 29 (April–June 1934): 18–29.

————. "Juvenile Crime." *Journal of Juvenile Research* 16 (January 1932): 66–76.

————. "The Behavior Problem Clinic and the Negro Child." *Journal of Negro Life* 9 (April 1931): 111–12, 123.

————. "Juvenile Delinquency and the Negro." *Opportunity* 9 (October 1931): 300–302.

Bederman, Gail. *Manliness and Civilization: A Cultural History of Gender and Race in the United States, 1880–1917.* Chicago: University of Chicago Press, 1995.

Beers, Clifford Whittingham. *A Mind That Found Itself: An Autobiography.* 7th ed. Garden City: Doubleday, Doran, 1948.

Bell, Ernest A. *Fighting the Traffic in Young Girls, or War on the White Slave Trade.* N.p.: G. S. Ball, 1910.

Bennett, James. *Oral History and Delinquency: The Rhetoric of Criminology.* Chicago: University of Chicago Press, 1981.

Binford, Jessie F. "Cook County (Illinois) Roadhouse." *Journal of Social Hygiene* 6 (May 1930): 257–64.

————. "Community Responsibility." *Welfare Magazine* 19 (February 1928): 143–48.

————. "Delinquent Geneva Girls and Co-Operation." *Institution Quarterly* 14 (December 1923): 141–44.

Bingham, Anne T. "Determinants of Sex Delinquency in Adolescent Girls Based on Intensive Studies of 500 Cases." *Journal of the American Institute of Criminal Law and Criminology* 13 (February 1923): 494–586.

Blackwell, James E. and Morris Janowitz, eds. *Black Sociologists: Historical and Contemporary Perspectives.* Chicago: University of Chicago Press, 1974.

Blanchard, Phyllis and Carlyn Manasses. *New Girls for Old.* New York: Macaulay, 1930.

Blumer, Herbert. *Movies and Conduct.* New York: Macmillan, 1933.

Blumer, Herbert and Philip M. Hauser. *Movies, Delinquency, and Crime.* New York: Macmillan, 1933.

Boas, Franz. "Growth and Development, Bodily and Mental, As Determined by Heredity and by Social Environment." In *The Child, the Clinic and the Court*. New York: New Republic, 1925. 178–88.

Bodine, William Lester. *Bodine's Reference Book on Juvenile Welfare: A Review of the Chicago Social Service System.* Chicago: W. L. Bodine, 1913.

Bogan, William J. *First Annual Report of Montefiore School, 1929–1930.* Chicago: n.p., 1930.

Bowen, A. L. "State Training School for Girls." *Institution Quarterly* 5 (1914): 43–45.

Bowen, Mrs. Joseph T. [Louise de Koven]. *Open Windows: Stories of People and Places.* Chicago: Ralph Fletcher Seymour, 1946.

———. "The Early Days of the Juvenile Court." In *The Child, the Clinic, and the Court.* New York: New Republic, 1925. 298–309.

Bowen, Louise de Koven. *Speeches, Addresses, and Letters of Louise de Koven Bowen.* Vols. 1 and 2. Ann Arbor: Edwards Brother, 1937.

———. *Growing Up with a City.* New York: Macmillan, 1926.

———. *Safeguards for City Youth at Work and at Play.* New York: Macmillan, 1914.

———. *The Colored People of Chicago.* Chicago: Juvenile Protective Association, 1913.

———. *The Girl Employed in Hotels and Restaurants.* Chicago: Juvenile Protective Association, 1912.

———. *Our Most Popular Recreation Controlled by the Liquor Interests: A Study of Public Dance Halls.* Chicago: Juvenile Protective Association, 1912.

———. *The Department Store Girl: Based upon Interviews with 200 Girls.* Chicago: Juvenile Protective Association, 1911.

———. *Five and Ten Cent Theatres: Two Investigations.* Chicago: Juvenile Protective Association, 1909 and 1911.

———. *Fighting to Make Chicago Safe for Children.* n.d.

Bowser, Benjamin P. "The Contributions of Blacks to Sociological Knowledge: A Problem of Theory and Role to 1950." *Phylon* 42 (Summer 1981): 180–93.

Boyce, Ella Ruth. "Magazine Articles on Parent Education." In *Parent Education: The First Yearbook,* edited by the National Congress of Parents and Teachers. Washington, DC: National Congress of Parents and Teachers, 1930. 130–52.

Braeman, John, Robert H. Bremner, and David Brody, eds. *Change and Continuity in Twentieth-Century America: The 1920s.* Columbus: Ohio State University Press, 1968. 351–98.

Breckinridge, Sophonisba P. *The Illinois Poor Law and Its Administration.* Chicago: University of Chicago Press, 1939.

———. "Social Workers in Cook County Courts." *Social Service Review* 12 (June 1938): 230–50.

———. "Chicago Housing Problem: Families in Furnished Rooms." *American Journal of Sociology* 16 (November 1910): 289–308.

Breckinridge, Sophonisba P., ed. *The Child in the City: A Series of Papers Presented at the Conference Held during the Chicago Child Welfare Exhibit.* Chicago: Department of Social Investigation, Chicago School of Civics and Philanthropy, 1925.

Breckinridge, Sophonisba and Edith Abbott. *The Delinquent Child and the Home.* New York: Charities Publication Committee, 1912.

Breckinridge, Sophonisba P. and Helen R. Jeter. *A Summary of Juvenile-Court Legislation in the United States.* Washington, DC: Government Printing Office, 1920.

Brenzel, Barbara. *Daughters of the State: A Social Portrait of the First Reform School for Girls in North America, 1856–1905.* Cambridge, MA: MIT Press, 1983.

Bronner, Augusta F. *A Comparative Study of the Intelligence of Delinquent Girls.* New York: Teachers College, Columbia University, 1914.

Bronner, Augusta F., William Healy, Gladys M. Lowe, and Myra E. Shimberg. *A Manual of Individual Mental Tests and Testing.* Boston: Little, Brown, 1938.

Bronner, Simon J. "Object Lesson: The Work of Ethnological Museums and Collections." In *Consuming Visions: Accumulation and Display of Goods in America, 1880–1920,* edited by Simon J. Bronner. New York: W. W. Norton, 1989. 217–54.

———. "Reading Consumer Culture." In *Consuming Visions: Accumulation and Display of Goods in America, 1880–1920,* edited by Simon J. Bronner. New York: W. W. Norton, 1989. 13–53.

Bronner, Simon J., ed. *Consuming Visions: Accumulation and Display of Goods in America, 1880–1920.* New York: W. W. Norton, 1989.

Brown, Dorothy M. *American Women in the 1920s: Setting a Course.* Boston: Twayne, 1987.

Brown, W. O. "Culture Contact and Race Conflict." In *Race and Culture Contacts,* edited by Edward B. Reuter. New York: McGraw-Hill, 1934. 34–47.

———. "The Negro Problem: A Sociological Interpretation." *Opportunity* 8 (November 1930): 330–33.

———. "Race Prejudice: A Sociological Study." Ph.D. diss., University of Chicago, 1930.

Brumberg, Joan Jacobs. " 'Ruined' Girls: Changing Community Responses to Illegitimacy in Upstate New York, 1890–1920." *Journal of Social History* 15 (Winter 1984): 247–87.

Bruno, Frank J. "Some Case Work Recording Limitations of Verbatim Reporting." *Social Forces* 6 (June 1928): 532–34.

Bryan, Mary Lynn McCree and Allen F. Davis, eds. *Years at Hull-House*. Bloomington: Indiana University Press, 1990.

Buchan, Evelyn. "The Delinquency of Girls." Master's thesis, University of Chicago, 1922.

Buhle, Mary Jo. *Feminism and Its Discontents: A Century of Struggle with Psychoanalysis*. Cambridge, MA: Harvard University Press, 1998.

Bulmer, Martin. *The Chicago School of Sociology: Institutionalization, Diversity, and the Rise of Sociological Research*. Chicago: University of Chicago Press, 1984.

———. "The Methodology of the Taxi-Dance Hall: An Early Account of Chicago Ethnography from the 1920s." *Urban Life* 12 (April 1983): 95–101.

Bulmer, Martin, Kevin Bales, and Kathryn Kish Sklar, eds. *The Social Survey in Historical Perspective*. Cambridge: Cambridge University Press, 1991.

———. "The Social Survey in Historical Perspective," in *The Social Survey in Historical Perspective*, edited by Martin Bulmer, Kevin Bales, and Kathryn Kish Sklar. Cambridge: Cambridge University Press, 1991. 1–48.

Burgess, Ernest W. "What Social Case Records Should Contain to Be Useful for Sociological Interpretation." *Social Forces* 6 (June 1928): 524–32.

———. "The Determination of Gradients in the Growth of the City." *Proceedings of the American Sociologist* 21 (1927): 178–84.

———. "The Study of the Delinquent as a Person." *American Journal of Sociology* 28 (May 1923): 657–80.

———. "The Moral Decay of the Modern Stage." In *The 1919 National Conference of Social Work*. Chicago: Rogers and Hall, 1920. 502–6.

Burgess, Ernest, ed. *The Urban Community: Selected Papers from the Proceedings of the American Sociological Society, 1925*. Chicago: University of Chicago Press, 1926.

Burleigh, Edith. "Principles of Parole for Girls." In *The Social Work of the Courts: Annual Report and Proceedings of the Tenth Annual Conference of the National Probation Association*. Albany, NY: National Probation Association, 1919. 156–65.

Burleigh, Edith N. and Frances R. Harris. *The Delinquent Girl: A Study of the Girl on Parole in Massachusetts*. New York: New York School of Social Work, 1923.

Burnet, Anne, M.D. "A Study of Delinquent Girls." *Institution Quarterly* 3 (June 30, 1912): 47–53.

Burnham, John Chynoweth. "The New Psychology: From Narcissism to Social Control." In *Change and Continuity in Twentieth-Century America: The 1920s*, edited by John Braeman, Robert H. Bremner, and David Brody. Columbus: Ohio State University Press, 1968. 351–98.

Burns, Mary Jane. "Twenty-Five Years of the Catholic Women's League of Chicago." *Catholic Charities Review* 2 (December 1918): 308–10.

Cahn, Susan. "Spirited Youth or Fiends Incarnate: The Samarcand Arson Case and Female Adolescence in the American South." *Journal of Women's History* 9 (Winter 1998): 152–80.

Calverton, V. F. and S. D. Schmalhausen, eds. *Sex in Civilization*. New York: Macaulay, 1929.

Carbaugh, Harvey C. *Human Welfare Work in Chicago*. Chicago: A. C. McClurg, 1917.

Carey, James T. *Sociology and Public Affairs: The Chicago School*. Beverly Hills: Sage, 1975.

Carlton-LaNey, Iris. "The Career of Birdye Henrietta Haynes, A Pioneer Settlement House Worker." *Social Service Review* 68 (June 1994): 259–63.

———. "Training African-American Social Workers Through the NUL Fellowship Program." *Journal of Sociology and Social Welfare* 21 (June 1994): 43–54.

Cavan, Ruth Shonle. "The Chicago School of Sociology, 1918–1933." *Urban Life* 11 (January 1983): 407–20.

———. *Business Girls: A Study of Their Interests and Problems*. Chicago: The Religious Education Association, 1929.

Chapin, F. Stuart. "The Relations of Sociology and Social Case Work." In *Proceedings of the National Probation Association*. New York: National Probation Association, 1920. 358–65.

Chauncey, George Jr. *Gay New York: Gender, Urban Culture, and the Making of the Gay Male World, 1890–1940*. New York: Basic Books, 1994.

———. "From Sexual Inversion to Homosexuality: The Changing Medical Conceptualization of Female 'Deviance.'" In *Passion and Power: Sexuality in History*, edited by Kathy Peiss and Christina Simmons with Robert A. Padgug. Philadelphia: Temple University Press, 1989. 87–117.

Cherry, David King. "Vocational Activities of Educated Negroes." Master's thesis, University of Chicago, 1931.

Chesney-Lind, Meda, and Randall G. Shelden. *Girls, Delinquency, and Juvenile Justice*. 2nd ed. Belmont, CA: Wadsworth, 1997.

Chicago Commission on Race Relations. *The Negro in Chicago: A Study of Race Relations and a Race Riot in 1919*. Chicago: University of Chicago Press, 1922.

Chideckel, Maurice, M.D. *Female Sex Perversion: The Sexually Aberrated Woman as She Is*. New York: Eugenics, 1935.

Children's Bureau. *A Study of Maternity Homes in Minnesota and Pennsylvania*. Washington, DC: Government Printing Office, 1926.

Chute, Charles L. "The Needs and Future of the Probation Service." In *The Social Service of the Courts: Proceedings of the Sixteenth Annual Conference of the National Probation Association*. New York: National Probation Association, 1923. 20–28.

Clapp, Elizabeth J. *Mothers of All Children: Women Reformers and the Rise of Juvenile Courts in Progressive Era America*. University Park, MD: Penn State University Press, 1998.

Cmiel, Kenneth. *A Home of Another Kind: One Chicago Orphanage and the Tangle of Child Welfare*. Chicago: University of Chicago Press, 1995.

Cohen, Lizabeth. *Making a New Deal: Industrial Workers in Chicago, 1919–1930*. New York: Cambridge University Press, 1990.

Connelly, Mark Thomas. *The Response to Prostitution in the Progressive Era*. Chapel Hill: University of North Carolina Press, 1980.

Cook, Inez M. and T. V. Goodrich. "How High School Pupils Spend Their Time." *The School Review* 36 (1929): 721–28.

Cook, Lloyd Allen. *Community Backgrounds of Education: A Textbook in Educational Sociology*. 1st ed. New York: McGraw-Hill, 1938.

"Cook County Juvenile Court." *Institution Quarterly* 7 (March 31, 1916): 52–55.

Cooper, Charles C. "The Necessity for Changes in Americanization Methods." In *The 1918 National Conference of Social Work*. Chicago: Rogers and Hall, 1919. 435–44.

Corman, Bertha. "Study of 446 Delinquent Girls with Institutional Experience." Master's thesis, University of Chicago, 1923.

Costin, Lela B. "Edith Abbott and the Chicago Influence on Social Work Education." *Social Service Review* 57 (March 1983): 94–11.

———. *Two Sisters for Social Justice: A Biography of Grace and Edith Abbott*. Urbana: University of Illinois Press, 1983.

Coughlin, Mary Foote. *A New Commandment: A Little Memoir of the Work Accomplished by the Shepherd Nuns in Chicago during a Half Century, 1859–1909*. Chicago: Sisters of the Good Shepherd, 1909.

Coughlin, Roger J. and Cathryn A. Riplinger. *The Story of Charitable Care in the Archdiocese of Chicago, 1844–1959*. Chicago: The Catholic Charities of Chicago, 1981.

Cranz, Galen. "Women in Urban Parks." *Signs* 5 (Spring 1980): S80–S95.

Cressey, Paul Goalby. "A Comparison of the Roles of the 'Sociological Stranger' and the 'Anonymous Stranger' in Field Research." *Urban Life* 12 (April 1983): 102–20.

———. *The Taxi-Dance Hall: A Sociological Study in Commercialized Recreation and City Life*. Chicago: University of Chicago Press, 1932; reprt., Montclair, NJ: Patterson Smith, 1969.

———. "The Closed Dance Hall in Chicago." Master's Thesis, University of Chicago, 1929.

Daniels, Harriet McDoual. *The Girl and Her Chance: A Study of Conditions Surrounding the Young Girl Between Fourteen and Eighteen Years of Age in New York City*. New York: Fleming H. Revell, 1914.

Davidson, Essie Mae. "Organized Boarding Homes for Self-Supporting Women in the City of Chicago." Master's thesis, University of Chicago, 1914.

Davis, Allen F. *Spearheads for Reform: The Social Settlements and the Progressive Movement, 1890–1914*. 2nd ed. New Brunswick, NJ: Rutgers University Press, 1984.

Davis, Clarence E. "Probation with Colored Cases." In *Community Treatment of Delinquency: Proceedings of the National Probation Association*. New York: National Probation Association, 1924. 243–45.

Davis, Edna Ruth. "A Comparison of Four National and Racial Groups." *Smith College Studies in Social Work* 13 (March 1933): 249–59.

Davis, Elizabeth Caroline. "State Institutional Care of the Feebleminded in Illinois." Master's thesis, University of Chicago, 1926.

Davis, Katharine Bement, Ph.D. *Factors in the Sex Life of Twenty-Two Hundred Women*. New York: Harper and Brothers, 1929.

Deegan, Mary Jo. "The Second Sex and the Chicago School: Women's Accounts, Knowledge, and Work, 1945–1960." In *A Second Chicago School? The Development of a Postwar American Sociology*, edited by Gary Alan Fine. Chicago: University of Chicago Press, 1995. 322–64.

———. *Jane Addams and the Men of the Chicago School, 1892–1918*. New Brunswick, NJ: Transaction, 1988.

Deegan, Mary Jo, ed. *Women in Sociology: A Bio-Biographical Sourcebook*. Westport, CT: Greenwood Press, 1991.

Dehey, Elinor Tong. "Sisters of the Good Shepherd." In *Religious Orders of Women in the United States: Accounts of Their Origin and of Their Most Important Institutions*, compiled by Elinor Tong Dehey. 1st ed. Hammond, IN: W. B. Conkey, 1913. 144–50.

Dell, Floyd. *Love without Money*. New York: Farrar and Rinehart, 1931.

———. *Love in the Machine Age: A Psychological Study of the Transition from Patriarchal Society*. New York: Farrar and Rinehart, 1930.

D'Emilio, John and Estelle Freedman. *Intimate Matters: A History of Sexuality in America*. New York: Harper and Row, 1988.

Devine, Edward T. and Mary Van Kleeck. *Positions in Social Work*. New York: New York School of Philanthropy, 1916.

Dewson, Mary W. "Probation and Institutional Care of Girls." In *The Child in the City*, edited by Sophonisba P. Breckinridge. Chicago: Chicago School of Civics and Philanthropy, 1912. 355–70.

Dexter, Robert C. "The Negro in Social Work." *The Survey* 46 (June 25, 1921): 439–40.

Dickinson, Robert Latou and Lura Beam. *The Single Woman: A Medical Study in Sex Education*. Baltimore: Williams and Wilkins, 1934.

Diner, Steven J. *A City and Its Universities: Public Policy in Chicago, 1892–1919*. Chapel Hill: University of North Carolina Press, 1980.

———. "Chicago Social Workers and Blacks in the Progressive Era." *Social Service Review* 44 (December 1970): 393–410.

Dobbs, Harrison A. "Institutional Care for Delinquent Children: A New Appraisal." *Annals of the American Academy* 151 (September 1930): 173–79.

Dodge, Mara. "One Female Prisoner Is of More Trouble than Twenty Males: Women Convicts in Illinois Prisons, 1835–1896." *Journal of Social History* 32 (Summer 1999): 907–30.

Donovan Frances R. *The Saleslady*. Chicago: University of Chicago Press, 1929.

———. *The Woman Who Waits*. Boston: Gorham Press, 1920.

Dorsey, James. *Up South: Blacks in Chicago's Suburbs, 1719–1983*. Bristol, IN: Wyndham Hall Press, 1986.

Drake, St. Clair and Horace R. Cayton. *Black Metropolis: A Study in The Negro Life in a Northern City*. New York: Harcourt, Brace, 1945.

Duberman, Martin Bauml, Martha Vicinus, and George Chauncey Jr., eds. *Hidden from History: Reclaiming the Gay and Lesbian Past*. New York: New American Library, 1981.

Dubin, Steven C. "The Moral Continuum of Deviancy Research: Chicago Sociologists and the Dance Hall." *Urban Life* 12 (April 1983): 75–94.

Du Bois, W. E. B. *Dusk of Dawn: As Essay toward an Autobiography of a Race Concept*. New York: Schocken Books, 1968.

Du Bois, W. E. B., ed. *Efforts for Social Betterment among Negro Americans*. Atlanta: Atlanta University Press, 1909.

Duis, Perry R. *The Saloons: Public Drinking in Chicago and Boston 1880–1920*. Urbana: University of Illinois Press, 1983.

Dummer, Ethel S. *Why I Think So: The Autobiography of an Hypothesis*. Chicago: Clarke-McElroy, n.d.

Dunlap, Knight. *Personal Beauty and Racial Betterment*. St. Louis: C. V. Mosby, 1920.

Earp, Edwin L. *A Community Study of the Religious Social Survey*. Philadelphia: American Baptist Publication Society, 1917.

Eaton, Allen. *A Bibliography of Social Surveys: Reports of Fact-Finding Studies Made as a Basis for Social Action; Arranged by Subjects and Localities*. New York: Russell Sage Foundation, 1930.

Eddy, John M. "Unsupervised Club Life among Girls Attending Secondary School." *Journal of Educational Sociology* 2 (1928): 210–20.

"Editorial." *Opportunity* 3 (August 1925): 1.

Edwards, G. Franklin. "E. Franklin Frazier." In *Black Sociologists: Historical and Contemporary Perspectives*, edited by James E. Blackwell and Morris Janowitz. Chicago: University of Chicago Press, 1974. 85–117.

Ehrenreich, John H. *The Altruistic Imagination: A History of Social Work and Social Policy in the United States*. Ithaca: Cornell University Press, 1985.

Eliot, Thomas D. "Objectivity and Subjectivity in the Case Record." *Social Forces* 6 (June 1928): 539–44.

———. "What Social Workers Think of Sociology." *Welfare Magazine* 17 (May 1926): 38–47.

———. *The Juvenile Court and the Community*. New York: Macmillan, 1914.

Elliott, Mabel Agnes. "A Correlation between Rate of Juvenile Delinquency and Racial Heterogeneity." *Welfare Magazine* 17 (July 1926): 5–15.

Ellis, Havelock. *Studies in the Psychology of Sex*. 3rd ed. Philadelphia: F. A. Davis, 1929.

Elowson, Margueritte Anita. "Some Aspects of the Cook County Juvenile Court in Relation to Readjustment of the Delinquent Girl." Master's thesis, University of Chicago, 1930.

Emerson, L. E. "A Psychoanalytic Study of a Severe Case of Hysteria." *Journal of Abnormal and Social Psychology* 7 (February–March 1913): 385–406.

Ewen, Elizabeth. "City Lights: Immigrant Women and the Rise of the Movies." *Signs* 5 (Spring 1980): S45–S65.

Ewen, Stuart and Elizabeth Ewen. *Channels of Desire: Mass Images and the Shaping of American Consciousness*. New York: McGraw-Hill, 1982.

Faderman, Lillian. *Odd Girls and Twilight Lovers: A History of Lesbian Life in Twentieth-Century America*. New York: Columbia University Press, 1991.

Faris, Robert E. L. *Chicago Sociology 1920–1932*. San Francisco: Chandler, 1967.

Farris, Robert E. and Warren Dunham. *Mental Disorders in Urban Areas: An Ecological Study of Schizophrenia and Other Psychoses*. New York: Hafner, 1960.

Fass, Paula S. *The Damned and the Beautiful: American Youth in the 1920s*. New York: Oxford University Press, 1977.

Feld, Barry C. "Abolish the Juvenile Court: Youthfulness, Criminal Responsibility, and Sentencing Policy." *Journal of Criminal Law and Criminology* 88 (Fall 1997): 68–136.

Fernald, Mabel Ruth, Mary Holmes, Steven Hayes, and Almena Dawley. *A Study of Women Delinquents in New York State*. New York: The Century Company, 1920.

Fine, Gary Alan, ed. *A Second Chicago School? The Development of a Postwar American Sociology*. Chicago: University of Chicago Press, 1995.

Firth, Maude Mary. "The Use of the Foster Home for the Care of the Delinquent Girls of the Cook County Juvenile Court." Master's thesis, University of Chicago, 1924.

Fish, Virginia Kemp. "Hull House: Pioneer in Urban Research during Its Creative Years." *History of Sociology* 6 (Fall 1985): 33–55.

Fitzpatrick, Ellen. *Endless Crusade: Women Social Scientists and Progressive Reform.* New York: Oxford University Press, 1990.

Flanagan, Maureen A. "Gender and Urban Political Reform: The City Club and the Woman's City Club of Chicago in the Progressive Era." *American Historical Review* 95 (October 1990): 1032–50, 1109–14.

Flexner, Bernard and Roger N. Baldwin. *Juvenile Courts and Probation.* New York: The Century Company, 1916.

Flyn, Frank T. "Judge Merritt W. Pinckney and the Early Days of the Juvenile Court in Chicago." *Social Service Review* 28 (March 1954): 20–30.

Folbre, Nancy. "The 'Sphere of Women' in Early-Twentieth-Century Economics." In *Gender and American Social Science: The Formative Years,* edited by Helene Silverberg. Princeton: Princeton University Press, 1998. 35–60.

Folks, Homer. "The Probation System, Its Value and Limitations." In *Proceedings of the Child Conference for Research and Welfare, 1910.* New York: G. E. Stechert, 1910. 224–32.

Foucault, Michel. *The History of Sexuality: An Introduction.* Vol. 1. New York: Vintage Books, 1990.

——— . *Power/Knowledge: Selected Interviews and Other Writings, 1972–1977,* edited by Colin Gordon. New York: Pantheon Books, 1977.

Frank, Henriette Greenebaum and Amalie Hofer Jerome, comps. *Annals of the Chicago Woman's Club for the First Forty Years of Its Organization, 1876–1916.* Chicago: Chicago Woman's Club, 1916.

Frankel, Emil. "Statistics on Juvenile Delinquency." *Social Service Review* 4 (December 1930): 563–74.

Franklin, Donna L. "Mary Richmond and Jane Addams: From Moral Certainty to Rational Inquiry in Social Work Practice." *Social Service Review* 60 (December 1986): 504–25.

Frazier, E. Franklin. "Traditions and Patterns of Negro Family Life in the United States." In *Race and Culture Contacts,* edited by Edward B. Reuter. New York: McGraw-Hill, 1934. 191–207.

——— . *The Negro Family in Chicago.* Chicago: University of Chicago Press, 1932.

——— . "Family Disorganization among Negroes." *Opportunity* 9 (July 1931): 204–7.

——— . "The Negro Family in Chicago." Ph.D. diss., University of Chicago, 1931.

——— . "Chicago: A Cross-Section of Negro Life." *Opportunity* 7 (March 1929): 70–73.

——— . "Round Table No. 2: Professional Education for Negro Social Workers." In *Proceedings of the National Conference of Social Work.* Chicago: University of Chicago Press, 1927. 639–41.

——— . "Is the Negro Family a Unique Sociological Unit?" *Opportunity* 5 (June 1927): 165–66.

——— . "The Pathology of Race Prejudice." *Forum* 77 (June 1927): 856–61.

——— . "Three Scourges of the Negro Family." *Opportunity* 4 (July 1926): 210–13, 234.

——— . "A Note on Negro Education." *Opportunity* 2 (March 1924): 75–77.

Freedman, Estelle B. "Separatism Revisited: Women's Institutions, Social Reform, and the Career of Miriam Van Waters." In *U. S. History as Women's History: New Feminist Essays,* edited by Linda Kerber, Alice Kessler-Harris, and Kathryn Kish Sklar. Chapel Hill: University of North Carolina Press, 1995. 170–88.

——— . *Their Sisters' Keepers. Women's Prison Reform in America, 1830–1930.* Ann Arbor: University of Michigan Press, 1984.

——— . "Bartelme, Mary Margaret." In *Notable American Women: The Modern Period,* edited by Barbara Sicherman, Carol Hurd Green, Ilene Kantror, and Harriette Walker. Cambridge, MA: Belknap Press of Harvard University Press, 1980. 60–61.

Furfey, Paul Hanly. *Social Problems of Childhood.* New York: Macmillan, 1929.

Gallichan, Walter M. *Sexual Apathy and Coldness in Women.* Boston: Stratford, 1930.

Garrett, Annette Marie. "The Administration of the Aid to Mothers' Law in Illinois 1917 to 1925." Ph.D. diss., University of Chicago, 1925.

Gary, Robenia Baker and Lawrence E. Gary. "The History of Social Work Education for Black People, 1900–1930." *Journal of Sociology and Social Welfare* 21 (March 1994): 67–83.

Gasgoyne, John J. "Standards of Probation Work." In *The Social Service of the Courts: Proceedings of the Sixteenth Annual Conference of the National Probation Association.* New York: National Probation Association, 1923. 29–31.

Geraghty, Thomas F. "Justice for Children: How Do We Get There?" *Journal of Criminal Law and Criminology* 88 (Fall 1997): 190–241.

Gesell, Arnold. "Handicapped School Children." In *Guidance of Childhood and Youth,* edited by Benjamin C. Gruenberg. New York: Macmillan, 1927. 294–301.

Getis, Victoria Lynn. "A Disciplined Society: The Juvenile Court, Reform, and the Social Sciences in Chicago, 1890–1930." Ph.D. diss., University of Michigan, 1994.

Gittens, Joan. *Poor Relations: The Children of the State of Illinois, 1818–1990.* Urbana: University of Illinois Press, 1994.

Goddard, Henry Herbert. *Juvenile Delinquency.* New York: Dodd, Mead, 1921.

——— . *Feeble Mindedness: Its Causes and Consequences.* New York: Macmillan, 1914.

Goddard, Henry Herbert and Helen F. Hill. "Delinquent Girls Tested by the Binet Scale." *Training School Bulletin* 8 (1911): 50–56.

Goldberg, Jacob A. and Rosamond W. Goldberg. *Girls on City Streets: A Study of 1400 Cases of Rape.* New York: Foundation Books, 1940.

Goodwin, Joanne. *Gender and the Politics of Welfare Reform: Mothers' Pensions in Chicago, 1911–1929.* Chicago: University of Chicago Press, 1997.

Gordon, Linda. *Heroes of Their Own Lives: The Politics and History of Family Violence: Boston 1880–1960.* New York: Penguin, 1988.

Gordon, Michael, ed. *The American Family in Social-Historical Perspective.* 3rd ed. New York: St. Martin's Press, 1983.

Gould, Margaret Anne. "A Historical Study of the House of the Good Shepherd, A Specialized Child-Caring Institution." Master's thesis, Loyola University, 1946.

Graham, Irene. "The Negro Family in a Northern City." *Opportunity* 8 (February 1930): 48–51.

———. "Family Support and Dependency among Chicago Negroes: A Study of Unpublished Census Data." *Social Service Review* 3 (December 1929): 541–62.

Greenberg, David F. *The Construction of Homosexuality.* Chicago: University of Chicago Press, 1988.

Greene, Ransom A., M.D. "Progress in Understanding and Control of the Feeble-Minded." *Annals of the American Academy* 151 (September 1930): 130–37.

Groves, Ernest R. The American Family. Chicago: J. B. Lippincott, 1934.

———. "Juvenile Delinquency." In *Guidance of Childhood and Youth,* edited by Benjamin C. Gruenberg. New York: Macmillan, 1927. 305–9.

Gruenberg, Benjamin C., ed. *Guidance of Childhood and Youth.* New York: Macmillan, 1927.

Guichard, Parris and Lester Brooks. *Blacks in the City: A History of the National Urban League.* Boston: Little, Brown, 1971.

Gullett, Gayle. "'City Mothers, City Daughters, and the Dance Hall Girls: The Limits of Female Political Power in San Francisco, 1913." In *Women and the Structure of Society: Selected Research from the Fifth Berkshire Conference on the History of Women,* edited by Barbara J. Harris and JoAnne K. McNamara. Durham, NC: Duke University Press, 1984. 149–59.

Haggerty, James E. "Training for Probation Workers in Colleges and Universities." In *The Social Service of the Courts: Proceedings of the Sixteenth Annual Conference of the National Probation Association.* New York: National Probation Association, 1923. 51–59.

Hall, Fred S., ed. *Social Work Year Book, 1935: A Description of Organized Activities in Social Work and in Related Fields.* New York: Russell Sage Foundation, 1935.

———. *Social Work Year Book, 1933: A Description of Organized Activities in Social Work and in Related Fields.* New York: Russell Sage Foundation, 1933.

———. *Social Work Year Book, 1929: A Description of Organized Activities in Social Work and in Related Fields.* New York: Russell Sage Foundation, 1930.

Hall, G. Stanley. *Adolescence: Its Psychology and Its Relations to Physiology, Anthropology, Sex, Crime, Religion and Education.* Vol. 2. New York: D. Appleton, 1904.

Haller, Mark H. "Policy Gambling, Entertainment, and the Emergence of Black Politics: Chicago From 1900 to 1940." *Journal of Social History* 24 (Summer 1991): 719–40.

Halley, Lois Kate. "A Study of Motion Pictures in Chicago as a Medium of Communication." Master's thesis, University of Chicago, 1924.

Hamilton, Mary E. *The Policewoman: Her Service and Ideals.* New York: Frederick H. Stokes, 1924.

Hapgood, Hutchin. *Types from City Streets.* New York: Funk and Wagnalls, 1910.

Harris, Ethel Ramsey. "A Study of Voluntary Social Activity among the Professional Negroes in Chicago." Master's thesis, University of Chicago, 1937.

Harvey, Lee. *Myths of the Chicago School of Sociology.* Avebury, England: Gower, 1987.

Haseltine, Helen D. "A History of the Chicago Home for Girls Founded in 1863 as The Chicago Erring Woman's Refuge for Reform." Master's thesis, University of Chicago, 1934.

Hauser, Philip Morris. "Motion Pictures in Penal and Correctional Institutions. A Study of the Reactions of Prisoners to Movies." Master's thesis, University of Chicago, 1933.

Hayner, Norman S. "Hotel Life and Personality." *American Journal of Sociology* 33 (March 1928): 784–95.

Haynes, George E. "Negro Migration—Its Effect on Family and Community Life in the North." In *Proceedings of the National Conference of Social Work.* Chicago: University of Chicago Press, 1924. 62–75.

———. "Race Riots in Relation to Democracy." *The Survey* (August 9, 1919): 697–99.

———. "The Basis of Race Adjustment." *The Survey* (February 1, 1913): 569–70.

———. "Cooperation with Colleges in Securing and Training Negro Social Workers for Urban Centers." In *Proceedings of the National Conference of Charities and Correction.* Fort Wayne, IN: Fort Wayne Printing, 1911. 384–87.

Healy, William. "How Does the School Produce or Prevent Delinquency?" *Journal of Educational Sociology* 6 (April 1933): 450–70.

——— . *The Individual Delinquent: A Text-Book of Diagnosis and Prognosis for All Concerned in Understanding Offenders.* Boston: Little, Brown, 1929.

——— . "The Constructive Values of Conflicts, Successes and Failures." In *Building Character: Proceedings of the Midwest Conference on Parent Education, February, 1928.* Chicago: University of Chicago Press, 1928. 132–60.

——— . "The Psychology of the Situation: A Fundamental for Understanding and Treatment of Delinquency and Crime." In *The Child, the Clinic and the Court.* New York: New Republic, 1925. 37–52.

——— . "Knowing Your Individual." In *The Social Service of the Courts: Proceedings of the Sixteenth Annual Conference of the National Probation Association.* New York: National Probation Association, 1923. 225–31.

——— . *Case Studies of Mentally and Morally Abnormal Types.* Cambridge, MA: Harvard University Summer School, 1912.

Healy, William and Augusta F. Bronner. *New Light on Delinquency and Its Treatment.* New Haven: Yale University Press, 1936.

——— . "Juvenile Detention Homes." *Annals of the American Academy* 151 (September 1930): 180–84.

——— . *Delinquents and Criminals: Their Making and Unmaking: Studies in Two American Cities.* New York: AMS Press, 1926.

——— . "Youthful Offenders: A Comparative Study of Two Groups, Each of 1,000 Young Recidivists." *American Journal of Sociology* 22 (July 1916): 38–52.

Healy, William, Augusta F. Bronner, Edith M. H. Baylor, and J. Prentice Murphy. *Reconstructing Behavior in Youth: A Study of Problem Children in Foster Families.* New York: Alfred A. Knopf, 1929.

Healy, William and Mary Tenney Healy. *Pathological Lying, Accusation, and Swindling.* Boston: Little, Brown, 1926.

Henderson, Charles Richmond. *Introduction to the Study of the Dependent, Defective, and Delinquent Classes and of Their Social Treatment.* 2nd ed. Boston: D. C. Heath, 1908.

Hill, Betty Marwood. "A Comparative Study of Delinquency in Four National Groups in Cook County Juvenile Court of 1930." Master's thesis, University of Chicago, 1932.

Hirsch, Elizabeth Frances. "A Study of the Chicago and Cook County School for Boys." Master's thesis, University of Chicago, 1926.

Hogan, David John. *Class and Reform: School and Society in Chicago, 1880–1930.* Philadelphia: University of Pennsylvania Press, 1985.

Hogkiss, Margaret. "The Influence of Broken Home and Working Mothers." *Smith College Studies in Social Work* 13 (March 1933): 259–74.

Hooker, Edith Houghton. *Life's Clinic: A Series of Sketches Written from between the Lines of Some Medical Case Histories.* New York: Association Press, 1918.

Hoover, David Henry. "A Study of Juvenile Probation in Cook County." Bachelor's thesis, University of Chicago, 1918.

Howard, Ronald L. "Sociology and the Family in the Progressive Era, 1890–1920." In *A Social History of American Family Sociology, 1865–1940,* edited by John Mogey. Westport, CT: Greenwood Press, 1981. 39–62.

——— . "From Ecology to Interaction: Family Sociology in the 1920s and 1930s." In *A Social History of American Family Sociology, 1865–1940,* edited by John Mogey. Westport, CT: Greenwood Press, 1981. 63–94.

Hoy, Suellen. "Caring for Chicago's Women and Girls: The Sisters of the Good Shepherd, 1859–1911." *Journal of Urban History* 23 (March 1997): 260–94.

Hoyt, Franklin Chase. *Quicksands of Youth.* New York: Charles Scribner's Sons, 1921.

Hughes, Everett, Charles Johnson, Jitsuichi Masuoka, Robert Redfield, and Louis Wirth, eds. *The Collected Papers of Robert Ezra Park.* Glencoe, IL: The Free Press, 1950.

Hunter, Joel D. "The History and Development of Institute for the Study of Children." In *The Child, the Clinic, and the Court.* New York: New Republic, 1925. 204–14.

Hurl, Lorna F. and David Tucker. "The Michigan County Agents and the Development of Juvenile Probation, 1873–1900." *Journal of Social History* 30 (Summer 1997): 907–35.

Hurley, Timothy D. "Origins of the Illinois Juvenile Court Law." In *The Child, the Clinic, and the Court.* New York: New Republic, 1925. 320–30.

Hurley, Timothy D., comp. *Origin of the Illinois Juvenile Court: Juvenile Courts and What They Have Accomplished.* 3rd ed. Chicago: The Visitation and Aid Society, 1907.

Huslin, Ralph G. *Salaries and Qualifications of Child Welfare Workers in 1941.* New York: Russell Sage Foundation, 1943.

Hutzel, Eleonore L. *The Policewoman's Handbook.* New York: Columbia University Press, 1933.

Illinois Association for Criminal Justice. *Illinois Crime Survey.* Chicago: Illinois Association for Criminal Justice and The Chicago Crime Commission, 1929; reprt., Montclair, NJ: Patterson Smith, 1968.

"Illinois State Training School for Girls." *Institution Quarterly* 3 (December 31, 1912): 49–52.

Insley-Casper, R. "The Negro Unmarried Mother of New York." *Opportunity* 12 (June 1934): 172–73.

Intercollegiate Wonder Book. Vols. 1 and 2. Washington, DC: Intercollegiate Club of Chicago, 1927.

Jacoby, A. L. "Some Individual Causes of Delinquency." In *Community Treatment of Delinquency: Proceedings of the National Probation Association.* New York: National Probation Association, 1924. 84–94.

Janowitz, Morris, ed. *W. I. Thomas on Social Organization and Social Personality: Selected Papers.* Chicago: University of Chicago Press, 1966.

Jenkins, Frederick Warren, and Bertha Fairfield, comps. *Bulletin of The Russell Sage Foundation Library, No. 14: The Social Survey.* New York: The Russell Sage Foundation Library, 1915.

Jeter, Helen Rankin. *The Chicago Juvenile Court.* Chicago: University of Chicago Libraries, 1922.

Johnson, Arlien. "Subsidies from Public Funds to Private Children's Institutions and Agencies in Chicago." *Social Service Review* 3 (June 1929): 169–206.

Johnson, Charles S. "Negro Personality Changes in a Southern Community." In *Race and Culture Contacts,* edited by Edward B. Reuter. New York: McGraw-Hill, 1934. 208–27.

Joint Committee on Negro Child Study in New York City. *A Study of Delinquent and Neglected Negro Children before the New York City Children's Court.* New York: Joint Committee on Negro Child Study in New York City, 1927.

Jones, Eugene Kinckle. "Social Work among Negroes." *Annals of the American Academy of Political and Social Science* 140 (November, 1928): 287–93.

———. "The Negro's Struggle for Health." In *Proceedings of the National Conference of Social Work, Fiftieth Annual Session.* Washington, DC.: n.p., 1923. 68–72.

Jones, Kathleen W. *Taming the Troublesome Child: American Families, Child Guidance, and the Limits of Psychiatric Authority.* Cambridge: Harvard University Press, 1999.

Juvenile Protective Association. *The "Block System" of the Juvenile Protective Association.* Chicago: Juvenile Protective Association, 1916.

Kammerer, Percy Gamble. "The Social Consequences of Illegitimacy." *Social Hygiene* 6 (April 1920): 161–80.

Kantowicz, Edward R. "The Ethnic Church." In *Catholicism, Chicago Style,* edited by Ellen Skerrett, Edward R. Kantowicz, and Steven M. Avella. Chicago: Loyola University Press, 1993. 1–28.

———. "Cardinal Mundelein of Chicago and the Shaping of Twentieth-Century American Catholicism." In *Catholicism, American Style,* edited by Ellen Skerrett, Edward R. Kantowicz, and Steven M. Avella. Chicago: Loyola University Press, 1993. 63–78.

———. *Corporation Sole: Cardinal Mundelein and Chicago Catholicism.* Notre Dame, IN: University of Notre Dame Press, 1983.

Karlan, Jules. *Chicago: Backgrounds of Education.* Chicago: Werkman's Book House, 1940.

Karpf, Maurice J. "Sociology and Social Work: A Retrospect." *Social Forces* 6 (June 1928): 511–19.

———. "Sociologists and Social Workers Meet." *The Family* 9 (April 1927): 39–45.

Kasius, Peter. "Venereal Disease Aspects of Delinquency." In *The Development of Juvenile Courts and Probation: Annual Report and Proceedings of the Nineteenth Annual Conference of the National Probation Association.* New York: National Probation Association, 1925. 147–54.

Kasson, John F. *Amusing the Million: Coney Island at the Turn of the Century.* New York: Hill and Wang, 1987.

Kawin, Ethel. "Anniversary of the Founding of the First Juvenile Court and the Establishment of the First Institute for Juvenile Research." *Institution Quarterly* 16 (March 1925): 94–99.

Kelley, Truman Lee. *Mental Aspects of Delinquency.* Austin: University of Texas Press, 1917.

Kerber, Linda, Alice Kessler-Harris, and Kathryn Kish Sklar, eds. *U.S. History as Women's History: New Feminist Essays.* Chapel Hill: University of North Carolina Press, 1995.

Kirschner, Don S. *The Paradox of Professionalism: Reform and Public Service in Urban America, 1900–1940.* Westport, CT: Greenwood Press, 1986.

Klein, Charlotte Ruth. "Success and Failure on Parole: A Study of 160 Girls Paroled from the State Training School at Geneva, Illinois." Master's thesis, University of Chicago, 1935.

Knupfer, Anne Meis. "'The Arm of the School Which Extends into the Home': The Visiting Teacher Movement, 1906 to 1940." *Teachers College Record* 100 (Spring 1999): 627–55.

———. *Toward a Tenderer Humanity and a Nobler Womanhood: African American Women's Clubs in Turn-of-the-Century Chicago.* New York: New York University Press, 1996.

Koenig, Rev. Msgr. Harry C., S.T.D., ed. *Caritas Christi, Urget Nos: A History of the Offices, Agencies, and Institutions of the Archdiocese of Chicago.* Vol. 2. Chicago: The Archdiocese of Chicago, 1981.

Koven, Seth and Sonya Michel, eds. *Mothers of a New World: Maternalist Politics and the Origins of Welfare States.* New York: Routledge, 1993.

Krughoff, Merrill F. *Salaries and Professional Qualifications of Social Workers in Chicago, 1935.* Chicago: University of Chicago Press, 1937.

Kunzel, Regina G. *Fallen Women, Problem Girls. Unmarried Mothers and the Professionalization of Social Work, 1890–1945.* New Haven: Yale University Press, 1993.

Ladd-Taylor, Molly. *Mother-Work: Women, Child Welfare, and the State, 1890–1930.* Urbana: University of Illinois Press, 1994.

Lal, Barbara Ballis. *The Romance of Culture in an Urban Civilization: Robert E. Park on Race and Ethnic Relations in Cities.* New York: Routledge, 1990.

Lasch, Christopher. "Social Pathologists and the Socialization of Reproduction." In *The American Family in Social-Historical Perspective,* edited by Michael Gordon. 3rd ed. New York: St. Martin's Press, 1983. 80–94.

———. *Haven in a Heartless World: The Family Besieged.* New York: Basic Books, 1977.

Lathrop, Julia C. "The Background of the Juvenile Court in Illinois." In *The Child, the Clinic, and the Court.* New York: New Republic, 1925. 290–97.

————— ."The Defective Child and the Juvenile Court." In *The Child, the Clinic, and the Court.* New York: New Republic, 1925. 224–27.

Laughlin, Clara E. *The Work-a-Day Girl.* New York: F. H. Revell, 1913; reprt., New York: Arno Press, 1974.

————— . *The Penny Philanthropist: A Story That Could Be True.* New York: Fleming H. Revell, 1912.

Leach, William. *Land of Desire: Merchants, Power, and the Rise of a New American Culture.* New York: Vintage, 1993.

————— ."Strategists of Display and the Production of Desire." In *Consuming Visions: Accumulation and Display of Goods in America, 1880–1920,* edited by Simon J. Bronner. New York: W.W. Norton, 1989. 99–132.

Lenroot, Katharine F. "Juvenile Detention Homes." In *Social Treatment of the Delinquent: Annual Report and Proceedings of the Fifteenth Annual Conference of the National Probation Association.* New York: National Probation Association, 1922. 92–100.

Levine, Murray and Adeline Levine. *A Social History of Helping Services: Clinic, Court, School, and Community.* New York: Appleton-Century-Crofts, 1970.

Levy, David M., M. D.. "Notes on Psychotherapy." *Social Service Review* 1 (March 1927): 78–83.

Lindeman, E. C. "Parent Education as a Social Movement." In *Parent Education: The First Yearbook,* edited by the National Congress of Parents and Teachers. Washington, DC: National Congress of Parents and Teachers, 1930. 10–16.

Lindner, Rolf. *The Reportage of Urban Culture: Robert Park and the Chicago School,* trans. Adrian Morris. Cambridge: Cambridge University Press, 1990.

Lintelman, Joy K. " 'On My Own': Single, Swedish, and Female in Turn-of-the-Century Chicago." In *Swedish-American Life in Chicago: Cultural and Urban Aspects of an Immigrant People, 1850–1930,* edited by Philip J. Anderson and Dag Lanck. Urbana: University of Illinois Press, 1992. 89–102.

"Little Journeys to Institutions of Interest." *Charity Watchman,* December 1919, 11–17.

Lou, Herbert. *Juvenile Courts in the United States.* Chapel Hill: University of North Carolina Press, 1927.

Lubove, Roy. *The Professional Altruist.* Cambridge, MA: Harvard University Press, 1965.

Lunbeck, Elizabeth. *The Psychiatric Persuasion: Knowledge, Gender, and Power in Modern America.* Princeton: Princeton University Press, 1994.

————— ." 'A New Generation of Women': Progressive Psychiatrists and the Hypersexual Female." *Feminist Studies* 13 (Fall 1987): 513–42.

Lundberg, Emma. *Unto the Least of These; Social Services for Children.* New York: D. Appleton-Century, 1947.

————— . *Children of Illegitimate Birth and Measures for Their Protection.* Washington, DC: Government Printing Office, 1926.

Lynd, Robert S. and Helen Merrell Lynd. *Middletown in Transition: A Study in Cultural Conflict.* New York: Harcourt Brace Jovanovich, 1937.

Lyon, F. Emory. "Home Neglect, A Factor in Delinquency: How May It Be Met?" In *Community Treatment of Delinquency: Proceedings of the National Probation Association.* New York: National Probation Association, 1924. 310–14.

Mangold, George B. *Problems of Child Welfare.* New York: Macmillan, 1928.

MacLean, Annie Marion. "Two Weeks in Department Stores." *American Journal of Sociology* 4 (May 1899): 721–41.

MacQueary, T. H. "Schools for Dependent, Delinquent, and Truant Children in Illinois." *American Journal of Sociology* 9 (July 1903): 1–23.

Martin, Paul R. *The First Cardinal of the West: The Story of the Church in the Archdiocese of Chicago.* Chicago: New World Publishing, 1934.

Matthews, Fred H. *Quest for an American Sociology: Robert E. Park and the Chicago School.* Montreal: McGill-Queen's University Press, 1977.

May, Elaine Tyler. "The Pressure to Provide: Class, Consumerism, and Divorce in Urban America, 1880–1920." In *The American Family in Social-Historical Perspective,* edited by Michael Gordon. 3rd ed. New York: St. Martin's Press, 1983. 154–68.

McChristie, Mary E. "What Is Success and What Is Failure?" In *1928 Proceedings of the National Probation Association.* New York: National Probation Association, 1928. 242–50.

McDowell, Mary E. "Hovels or Homes?" *Opportunity* 7 (March 1929): 74–77, 100.

McKee, James B. *Sociology and the Race Problem: The Failure of a Perspective.* Urbana: University of Illinois Press, 1993.

McKeever, William A. *Training the Girl.* New York: Macmillan, 1916.

————— . *Industrial Training of the Girl.* New York: Macmillan, 1914.

McKenzie, R. D. "The Ecological Approach to the Study of the Human Community." In *The Urban Community: Selected Papers from the Proceedings of the American Sociological Society, 1925,* ed. Ernest Burgess. Chicago: University of Chicago Press, 1926.

Mead, Margaret. *Coming of Age in Samoa.* New York: Morrow Quill Paperbacks, 1928.

Meis, Caroline. "Personnel Standards and Salaries of Social Workers in the Children's Agencies in Chicago." Master's thesis, University of Chicago, 1934.

Melendy, Royal L. "The Saloon in Chicago." *American Journal of Sociology* 6 (November 1900): 289–306.

Menken, Alice D. "A Social Aspect of the Unmarried Mother." *Journal of Delinquency* 7 (March 1922): 99–103.

Mennel, Robert M. "Ethel Sturges Dummer." In *Notable American Women: The Modern Period*, edited by Barbara Sicherman, Carol Hurd Green with Ilene Kantror and Harriette Walker. Cambridge, MA: Belknap Press of Harvard University Press, 1980. 208–10.

———. *Thorns and Thistles: Juvenile Delinquents in the United States 1825–1940*. Hanover, NH: University Press of New England, 1973.

Meyerowitz, Joanne J. *Women Adrift: Independent Wage Earners in Chicago, 1880–1930*. Chicago: University of Chicago Press, 1988.

Millis, Savilla. *The Juvenile Detention Home in Relation to Juvenile Court Policy: A Study of Intake in the Cook County Chicago Juvenile Detention Home*. Chicago: University of Chicago, Graduate School of Social Service Administration, 1927.

Minehan, Thomas. *Boy and Girl Tramps of America*. New York: Farrar and Rinehart, 1934.

Miner, Maude E. "The Policewoman and the Girl Problem." *Proceedings of the National Probation Association*. New York: National Probation Association, 1920. 134–43.

Mogey, John, ed. *A Social History of American Family Sociology, 1865–1940*. Westport, CT: Greenwood Press, 1981.

Monahan, Florence. *Women in Crime*. New York: Ives Washburn, 1941.

Monroe, Day. *Chicago Families: A Study of Unpublished Census Data*. Chicago: University of Chicago Press, 1932.

Moore, Howard. *The Care of Illegitimate Children in Chicago*. Chicago: Juvenile Protective Association, 1912.

Morton, Marian J. "Fallen Women, Federated Charities, and Maternity Homes, 1913–1973." *Social Service Review* 62 (March 1988): 61–82.

Moses, Earl R. *The Negro Delinquent in Chicago*. Washington, DC: Washington Public Schools, 1936.

———. "Delinquency in the Negro Community." *Opportunity* 11 (October 1933): 304–7.

Mowrer, Ernest W. *Family Disorganization: Introduction to a Sociological Analysis*. Chicago: University of Chicago Press, 1927.

Mueller, John Henry. "The Automobile: A Sociological Study." Ph.D. diss., University of Chicago, 1929.

Muncy, Robyn. *Creating a Female Dominion in American Reform 1890–1935*. New York: Oxford University Press, 1991.

Myerson, A., M.D. "Hysteria as a Weapon in Marital Conflicts." *Journal of Abnormal and Social Psychology* 10 (1915–1916): 1–10.

Naether, Carl A. *Advertising to Women*. New York: Prentice-Hall, 1929.

Nasaw, David. *Going Out: The Rise and Fall of Public Amusements*. New York: Basic Books, 1993.

National Congress of Parents and Teachers. *Parent Education: The First Yearbook*. Washington, DC: National Congress of Parents and Teachers, 1930.

National Urban League. "1912–1913 Report." In *Black Heritage in Social Welfare 1860–1930*, compiled and edited by Edyth L. Ross. Metuchen, NJ: Scarecrow Press, 1978. 240–42.

———. "Result of the 1912–1913 Program." *Bulletin of the National League on Urban Conditions among Negroes* 3 (November 1913): 10–11.

Neuman, R. P. "Masturbation, Madness, and the Modern Concepts of Childhood and Adolescence." *Journal of Social History* 8 (Spring 1975): 1–27.

"New Boarding Homes for Chicago." *Catholic Charities Review* 5 (October 1921): 274.

Nichols, Franklin O. "The Aim and Scope of Social Hygiene." *Opportunity* 1 (April 1923): 8–10.

Noll, Steven. *Feeble-Minded in Our Midst: Institutions for the Mentally Retarded in the South, 1900–1940*. Chapel Hill: University of North Carolina Press, 1995.

Odem, Mary E. *Delinquent Daughters: Protecting and Policing Adolescent Female Sexuality in the United States, 1885–1920*. Chapel Hill: University of North Carolina Press, 1995.

Odem, Mary E. and Steven Schlossman. "Guardians of Virtue: The Juvenile Court and Female Delinquency in Early Twentieth-Century Los Angeles." *Crime and Delinquency* 37 (April 1991): 186–203.

Ogburn, William F. "The Changing Family with Regard to the Child." *Annals of the American Academy* 151 (September 1930): 20–24.

Ordahl, Louise E. and George Ordahl. "A Study of Delinquent and Dependent Girls at Geneva." *Institution Quarterly* 9 (September 30, 1918): 56–60.

Osborn, Phyllis Rae. "A Study of the Detention of Two Hundred Six Children." Master's thesis, University of Chicago, 1931.

Otis, Margaret. "A Perversion Not Commonly Noted." *Journal of Abnormal and Social Psychology* 8 (April–May, 1913): 113–16.

Pacyga, Dominic A. *Polish Immigrants and Industrial Chicago: Workers on the South Side, 1880–1922*. Columbus: Ohio State University Press, 1991.

Park, Robert E. and Ernest W. Burgess. *Introduction to the Science of Sociology*. Chicago: University of Chicago Press, 1924.

Park, Robert E., Ernest W. Burgess, and Roderick D. McKenzie. *The City*. Chicago: University of Chicago Press, 1925; reprt., University of Chicago Press, 1967.

Parker, Elisabeth. "Personnel and Organization in the Probation Department of the Juvenile Court of Cook County (1899–1933)." Master's thesis, University of Chicago, 1934.

Pascoe, Peggy. *Relations of Rescue: The Search for Female Moral Authority in the American West, 1874–1939.* New York: Oxford University Press, 1990.

Patrice, Sister Mary. "Psycho-Social Factors in the Case Histories of Seventy Girls Admitted to the House of the Good Shepherd." Master's thesis, Loyola University, 1955.

Peiss, Kathy. *Hope in a Jar: The Making of American's Beauty Culture.* New York: Henry Holt, 1998.

———. " 'Charity Girls' and City Pleasures: Historical Notes on Working-Class Sexuality, 1880–1920." In *Passion and Power: Sexuality in History*, edited by Kathy Peiss and Christina Simmons with Robert A. Padgug. Philadelphia: Temple University Press, 1989. 57–69.

———. *Cheap Amusements: Working Women and Leisure in Turn of-the-Century New York.* Philadelphia: Temple University Press, 1986.

Peiss, Kathy and Christina Simmons with Robert A. Padgug, eds. *Passion and Power: Sexuality in History.* Philadelphia: Temple University Press, 1989.

Perkins, Nellie L. "Mental and Moral Problems of the Woman Probationer." In *Probation and the Prevention of Delinquency: Proceedings of the Seventh Annual Conference of the National Probation Association.* New York: National Probation Association, 1924. 91–105.

Persons, Stow. *Ethnic Studies at Chicago, 1905–1945.* Urbana: University of Illinois Press, 1987.

Pinckney, Merritt W. "The Juvenile Court." In *The Child in the City; A Series of Papers Presented at the Conference Held during the Chicago Child Welfare Exhibit*, edited by Sophonisba Breckinridge. Chicago: Chicago School of Civics and Philanthropy, 1912. 315–26.

———. "The Delinquent Girl and the Juvenile Court." In *The Child in the City; A Series of Papers Presented at the Conference Held during the Chicago Child Welfare Exhibit*, edited by Sophonisba Breckinridge. Chicago: Chicago School of Civics and Philanthropy, 1912. 349–54.

Platt, Anthony M. *E. Franklin Frazier Reconsidered.* New Brunswick, NJ: Rutgers University Press, 1991.

———. *The Child Savers: The Invention of Delinquency.* 2nd ed. Chicago: University of Chicago Press, 1977.

Platt, Jennifer. *A History of Sociological Research Methods in America 1920–1960.* Cambridge: Cambridge University Press, 1996.

———. "The Chicago School and Firsthand Data." *History of the Human Sciences* 7 (1994): 57–80.

Pleck, Elizabeth. "Challenge to Traditional Authority in Immigrant Families." In *The American Family in Social-Historical Perspective*, edited by Michael Gordon. 3rd ed. New York: St. Martin's Press, 1983. 504–17.

———. "A Mother's Wages." In *Heritage of Her Own: Toward a New Social History of American Women*, edited by Nancy F. Cott and Elizabeth Pleck. New York: Simon and Schuster, 1979. 367–92.

Pois, Joseph. "The Recruitment of Police." Ph.D. diss., University of Chicago, 1929.

Polkinghorne, Donald E. *Narrative Knowing and the Human Science.* Albany: State University of New York Press, 1988.

Practical Rules for the Use of the Religious of the Good Shepherd for Direction of the Classes. St Paul, MN: Convent of the Good Shepherd, 1943.

Pringle, Ralph W. *Adolescence and High-School Problems.* Boston: D.C. Heath, 1922.

Proceedings of the Child Conference for Research and Welfare, 1910. New York: G. E. Stechert, 1910.

Proceedings of the Conference in the Care of Dependent Children. Washington, DC: Government Printing Office, 1909.

Proceedings of the National Conference of Social Work, Fiftieth Annual Session. Washington, DC: National Conference of Social Work, 1923.

Proceedings of the Twelfth Annual Conference on the Education of Dependent, Truant, Backward and Delinquent Children. Baltimore, Maryland: n.p., 1915.

Puttee, Dorothy Frances and Mary Ruth Colby. *The Illegitimate Child in Illinois.* Chicago: University of Chicago Press, 1937.

Queen, Stuart Alfred, Walter Blaine Bodenhafer, and Ernest Bouldin Harper. *Social Organization and Disorganization.* New York: Thomas Y. Crowell Company, 1935.

Quinlan, Emma. "Cases Cared for by the Chicago Juvenile Court and the House of the Good Shepherd." *Catholic Charities Review* 9 (June 1925): 208–13.

Ransom, John Edward. *A Study of Mentally Defective Children in Chicago.* Chicago: Juvenile Protective Association, 1914.

Reckless, Walter. *Vice in Chicago.* Chicago: University of Chicago Press, 1933.

Reed, Dorothy. *Leisure Time of Girls in a "Little Italy."* Portland, OR: n.p., 1932.

Reeves, Margaret. *Training Schools for Delinquent Girls.* New York: Russell Sage Foundation, 1929.

Reilly, Philip R. *The Surgical Solution: A History of Involuntary Sterilization in the United States.* Baltimore: Johns Hopkins Press, 1991.

Reuter, Edward B., ed. *Race and Culture Contacts.* New York: McGraw-Hill, 1934.

Rhoades, Mabel Carter. *A Case Study of Delinquent Boys in the Juvenile Court of Chicago.* Chicago: University of Chicago, 1907.

Richardson, Dorothy. *The Long Day: The Story of a New York Working Girl*, edited by William L. O'Neill. Chicago: Quadrangle Books, 1972.

Richmond, Mary. *Social Diagnosis*. New York: Russell Sage Foundation, 1917.

Richmond, Winifred, Ph.D. *The Adolescent Girl: A Book for Parents and Teachers*. New York: Macmillan, 1925.

Riley, Ralph J. *A Working Manual for Juvenile Court Officers*. Chicago: University of Chicago Press, 1932.

Rood, Alice Quan. "Social Conditions among the Negroes on Federal Street between Forty-Fifth Street and Fifty-Third Street." Master's thesis, University of Chicago, 1924.

Rosenthal, Marguerite G. "The Children's Bureau and the Juvenile Court: Delinquency Policy, 1912–1940." *Social Service Review* 60 (June 1986): 303–18.

Ross, Dorothy. "Gendered Social Knowledge: Domestic Discourse, Jane Addams, and the Possibilities of Social Science." In *Gender and American Social Science: The Formative Years*, edited by Helene Silverberg. Princeton: Princeton University Press, 1998. 235–64.

———. *The Origins of American Social Science*. Cambridge: Cambridge University Press, 1991.

Ross, Edith L., comp. and ed. *Black Heritage in Social Welfare 1860–1930*. Metuchen, NJ: Scarecrow Press, 1978.

Rothman, David J. *The Discovery of the Asylum: Social Order and Disorder in the New Republic*. Boston: Little, Brown, 1971.

Rudwick, Elliott. "W. E. B. Du Bois as Sociologist." In *Black Sociologists: Historical and Contemporary Perspectives*, edited by James E. Blackwell and Morris Janowitz. Chicago: University of Chicago Press, 1974. 25–55.

Runyon, Gertrude Louise. "State Institutional Care of the Epileptic in Illinois." Master's thesis, University of Chicago, 1931.

Russell, Daniel. "The Road House: A Study of Commercialized Amusements in the Environs of Chicago." Master's thesis, University of Chicago, 1931.

Ryerson, Ellen. *The Best-Laid Plans: America's Juvenile Court Experiment*. New York: Hill and Wang, 1978.

Rynbrandt, Linda J. *Caroline Bartlett Crane and Progressive Reform: Social Housekeeping as Sociology*. New York: Garland, 1999.

Sadler, Ann. "The Ideal Policewoman." *Welfare Magazine* 19 (May 1928): 638–44.

Sager, Gertrude Eileen. "Immigration. Based Upon a Study of the Italian Women and Girls of Chicago." Master's thesis, University of Chicago, 1914.

Scharff, Virginia. *Taking the Wheel: Women and the Coming of the Motor Age*. New York: The Free Press, 1991.

Schlossman, Steven. *Love and the American Delinquent: The Theory and Practice of "Progressive" Juvenile Justice, 1825–1920*. Chicago: University of Chicago Press, 1977.

Schlossman, Steven and Stephanie Wallach. "The Crime of Precocious Sexuality: Female Juvenile Delinquency in the Progressive Era." *Harvard Educational Review* 48 (February 1978): 65–94.

Schneider, Eric C. *In the Web of Class: Delinquents and Reformers in Boston, 1810s–1930s*. New York: New York University Press, 1992.

Schoff, Hannah Kent. *The Wayward Child: A Study of the Causes of Crime*. Indianapolis: Bobbs-Merrill, 1915.

Sedlak, Michael W. "Young Women and the City: Adolescent Deviance and the Transformation of Educational Policy, 1870–1960." *History of Education Quarterly* 23 (Spring 1983): 1–28.

———. "Youth Policy and Young Women, 1870–1972." *Social Service Review* 56 (September 1982): 448–64.

Seigfried, Charlene Haddock. "Socializing Democracy: Jane Addams and John Dewey." *Philosophy of the Social Sciences* 29 (June 1999): 207–30.

Shanabruch, Charles. *Chicago's Catholics: The Evolution of an American Identity*. Notre Dame, IN: University of Notre Dame, 1981.

Shaw, Clifford with Frederick M. Zorbaugh, Henry D. McKay, and Leonard S. Cottrell. *Delinquency Areas: Study of the Geographic Distribution of School Truants, Juvenile Delinquents, and Adults Offenders in Chicago*. Chicago: University of Chicago Press, 1929.

Shaw, Stephanie. *What a Woman Ought to Be and to Do: Black Professional Women Workers during the Jim Crow Era*. Chicago: University of Chicago Press, 1996.

Sheahan, Marie. "A Catholic School of Sociology." *Catholic Charities Review* 5 (June 1921): 196–98.

Shireman, Charles H. and Frederic G. Reamer. *Rehabilitating Juvenile Justice*. New York: Columbia University Press, 1986.

Shorter, Edward. *A History of Psychiatry: From the Era of the Asylum to the Age of Prozac*. New York: John Wiley and Sons, 1997.

Sicherman, Barbara, Carol Hurd Green with Ilene Kantro and Harriette Walker, eds. *Notable American Women: The Modern Period*. Cambridge, MA: Belknap Press of Harvard University Press, 1980.

Silverberg, Helene, ed. *Gender and American Social Science: The Formative Years*. Princeton: Princeton University Press, 1998.

Simmons, Christina. "Modern Sexuality and the Myth of Victorian Repression." In *Passion and Power: Sexuality in History*, edited by Kathy Peiss and Christina Simmons with Robert A. Padgug. Philadelphia: Temple University Press, 1989. 157–77.

Skerrett, Ellen. "The Irish in Chicago: The Catholic Dimension." In *Catholicism, Chicago Style*, edited by Ellen Skerrett, Edward R. Kantowicz, and Steven M. Avella. Chicago: Loyola University Press, 1993. 29–62.

Skerrett, Ellen, Edward R. Kantowicz, and Steven M. Avella. *Catholicism, Chicago Style*. Chicago: Loyola University Press, 1993.

Sklar, Kathryn Kish. "Hull-House Maps and Papers: Social Science as Women's Work in the 1890s." In *Gender and American Social Science: The Formative Years*, edited by Helene Silverberg. Princeton: Princeton University Press, 1998. 127–55.

——— . *Florence Kelley and the Nation's Work*. New Haven: Yale University Press, 1995.

——— . "The Historical Foundation of Women's Power in the Creation of the American Welfare State, 1830–1930." In *Mothers of a New World: Maternalist Politics and the Origins of Welfare States*, edited by Seth Koven and Sonya Michel. New York: Routledge, 1993. 43–93.

——— . "Who Funded Hull House?" In *Lady Bountiful Revisited: Women, Philanthropy, and Power*, edited by Kathleen D. McCarthy. New Brunswick: Rutgers University Press, 1990. 94–118.

Smith, Carrie Weaver. "Can the Institution Equip the Girl for Normal Social Relationships?" In *Proceedings of the National Conference of Social Work*. Chicago: University of Chicago Press, 1925. 108–20.

Smith, Edith Livingston and Hugh Cabot, M.D. "A Study in Sexual Morality." *Journal of Social Hygiene* 2 (October 1916): 527–47.

Smith, T. V. and Leonard D. White, eds. *Chicago: An Experiment in Social Science Research*. Chicago: University of Chicago Press, 1929.

Smith-Rosenberg, Carrol. "Discourse of Sexuality and Subjectivity: The New Woman, 1870–1936." In *Hidden from History: Reclaiming the Gay and Lesbian Past*, edited by Martin Bauml Duberman, Martha Vicinus, and George Chauncey Jr. New York: New American Library, 1981. 264–80.

Snitow, Ann, Christine Stansell, and Sharon Thompson, eds. *Powers of Desire: The Politics of Sexuality*. New York: Monthly Review Press, 1983.

Snodgrass, Jon. "William Healy (1869–1963): Pioneer Child Psychiatrist and Criminologist." *Journal of the History of the Behavioral Sciences* 20 (October 1984): 332–39.

Somerville, Siobhan. "Scientific Racism and the Emergence of the Homosexual Body." *Journal of the History of Sexuality* 5 (Summer 1994): 243–66.

Spaulding, Edith R., M.D. *An Experimental Study of Psychopathic Delinquent Women*. New York: Rand McNally, 1923.

Spear, Allan H. *Black Chicago: The Making of a Negro Ghetto 1890–1920*. Chicago: University of Chicago Press, 1967.

Spence, Donald. *Narrative Truth and Historical Truth: Meaning and Interpretation in Psychoanalysis*. New York: W. W. Norton, 1982.

Spingarn, Arthur B. *Laws Relating to Sex Morality in New York City*. New York: The Century Company, 1926.

Staiger, Janet. *Bad Women: Regulating Sexuality in Early American Cinema*. Minneapolis: University of Minnesota Press, 1995.

Stanfield, John H. *Philanthropy and Jim Crow in American Social Science*. Westport, CT: Greenwood Press, 1985.

"State Aid Sustained in Illinois." *Catholic Charities Review* 1 (December 1917): 309–10.

State of Illinois. *Laws of the State of Illinois Enacted by the Forty-First Assembly*. Springfield, IL: Phillips Brothers, 1899.

"State Training School for Girls Notes." *Institution Quarterly* 9 (June 30, 1918): 68–69.

"State Training School for Girls." *Institution Quarterly* 4 (June 30, 1913): 118–19.

Stehno, Sandra. "Foster Care for Dependent Black Children in Chicago 1899–1934." Ph. D. diss., University of Chicago, 1985.

Stern, Leon. "Detention Homes for Children." In *Social Work Year Book, 1933: A Description of Organized Activities in Social Work and in Related Fields*, edited by Fred S. Hall. New York: Russell Sage Foundation, 1933. 129–31.

——— . "Report of the Committee on Training for Probation Work." In *Probation and the Prevention of Delinquency: Proceedings of the Seventh Annual Conference of the National Probation Association*. New York: National Probation Association, 1924. 172–79.

Stone, Esther, M.D. "A Plea for Early Commitment to Correctional Institutions of Delinquent Children, and an Endorsement of Industrial and Vocational Training in These Institutions." *Institution Quarterly* 9 (March 31, 1918): 60–66.

Stone, Lawrence, ed. *Schooling and Society: Studies in the History of Education*. Baltimore: Johns Hopkins University Press, 1976.

Strange, Carolyn. *Toronto's Girl Problem: The Perils and Pleasures of the City, 1880–1930*. Toronto: University of Toronto Press, 1995.

Strickland, A. *History of the Chicago Urban League*. Urbana: University of Illinois Press, 1966.

Talbert, Ernest L. *Opportunities in School and Industry for Children of the Stockyard District*. Chicago: University of Chicago Press, 1912.

Tanenhaus, David S. " 'Rotten to the Core': The Juvenile Court and the Problem of Legitimacy in the Progressive Era." In *A Noble Social Experiment? The First 100 Years of the Cook County Juvenile Court 1899–1999*, edited by Gwen Hoerr McNamee. Chicago: The Chicago Bar Association and the Children's Court Centennial Committee, 1999. 24–28.

——— . "Policing the Child: Juvenile Justice in Chicago, 1870–1925." Ph.D. diss., University of Chicago, 1997.

Taylor, Josephine Gordon. "The Development of Social Service at Cook County Hospital, 1911–1933." Master's thesis, University of Chicago, 1935.

Tentler, Leslie Woodcock. *Wage-Earning Women: Industrial Work and Family Life in the United States, 1900–1930.* New York: Oxford University Press, 1979.

Terman, Lewis M. and Catharine Cox Miles. *Sex and Personality: Studies in Masculinity and Femininity.* New York: McGraw-Hill, 1936.

"The Chicago Big Sisters." *Catholic Charities Review* 5 (February 1921): 91–92.

"The Good Shepherd's Black Sheep." *American Mercury* 26 (June 1932): 150–57.

"The Story of Four Girls." *Institution Quarterly* 3 (December 31, 1912): 28–29.

Thom, Douglas A., M.D. *Normal Youth and Its Everyday Problems.* New York: D. Appleton-Century, 1932.

Thomas, Evan Ames. "The Sociology of William I. Thomas in Relation to the Polish Peasant." Ph.D. diss., University of Iowa, 1986.

Thomas, Jesse O. "A Social Program to Help the Migrant." *Opportunity* 2 (March 1924): 71–73.

Thomas, William Isaac. *The Unadjusted Girl: With Cases and Standpoint for Behavior Analysis.* Boston: Little, Brown, 1937.

——— . "Race Psychology: Standpoint and Questionnaire, with Particular Reference to the Immigrant and the Negro." *American Journal of Sociology* 17 (May 1912): 725–75.

——— . *Sex and Society: Studies in the Social Psychology of Sex.* Chicago: University of Chicago, 1907.

——— . "The Adventitious Character of Women." *American Journal of Sociology* 12 (July 1906): 32–44.

Thomas, William I. and Florian Znaniecki. *The Polish Peasant in Europe and America,* edited by Eli Zaretsky. Urbana: University of Illinois Press, 1996.

Thomas, William I. and Dorothy Swaine Thomas. *The Child in America: Behavior Problems and Programs.* New York: Alfred A. Knopf, 1928.

Thompson, Joseph J. *Diamond Jubilee of the Archdiocese of Chicago.* Des Plaines, IL: St. Mary's Training School Press, 1920.

Thurston, Henry W. "The Training of Probation Officers in Schools of Social Work." In *The Social Service of the Courts: Proceedings of the Sixteenth Annual Conference of the National Probation Association.* New York: National Probation Association, 1923. 45–51.

Tice, Karen W. *Tales of Wayward Girls and Immoral Women: Case Records and the Professionalization of Social Work.* Urbana: University of Illinois Press, 1998.

Tiffin, Susan. *In Whose Best Interest? Child Welfare Reform in the Progressive Era.* Westport, CT: Greenwood Press, 1982.

Tinney, Mary C. "Catholic Charities with Illustrations from Chicago." Master's thesis, University of Chicago, 1910.

Trattner, William I. *From Poor Law to Welfare State: A History of Social Welfare in America.* 2nd ed. New York: The Free Press, 1979.

Trent, James W., Jr. *Inventing the Feeble Mind: A History of Mental Retardation in the United States.* Berkeley and Los Angeles: University of California Press, 1994.

Trotter, Ann Elizabeth. *Housing of Non-Family Women in Chicago.* Chicago: Chicago Community Trust, 1921.

True, Ruth S. *The Neglected Girl.* New York: Russell Sage Foundation, 1914.

Tuttle, Rosemary. "The Big Sister." *Catholic Charities Review* 9 (February 1925): 68–69.

Two Crowded Years: Being Selected Addresses, Pastorals, and Letters Issued during the First Twenty-Four Months of the Episcopate of the Most Rev. George William Mundelein, D.D. Chicago: Extension Press, 1918.

Tyack, David and Elisabeth Hansot. *Learning Together: A History of Co-Education in American Schools.* New York: Russell Sage Foundation, 1990.

Tylor, Peter. "Denied the Power to Choose the Good: Sexuality and Mental Defect in American Medical Practice 1850–1920." *Journal of Social History* 10 (June 1977): 472–89.

University of Chicago Local Community Research Committee. *Social Research Base Map of the City of Chicago.* Chicago: University of Chicago Press, 1926.

Vanuxem, Mary. *Education of Feeble-Minded Women.* New York: Teacher College Press, 1925.

Van Waters, Miriam. *Youth in Conflict.* New York: Republic, 1925.

——— . "What Is the Test of Success?" In *Proceedings of the National Conference of Social Work.* Chicago: University of Chicago Press, 1925. 117–20.

——— . "The Delinquent Attitude." In *Community Treatment of Delinquency: Proceedings of the National Probation Association.* New York: National Probation Association, 1924. 72–79.

——— . "Who Are Successful Workers with Delinquents?" In *Community Treatment of Delinquency: Proceedings of the National Probation Association.* New York: National Probation Association, 1924. 26–41.

Veblen, Thorstein. *The Theory of the Leisure Class.* New York: Penguin Books, 1994.

Venkatesh, Sudhir Alladi. "Gender and Outlaw Capitalism: A Historical Account of the Black Sisters United 'Girl Gang.' " *Signs* 23 (Fall 1998): 683–709.

Vice Commission of Chicago. *The Social Evil in Chicago.* Chicago: Gunthorp, 1911.

Wacker, Fred R. *Ethnicity, Pluralism, and Race: Race Relations Theory in America Before Myrdal.* Westport, CT: Greenwood Press, 1983.

Walkowitz, Daniel J. "The Making of a Feminine Professional Identity: Social Workers in the 1920s." *American Historical Review* 95 (October 1990): 1051–75.

Walsh, John Patrick. "The Catholic Church in Chicago and Problems of an Urban Society: 1893–1915." Ph.D. diss., University of Chicago, 1948.

Walter, Henriette R. *Girl Life in America: A Study of Backgrounds*. New York: The National Committee for the Study of Juvenile Reading, 1927.

Warner, Florence Mary. *Juvenile Detention in the United States*. Chicago: University of Chicago Press, 1933.

Warren, Margaret Elizabeth. "Salaries, Education, Training and Experience of Social Workers in Six Family Welfare and Relief Agencies in Chicago." Ph.D. diss., University of Chicago, 1933.

Washington, Forrester B. "Negroes." In *Social Work Year Book, 1933: A Description of Organized Activities in Social Work and in Related Fields*, edited by Fred S. Hall. New York: Russell Sage Foundation, 1933. 313–18.

——— . "What Professional Training Means to the Social Workers." *Annals of the American Academy of Political and Social Science* 127 (September 1926): 165–69.

Webster, Albert Ellis. "The Relation of the Saloon to Juvenile Delinquency." Ph.D. diss, University of Chicago, 1912.

Weeks, Jeffrey. "Movements of Affirmation: Sexual Meanings and Homosexual Identities." In *Passion and Power: Sexuality in History*, edited by Kathy Peiss and Christina Simmons with Robert A. Padgug. Philadelphia: Temple University Press, 1989. 70–86.

Weiner, Lynn Y. "Maternalism as Paradigm: Defining the Issues." *Journal of Women's History* 5 (Fall 1993): 96–115.

Weiss, Nancy J. *The National Urban League, 1910–1940*. New York: Oxford University Press, 1974.

West Dorothy. "Mammy." In *The Richer, The Poorer: Stories, Sketches, and Reminiscences*. New York: Doubleday, 1995.

White House Conference on Child Health and Protection. *The Delinquent Child*. New York: The Century Company, 1932.

——— . *White House Conference, Addresses and Abstracts of Committee Reports*. New York: The Century Company, 1930.

Wile, Ira S. "The Sex Problems of Youth." *Journal of Social Hygiene* 16 (October 1930): 413–27.

——— . "Sex and Normal Human Nature." In *Sex in Civilization*, edited by V. F. Calverton and S. D. Schmalhausen. New York: Macaulay, 1929. 600–620.

Wilson, Otto. *Fifty Years' Work with Girls, 1883–1933: A Story of the Florence Crittenton Home*. Alexandria, VA: The National Florence Crittenton Mission, 1933.

Wilson, Samuel Paynter. *Chicago and Its Cess-Pools of Infamy*. Chicago: Samuel Paynter Wilson, 1910.

Woods, Robert A. and Albert J. Kennedy. *Young Working Girls: A Summary of Evidence from Two Thousand Social Workers*. Boston: Houghton-Mifflin, 1913.

Wooldridge, Clifton F. *Twenty Years a Detective in the Wickedest City in the World*. Chicago: Clifton F. Wooldridge, 1908.

Woolley, Helen T. "Personality Trends in Children." In *The Child, the Clinic and the Court*. New York: New Republic, 1925. 53–65.

Work, Monroe N. "Problems of Negro Urban Welfare." *Southern Workman*, January 1924, 10–16.

Worthington, George E. and Ruth Topping. *Specialized Courts Dealing with Sex Delinquents: A Study of the Procedure in Chicago, Boston, Philadelphia and New York*. New York: F. H. Hitchcock, 1925.

——— . "The Morals Court of Chicago." *Social Hygiene* 7 (October 1921): 351–411.

Young, Erle Fiske. "The Scientific Study of Social Case Records." *Journal of Applied Sociology* 9 (January 1925): 283–89.

——— . "The Social Base Map." *Journal of Applied Sociology* 9 (December 1924): 202–6.

Young, Kimball. "A Sociological Study of a Disintegrated Neighborhood." Master's thesis, University of Chicago, 1918.

Zabel, William LeRoy. "Street Trades and Juvenile Delinquency." Master's thesis, University of Chicago, 1918.

Zorbaugh, Harvey W. *The Gold Coast and the Slum*. Chicago: University of Chicago Press, 1929.

——— . "The Dweller in Furnished Rooms: An Urban Type." In *The Urban Community: Selected Papers from the Proceedings of the American Sociological Society, 1925*, edited by Ernest Burgess. Chicago: University of Chicago Press, 1926. 98–105.

Zuerner, William F. "Detention Homes Report of the Committees." In *The Social Service of the Courts: Proceedings of the Sixteenth Annual Conference of the National Probation Association*. New York: National Probation Association, 1923. 111–16.

Index

Abbott, Edith: and probation officers, 7; and social workers, 7, 54; and affiliation with University of Chicago, 14, 18; and sociological research, 14–16, 25; formation of public policy of, 14–17, 25; and Robert Park, 19; concepts of female delinquency of, 92. *See also* Chicago School of Civics and Philanthropy (CSCP)

Abbott, Grace, and the Immigrant Protective League, 17

accommodation: of African Americans, 5, 21, 25, 26, 63; of immigrants, 5, 16, 17, 25, 26, 32. *See also* assimilation; Chicago School of Sociology

Addams, Jane: and Hull House activities, 5, 13, 25, 111, 164; and Chicago School of Sociology, 13, 18

Adler, Herman: theory of feeblemindedness of, 38; theory of psychopathics of, 40

adoption, babies: at the Chicago Home for Girls, 126; at the State Industrial School for Delinquent Girls, 144

adventuress, 33. *See also* William I. Thomas

advertisements, and women, 68–69

African Americans: discrimination of, 27, 29, 61, 62, 92; and social work, 59, 62. *See also* disorganization; Chicago School of Sociology

alcoholism, and degeneracy, 36

Altgeld, John, 163

Americanization: of immigrant girls, 2, 84, 85, 87; at Hull House, 16–17; at Chicago Home for Girls, 130, 137. *See also* accommodation; amusements, commercial; Bartelme, Mary

Amigh, Ophelia: and cruelty at State Industrial School for Delinquent Girls, 139–40, 149, 154–55; and sterilization of delinquent girls, 142; letters from reformed girls to, 148–49; at Chicago Home for Girls, 154

amorality, 5, 20, 32. *See also* William I. Thomas

amusements, commercial: and scripts, 2, 7, 67–68, 69–70; and working-class girls, 7, 28, 33, 51, 67–68, 69–70, 71, 73–74; and sociological studies, 16, 20–21, 71–72; as source of female delinquency, 50, 51, 67, 71–73, 84, 116, 126, 141. *See also* Juvenile Protective Association (JPA)

anthropometry, and delinquency, 37, 213

assimilation, of African Americans, 5, 26–27, 30–31, 60. *See also* accommodation

Atlanta Neighborhood Union, 60

Atlanta University, 7, 60

Aussage test, 39, 114

automobiles, and mobility of youth, 69

autoeroticism, 144, 156. *See also* masturbation

Bartelme, Mary: and interactions with delinquent girls, 3–4, 54, 82, 84–86, 87, 94–95, 104–05; and Chicago Home for Girls, 10, 95, 122, 127, 138; and ideas about probation work, 59; appointment as juvenile judge of, 84; maternalist beliefs of, 121; and House of the Good Shepherd, 172. *See also* Mary Clubs

Bartzen, Peter, 52